TALK THE TALK

WRITER'S DIGEST BOOKS

writersdigestbooks.com
Cincinnati, Ohio

 Published by Writer's Digest Books, an imprint of F+W Publications, Inc., 4700 East Galbraith Road, Cincinnati, OH 45236. (800) 289-0963. First edition.

Visit our Web site at www.writersdigest.com for information on more resources for writers.

To receive a free weekly e-mail newsletter delivering tips and updates about writing and about Writer's Digest products, register directly at our Web site at http://newsletters.fwpublications.com.

10 09 08 07 06 5 4 3 2 1

Distributed in Canada by Fraser Direct, 100 Armstrong Avenue, Georgetown, ON, Canada L7G 5S4, Tel: (905) 877-4411
Distributed in the U.K. and Europe by David & Charles, Brunel House, Newton Abbot, Devon, TQ12 4PU, England, Tel: (+44) 1626 323200, Fax: (+44) 1626 323319, E-mail: postmaster@davidandcharles.co.uk
Distributed in Australia by Capricorn Link, P.O. Box 704, Windsor, NSW 2756 Australia, Tel: (02) 4577-3555

Library of Congress Cataloging-in-Publication Data
Reid, Luc.
Talk the talk : the slang of 65 American subcultures / by Luc Reid.
p. cm.
Includes bibliographical references (p. 384) and indexes.
ISBN-13: 978-1-58297-423-1 (pbk. : alk. paper)
ISBN-10: 1-58297-423-3
1. English language--United States--Slang--Dictionaries. 2. Americanisms--Dictionaries. I. Title.

PE2846.R43 2006
427'.73--dc22

2006015738

Edited by Michelle Ehrhard
Designed by Claudean Wheeler
Production coordinated by Robin Richie

DEDICATION/ ACKNOWLEDGMENTS

If you find anything you dislike or disagree with in this book, those things are entirely my fault. For everything you may find interesting or useful, a good portion of the appreciation is due to the people below, without whom this book would be just another one of my crazy ideas. I owe debts of gratitude to:

MICHELLE EHRHARD, an MS moose among editors, who put up with too many suggestions and made room for a publishing grom; My friend and agent, **NADIA CORNIER**, who immediately thought of me when she heard the phrase "weird reference book," then sold the angle and put me over; **ETHAN AND LILY**, the first people I think of when I hear the word "super," who patiently waited until I had more time for play flights; **JEN**, the filthiest of filthy nectar; **PAT REID**, who spent years rustling the chuck for the whole remuda and posted a record parental average, **JAMES REID**, the most supportive elmer a harmonic could wish for; **SEAN REID**, whose help almost allowed me to keep the shiny side up on a photographers section, and **KYM TAYLOR**, whose help almost got enough artistes in my troupe of dancer terms to get it on the show; **THE MEMBERS OF CODEX AND LEECON 2006**, who grokked what I was doing and who are egoscanning this right now to see if they've been Tuckerized in the quotes. (They haven't. Sorry.) **NICK ROBERTS**, **JOY MARCHAND**, and **KYLE LAVALLE**, who among them helped me sling all the ink I needed into the tattoo section; **MARY ROBINETTE KOWAL**, to whom a big vagabond salute for her crucial help in the field of dolly shaking; **STEVE BEIN**, who made his save vs. insanity while he waited for me to finish this tunnel of fun; **RACHEL ANN DRYDEN**, to whom gramercy in very sooth for helping me put out my carbon condition;

CATHY BOLLINGER, who provided pass-along terms and patiently waited while I forced this manuscript; **LINDA SWANSON**, who found elegant solutions to my timing issues so that I could get this program live; **JUD ROBERTS**, who gave me details from his law enforcement experience that helped me make game and find the shooters in drug slang; **NORMA JEAN ALMODOVAR**, who gave me the beta to help avoid cratering on sex worker slang; And **YOU**, that wonderful person whose help was invaluable as I wrote this book but whom I have negligently forgotten to include, which omission grieves me even now: mad, mad, mad, mad props.

ABOUT THE AUTHOR

Luc Reid lives in Jacksonville, Florida, with his wife, Jennifer St. John, and children. He's a past winner of the Writers of the Future contest and is the founder of the neo-pro writers' group Codex (www.codexwriters.com), which promotes the exchange of information, ideas, and writing wisdom among pro-level writers, facilitates rapid (seven days or less) short fiction critiques, provides a place for a centralized compilation of writing resources, knowledge, and connections, and sponsors workshops and other career- and skill-building events. His short stories have appeared in Galaxy Press anthologies. He also writes novels and books for young adults. You can learn more about him at his Web site www.lucreid.com.

TABLE OF CONTENTS

Introduction 1

AMERICANS IN ANTARCTICA 11

ANIME AND MANGA FANS 15

ASTROLOGERS AND ASTROLOGISTS 24

BEEKEEPERS 30

BICYCLISTS AND MOUNTAIN BIKERS 34

BIRDERS 41

BODYBUILDERS 45

CARNIVAL WORKERS 55

CAT FANCIERS 65

CAVERS AND SPELUNKERS 69

CIRCUS PEOPLE 72

COIN AND MONEY COLLECTORS 81

CON ARTISTS AND SCAMMERS 87

COWBOYS AND RODEO RIDERS 102

DRUG PUSHERS AND USERS 107

FLYFISHERS AND SPORT FISHERMEN 119

FURRIES 122

GAMBLERS AND POKER PLAYERS 127

GARDENERS 134

GAY, LESBIAN, TRANSGENDERED, AND BISEXUAL PEOPLE 137

GOTHS 147

GRAFFITI WRITERS 152

GUN ENTHUSIASTS 156

HACKERS AND PROGRAMMERS 159

HAM RADIO OPERATORS 166

HIKERS AND BACKPACKERS 171

HISTORICAL REENACTORS 176

HOT RODDERS 180

HUNTERS 185

KAYAKERS, CANOERS, AND RAFTERS 189

MAGICIANS 195

MEDIUMS, CHANNELERS, AND SPIRITUALISTS 200

MODEL BUILDERS AND RADIO-CONTROLLED MODEL ENTHUSIASTS 207

MODEL RAILROADERS AND RAILFANS 212

MOTORCYCLISTS (BIKERS) 215

NATURISTS AND NUDISTS 221

ONLINE GAMERS 223

PARAPSYCHOLOGISTS 230

POLITICIANS AND POLITICOS 235

PRISONERS 243

PRO WRESTLING FANS 248

PROSTITUTES AND OTHER SEX WORKERS 257

PUNK ROCKERS AND STRAIGHT EDGERS 262

PUPPETEERS 265

RENAISSANCE FAIREGOERS 270

ROCK CLIMBERS 275

ROLE-PLAYING GAMERS 283

RV OWNERS 288

SCI-FI AND FANTASY FANS 293

SCUBA DIVERS 305

SKATEBOARDERS 309

SKIERS 313

SKINHEADS 316

SKYDIVERS AND BASE JUMPERS 319

SNOWBOARDERS 324

SOCIETY FOR CREATIVE ANACHRONISM MEMBERS (SCADIANS) 327

STAMP COLLECTORS (PHILATELISTS) 332

SURFERS 336

SUSTAINABLE LIVING ADVOCATES 341

TATTOO ARTISTS AND TATTOO ENTHUSIASTS 345

THESPIANS AND STAGE CREW 348

TRUCKERS 353

UFO BELIEVERS 356

WICCANS, WITCHES, AND NEO-PAGANS 362

Appendix:
THE LANGUAGE OF HIP HOP 372

Bibliography 384

Index of Terms 395

Introduction

This is only the introduction. If you want to dive right into the terms, my feelings won't be hurt. On the other hand, if you read the introduction you'll find out some interesting things about skiers, Eskimos, and in what beneficial ways this book is not like the *Oxford English Dictionary*. Your call.

SPEAKING LOUDER THAN WORDS

Subculture slang is more than a specialized vocabulary. Adopting slang is a way to invite people in or to keep casual onlookers out; a way to show your attitude toward what you're doing while you do it; of confirming or denying relationships; of marking your particular territory in the strange countries of stamp collecting, gambling, bodybuilding, or any of the other subcultures this book covers.

Subculture slang is illuminating too because knowing what kinds of terms a subculture adds to the language tells us something about what's important to that subculture. The classic example is the number of Eskimo* words for snow: As I'm sure you've heard, there are hundreds.

* Some people prefer the term "Inuit," but Inuit is just one of five Eskimo languages, so it would be technically wrong for me to use the word here. I didn't want to bore you with that explanation, but I figured if you were willing to follow the asterisk, you must really want to know.

But actually, there aren't. Depending on which Eskimo dialects you count, how many forms of the word you allow, and what you consider snow versus not snow (no fair including ice!), you'll come up with different totals. If we're talking about different forms or characters of snow-the-substance, I come up with nine Eskimo words for "snow." **

Nine's a pretty respectable number. You can cover a lot of ground with nine kinds of snow. In standard English, again by my count and eliminating straight synonyms, I come up with five: "snow," "snowflake," "slush," "sleet," and "graupel" (I had to look that last one up, by the way). We probably wouldn't even come that close to the Eskimos except that English has more words than any other language, anywhere from 600,000 to around a million of them, depending on whom you ask.

So, five English words for snow. Now let's compare that non-slang vocabulary from a culture that deals with a lot of cold weather (Eskimos) to the total vocabulary of a subculture that deals with a lot of cold weather: skiers, say. Skiers have a wide variety of terms for distinct types of snow; I can count at least seven: "powder," "sugar snow," "crust," "dust on crust," "breakable crust," "mashed potatoes," and "crud" (which is used here in a technical sense, meaning snow

** I guess I underestimated your thirst for knowledge: Apparently you want to know how I came up with the number nine. Well, there's a linguistics professor named Anthony C. Woodbury who went through a dictionary of one of the Eskimo dialects—Yup'ik, in this case—and identified the separate lexemes that described different kinds of snow. A lexeme is a basic word form, so for instance, "snow," "snowing," and "snowy" are all based on the lexeme "snow."

Dr. Woodbury identified fifteen Yup'ik lexemes for snow, and six of those were words describing ice, weather, or things made out of snow, which in my book—this one—don't count. So, 15 - 6 = 9. If you want to make your own count, you can follow my footsteps by consulting the bibliography, where Dr. Woodbury's summary and the Eskimo dictionary itself are referenced.

that's a mixture of slippery and lumpy parts). And of course we're talking about English-speaking skiers who therefore also use those five English words for snow.

So, if you'll allow me to count the skier terms as "words," which I admit is a cheap trick on my part, we get a final score of nine for Yup'ik Eskimos and 7 + 5 = 12 for American skiers. In a shocking upset, American skier slang wins over non-slang Eskimo vocabulary.

There are two insights we can take from this. First, Eskimos may think about snow a lot, but it's possible that skiers—some of whom spend most of the year in balmy climates—think about snow *more* even than Eskimos, whose survival depends on understanding winter weather. Second, if you want to become a skier, hang out with skiers, or write about skiers, you have some vocabulary to learn. Fortunately, you came to the right place.

Talk the Talk provides the means to understand and get comfortable with the terms used in conversation among people in a wide variety of subcultures. It's not possible for me to cover every American subculture in one book, but in terms of modern-day, American subcultures, this one book covers a lot of ground, especially in pointing out where sixty-five intriguing groups of people have focused their attention, by showing you the words they use.

WHAT DOES AND DOESN'T THIS BOOK COVER?

Since I had to draw the line somewhere, you won't find professional subcultures here, with some exceptions for non-standard professions like prostitution, drug dealing, and con games. You also won't find regional idioms, religious groups (again with a couple of non-standard exceptions), or pop culture: no instant messaging speak or MTV expressions. However, it seemed important to include something about hip hop, to which I've devoted the appendix.

Nor does this book contain general slang that just anybody would use. There are several general-purpose slang dictionaries available that serve that purpose, and you'll find them listed in the bibliography. Because of the enormity of the American slang vocabulary, none of these dictionaries is close to comprehensive despite some very good work on the part of slang lexicographers. If you compare them to one another, you'll find that each book includes many terms that others leave out.

In this book, you also won't find words that outsiders use about a subculture. This book is about what's going on inside those groups, not about what outsiders think.

What you *will* find are the languages of the most interesting and widespread American hobbies, preoccupations, shared interests, and obsessions, from railroad enthusiasts to wrestling fans, snowboarders to scuba divers, goths to cowboys.

While this is a reference book—and one that takes its job very seriously—it's also intended to be entertaining enough to browse through or read. One of the great joys of researching this book was discovering how creative and playful people can be in all walks of life. Don't take my word for it: Look up how scuba divers refer to sea sickness, or what a computer programmer means by "the Vulcan nerve pinch," or how bikers (the motorcycle kind) refer to dogs that rush out at them as they're riding past.

Each section contains an introduction to the subculture, with a few brief notes about that group's speech, concerns, and attitudes. This is followed by an alphabetical list of terms.

Throughout the book, you'll occasionally see terms that are used in more than one subculture. For instance, both rock climbers and snowboarders talk about cratering (falling and hitting the ground)—although for snowboarders it's a gentler process than for rock climbers.

THIS IS NOT THE *OXFORD ENGLISH DICTIONARY*

To give you an idea of how this book is (and has to be) different from a dictionary, I'd like to talk briefly about the superstar of language reference books, the *Oxford English Dictionary*.

Lexicographers (dictionary compilers) at the *OED* compile material in the following way: Over the course of years, volunteers read books, magazines, and other material—even Web sites—and gather meaningful quotes that use words the lexicographers want to define. By cross-referencing these quotes, the lexicographers infer various meanings of a word and write them down. And more power to them.

By contrast, what I've done for *Talk the Talk* is to find knowledgeable individuals and groups who are part of a particular subculture and who have documented some of that subculture's language (or who could be begged, tricked, cajoled, or shamed into doing so). I've then stood on their shoulders (so to speak) and distilled the most pertinent terms into this book.

Which means not only that I was able to finish this book much more quickly than the first edition of the *OED* was finished (one very hectic year for me versus seventy-one years for them—although I admit their project was a little larger than mine), but also that I didn't have to wait for books or magazines to mention the terms we have here or for them to gain any kind of broad acceptance. No, these terms have taken the fast track to glory, going as directly as possible from the mouths of the speakers to the pages you hold in your hand. The con artist slang here is not forties era gangster speak, and the surfer slang is not circa 1965, but rather the new and current terms being used by these subcultures. I'd be surprised if you could find the majority of terms as they are documented here in *any* other book (including the *OED*, where they probably ought not to be anyway).

Unfortunately, a book like this can't be (and shouldn't be) comprehensive. Subculture slang terms range from universally-known to barely heard-of, have local variations, use terms that are not exclusive to a particular subculture, are subject to differing opinions on their exact meaning, and otherwise vary enormously. Instead of trying to get everything, I've done my best to document the most useful, widespread, and interesting terms.

And not every member of a particular subculture will be familiar with all of the words documented here for that subculture: Don't think for a minute that every parapsychologist knows or cares about astral projection or that any con artist can perform a salami attack on command.

In order to minimize the danger of incorrect entries, virtually every term in this book has been verified against at least two (and often three or more) sources to be sure it's correct and in current use among a significant portion of the subculture.

Quotations from members of the various subcultures are included for many terms to illustrate usage. Not all quotations are from written sources, and often I don't have access to personal information about the speaker, which is why many of the quotes are attributed only in a general way. I've found quotations at Web sites, on Internet discussion groups, and in spoken conversations, among other sources.

ABOUT FORMAT

The symbol **(!)** appears next to any term that should be used with caution. Often the term is derogatory, but it can also signify, among other things, that the term (1) is somewhat outdated; (2) means something different than might be expected; or (3) is erroneously thought by outsiders to be used in the subculture in question, in which case it is included only to point out that it isn't used.

Whenever a term has synonyms, they are listed in parentheses before the definition. When one of these synonyms is underlined, that means that a more detailed entry for that word is available in the same subculture section.

SLANG VS. JARGON

Talk the Talk doesn't cover technical terms, which is to say words and phrases used to refer to very particular things inside a subculture that are not readily comprehensible to someone unfamiliar with the focus of that group, whether that focus is stamps, sex, motorcycles, or marionettes.

There were four reasons for this decision. First, lists of technical terms would be 99.95% useless to you and me for the simple reason that you really have to know something substantial about model railroading to understand the purpose of an automatic block signal, or about swords to appreciate the relative merits of the flamberge versus the wakizashi.

Second, there isn't room to document all the technical terms for each of the subcultures. The book would have fluffed up to thousands of pages of dense text and cross-references, and it would have cost hundreds of dollars.

Third, there's no way I could learn enough about each of these subcultures in less than a couple of decades or so to intelligently define all of their technical terms.

And finally, technical terms make a boring read. I'm not saying there's nothing interesting about automatic block signals; I'd hazard a bet they can be a lively subject of conversation under the right circumstances. By leaving these terms out, though, we're left with terms that help us understand the subculture itself, terms that represent the distilled wit and charm of a lot of intriguing people.

If you need to understand the technical fascinations of a subculture, you can use the bibliography as a jumping-off point. Starting with this book will give you a foundation for friendly conversation with the people in a given subculture, but it's not meant to be a substitute for actually knowing the material.

IF YOU NEED TO KNOW MORE

In addition to the bibliography you'll find at the end of this book, an updated bibliography appears on the book's Web site at www.subculturetalk.com. You'll notice that the bibliography has many more Web resources than books and magazines. There's a reason for that: Most of these subcultures aren't grand and formal entities, but collections of individuals with shared interests, whose unusual ways of speaking among friends or acquaintances with those same interests don't often find their way onto paper.

The Web, being a cheaper, faster, and easier place to publish, contains a wealth of information on subcultures. Not everything you'd ever want to know, but certainly a lot. Good Web resources include discussion groups (online forums), personal Web pages, association Web pages, and encyclopedia-type articles. In this last category, Wikipedia (www.wikipedia.org) is a top-notch resource. There aren't many places where you can type in a term like "neo-pagan" or "straight edge" and get a well-informed article with links. Magazines, associations, and clubs are also good sources of information.

Ultimately, though, the only way to fully understand a subculture is to become a part of it.

FOR WRITERS

One of the key purposes of this book is to provide a unique reference for writers who want to write about characters or real people from a given subculture. For you, my colleagues, I have a few suggestions:

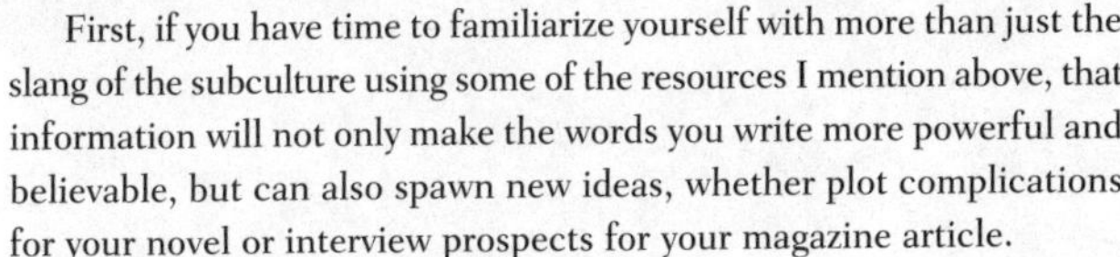

First, if you have time to familiarize yourself with more than just the slang of the subculture using some of the resources I mention above, that information will not only make the words you write more powerful and believable, but can also spawn new ideas, whether plot complications for your novel or interview prospects for your magazine article.

Second, keep in mind that these subcultures are not often homogenous: Close scrutiny breaks them into sub-subcultures that vary in speech, attitude, and concerns.

Third, I'd like to suggest reading the entire section on the subculture you're writing about. I've done my best to keep the sections to the point and fun to read, and knowing the full range of terms used in that subculture—especially what they tend to emphasize or focus on—may help you get inside the head of your character or story subject.

Finally, you may want to use these terms sparingly. While it varies from one subculture to another, most of what people in subcultures say is regular English of one kind or another, with terms like the ones in this book sprinkled throughout the conversation. Of course, even that sprinkling might make the conversation impenetrable to anyone outside that subculture—with the exception of readers of this book.

Americans in Antarctica

Antarctica is a roughly circular continent about one and a half times the size of the continental United States. It used to be a tropical paradise full of dinosaurs, but now it's an icy wasteland populated by birds, seals, and the occasional scientist.

When I first considered including Antarctic slang in a book about American subcultures, it occurred to me that people working in Antarctica are neither a subculture nor American. As it turns out, I was wrong on both counts, at least as regards people who work at McMurdo Station near the Ross Ice Shelf. McMurdo is a permanent American research station, and slang thrives there.

This particular lexicon covers American Antarctic slang; citizens of the U.K. and New Zealand living in Antarctica have some of their own slang terms.

In addition to the social slang you'll see below, a variety of military terms are used in Antarctica, especially when referring to supply planes and to special gear. And of course, Antarctic scientists—"beakers"—have a wide selection of technical jargon to work with.

When all of these pieces come together, Antarctic slang sounds like the kind of talk you'd hear from a bunch of scientists penned up during a record cold Minnesota winter with nothing but canned food and some large tractors.

(!) ANTARCTIC 10: A person of the opposite sex who might not be considered a "10" in a Manhattan bar but who begins to look pretty attractive after a few months of seeing no new people. Can be considered derogatory, especially if used outside of Antarctica.

BAG DRAG: The process of taking luggage to be weighed in preparation for flying out of Antarctica, usually at an inconvenient time. Flights are often cancelled, so a bag drag is frequently a wasted effort.

> "Well, I just finished my **bag drag**, where I turned in all my checked baggage for my flight tomorrow."
>
> - FORMER ASTROPHYSICS STUDENT TED KISNER

BEAKER: A scientist.

see also: *jafa*

BIG EYE: Antarctic summer insomnia caused by the overabundance of sunlight.

> "We've been operating in an insomniac time warp. The **Big Eye**, some call it."
>
> - ENVIRONMENTAL JOURNALIST MARYANN BIRD

BOOMERANG: A flight to Antarctica that has to turn back rather than complete the trip. The usual causes of a boomerang are bad weather or mechanical failure.

BUNNY BOOTS: Big, white, very warm boots that are insulated in part with wool felt. The wool felt is sometimes referred to as rabbit fur (which of course it isn't), giving rise to the term.

CHCH: Pronounced "Cheech." A slang name for Christchurch, New Zealand, which is a launching point for American Antarctic expeditions.

> "[The plane] had mechanical problems, and so we boomeranged back to **ChCh** after one hour aloft."
>
> - ANTARCTIC WORKER DOUG COWEN

THE CRUD: Also known as "The McMurdo Crud," The Crud is any cold or flu-like illness carried in by a large group of new arrivals. When there are few new arrivals, there is little illness because new diseases are not being introduced to the group.

DV: A distinguished visitor: a VIP.

DOME SLUG: Someone who stays inside the station. The Antarctic equivalent of a homebody.

see also: house mouse

ECW GEAR: Extreme Cold Weather gear, which is to say any special clothing used to keep the cold at bay, such as bunny boots.

see also: bunny boots

> "I was scheduled to get my **ECW gear** the morning after my arrival."
>
> - ANTARCTIC WORKER IRMA HALE

(!) FNG: (Pronounced "FIN-jee") Short for "f***ing new guy," an uncomplimentary term for new arrivals in Antarctica.

FRESHIES: Fresh fruits and vegetables, available only when flown in. Freshies are a coveted resource.

HELO: Short for "HELicOpter."

> "When I arrived at the **helo** hanger I found Steve already there."
>
> - ANTARCTIC WORKER KEITH DREHER

HERBIE: The worst storms affecting the American base, McMurdo Station, which arrive off the ocean from the south. Short for "hurricane force blizzards."

HOLLYWOOD SHOWER: A personal shower that lasts longer than two minutes. The term is borrowed from the American Navy, and used because liquid water is hard to come by at Antarctic bases.

HOUSE MOUSE: A person on temporary janitorial duty at the station, i.e., someone who stays in and cleans while others go out into the field.

see also: dome slug

THE ICE: Antarctica. Being in Antarctica is known as being "on the Ice."

> "These are very harsh and extreme conditions, and we have to discern who would do well in that environment and if they are psychologically qualified to remain on **the Ice** for the winter."
>
> - PSYCHOLOGIST DR. TONI ANKER

(!) JAFA: An uncomplimentary term for an Antarctic scientist. Jafa is an acronym for "just another f***ing academic."

see also: beaker

MACTOWN: McMurdo Station, the U.S. research base in Antarctica.

MAINBODY: The warmest and brightest of the three seasons recognized by McMurdo Station.

MEDEVAC: Bringing a person back from Antarctica early due to medical problems. Short for "medical evacuation."

OLD ANTARCTIC EXPLORER: Anyone who has been in Antarctica through an entire winter or several summers.

PAX: Airplane passengers; the term is borrowed from the military.

> "It makes me wonder how many of those **PAX** will get to observe the eclipse from start to finish."

SELF-DEPLOYING CARGO: Passengers (because they get off the plane under their own power).

TOAST: A deranged state that results from spending a winter in Antarctica. An Antarctic winter is said to be a harrowing experience, and persons who have lived through one may need a period of leave in Christchurch, New Zealand (a.k.a. ChCh) to regain some feeling of normalcy.

TRAVERSE: A trip across the Antarctic ice (as opposed to a flight above it). Specially modified agricultural or older military tractors are used for traverses.

U-BARREL: A 55-gallon, bright yellow barrel used for collecting urine in places where more advanced plumbing is not available.

WEATHER GUESSER: A meteorologist.

see also: beaker, jafa

WINTER-OVER: Also "winterover." 1) To stay in Antarctica from about March through November, i.e., through the local winter. 2) Someone who has spent the winter in Antarctica.

see also: toast, old Antarctic explorer

Anime and Manga Fans

Anime and manga are a particular Japanese style of drawing in animation and comic books, respectively. Anime and manga characters tend to be illustrated with very large eyes and extremes of expression. Flamboyant dress, strange hairstyles, and unusual hair colors are also common, although it could be argued that the same is true of teenagers, one of the target markets for anime.

In Japan, "anime" is a generic term for any kind of animation, and "manga" is a generic term for any kind of comic book. In America, by contrast, these two words are used more narrowly, to refer only to the "anime" style of animation.

Fans of anime and manga use slang that is unlike most subcultural slang in this book in that most anime terminology, not surprisingly, is derived from Japanese. This makes for some oddities. First, there may be variations in how words are spelled, since Japanese can be transcribed into our Latin alphabet in different ways. For instance, a sustained "i" sound (as in the word "machine," but held longer) is often transcribed as "ii." but sometimes as "ī."

Second, some anime slang comes from Japanese words that themselves are based on English words. In fact, the word "anime" is a typically Japanese shortening of the English word "animation."

Surprisingly, some features of the anime drawing style itself also have an American origin. For instance, the large eyes widely associated with anime were popularized in the work of Japanese animator Osama Tezuka, who was inspired by early Disney films and other American cartoons.

Sexuality in anime is an odd subject. When anime began in the 1950s, it was produced with children and teenagers in mind and was drawn innocently. Young people are still the primary market, but these days even anime for young people feature a lot of young women who dress provocatively, and a variety of anime for older teens and adults has emerged that ranges from mildly suggestive to flagrantly pornographic. The odd contrast between innocence and highly sexual content is similar to what goes on in the overlapping subculture of furries, fans of anthropomorphic animal characters.

RELATED SUBCULTURES:

Furries, Sci-Fi and Fantasy Fans

ANIME: (usually pronounced "ann-ee-MAY," although a more purely Japanese pronunciation would be "ah-nee-meh;" sometimes spelled "animé" in a mistaken application of French spelling to Japanese) In America, a Japanese style of animation and storytelling that tends to focus on characters and emotions. Its characters are commonly depicted with large eyes and exaggerated facial expressions. Anime often involves science fiction and fantasy elements such as monsters, high technology, ghosts, demons, or superheroes. Main characters tend to be young adults or children.

The word "anime" can refer to the genre in general or to a particular anime episode. It can be used as a singular or plural noun ("animes" is not a word) or as an adjective.

"Anime" can also be used to refer to comics drawn in this same

style, although these are more often called manga.

see also: Japanimation, manga

> "You also have to remember that most of those **anime** were based on manga which were very popular (like *3x3 Eyes*, *RKenshin*, *KOR*, *Ranma*, *A!MG*)."

ANIPARO: In manga (Japanese-style comics), an anime parody, in which characters are taken from other manga and anime works and used in humorous stories.

BISHOJO OR BISHOUJO: "Beautiful girl," a word used more widely in anime cartoons than in American ones, since anime has an unusually high ratio of very young women to other characters.

see also: bishonen

> "In the age of *Negima* [an anime program] and endless **bishoujo** game conversions, a simple four-girl harem is a breath of fresh air."

BISHONEN OR BISHOUNEN: A somewhat feminine-looking boy, or a "pretty boy," a fairly common anime character type. A bishonen may be gay and/or a crossdresser, or he may simply be "pretty" or androgynous.

see also: bishojo

CHARA: (the more Japanese-style pronunciation is "KAH-rah;" also pronounced "KEH-ruh") An anime character. The word "character" is also used.

> "I got pretty far, but I can't think of any anime **charas** that start with Q or X."

CHIBI: Small, short, young, or junior. A chibi character might be younger than the other characters or may be unnaturally short.

see also: chibi eyes

CHIBI EYES: The characteristic, big, child-like eyes used in anime.

see also: chibi

CON: Anime convention; a gathering of anime fans. Cons often include a variety of anime-related merchandise, signings by anime artists and voice actors for anime shows, showings of anime, etc. Fans often dress as favorite characters.

Other subcultures who hold similar gatherings include science fiction and fantasy fans and furries.

see also: cosplay

COSPLAY: (pronounced "KOSS-play") A costume play. At anime conventions (cons), many attendees dress as favorite anime characters and act out anything from a simple skit to an elaborate production with special effects.

see also: cons

DIGISUB: A digital copy of an anime that fans have translated and subtitled for English-speaking fans.

see also: fansub

DOUJINSHI OR DOJINSHI: (pronounced "doe-JEEN-shee") Fan-produced books, magazines, or CDs of comic book stories (manga) based on popular anime and manga characters. The use of the characters being illustrated is generally not authorized by the copyright holders, but are usually distributed through fan channels.

Many doujinshi creatively imagine the characters' sex lives, although this is by no means a characteristic of all doujinshi.

see also: manga, hentai, fanfic

DRAMA CD: (*synonyms: image album, manga CD*) A CD of music designed to accompany a particular manga.

DUB: A Japanese anime in which the original Japanese dialog has been replaced with English for English-speaking audiences. Some fans prefer subtitled programs to dubs.

Also used as a verb, or as an adjective in the form "dubbed." Not unique to anime, but an important word in the anime lexicon.

see also: fanduh

ECCHI: (*synonyms: etchi, H*): (pronounced "EH-chee") From the Japanese word for the letter "H," used as shorthand for the word hentai, which means, very roughly, "sexual perversion." Both "hentai" and "ecchi" are used to describe anime, but "hentai" has a stronger connotation of sexual content and kinkiness, approximately "anime pornography," whereas "ecchi" has a milder connotation, roughly along the lines of "anime erotica."

"H-" is sometimes added to terms to indicate that the material is "ecchi," e.g., "H-anime" or "H-manga."

see also: hentai, lemon

"*Bubblegum Crisis* (both incarnations) has a female cast a good deal more mature than the SM crew, and there's only the standard token anime nude shots, nothing **ecchi** or hentai."

ETCHI: *(synonyms: ecchi, H)* Anime erotica.

EYECATCH: Two brief pieces of animation or still shots usually used to transition from an anime program to a commercial and back, but sometimes included even in programs that don't have commercials (especially Original Anime Videos, or OAVs).

FACE FAULT: A sudden, exaggerated facial expression of discomposure or disbelief from an anime character, used regularly in anime comedy.

FAN SERVICE: (occasionally "fanservice") Scenes or details of scenes that have little or nothing to do with the storyline but that are provided to titillate or excite fans. Fan service often refers to a shower scene or other gratuitous element intended to excite teenaged male viewers. However, it can also refer to any cool visual effect that doesn't particularly further the story.

"What anime [has the best] **fanservice** that doesn't actually go into hentai [pornography]?"

FANDUB: An anime video originally recorded in Japanese that has been overdubbed (dubbed) into English by fans for other fans. Fandubs are rare; much more common are anime with fan-added subtitles, fansubs.

see also: fansub

FANFIC: *(synonym: fanfiction or fan fiction)* Stories written by fans about characters in popular anime and manga. Generally, these aren't approved by the copyright owners, but since they are usually offered for free (often on the Web), they don't tend to cause legal trouble. Like doujinshi (fan comic books) and anime and manga themselves, fanfics range from innocent to lurid.

see also: doujinshi

FANFICTION OR FAN FICTION: *(synonym: fanfic)* Stories written by fans about characters in popular anime.

FANSUB: An anime that fans have translated from Japanese into English and subtitled. Fansubs are often made available to other fans for the cost of the tape or disk onto which they're copied. Since fansubs are normally done of programs for which no official English version exists, they're generally tolerated by the copyright holders.

see also: *digisub*

GARAGE KIT: A model kit for an anime or manga character. The kits were originally made by fans at home (hence the term), but have become a commercial item.

H: *(synonyms: ecchi, etchi)* Anime erotica.

HENSHIN: 1) A flashy transformation scene, in which an anime character transforms into a more powerful version of her- or himself, e.g., a superhero. 2) An anime show that focuses on a character who transforms into a more powerful form.

> "The most disgusting **henshin** sequence is in *Demon Fighter Kocho*."

HENTAI: 1) Pornographic anime. Similar to ecchi (erotic anime), but with a stronger component of sex or kinkiness. 2) An insult sometimes used by a female anime character toward a male anime character, roughly corresponding to "pervert!"

The original Japanese meaning of the word is roughly "transformation."

see also: *ecchi, lemon*

IMAGE ALBUM: *(synonyms: manga CD, drama CD)* A CD of music intended to accompany the reading of a particular manga.

(!) JAPANIMATION: Roughly a synonym for "anime," except that the term originated in America and is not in wide favor among anime fans, some of whom consider it derogatory.

Alternatively, it can be used to refer to earlier, cruder Japanese animation, whether in a derogatory sense or not.

see also: *anime*

KEYFRAME: A single, carefully-rendered frame (still picture) used in an animation. A lead animator draws the keyframes, and lesser animators draw the transitions from one keyframe to the next.

LEMON: Anime intended for mature viewers. Not quite "hentai" (pornographic) or even "ecchi" (erotic), but containing mildly sexual material. "Lemon" is a noun; the adjective form (which is not as widely used) is "lemony."

see also: ecchi, hentai

"Case in point, the panel that never ends at Anime North spent 90 percent of the time I was present discussing **lemon** fics."

MAGICAL GIRL: *(synonyms: mahou shoujo or maho shojo, majoko)* A type of character and subgenre of anime aimed mainly at pre-teen girls. Magical girl characters are expected to save the world with their powers. They may have always had magical powers, or may be gifted with them in order to face some variety of evil.

Magical girls generally experience a transformation (henshin) scene to become their magical selves and tap into their various powers and abilities. In most cases they expend great effort to hide their gifts from everyone else.

see also: henshin

MAHOU SHOUJO OR MAHO SHOJO: *(synonyms: magical girl, majoko)* A girl anime character with magical powers who must save the world.

MAJOKO: *(synonyms: magical girl, mahou shoujo or maho shojo)* A girl anime character with magical powers who must save the world.

MANGA: (pronounced "mahn-gah" or, if you want to be more American about it, "MAN-gah") Anime-style comic books, sometimes of very large size and often including episodes from a variety of series.

"Manga" can be used either to refer to a specific book or to the entire genre. It serves as either a singular or plural noun (there is no such word as "mangas"), and can also be used to refer to animation, although the preferred term for animation is "anime."

Manga have been around for centuries, but were popularized in roughly their current form in the mid-twentieth century. They are generally written for a wide audience (as contrasted with anime, which tend to target a specific age group and gender), so that while you may see schoolchildren and college students reading manga, it's also not uncommon to see a middle-aged businessman reading one on a commuter train.

Notwithstanding the wide audience idea, there are also erotic and pornographic manga.

see also: anime, ecchi, hentai

MANGA CD: (*synonyms: image album, drama* CD) A CD of music designed to accompany a particular manga.

MANGAKA: A manga artist. One who creates manga.

MECHA: (pronounced "MEH-ka") In anime, any kind of large, mechanical device, especially a giant, battling robot.

> "The only problem is there are lots of thing that **mecha** do that people don't. (Last time I checked, I couldn't fire rockets built into my feet.)"

MOOK: (pronounced to rhyme with "look") A large, soft-covered, floppy book, usually of manga. "Mook" is a portmanteau of "magazine" and "book."

OAV: (*synonym: OVA*) Original Anime Video: an anime series never broadcast on TV, but instead sold only on video or DVD. "OAV" can mean either an entire miniseries or an individual episode.

OAVs tend to comprise fewer than 10 episodes, each shorter than an hour. A large number of OAVs are released each year.

OVA: (*synonym: OAV*) Original video animation; direct-to-video anime.

(!) OTAKU: In American usage, a hard-core anime fan. The Japanese usage roughly corresponds to "obsessive geek" and can apply to anything, not just anime. Derogatory in Japanese usage, it's perfectly okay in American.

> "He's not just an otaku, he's an uber-**otaku**. *Geeez.*"

SEIYUU: (pronounced "say-yooo") A voice actress or voice actor for anime.

SHOJO OR SHOUJO: Girl, girl-related, or anime/manga intended for girls. Shojo anime are targeted at girls and tend to revolve around girl main characters, often includ-

ing romance in the storyline. The shojo drawing style tends to be more gentle and sweet than that of more boy-oriented anime.

see also: bishojo, shonen

SHONEN OR SHOUNEN: Boy, boy-related, or anime/manga intended for boys. Shojo anime tend to focus on battles, showdowns, giant robots, and things that explode.

see also: shojo, bishonen

SHONEN AI OR SHOUNEN AI: Anime in which pairs of boys (sometimes pretty boys, i.e. bishonen) are attracted to one another. Shonen ai anime are usually intended for girls.

SIDE STORY: A spin-off manga or anime that focuses on secondary characters from an existing, popular anime.

SUB: Subtitled, or an anime that is subtitled. Anime fans vary in whether they preferred subbed or dubbed programs.

SUPERDEFORMED OR SD: An anime/manga style that uses huge heads and extreme expressions, often as a parody.

YAOI: Anime about boys in love with boys.

see also: shonen ai

> "Maybe in a hundred years' time, gays might live out lives as portrayed in those yummy **yaoi** mangas and doujinshis."

YURI: Lesbian storylines in anime, or anime mainly about lesbian characters. Not as common in anime as storylines about male homosexuality, which are called yaoi or bishonen ai. Sometimes explicit, sometimes not.

Astrologers and Astrologists

Much of astrology is concerned with the Zodiac, a collection of twelve constellations that divide the sky into twelve sections. Like much of astrology, the Zodiac comes to us from the ancient Greeks, who also contributed to astrology the classical elements (earth, air, water, and fire) and the traits associated with the different planets.

Astrology is deeply concerned with angles, in the sense of comparing different places on a circle, measured in degrees. If you divide the rim of a circle into three hundred and sixty equal-sized sections, each of those sections is one degree, and the number of sections between two points on that circle tells you the size of the angle between it. All of this will have been painfully obvious to you if you remember geometry class, but personally my main recollections of geometry class are of our teacher recounting episodes of the television show *Square Pegs*, and I had been confused initially because I was thinking of angles as those pointy things (which of course, they are also).

Many astrology terms come in complements or groups, such as grouping the signs of the Zodiac into the classical elements as earth signs, air signs, fire signs, and water signs; dignity and detriment; etc. Astrology is a complicated view of the universe where everything is maintained in a delicate balance. Perhaps this is why the slang of astrology is so hifalutin.

AFFLICTED: In reference to a planet, at an unfavorable angle to another planet or position in the sky.

> "I would agree with you if you were to say that **afflicted** planets in Gemini might indicate a psychological disorder, and likewise planets in Virgo."

AIR SIGN: A sign of the Zodiac associated with the classical element air. The air signs are Gemini (the Twins), Libra (the Scales), and Aquarius (the Water Bearer). Air signs are associated with the intellect.
see also: Zodiac

ANGLES: The four main directions used in a horoscope, figured in reference to a particular location at a particular time. The angles comprise four quarters, at 0 degrees (the ascendant, which is to say the starting point of the horoscope), 90 degrees (the imum coeli), 180 degrees (the descendant), and 270 degrees (the medium coeli or midheaven).
see also: ascendant

> "The rest of 'proper' astrology is all about **angles**, and therefore connections."

ASCENDANT: *(synonym: rising sign)* The part of the heavens that are just over the eastern horizon at the place and time for which a particular horoscope is cast. For an individual, then, the ascendant is the sign of the Zodiac that's just over the eastern horizon at the place and time of birth. The ascendant is said to indicate key traits.
see also: angles

ASPECT: The distance of one planet to another planet or to a significant point in the sky in terms of degrees of a circle. If you think of the Earth as being surrounded by that circle, then for instance you can conceive of two planets on opposite sides of the Earth as being 180 degrees away from each other—that is, halfway around the circle.

The word "aspect" only refers to specific, significant angles, each of which has a name. These names are sextile (sixty degrees), square (ninety degrees, i.e. a corner or right angle), trine (one hundred twenty degrees),

and opposition (one hundred eighty degrees: the far side of the circle).

The following angles are counted aspects by some astrologers and not by others: semisextile (thirty degrees) and quincunx (one hundred fifty degrees).

ASTROLOGER: A professional who studies the influence of celestial bodies on earthly events.

see also: *astrologist*

ASTROLOGIST: Anyone who studies the influence of celestial bodies on earthly events; often implies a non-professional.

CHART: (*synonym:* *horoscope*) A map used for astrology.

COMBUST: In reference to a planet, near to or directly in line with the sun when seen from a particular place on earth. A celestial body that is combust is generally considered weakened in its influence on the Earth.

> "Jupiter is **combust** the Sun ruler ninth, indicating that Kerry may burn out before the election or commit some major error regarding foreign policy."

COMPOSITE CHART: A horoscope based on two times and places, designed to show the relationship between two subjects. Particularly, a horoscope that uses two people's birth dates to look at the relationship between the two.

CUSP: The boundary between the areas of two different signs of thepes) in the heavens.

see also: *Zodiac, house*

> "No, I know the exact time of my birth and wasn't born on the **cusp**."

CYCLE: In reference to a planet, the amount of time it takes to travel through all the signs of the Zodiac.

DETRIMENT: A condition of a celestial body in which it is opposite its natural location, and therefore weaker than usual in influence.

see also: *dignity*

DIGNITY: A condition in which a planet or moon is in what is considered its natural place in the heavens. The influence of such a heavenly body is generally considered to be stronger than in most other situations, and it is said to be "dignified."

see also: *detriment*

DIRECT: In reference to heavenly bodies, moving through the Zodi-

ac in the usual order, for instance Capricorn to Aquarius to Pisces, instead of the reverse.

see also: retrograde

EARTH SIGN: A sign of the Zodiac associated with the classical element earth. The earth signs are Taurus (the Bull), Virgo (the Virgin), and Capricorn (the Goat). Earth signs imply practicality and groundedness.

see also: Zodiac

FIRE SIGN: A sign of the Zodiac associated with the classical element fire. The fire signs are Aries (the Ram), Leo (the Lion), and Sagittarius (the Archer). Fire signs are connected with passion and energy.

see also: Zodiac

FIXED STAR: A star that never appears to move. Fixed stars do change position relative to earth, but very slowly compared to most other stars.

HORARY ASTROLOGY: Use of astrology to make a chart of the heavens based on a particular moment in time and answer questions about that moment.

see also: mundane astrology, natal astrology

HOROSCOPE: *(synonym: chart)* A map of the heavens in relation to Earth, specific to a particular time and place. A natal chart, which is a horoscope based on the time and place of a person's birth, is the most common type of horoscope.

HOUSE: The twelve sections into which astrology divides the sky. At any given time, a house is ruled by one particular sign of the Zodiac. As the constellations turn in reference to the Earth, the signs move through the houses, so that the houses are not permanently associated with particular signs. The band of sky that is just above the eastern horizon is called the "First House;" the one above (west of) that is the "Second House;" etc.

There is some debate among astrologers as to what exact system of houses should be used.

see also: Zodiac

"The third **house** is not a powerful position for the Sun, nor is the sign Cancer, for here the Moon disposes of it and overshadows it with romantic, sentimental lunar values."

INFERIOR PLANET: A planet located closer to the Sun than Earth, i.e., either Venus and Mercury.

LORD: (*synonym: ruler or ruling planet*) A planet associated with a particular sign.

LUNAR MANSION: One of twenty-eight divisions of the celestial sphere reflecting the location of the moon on each day of the lunar month.

MAKE A STATION: For a celestial body to appear to stop moving in the heavens when its motion seems to change direction from the perspective of someone on Earth. It's counterintuitive that a planet should be going through the sky in one direction and then suddenly reverse itself, because the planets don't really change direction. The appearance of the change is due to the differing speeds of planetary orbits. In astrological terms, the influence of a celestial body making a station is considered exceptionally strong.

> "Finally, it should be noted that in October, Saturn will **make a station**."

MUNDANE ASTROLOGY: A type of astrology used to ask questions about world affairs or general events instead of about specific people.

see also: natal astrology, horary astrology

NATAL ASTROLOGY: A type of astrology that deals with individuals, based on a horoscope made up for a specific person's date and time of birth.

see also: horary astrology, mundane astrology

ORB: A distance a celestial body may be away from a particular location and still have the effect of being in that position. For instance, two planets in opposition (that is, on opposite sides of the Earth from one another), can be at slightly more or less than a 180° angle and still be considered in opposition; the orb is the allowable variance from 180°.

PLANET: A celestial body with major astronomical significance within our solar system. The Earth itself is not a planet from an astrological point of view since it is considered the center of the celestial sphere. Astrologically, the Earth is not a "planet," but the Moon and the Sun are.

PROGRESSION: The drawing of a horoscope based on a time after a given person's birth in order to examine that person's future.

RETROGRADE: In reference to heavenly bodies, moving contrary to

the order of the Zodiac, for instance Sagittarius to Scorpio to Libra, instead of the reverse. A body in retrograde may have a reduced influence, or may represent a return of some kind in a person's life.

see also: direct

RISING SIGN: *(synonym: ascendant)* The part of the heavens that form the basis of a horoscope.

RULER OR RULING PLANET: *(synonym: lord)* A planet associated with a particular sign of the Zodiac. Some planets are associated with one sign, others with two.

SIGN: Any of the twelve figures of the Zodiac, each considered to encompass one-twelfth of the celestial sphere. The signs are Aries (the Ram), Taurus (the Bull), Gemini (the Twins), Cancer (the Crab), Leo (the Lion), Virgo (the Virgin), Libra (the Scales), Scorpio (the Scorpion), Sagittarius (the Archer), Capricorn (the Goat), Aquarius (the Water Bearer), and Pisces (the Fish).

A reference to a person's "sign" is specifically a reference to the person's Sun sign, the place in the heavens where the Sun was located when the person was born.

see also: Sun sign, Zodiac

SUN SIGN: The sign of the Zodiac that is most strongly associated with a person. If someone says "I'm a Pisces," it means that the Sun was in Pisces when born.

see also: Zodiac

SUPERIOR PLANET: Any planet located farther from the Sun than Earth, i.e., Mars, Saturn, Jupiter, Uranus, Neptune, or Pluto.

SYNASTRY: The practice of comparing two horoscopes based on two individuals' birth dates to make observations about the relationship between those individuals.

TRANSIT: The movement of a planet through a particular sign of the Zodiac.

WATER SIGN: A sign of the Zodiac associated with the classical element water and with emotion and intuition. The water signs are Cancer (the Crab), Scorpio (the Scorpion), and Pisces (the Fish).

see also: Zodiac

ZODIAC: A band of constellations (the twelve signs) that surround the Earth. The twelve signs of the Zodiac define separate areas in the heavens (the houses), which are central to working out horoscopes.

see also: sign, house

Beekeepers

★ ★ ★ ★ ★ ★

Harvesting honey—sometimes one hundred pounds or more per year from a single hive—is the greatest single motivation for keeping bees, but there are other potential benefits: Bees provide top-notch pollination for gardens; many beekeepers find working with and observing bees to be relaxing; bees' range of intriguing behaviors make an interesting subject of study; and beehives can provide a variety of useful products in addition to honey.

Among the other products a hive can supply are beeswax; propolis, a resinous gum that bees use to seal cracks in a hive and that is reputed to have a number of health benefits; package bees and queen bees for sale to other beekeepers; and royal jelly, a special bee food produced by nurse bees, also said to have health benefits. Bees themselves are even used as medicine when they are made to sting people in a practice called apitherapy. Bee venom is thought by some to provide relief from arthritis, multiple sclerosis, and other inflammatory and degenerative diseases. Scientific studies of bee venom are ongoing.

Many beekeepers take part in secondary hobbies that relate to beekeeping, such as carpentry (to build frames, supers, and hives), gardening (to benefit from the bees' pollination services), and various hobbies in which they make finished goods from bee products, such as foods, natural cosmetics, candles, soap, and mead (honey wine).

★ ★ ★ ★ ★ ★

ABSCOND: For bees, to abandon the hive as a group, usually because of disease, heat, a wax moth infestation, or other trouble.

ALARM ODOR: A chemical released by a bee to warn other bees of danger.

BALL: For bees, to gang up on and attack an unacceptable queen, maiming or killing her.

"The new hive **balled** their queen, so I inspected the old hive, too."

BEE BLOWER: A device that creates a strong wind to blow bees off honey for harvesting.

BEE SPACE: Open areas within a hive, about 1/4" to 3/8" wide, that are large enough to allow bees to move through but too small to build combs in. Bee space is essential to proper beekeeping.

"Our problem is that one frame ... has warped somehow, and the bees are correcting the **bee space** violation by making wild comb."

BEE SUIT: White or pale-colored overalls used as protection when working with bees. A veil usually provides protection for the face.

BEE YARD OR BEEYARD: An area with a number of beehives in it; an apiary.

"Other than that, put a nice high shrub around your **bee yard**, and people probably won't even know they're there."

(!) BEE-HAVER: (pronounced "BEE-HAVvur") A derogatory term for a person who has beehives but doesn't take proper care of the bees.

"And I've had to learn a ton to try and be a good bee 'keeper' and not just a **bee 'haver'**."

BROOD: Bee eggs, bee larvae, and bee pupae; that is, any group of bees that aren't fully mature.

CLUSTER: A clump of bees clinging to one another and hanging from an object. Clusters appear when bees swarm, when they seek a new hive, and in cold weather.

COLONY: All of the bees living in a particular hive.

DEQUEEN: To remove a queen from a hive.

see also: requeen

DRIFT: For a bee, to lose its way and go to a different hive than the one in which it has been living.

"By that time, some of the bees had totally **drifted** out of some hives, but he tried again to equalize the bees and added a queen to each."

- BEE SPECIALIST DR. PHIL TORCHIO

FRAME: A wooden rectangle stacked into a hive and designed as a place for bees to build a comb.

GRAFT: To take a worker bee larva and place it in an extra-large, sometimes man-made cell in the hive, which when done properly causes the larva to become a queen.

GUM OR GUM HIVE: A beehive in a hollow log or chunk of hollow tree. These are not a legal way to keep bees in the U.S., since gum hives don't allow access to check for disease.

HONEYFLOW OR HONEY FLOW: *(synonym: nectarflow)* The time when the most nectar is available to bees and the most honey is produced.

"To determine if a **honey flow** is on, lots of 'to and fro' traffic at the entrance is a good sign."

NECTARFLOW: *(synonym: honeyflow or honey flow)* Peak honey-producing time.

NUC OR NUCLEUS: An unusually small hive, used for starting a new colony or raising queens.

PACKAGE BEES: A quantity of bees, weighing between two and five pounds and normally including a queen, which is packed in a screen cage for transportation. Package bees usually have sugar water with them to feed the bees while in transit.

see also: queen cage

PLAY FLIGHT: An excursion a short distance from the hive by a group of young bees who are getting familiar with the neighborhood.

QUEEN CAGE: A screened enclosure, small enough to be held in one hand, used to ship a queen bee with (usually) a wad of sugary candy as nourishment and a few attendant bees.

see also: package bees

QUEENRIGHT: In reference to a hive or colony of bees, having a queen.

"I thought they wouldn't forage if they weren't **queenright**."

REQUEEN: To put a queen bee back into a hive.

see also: dequeen

ROBBER BEE: A bee that has given up on hard work and that tries to steal either honey from another hive or honey that the beekeeper has removed.

SLUMGUM: The junk left over after beeswax is melted, containing dead bees, dirt, and other refuse.

SMOKER: A metal container that produces smoke to be blown into hives in order to scare off the bees.

SUPER: (as a noun) A box-shaped section of hive in which bees are intended to make honey. (as a verb) To put a super into a hive with the expectation that the bees will soon be making honey.

"Having taken the crop **supers** off in anticipation of the move, I now have a very crowded hive."

Bicyclists and Mountain Bikers

★ ★ ★ ★ ★ ★

Bicyclists include at least four major groups: mountain bikers, BMX bikers, road bikers/racers, and people who ride mainly for transportation or exercise. The first three groups—the more serious bikers—each use variations on general biking slang. For example, mountain bikers have a wide variety of words for crashing and for different types of crashes, and racers have terms to refer to packs of riders and the effects of being in or out of such a group.

In addition to slang, any type of rider might use technical jargon for parts of a bike, bike brands, maintenance procedures, and the like, and BMX bikers have an additional stock of names for BMX biking tricks.

While bicycling as a whole is well over a century old, BMX biking originated in the late 1960s, and mountain biking didn't fully emerge until the 1980s.

Many mountain bikers have experience with other mountain-related sports, such as rock climbing, skiing, and snowboarding, so certain terms—"yard sale," for instance—are shared between mountain bikers and other subcultures.

RELATED SUBCULTURES:

Hikers and Backpackers

★ ★ ★ ★ ★

ALL-TERRAIN BIKING OR ATB: *(synonym: mountain biking or MTB)* A type of off-road biking done with specialized bikes on sloped terrain.

ANCHOR: A family member (especially a child) whose existence prevents a biker from riding some of the time. Not meant to be a derogatory term, at least not on a conscious level.

APEX: (as a noun) The sharpest part of a curve or turn. (as a verb) To minimize the distance traveled when taking a curve by targeting the inside of the curve at the apex.

> "Focusing on the **apex** will draw you right to it."
>
> - MOUNTAIN BIKING INSTRUCTOR DUANE FORTH

AUGER: To crash face-first into dirt.

see also: biff, stack

BSG: A "bike store guy." A person who works in a bike store.

BABYHEADS: A scattering of rocks about the size of a baby's head clustered on a mountain biking trail, which can topple unwary bikers.

see also: death cookies

BACON: Scabby biking wounds.

see also: road rash, crayon

(!) BETTY: A generic name for a female rider, used most often by male riders. May not be universally appreciated.

BIFF: *(synonym: chunder)* To crash or wipe out.

see also: auger, stack, wash out, yard sale

(!) BOING-BOING: *(synonym: dual boinger)* A derogatory term for a full suspension bike, i.e., one that allows the wheels to move up and down by small amounts without the entire bike frame moving also.

BOMB: To bike at great speed and with little concern for obstacles.

BONK: To be unable to muster any additional energy and fail to complete the ride. The word is a cartoon description of the sound the rider and bike make when the rider falls over from exhaustion.

BOULDER GARDEN: A part of a riding trail littered with boulders.

BRAIN BUCKET: *(synonyms: lid, skid lid)* A bike helmet.

BRING HOME A CHRISTMAS TREE: To crash through foliage and find that a few branches decided to come along for the ride.

BUNNY HOP: (as a noun) Bouncing a bike into the air while riding it. This is done by crouching, then springing up. Usually done to clear an obstacle. (as a verb) To jump a bike over a small obstacle.

CANYON: The space between two ramps, where a BMX biker does not want to land.

CATCH AIR: *(synonym: get air)* To jump or bounce completely off the ground while riding: Air is the visible gap between the bike and the ground.

"I went faster than 20 m.p.h. the whole way, **catching** huge **air** and making five water crossings."

CHAIN SUCK: A condition in which the bicycle chain becomes jammed between the bike's frame and its chain rings (the toothed wheels that normally move the chain).

CHUNDER: *(synonym: biff)* To crash or wipe out.

CLEAN: To get through a difficult section of a trail without crashing, falling, or putting a foot on the ground (dabbing).

CLIP OUT: To remove a foot from a toe clip. Toe clips keep feet firmly on the pedals while riding. Being unable to clip out can cause accidents or embarrassing toppling incidents.

"As my bike, body, and pedals accumulated more and more grime, it became progressively harder and harder to **clip out**."

CORE SAMPLE: (as a noun) A wound given to a biker by an unplugged handlebar. Since handlebars are usually made of hollow metal tubing, an unplugged tube can have a cookie cutter effect. (as a verb) For an unplugged handlebar to wound a biker.

CORNDOGGED: Covered in dirt from a fall.

CRANIAL DISHARMONY: Discomfort brought on by falling off the bike and smacking one's head against something.

CRANK: *(synonyms: hammer, sprint)* To pedal hard in order to pull ahead of other riders.

CRAYON: To leave blood on rock or asphalt after a crash or fall.

DFL: In last position by the end of the ride or race. Short for "dead f**king last."

DAB: To put a foot down in order to stabilize the rider on the bike. Not considered an elegant move.

"A riding bud pointed it out to me. He said 'hey, why you always unclipping for the technical sections?' ... umm, in case I need to **dab**!"

DANCE: To stand on the pedals and ride in a standing position.

DEATH COOKIES: A group of smallish rocks that can knock a bike off course.

see also: babyheads

DEATH MARCH: A ride that turns out to be much more grueling than planned.

see also: three-hour tour, epic

DIALED IN: In reference to a bike, set up perfectly for the rider.

"Once I get the bike **dialed in**, then it's a moot point, as I generally never change the positioning."

DRILLIUM: The fictitious substance out of which parts of a bike are said to be made when the part in question has holes in it to make it lighter.

"Without liberal amounts of **drillium**, I can't see anyone getting a useable and durable geared bike under about 16 lbs."

DUAL BOINGER: (*synonym: boing-boing*) A bike with front and rear suspension.

ENDO: An experience in which the rider flies forward over the handlebars (unintentionally). Said to be short for "end over end."

"Endo" has also been used in BMX biking in the past to refer to a front wheelie, i.e., a move in which the only part of the bike touching the ground is the front wheel.

EPIC: In reference to a ride, extraordinarily long or difficult.

see also: three-hour tour, death march

FDGB: A whimsical term for a crash, short for "fall down, go boom." Since it's hard to be whimsical after crashing, generally used to describe other people's crashes.

"If you're riding on the brake lever hoods, sudden rotation of the bars could cause your hands to lose contact, possibly causing a **FDGB**."

(!) **FRED:** A multipurpose derogatory term for a bike rider, normally used to label people who have expensive equipment but don't ride often. Alternatively, can be used to deride a commuter, newbie, or anyone who rides a bike but who isn't devoted to riding.

GET AIR: *(synonym: catch air)* To get off the ground; to jump.

GIBLETS: Any attractive gee-gaws that can be purchased and attached to a bike.

GONZO: Dangerous or treacherous, whether in regard to a feature of a trail, a particular ride, or the rider.

> "I use the same method to clear railroad tracks (and when I'm really feeling **gonzo**, double railroad tracks)."

GRANNY GEAR: A very low gear, one which is easy to pedal; not present on most serious mountain bikes.

GRAVITY CHECK: A fall.

(!) **GUTTER BUNNY:** Anyone who commutes by bicycle.

HAMMER: *(synonyms: crank, sprint)* To pedal hard in order to pull ahead of other riders.

HAMMERHEAD: A person who habitually rides hard or fast.

HUCK: To jump wildly off a mountain bike, usually when it is about to crash.

INVOLUNTARY DISMOUNT: A crash.

LAUGHING GROUP: In a bike race, a bunch of riders who keep pace with each other. In Europe, often known as a "gruppetto" or "autobus."

LAUNCH: (as a verb) To jump the bike into the air. (as a noun) In a jump, the moment the bike leaves the ground.

see also: catch air

LID: *(synonyms: brain bucket, skid lid)* A bike helmet.

LUNCH: To destroy part of a bike. The wreckage is said to be "lunched."

see also: taco, potato chip, prang

MOUNTAIN BIKING OR MTB: *(synonym: all-terrain biking or ATB)* A type of off-road biking done with specialized bikes on sloped terrain.

NARD GUARD: Male protective gear for biking.

ORGAN DONOR: Anyone who rides without a helmet.

POTATO CHIP: A wheel that has been bent in a crash.

see also: *taco, lunch*

PRANG: To hit something and damage oneself or one's bike.

see also: *lunch*

RETRO-GROUCH: A rider who uses old equipment and isn't fond of the newer, lighter, faster stuff.

'RHOID BUFFING: Riding down a slope so steep that the rear wheel of the bike hits your backside.

"I turn around and do the **'rhoid buff** decent."

RIDER: Someone who rides a bicycle (a much more common term than "biker" or "bicycler").

ROAD RASH: Scrapes sustained during biking.

see also: *bacon, crayon*

(!) ROADIE: A rider who bikes on roads rather than trails. Can be derogatory, particularly if coming from a trail biker.

ROCKET FUEL: Coffee.

ROOST: To stop suddenly, spraying another rider with dirt.

SIT IN OR SIT ON: To bike in the wake of other, harder-working riders without taking a turn at the front.

"There is no shame in wheelsucking —some of the best racers are those who **sit in** all race and then win with a well-timed move."

SKID LID: (*synonyms:* *brain bucket, lid*) A bike helmet.

SLICKS: Mountain bike tires with no tread, sometimes used when riding mountain bikes on pavement.

SPIT OUT: Left behind by a group of faster riders. A rider who is unable to keep pace with a group is said to have been "spit out."

"If and when this sport gets big enough on the pro side not to need your entry fees anymore, you'll get **spit out** the back so fast you'll get whiplash."

SPRINT: (*synonyms:* *hammer, crank*) To pedal hard in order to pull ahead of other riders.

STACK: (as a noun) A crash. (as a verb) To crash.

see also: *auger, biff, wash out*

STEED: A bike, often used in the possessive ("my steed").

"If you're dealing with a mountain bike-style **steed**, invest the bucks to replace the knobby tires with slicks."

TACO: A wheel that has been practically folded in half in a crash.

see also: potato chip, lunch

TEA PARTY: Any point when a group of riders take a break to talk.

> "After group photos taken by an obliging biker who had just arrived, Rod left for home and the rest of us had an extended '**tea party**' before leaving."

THRASH: To ride roughly, especially when eroding the trail.

> "My only complaint about carbon fiber is that the clearcoat gets scratched up pretty easily and looks like hell—particularly when you **thrash** it around on rocks (granted, I didn't look very good afterward either)."

THREE-HOUR TOUR: A ride that looks easy but turns out to be difficult and long.

see also: death march, epic

TI: (pronounced with a long "i," as in "bike") Short for titanium, a substance used in many newer bike parts.

UNOBTAINIUM: An imaginary expensive substance. Any bike part one can't afford is said to be made of unobtainium.

VEGETABLE TUNNEL OR VEGGIE TUNNEL: A narrow track overshadowed by foliage, which requires the rider to bend down in order to avoid a face full of branches.

WALL: A very steep slope.

WASH OUT: To lose traction with the front of the bike and crash.

see also: biff, stack

> "When I get on [that brand of] bikes, I **wash out** in the first sharp corner!"

WILD PIGS: Brake pads that haven't been set up or adjusted properly and that screech when used.

WINKY: A reflector.

WRENCH: A bike mechanic.

YARD SALE: A serious crash that results in a rider's gear being spread around as though on display.

see also: biff

> "The benign crashes at HPV races versus '**yard sale**' piles of bent and broken bike parts and bleeding riders in conventional races are proof enough."

Birders

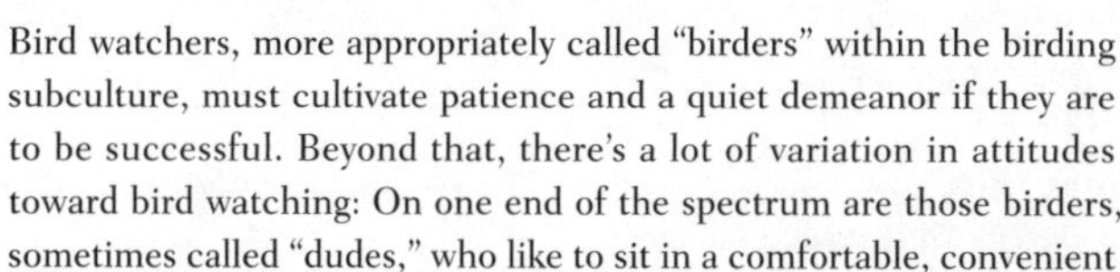

Bird watchers, more appropriately called "birders" within the birding subculture, must cultivate patience and a quiet demeanor if they are to be successful. Beyond that, there's a lot of variation in attitudes toward bird watching: On one end of the spectrum are those birders, sometimes called "dudes," who like to sit in a comfortable, convenient location in good weather and see what flies by. At the other end are hell-bent, rare-bird enthusiasts who will run out the door at the first rumor of a Dusky Warbler, and who are sometimes uncharitably known as "twitchers."

Most birders use some kind of telescopic equipment, such as binoculars, telescopes, or spotting scopes to observe birds from a distance.

Many birders maintain one or more lists of birds they have spotted. Some examples are life lists, which include every sighting the birder has ever made; national lists; state lists; and year lists.

ACCIDENTAL: Any bird seen outside its usual range that doesn't normally wander. Also used as an adjective.

see also: *casual*

ASIAN FLU OR ASIAN FLEW: A condition that sometimes afflicts birders with the mistaken belief that they've sighted a rare Asian bird reported to be in the area.

BOP: 1) Bird of Paradise. 2) Bird of Prey.

BIRDER: A birdwatcher, usually someone who knows a bit about birds and doesn't mind a little inconvenience in the cause of seeing them.

BUTTER BUTT: (*synonym: rump*) A Yellow-Rumped Warbler.

CASUAL: A bird that's out of its normal range, belonging to a species known to wander.

see also: *accidental*

CRIPPLER: A rare bird so impressive or beautiful that it temporarily renders the birder awestruck and unable to move on.

"So, if I see a '**crippler**' in international waters, where do I put the tick?"

CULL: The common gull.

DABBLER: Any type of duck that doesn't typically dive under water.

DARK LARK: A European Starling.

DIP: (as a verb) To be in the vicinity of a bird but to miss seeing it. Also to dip out. (as a noun) A bird that was in the area but that the birder missed.

see also: *dip out*

"Amazingly, we **dipped** on *chickadee*!"

DIP OUT: To miss a bird that one was trying to find while it is in the area. Also, to dip.

see also: *dip*

DIVER: Any kind of duck that regularly dives under water.

DUDE: A fair-weather birder, willing to go only modest distances and to comfortable locations in good weather for birdwatching.

"I'm not a novice either, but I now feel like I have the word '**dude**' stamped across my clothing."

FINK: A finch.

GASHAWK: An airplane.

GEE-FINK: An American Goldfinch.

GRIP OFF: 1) To claim to see a bird no one else saw. 2) To succeed in seeing a bird someone else wanted to see but missed. With this usage, there's always someone being gripped: The birder has gripped someone off.

see also: dip, dip out

"It's not a case of **gripping off** people. The purpose of making the sighting public knowledge (which I didn't particularly agree with at the time) is to make birders aware that there is a major rarity in the area, and to keep their eyes open at other sites."

GROWL: A Great Horned Owl.

HONKER: A Canada Goose.

JINX BIRD: A fairly common bird that a particular birder has never been able to spot.

"My **jinx bird**, however, was Henslow's Sparrow."

JIZZ: The general set of characteristics and behaviors of one species of bird.

"The bird adopted the stance and general **jizz** more indicative of (white morph) Eastern Reef Heron (Egretta sacra) ... but in a freshwater swamp!"

JUNGLE FOWL: Chickens.

LBJ: "Little brown job." Any small, brown bird, easily confused for a number of other small, brown birds and therefore difficult to identify.

LAWN CARP: Western Canada Geese, when seen in populated areas.

LIFE LIST: The list of all birds that a given birder has seen and identified in the wild.

LIFER: A species of bird that a given birder is seeing for the first time.

MEGATICK: A sighting of a bird that few birders have seen.

MOO-TWEET: A Cowbird.

MUDPECKER: Any shore bird that walks in the mud.

PATCH: A particular birder's familiar birding area.

PEEP: A Calidris Sandpiper.

PIE: A Magpie.

PIG: A Rock Dove (a species of pigeon).

PISH: To make a noise that sounds kind of like "pish" in hopes of getting a bird to call out a response.

> "Just up the trail not fifty yards, I **pished** a male painted redstart to within 18 inches of my face."

ROCKPECKER: Any shore bird that prefers rocky terrain.

RUMP: *(synonym: butter butt)*: A Yellow-Rumped Warbler.

SCOPE: To use a spotting scope (a type of telescope often used in birding) to pick out birds.

SHARPIE: A Sharp-Shinned Hawk.

SPATULA: A Shoveler.

SPRAWK: A Sparrowhawk.

STRINGER: A person who regularly makes sightings that other birders doubt.

see also: stringy

STRINGY: In reference to a bird sighting, questionable or unlikely.

see also: stringer

> "There was the regular grey phase Northern Wheatear as well as Spotted Flycatcher and Common Redstart *and* a rather **stringy** Marmosa's Warbler."

TV: A Turkey Vulture.

TAIL: A Red-Tailed Hawk.

TRASH BIRD: A bird that's very common in a particular area.

TWITCH: To run off to see a rare bird after finding out it has been sighted in the area.

see also: twitcher

(!) TWITCHER: A birder who obsessively goes out to follow up on sightings of rare birds in order to spot them and check them off from a list. (Mildly derogatory.)

Bodybuilders

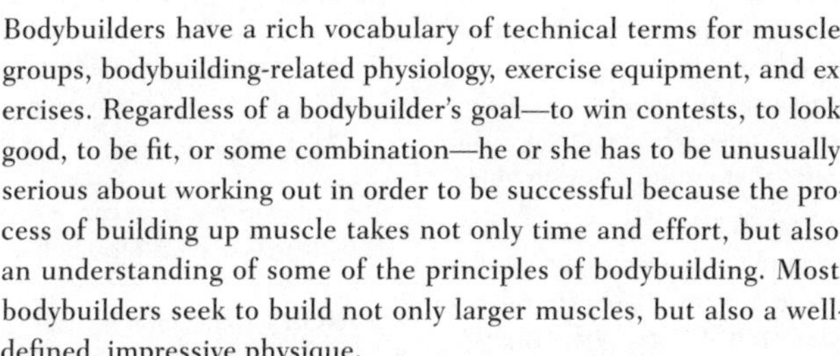

Bodybuilders have a rich vocabulary of technical terms for muscle groups, bodybuilding-related physiology, exercise equipment, and exercises. Regardless of a bodybuilder's goal—to win contests, to look good, to be fit, or some combination—he or she has to be unusually serious about working out in order to be successful because the process of building up muscle takes not only time and effort, but also an understanding of some of the principles of bodybuilding. Most bodybuilders seek to build not only larger muscles, but also a well-defined, impressive physique.

One of the interesting things about bodybuilder slang is the number of terms that have positive connotations in bodybuilding but negative ones in everyday use, for example, "cheating," "freak," and "failure." In bodybuilding, a cheating freak who experiences regular failure—that is, an extremely muscular bodybuilder who exercises muscles past the point of exhaustion by switching muscle groups—is a proud success.

ABS: Abdominal muscles.

BENCH: A specialized piece of furniture for weight training, usually padded and about four feet long. The bodybuilder lies or sits on the bench, depending on the exercise.

BIS: *(synonyms: guns, pythons, pipes)* (pronounced to rhyme with "eyes") Biceps; the muscles on the inside upper arm that move the forearm. In the classic "strong man" pose, the biceps are the ones that are supposed to bulge.

(!) BITCH TITS: The slang term for a condition called gynecomastia (which is an almost literal but more refined Greek translation of "bitch tits"). Men afflicted with this condition develop breasts. Gynecomastia can result from steroid usage and is undesirable .

BLAST: *(synonyms: thrash, fry, torch)* To work a muscle group very hard for a long time.

BODY COMPOSITION: The relative proportions of fat and muscle in a person's body. Bodybuilders tend to be keenly interested in body composition and not particularly interested in weight.

BOTTOMS: *(synonym: glutes)* The gluteus maximus.

BUFF: *(synonyms: buffed, cut, defined, ripped, shredded, sliced, sliced and diced)* Having prominent, clearly-defined muscles.

BUFFED: *(synonyms: buff, cut, defined, ripped, shredded, sliced, sliced and diced)* Having a well-developed, muscular body. Usually implies having clean lines rather than being bulky with muscle.

see also: full, flat, definition

> "Too bad more hot animated female superheroes don't get this **buffed**."

BULK UP: To become heavier by adding both muscle and fat.

BURN: 1) A painful sensation that occurs when overloading a muscle, which makes it sound like a bad thing, but it's actually an indication of a good workout that is building muscle. It's caused by the release of lactic acid in the muscle. Often used in the phrase "feel the burn." 2) As a verb, to lose body fat.

CAP: *(synonym: delts)* Shoulder muscles.

CARB UP: To eat foods high in carbohydrates. Some bodybuilders carb up before a contest to achieve the best muscle appearance, but the process is tricky to get just right.

CHEAT: To use improper form to propel a weight after the muscles being worked can no longer perform. Some bodybuilders believe a small amount of strategic cheating is helpful.

see also: cheat reps

"You can do a **cheat** curl that is ballistic or a cheat curl which is explosive."

CHEAT REPS: Extra repetitions (reps) achieved through improper form, which is to say through cheating.

see also: cheat

CLEAN AND JERK: A two-stage lift used in competitions: The competitor lifts the weight to shoulder level (the clean), then pushes it above the head (the jerk).

see also: snatch

CLOSE SPOT: *(synonym: spot)* To stand ready to assist a weightlifter.

COMPULSORY POSE: *(synonym: mandatory pose)* A set number of poses in a bodybuilding contest in which competitors are evaluated by judges to assess overall muscle development.

see also: posing routine, posedown

CUT: *(synonyms: buffed, buff, defined, ripped, shredded, sliced, sliced and diced)* Having prominent, clearly-defined muscles.

CUT UP: (as a verb) To reduce body fat so as to increase muscle definition. (as an adjective) Having good muscle definition.

see also: buffed

CYCLE: (as a noun) A period during which a bodybuilder is focusing on one aspect of training, for instance, bulking up with more muscle. (as a noun) A period during which a bodybuilder takes steroids or other performance-enhancing drugs. (as a verb) To take steroids or other performance-enhancing drugs for a limited period of time.

see also: juice

DEFINED: *(synonyms: buffed, buff, cut, ripped, shredded, sliced, sliced*

and diced) Having prominent, clearly-defined muscles.

DEFINITION: *(synonym: separation)* Possession of low body fat with lots of clearly-defined muscle.

see also: buffed, cut up

DELTS: *(synonym: cap)* The deltoid muscles, the muscles on either shoulder that stretch from near the end of the collarbone to about midway down the upper arm.

DIAL IT IN: To train and diet so as to optimize muscle definition for an upcoming contest.

DIME: A ten-pound plate used on an Olympic barbell.

see also: nickel, Olympic plate, quarter, spare change

FAILURE: The point at which a muscle group is completely exhausted: The bodybuilder can't perform additional reps without cheating. At this point, the muscle group is said to have been "exercised to failure."Exercising the muscle to failure stimulates muscle growth.

> "I believe both are achievable without going to **failure**, except once in a while when testing one's max."

FLAT: Poor, in regard to muscle definition. Can result from overtraining, not drinking enough water, poor nutrition, or not working out enough.

see also: buffed, full

FLUSH: To do many repetitions in order to cause a lot of blood to rush to a muscle and deliver more nutrients to it.

FORCED REP: A repetition of a lift assisted by a spotter, usually after the muscle has reached the point of failure, i.e. the muscle is exhausted and cannot do the lift on its own any more.

see also: failure, spotter, spot

(!) FREAK: A compliment: a freak is a bodybuilder with really, really enormous muscles, next to whom most hard-core bodybuilders look like 198-pound weaklings. Sometimes used by non-bodybuilders as an insult.

FREE POSING ROUND: *(synonym: posing routine)* A round of a bodybuilding contest during which bodybuilders pose.

FREE WEIGHTS: Weightlifting equipment that consists only something to lift, for example,

dumbbells and barbells. This is in contrast to, for instance, exercise machines in gyms.

FRENCH PRESS: *(synonym: skull crusher)* An exercise in which a barbell is taken from a rack over the head to be lifted over the chest.

FRY: *(synonyms: thrash, blast, torch)* To work a muscle group very hard, repeatedly.

FULL: In regard to muscles, pressing out against the skin in a desirable way. Full muscles are good, while flat muscles are bad. Not quite the same as buffed, since "full" refers to the size and prominence of the muscle instead of its definition.

see also: buffed, flat, definition

GEAR: 1) Anabolic steroids. 2) Paraphernalia related to steroid use.

see also: juice

GLUTES: *(synonym: bottoms)* The two gluteus maximus muscles: the largest muscles in the buttocks.

GOLDEN HOUR: The hour after a workout, in which some bodybuilders believe the body can absorb certain nutrients (especially protein) better than at other times. This idea does not have universal acceptance.

GRIND IT OUT: Suffer through a difficult workout.

"My partner and I were **grinding out** some full squats the other day, and this guy comes over and ask us to spot him on the leg press."

GUNS: *(synonyms: bis, pythons, pipes)* Biceps.

(!) GYM RAT: A person who hangs around a gym even when not working out. Can be derogatory.

HAMS: *(synonym: thigh biceps)* The hamstrings: the three muscles in the back of the upper leg.

HARDBODY: A female bodybuilder in excellent shape, with very good muscle tone.

ISOLATION: The practice of exercising one muscle or muscle group to build it up more quickly.

JUICE: *(synonyms: 'roids, sauce)* Anabolic steroids, taken to increase performance or to gain weight.

see also: bitch tits

LATS: The latissimus dorsi, a muscle that tapers from the middle of the lower back nearly up to the armpit.

MANDATORY POSE: *(synonym: compulsory pose)* A bodybuilding contest pose used to gauge overall muscle development.

MAX OUT: For a bodybuilder to lift the most weight she possibly can.

see also: one rep max

> "Many people think that if you want to know how much you can lift for one rep you can simply look it up in a chart and avoid any chance of injury. Others feel that there simply is no reason to **max out**."
>
> - WEIGHTLIFTING EQUIPMENT COMPANY OWNER AND BODYBUILDER MIKE WESTERDAL

MEGADOSE: *(synonym: shotgun)* To use a large amount of a performance-enhancing drug.

MUSCLE CONFUSION: A state that results from varying a workout routine so that the muscles trained don't get used to the demands of training. If a workout is not varied, a muscle group can become too efficient at a particular exercise and stop getting much benefit from it. Despite the sound of the term, muscle confusion is usually desirable.

NATURAL CONTEST: A bodybuilding contest in which bodybuilders who use performance-enhancing drugs are not permitted to compete.

NEGATIVE OR NEGATIVE REP: The second half of a weightlifting repetition, in which the bodybuilder lowers or releases the weight slowly against gravity.

NICKEL: A five-pound plate used on an Olympic barbell.

see also: dime, Olympic plate, quarter, spare change

OIL: Synthol, a banned substance some bodybuilders inject to increase apparent muscle size.

OLYMPIC PLATE: *(synonym: plate)* A type of barbell plate with a large hole; by contrast, a standard plate has a smaller hole. The bar in any given barbell is sized either for Olympic plates or standard plates. Olympic plates are generally forty-five pounds each; plates smaller than this are referred to as spare change: nickels, dimes, and quarters.

see also: dime, nickel, quarter, spare change

ON THE MONEY: *(synonyms: on time, peaking)* Having optimum muscle definition for a competition.

ON TIME: *(synonyms: on the money, peaking)* Having achieved top-notch muscle definition, generally for a competition. Getting on time is called dialing it in.

ONE REP MAX: Also "1RM." The maximum weight a bodybuilder can lift one time.

see also: max out

PEAKING: *(synonyms: on time, on the money)* Having optimum muscle definition for a competition.

PECS: Pectoral muscles: the two prominent chest muscles.

PIPES: *(synonyms: bis, guns, pythons)* Biceps.

PLATE: *(synonym: Olympic plate)* An Olympic-standard weight, used for increasing the weight of a barbell.

POSEDOWN: The final round of a bodybuilding contest, in which contestants present poses of their own selection.

see also: posing routine, compulsory pose

POSING ROUTINE: *(synonym: free posing round)* A later round of a bodybuilding contest in which bodybuilders present poses of their own choice, usually to music.

see also: compulsory pose, posedown

POUNDAGE: *(synonym: resistance)* The amount of weight lifted or otherwise manipulated in an exercise.

POWERLIFTING OR POWER LIFTING: A type of weightlifting event that features three types of lift: the squat, the deadlift, and the bench press.

PROGRAM: *(synonym: routine)* A sequence of exercises.

PUMP: (as a noun) The experience of having an intensive workout fill a muscle with blood, making it look larger. (as a verb) to get a muscle to a pumped state.

Not to be confused with the much more common slang term "pumped" in the sense of "enthusiastic."

> "Work one group, and immediately work the antagonistic group while you still have the **pump** from the first set."

PUMP IRON: To lift weights.

PYRAMIDING: Performing progressively fewer repetitions (reps)

and adding progressively more weight on a particular exercise during a given workout. This is a common technique; doing more reps with lower weight (high reps) is considered a good approach to warming up a muscle group.

PYTHONS: *(synonyms: bis, guns, pipes)* Biceps.

QUADS: The quadriceps: the muscle groups at the front of the thigh.

QUARTER: A twenty-five-pound weight used on an Olympic-style barbell.

see also: dime, nickel, Olympic plate

REP: One complete movement of a weightlifting exercise. "number of reps" means the number of times the bodybuilder does the exercise.

RESISTANCE: *(synonym: poundage)* Weight being lifted.

RIPPED: *(synonyms: buffed, buff, cut, defined, shredded, sliced, sliced and diced)* Having prominent, clearly-defined muscles.

'ROID RAGE: Uncontrolled anger brought on by steroid use.

see also: juice, bitch tits

'ROIDS: *(synonyms: juice, sauce)* Anabolic steroids.

ROUTINE: *(synonym: program)* A sequence of exercises; a full workout. A bodybuilder's routine often changes from one session to the next.

SAUCE: *(synonyms: juice, 'roids)* Anabolic steroids.

SEPARATION: *(synonym: definition)* The extent to which muscles are prominent and clearly-defined.

SET: The collection of repetitions, or reps, a bodybuilder does of an exercise at one time. For example, a bodybuilder might do three sets of eight reps each on a particular machine.

see also: rep

SHOTGUN: *(synonym: megadose)* To use far more than the suggested amount of a performance-enhancing drug. Generally a very bad idea.

see also: bitch tits

> "You'll probably think it's great if you **shotgun** the amount of T he did to get to where he was."

SHREDDED: *(synonyms: buffed, buff, cut, defined, ripped, sliced, sliced and diced)* Having prominent, clearly-defined muscles.

SIX PACK: *(synonym: washboard)* An abdominal muscle so well-defined that individual sections of the muscle stand out. (It looks like multiple muscles, but it's really just one muscle with some bands across it.)

SKULL CRUSHER: *(synonym: french press)* The skull crusher is an exercise in which a barbell is taken from a rack over the head to be lifted over the chest. (The same exercise as the french press.)

SLICED: *(synonyms: buffed, buff, cut, defined, ripped, shredded, sliced and diced)* Having prominent, clearly-defined muscles.

SLICED AND DICED: *(synonyms: buffed, buff, cut, defined, ripped, shredded, sliced)* Having prominent, clearly-defined muscles.

SNATCH: The snatch is a lift used in competition: The arms are held straight to carry the weight from the floor to above the head in one motion.

see also: clean and jerk

SPARE CHANGE: Smaller plates with a hole designed for an Olympic barbell (as opposed to a standard barbell, which has a smaller hole). Olympic plate generally refers to a forty-five-pound weight, so the smaller Olympic plates are called spare change in general and nickels, dimes, and quarters specifically.

see also: Olympic plate, nickel, dime, quarter

SPOT: *(synonym: close spot)* To stand ready to assist a weightlifter, for instance, in case the lifter has worked a muscle group to failure and can't put the weights back on their rack. Spotters sometimes help as well, but are primarily around for safety.

see also: spotter

"I realized that she couldn't **spot** *me*, but really wanted me to spot her."

SPOTTER: A person who stands by a weightlifter in case he or she needs assistance.

see also: spot

STACK: (as a verb) To take multiple performance-enhancing drugs at the same time with the intention of getting them to work together to unusually good effect. (as a noun) A group of performance-enhancing drugs taken at the same time.

see also: shotgun

> "His trainer says he's been stacking anabolic steroids, human growth hormone, insulin, caffeine and Ny-quil. Now that's a **stack**."

STANDARD PLATE: A type of barbell plate with a small hole, as opposed to the larger-holed Olympic plate.

see also: Olympic plate

SUPERSET: Two complementary exercises performed one immediately after the other.

see also: tri-set

SYMMETRY ROUND: The stage of a contest in which bodybuilders stand more or less relaxed in a pose that allows judges to gauge how evenly their muscles are developed.

THIGH BICEPS: *(synonym:* hams*)* The hamstrings: the three muscles in the back of the upper leg.

THRASH: *(synonyms: blast, fry, torch)* To work a muscle group to the point where it can no longer perform an exercise (i.e., to failure) multiple times during a workout; working out in a high-intensity way.

> "You don't really want to **thrash** your back right out of the gate."

TORCH: *(synonyms:* thrash, *blast, fry)* To work a muscle group very hard, repeatedly.

TRI'S OR TRIS: Triceps; the muscles on the outside of the upper arm.

TRI-SET: A group of three related exercises done one immediately after the other.

see also: superset

WASHBOARD: *(synonym:* six pack*)* A well-developed abdominal muscle.

Carnival Workers

Carnivals have a reputation for small-scale cheating and rigged games, and while there are certainly honest carnivals, the reputation isn't entirely unearned. In a recent investigation by Kessler International, a firm that specializes in protection against fraud and theft, only a little more than 25 percent of carnivals they reviewed treated their patrons honestly across the board.

So it's no surprise that carnival slang deals with getting money from carnival attendees by whatever means is most efficient and that some key terms in con artist slang (see page 87) are also used at carnivals.

Along with carnival slang itself, the language of carnival workers includes Ciazarn, a Pig-Latin-like "language" that allows them to speak to one another without being understood by patrons.

Many carnival games and concessions are privately owned: Their proprietors rent space, access to utilities, and so forth from the carnival owner. Other carnivals may be made up of concessions owned by the same organization that owns the carnival as a whole. Thus carnival workers include carnival owners and their employees, as well as independent concession owners and their employees.

Carnival slang is a particularly enduring kind of speech; many of the terms in use today originated in the early days of carnivals. This isn't surprising, since slang tends to have a lot of strength among subcultures that want to set themselves apart and to speak without being understood by outsiders. And why would any self-respecting flattie want to educate the chumps?

RELATED SUBCULTURES:

Circus People, Magicians, Pro Wrestling Fans, Con Artists and Scammers

40-MILER OR 50-MILER: Any younger person who has very recently joined the carnival and is expected to get homesick and leave before the carnival gets forty (or fifty) miles down the road.

> "The old timers all called me a **forty miler**. Not this kid."
>
> - FORMER CARNIVAL WORKER KELLY BELL

86'ED: *(synonym: disqualified)* Banned from the carnival grounds. This can apply to either a person working the carnival or to a visitor.

ADD 'EM UP: *(synonym: count store)* Any carnival game where points are added to try to reach a certain score.

ADVANCE MAN: A carnival employee who takes care of details like licenses, rentals, etc., before the carnival arrives in town.

AGENT: A person who works a carnival game, especially if the game is dishonest.

see also: jointee

ALIBI STORE: A carnival game with unwritten or slippery rules. A person who wins such a game will generally get an explanation

of how her apparent win actually broke the rules, along with a more attractive offer to play again, often for a bigger prize.

ANNEX: An area at a sideshow where an extra show (the blowoff) is available.

see also: blowoff

> "The couple and their two daughters were pretty much the show, except for the **annex** attraction, Lola Conklin."
>
> - "THE CZAR OF BIZARRE" JOHNNY MEAH

BACK END: The far side of the carnival, where the best rides and shows are usually kept in order to draw crowds through the entire length of the grounds.

BAG MAN: Any local official bribed to allow the carnival to operate without interference.

BALLY OR BALLYHOO: A pitch outside a sideshow intended to draw customers. The bally sometimes includes brief appearances by the performers, or it can comprise a mini-performance offered for tips.

(!) BARKER: Not a common term at most carnivals; mentioned here to make it clear that it's best to avoid it. Used mainly by people who don't work at carnivals for a person who speaks to attract customers to a sideshow, although it is used professionally at a minority of carnivals. At most carnivals, this person is called a talker.

see also: talker

BEEF: A complaint from a customer, policeman, etc., about a carnival attraction. More generally, a disagreement.

BLADE GLOMMER: A sword swallower.

BLOWOFF: An extra show offered after a sideshow (or less often, after a popular ride).

BOUNCER: A fake, rubber, deformed fetus (as opposed to a real, preserved, deformed fetus) displayed as an oddity in a side show.

see also: pickled punk

BOZO: An irritating clown at a dunk tank attraction who insults carnival patrons in order to goad

them into paying money to try to dunk him.

BUILD-UP: A type of carnival game in which winning more than once can earn larger prizes; additional plays are often more expensive than the first one.

"The Break a Dish game is not a **build-up** game. It's a tough game, and there's only one prize, a big tiger or some other stuffed toy."

CALL: (as a noun) Anything shouted out to passing carnival patrons to entice them to consider a particular game. (as a verb) To use a call.

(!) CARNEY OR CARNY OR CARNIE: 1) A carnival worker. This term is sometimes considered derogatory. Carnival workers tend to prefer terms like "agent" or "operator" (for a person operating a game of chance), "talker" (for a person who speaks to the public at a sideshow), or more generally showman. 2) The carnival worker "language" more commonly called Ciazarn.

CENTER JOINT: A carnival game open on more than one (often four) sides, so that it can handle more patrons.

CHUMP: *(synonyms: mark, towner or townie, sucker, clem)* A carnival patron.

CIAZARN: (pronounced "KEE-uhz-arn") A fake language used by workers at carnivals to speak without being understood by carnival patrons.

To speak Ciazarn, simply add the sound "ee-uhz" after the first letter of each word. For instance "Tee-uhz-ell hee-uhz-im hee-uhz-ee kee-uhz-an wee-uhz-in thee-uhz-ee tee-uhz-ed-dy bee-uzh-ear." ("Tell him he can win the teddy bear.")

The word "Ciazarn" is of course just "carn" in Ciazarn.

Also called Carney.

CIRCUS JUMP: A move from one carnival location to the next that's difficult to manage in the available time.

CLEM: *(synonyms: mark, towner or townie, sucker, chump)* A carnival patron.

COOK SHACK: A place where carnival workers eat. A cook shack is infrequently open to the public.

COUNT STORE: *(synonym: add 'em up)* A carnival game based on point totals.

CRACK: A tried and true phrase the operator of a carnival game uses to get the best possible reaction from a carnival patron.

CUT UP JACKPOTS: For carnival workers, to tell exaggerated stories about things they've done at carnivals in the past.

DISQUALIFIED: *(synonym: 86'ed)* Kicked out of a carnival.

DONIKER: A rest room.

> "Got in line; got our various tickets, our agenda, and T-shirts; entered the park; and proceeded to our first attraction: the **doniker**."

DONIKER JOINT: A concession located in an undesirable location, for instance next to a restroom.

DRAW: Small amounts of money advanced to carnival help against wages, since regular wages are often not paid until the carnival has packed up.

EDUCATED: Too knowledgeable to be cheated at a carnival game. Refers to a carnival patron who knows the various ways games are rigged.

FIREBALL OR FIREBALL SHOW: A carnival where the owner allows pretty much any kind of behavior from the people running the concessions on the lot. A fireball may include lewd attractions, highly dishonest games, etc.

FIRST COUNT: The right to be the first person to count money or tickets. Having first count offers the best opportunity to ensure one is not being cheated or to potentially skim a little off the top.

FLASH: Showy prizes or other glitz shown at a carnival game to attract patrons. Flash may not be winnable, depending on how honest the game is.

FLAT JOINT: *(synonym: flat store)* A carnival game rigged so that it can't be won.

FLAT STORE: *(synonym: flat joint)* A carnival game rigged so that it can't be won.

see also: flattie

> "A good **flat-store** man learns how to bleed his mooch for every quarter he can get."
>
> - WRITER AND FORMER CARNIVAL TALKER DAN FANTE

FLATTIE: A person who runs a dishonest game, particularly one that is impossible to win (known as a flat store).

FRONT: The length of the side or sides of a carnival concession that that are open to allow carnival patrons to be served. Comparable to a storefront on a downtown street.

GAFF: Any gimmick used to rig or fake a carnival attraction. For example, a gaffed game is rigged to be difficult or impossible to win; a gaffed exhibit is fake.

GEEK: A carnival performer whose act consists of acting wild or doing disgusting things, for instance, biting the heads off live chickens. Less common now than they once were.

GO SOUTH: To steal money from an employer.

GRAB JOINT: A food concession that has no seating.

GRIND SHOW: A carnival attraction where people can enter at any time (as opposed to one that offers performances on a schedule).

G-TOP: A gambling tent for carnival workers, not open to the public, which opens after the carnival closes for the day. Food and other items may be for sale in the G-top as well.

HANDLE: The name or nickname used by a carnival worker.

HANKY-PANK: Counter-intuitively, a hanky-pank is a game that isn't rigged or one that produces a win every time. It generally yields prizes that are worth much less than the price of the game.

> "Your best bet is to play the **hanky panks**, where you are playing against other players and someone has got to win."
>
> - Coney Island sideshow man Todd Robbins

HEAT: Trouble at a carnival site, whether between carnival workers or between the carnival and the town.

HOLE: A space available for rent to a concession operator (an agent). One concession may require multiple holes, depending on how much space it needs (i.e. how much front).

HOT SNAKE: A poisonous snake used in a carnival show.

INSIDE TALKER: *(synonym: lecturer)* A carnival worker who speaks to patrons inside a show tent.

JOINT: *(synonym: store)* Any concession at a carnival. Joints may be tents or trailers, and may be "line-up joints," with only one side facing the public, or "center joints," with two or more sides facing the public.

JOINTEE: A person who works a carnival game.

see also: agent

> "If the **jointee** is an old guy and he only has large plush to win, walk away fast."
>
> - CONEY ISLAND SIDESHOW MAN TODD ROBBINS

JUMP: In reference to a carnival, to move from one town to another.

KEY TO THE MIDWAY: *(synonyms: light bulb grease, left-handed monkey wrench)* A pretend object that carnival workers may send annoying children to find.

KICK: Any place (pocket, pouch, etc.) a carnival worker keeps his or her money.

LECTURER: *(synonym: inside talker)* A carnival worker who speaks to patrons inside a show tent.

LEFT-HANDED MONKEY WRENCH: *(synonyms: light bulb grease, key to the midway)* A pretend object that carnival workers may send annoying children to find.

LIGHT BULB GREASE: *(synonyms: left-handed monkey wrench, key to the midway)* A pretend object that a carnival worker may send an annoying kid to fetch . This is a favored means of shooing away children.

> "I passed through the gauntlets of fetchin' **light bulb grease** and left-handed wrenches."
>
> - FORMER CARNIVAL WORKER KELLY BELL

LOC: (pronounced "loke") The location of a carnival concession.

see also: hole, joint

LOT: The location of the carnival as a whole; the midway.

see also: midway

LOT LICE: People who go to a carnival to look, but don't spend any money.

(!) MARK: *(synonyms: towner or townie, sucker, clem, chump)* Broadly, any carnival patron; but used especially to imply an

individual targeted to be tricked out of his money. Note that this is the same term favored by con artists for their intended victims (see page 95).

see also: mooch

MIDWAY: The entire carnival, including games, rides, concessions, shows, etc.

see also: lot

MITT CAMP: A fortune-telling concession.

MONEY STORE: A carnival game that offers cash as a prize.

see also: joint

MOOCH: A carnival patron who looks to be easy to separate from his or her money.

see also: mark

> "[He] stands in a midway game waving hoops or baseballs at people, calling to **mooches** passing by to come over and play his game."
>
> - WRITER AND FORMER CARNIVAL WORKER DAN FANTE

NUT: The expense of running a carnival, or its break-even point; a carnival has to "make the nut" before it brings in profit.

OUTSIDE TALKER: A carnival worker who entices people to buy tickets for a show; typically, he or she stands outside the tent or trailer housing the event.

see also: talker, barker, inside talker

OVERCALL: For the operator of a carnival concession to call out to a carnival patron before he or she is in the area belonging to the concession in question; that is, to try to steal patrons from someone else's turf.

PATCH: (as a verb) To fix a problem that arises from a crooked carnival concession, or to pay bribes to local law enforcement. (as a noun) A carnival worker whose job is to pay patch.

PICKLED PUNK: A deformed fetus preserved in formaldehyde and displayed in a side show. Not a term often used with the public.

see also: bouncer, punk

> "During this time, a dollar ding is done showing a very fine '**pickled punk**' 'til part two."
>
> - SHOWMAN WARD ALEXANDER

PITCH: A lecture designed to sell something. Descended from old-time medicine shows.

PLAY A MARK: To keep a carnival patron at a game long enough for him or her to lose as much money as possible; more broadly, to milk a carnival patron dry by any means.

see also: mark

PROPOSITION OR PROP: The business deal offered by a carnival owner to an independent concession owner; includes all monetary terms, percentages, additional fees, etc.

PUNK: A child.

RANGY: (pronounced "RAN-ghee," not "RANE-jee") Jumpy, agitated, or out of control. Can be used to describe an upset patron at a carnival game, a rowdy show, or even an animal that's out of sorts.

REHASH: To give a carnival patron a free play at a game after the patron loses, or to get the patron to pay for another play. More broadly, to reuse anything.

RIDE JOCK: A carnival worker who operates a ride.

ROUGHY: Carnival workers employed by the carnival owner rather than by owners of carnival concessions. Roughies take care of a variety of tasks, such as collecting money from concession operators, and hiring new workers.

SHILL: *(synonym: stick)* A person who pretends to be a regular carnival patron while working for a concession operator in any kind of deception that may encourage a carnival patron to spend more money. For example, a shill might succeed immediately at winning a big prize, making it appear that the game can be won and that the big prizes are actually given out when this might not really be the case.

SHOWMAN: A carnival worker. Carnival workers usually prefer this term to "carney."

SIMP HEISTER: A Ferris wheel.

SINGLE-O: A show with only one attraction (as opposed to a show with multiple attractions, such as a "ten-in-one").

see also: ten-in-one

SLICK: To catch someone doing something dishonest.

SLUM: Cheap prizes that cost far less than the price of playing the game.

SPOOF: Any small-scale deceit.

see also: gaff

STICK: *(synonym: shill)* A concession employee posing as a carnival patron.

STORE: *(synonym: joint)* A carnival concession.

STRONG: 1) Aggressive or successful. 2) In reference to a show, provocative; for instance, offering full or partial nudity.

SUCKER: *(synonyms: mark, towner or townie, clem, chump)* A carnival patron.

TALKER: Someone who talks to carnival patrons, whether to entice them to buy a ticket or to guide them through. The person who sells the tickets this way is called the outside talker (not usually called a barker; "barker" is not a word used at most carnivals). The person who speaks to patrons inside the tent is called the lecturer or inside talker.

see also: barker, showman, outside talker, inside talker

TEN-IN-ONE: A show with roughly ten attractions; for example, a freak show with a fat lady, a mummified devil baby, a contortionist, and six to eight other oddities.

see also: single-O

TIP: The potential audience for a carnival show, whom the outside talker tries to convince to buy tickets. "Turning the tip" means getting patrons to buy tickets to the show.

TOWNER OR TOWNIE: *(synonyms: mark, sucker, clem, chump)* A carnival patron.

WIDE OPEN: In reference to the carnival as a whole, immune from action by the local authorities, generally as a result of bribery, and therefore operating without restraint. For instance, such a show might cheat patrons flagrantly or include unusually raunchy girl shows.

Cat Fanciers

Cat lovers have been around since antiquity, but the subculture of cat fanciers didn't emerge until the late nineteenth century when groups began to get together to document breeding of cats and to hold cat shows. The language of cat shows seems to have been largely set in this period, so that the cat fancy terms used today (like "queen" and "cattery") have a bit of a quaint sound to an outsider.

The term "cat fancier" implies something beyond the more general term "cat lover," in that cat fanciers are normally interested in pedigreed cats, cat breeding, and cat shows. The Cat Fanciers' Association, an American organization founded in 1906, sponsors many of the cat shows that occur around the United States. Currently there are well over a hundred American cat shows each year.

Pedigreed cats can have long and grand names that include the cattery where the animal was born; the cattery that currently owns the animal, if it's not a pet; and abbreviations for prizes won. A few of these abbreviations are CH (Champion), GC (Grand Champion), BW (Best of Breed Winner), and RW (Regional Winner).

ALLBREED OR ALL BREED: Including cats of all breeds and coat lengths, as for example in "allbreed judge" or "all breed show."

"By the end of the show, Vincent had won a 5th, 4th and 2nd in longhairs and a 3rd in **allbreed**, giving him a total of 1,150 points."

ALTER: To remove a cat's reproductive organs: to "fix," "spay," "neuter," etc. A spayed or neutered cat is said to be an "altered" cat.

ANY OTHER VARIETY OR AOV: Describes a purebred, registered cat that doesn't meet the usual show requirements for its breed. For instance, Manx cats are not supposed to have tails, but every once in a while a very nice Manx with a tail comes along, and if it participates in a cat show it does so in the Any Other Variety class, competing against a variety of other elegant misfits rather than against others of its own breed.

BREED TRUE: To produce a kitten that looks very similar to its parents.

"One of her latest litter is a little *orange*-point tom! She's hoping he'll **breed true**."

CALL: In reference to a pedigreed female cat (queen), to make characteristic noises that show she's in heat. Alley cats may yowl, but queens call.

CAT FANCIER: Generally, a person who likes cats. Often used more specifically to refer to cat enthusiasts who are involved in cat breeding or cat shows.

see also: cat fancy

CAT FANCY: The general phenomenon of enthusiasm for cats. Sometimes used more narrowly to refer to activities like cat breeding and cat shows.

see also: cat fancier

CATTERY: 1) A registered cat breeding establishment. An individual cat breeder registers the name of his or her cattery. This designation becomes part of the name of each of the cats born there. See prefix for more information on cat naming. 2) A place where cats are boarded temporarily.

see also: prefix

CRYPTORCHID: (pronounced "crip-TOR-kid") A male cat whose testicles haven't descended. This condition disqualifies a cat from appearing in a show.

see also: monorchid

DAM: A cat's mother.

see also: queen, sire

"If the sire and the **dam**'s **dam** and the **dam**'s sire's parents have all tested negative, you have a cat which should not develop P.K.D."

EXHIBITOR: A person showing a cat at a cat show.

HOUSEHOLD PET: The cat show term for an unregistered or mixed breed cat. (Not derogatory.)

"I am planning to show her as a **household pet**—she isn't a pedigree—to help me decide if I truly want to get a show cat."

HYBRID: A cat whose parents are of two different breeds. If a hybrid meets the standard for one or the other of its parent's breeds, it can be registered as being of that breed.

MONORCHID: (pronounced "mon-OR-kid") A male cat with only one descended testicle.

see also: cryptorchid

ODD-EYED: Having a different color for each eye.

PAPERS: A cat's registration and pedigree.

"Stud is expensive, and if your cat is not a pure-breed with **papers**, you may find it difficult to find a breeder that is willing to sire 'mongrel' kittens."

PEDIGREED: In reference to a cat, having documented ancestors three or more generations back.

see also: registered

PREFIX: In a registered cat's full name, the cattery where that cat was born. For example, in the name Londinium's Tiger of Wallaby, DM, "Londinium," the name of a (fictitious) cattery where Tiger was born, is the prefix.

see also: cattery, suffix, title

QUEEN: A registered, breeding, female cat.

see also: dam, stud cat

RANDOM BRED: A cat that is not recognized as a particular breed, or whose ancestry isn't documented (i.e., a non-pedigreed cat).

see also: pedigreed, hybrid

> "The only reason that many **random-bred** offspring of Siamese tend to be black is that many Siamese are seal point."

REGISTERED: In reference to a cat, documented in terms of immediate ancestry with a cat registering association.

see also: pedigreed

SHOW QUALITY: In reference to a registered cat, meeting the requirements for its specific breed to the extent that it can compete within that breed at cat shows.

SIRE: A cat's father.

see also: dam

STUD CAT: A registered, breeding, male cat.

see also: sire, queen

SUFFIX: In a registered cat's full name, the name of the cattery that currently owns the cat, if any. For instance, the cat name Londinium's Tiger of Wallaby, DM, "Wallaby," the name of a (fictitious) cattery, is the suffix. If a cat changes ownership, the suffix must be officially removed to be replaced with a new suffix.

see also: prefix, cattery

TITLE: An abbreviation at the beginning or end of a cat's name, earned from placement in shows and/or success in shows by the cat's offspring.

see also: suffix, prefix

TOM: A male cat with its reproductive organs intact, that is, that hasn't been altered.

see also: stud cat

Cavers and Spelunkers

★ ★ ★ ★

Among the important things to understand about cave exploration slang are the differences between the terms "caver," "spelunker," and "speleologist."

A "caver" is a person who learns effective and safe cave exploration techniques and who practices them. The designation applies even to very new cavers, as long as they are trying to learn the right way to do things.

"Spelunker" is a less cut-and-dried term. It is sometimes used to mean the same thing as "caver," but more often is a derogatory term for a person who explores caves without being well equipped, prepared, or trained.

A "speleologist" is a person who explores caves primarily to gather information. A speleologist may have a degree in geology, biology, hydrology, or some other related field or may simply have studied on his or her own.

Cavers and speleologists (and occasionally spelunkers) may know a long list of words for different rock forms, terms like "bedding grike," "flap," "bench," "hornito," "keyhole," "lava hands," "lavacicle," "pudding," and "swirlhole."

RELATED SUBCULTURES:

Rock Climbers, Hikers and Backpackers

★ ★ ★ ★ ★ ★

ACTIVE CAVE: A cave with water flowing through it.

AIR RAPPEL: The activity of falling into a pit.

(!) ARMCHAIR CAVER: *(synonym: virtual caver)* A person involved in the caving subculture who spends time with books, Web sites, and other sources of caving material, but who doesn't actually go caving. Can be a non-derogatory term for an experienced caver who no longer goes caving or either a derogatory or non-derogatory term for a person who doesn't have any substantial experience with caving.

BIG-NAME CAVER OR BNC: A person recognized as a caving authority.

> "In the '50s and '60s the best way to become an NSS **BNC (Big-Name Caver)** was to advance mankind's scientific knowledge by publishing a book entitled *Caves of [Your State]*."

BOOBTUBE: A long, flexible tube used to drink water from hard-to-reach sources.

BOOTY: First visits to previously unexplored passages of a cave.

see also: scoop

> "I hate it that the ones who run the grottos have a hard time dealing with the fact that people just come in and scoop **booty**."

CAVE DIVING: Exploring underwater caves with scuba equipment.

CAVER: A person who explores caves. See the introduction to this section for the differences between caver, spelunker, and speleologist.

CHEMICAL PERSUASION: *(synonym: rock solvent)* Explosives used to open cave passages.

> "I'm hoping to be free to drive up the following weekend to see if my little bit of **chemical persuasion** has let me into miles of new cave system."

ENTRANCE FEVER: A pressing urge to leave a cave.

> "I had severe **entrance fever** by then because I never pee in a cave."

FALSE FLOOR: A sheet of rock that has formed over another type of rock that has since eroded away, leaving a gap, hole, pit, or void underneath.

FLATTENER: A passage that is so low that the only way to get through it is to worm through on one's belly.

FOUL AIR: In a cave, air that has too much carbon dioxide to be safe to breathe for long.

GROT HOLE: A cave that dead-ends quickly and is not worth exploring.

GROUND TROG: An above-ground search for cave entrances.

NERD GATE: A natural barrier in a cave passage that's fairly easy to get past, such that it keeps out only casual cave explorers.

> "This traverse is about sixty feet in the air along one wall. It's a great **nerd gate**."

PIG: A long container for carrying loose objects, made by attaching parts of two large, plastic bottles to one another. A pig can be strapped on in such a way that it doesn't interfere when crawling or otherwise cause a person to move awkwardly.

PITCH: A vertical drop in a cave.

ROCK SOLVENT: *(synonym: chemical persuasion)* Explosives used to remove caving obstacles.

ROOF SNIFFING: Edging through a passage nearly filled with water, where there's only a small amount of air between the top of the water and the ceiling. The caver needs to "sniff" the air from that little gap.

ROUT: To head out of a cave.

> "Bob and Pete now decided to **rout** while Keith and Frank continued surveying in side leads."

(!) SCOOP: 1) To be the first person known to enter a cave or passage. 2) To progress through caves in order to be first person to get to as many passages as possible, not stopping to explore. Can be derogatory.

SPELEOLOGIST: A person who studies caves. See the introduction to this section for the differences between caver, spelunker, and speleologist.

(!) SPELUNKER: A person who explores caves; sometimes carries the implication of a person who doesn't know or much care about good caving practices. See the introduction to this section for the differences between caver, spelunker, and speleologist.

TROG UP: To don caving clothing and gear in preparation for entering a cave.

TWILIGHT ZONE: The part of a cave that doesn't receive direct sunlight and gradually shades from light to full darkness.

VIRTUAL CAVER: *(synonym: armchair caver)* A person who is interested in caving but who doesn't go caving.

Circus People

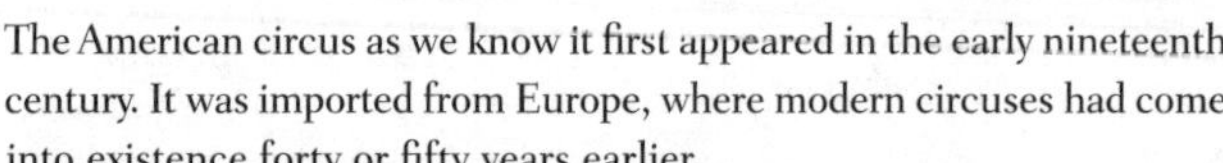

The American circus as we know it first appeared in the early nineteenth century. It was imported from Europe, where modern circuses had come into existence forty or fifty years earlier.

Much modern American circus slang emerged during the early years of the circus and has remained consistent over the decades since. It has incorporated terms from European circuses and through them a few from the gypsy language, Romany, since many European circuses included gypsy performers.

Circuses have lost much of their popularity since the 1960s as other forms of entertainment have become common. Over that time, a new type of circus has developed in contrast to the traditional shows of varied acrobat, clown, and performing animal acts. This movement, called "Cirque Nouveau," combines theatrical storytelling with acrobatics and spectacle.

What we now call a carnival originated as the part of a circus that was outside the big top. These additional entertainments grew over time, eventually becoming completely separate organizations. Because of this history, much carnival worker slang is shared with circus folk.

RELATED SUBCULTURE:

Carnival Workers

ANNIE OAKLEY: *(synonyms: ducat or ducket, comp)* A free pass to the show.

"The big shows never forget him, and when they arrive in Portland, Doc is always presented with a generous supply of '**Annie Oakleys**.'"

ANNOUNCER: *(synonyms: fancy pants, gaffer)* The Master of Ceremonies.

ARTIST: *(synonym: artiste)* A performer.

ARTISTE: *(synonym: artist)* (pronounced "ar-TEEST") A performer.

AUGUSTE CLOWN: A type of foolish clown, usually with white makeup on the whole face or around the eyes and mouth.

BACK DOOR: The performers' entrance to the circus tent.

BACK YARD OR BACKYARD: An area behind the big top, hidden from the public, where performers dress, repairs are made, animals are prepared for performances, and other preparations are made during the show.

see also: big top

BALLYHOO: Any means of raising excitement and focusing the crowd's attention before an act, especially an energetic speech.

"Mostly he is one hell of a good showman, taking his style from snake oil peddlers and **ballyhoo**, with a nice touch of Elmer Gantry revivalist frenzy thrown in."

BIG TOP: The main show tent, where the main performance takes place.

see also: top

BILL: (as a noun) A poster advertising the circus. (as a verb) To put up circus posters.

see also: hit, herald, paper

BLOWDOWN: The knocking down of a tent by a storm or high wind.

"The circus were the victim of a **blowdown** and were showing without a tent! I expected that they were downhearted, but they were not, especially as the tent was not repairable!"

BLUES: *(synonym: stringers)* The least expensive seats.

see also: grandstands, stalls

BOSS CANVASMAN: (*synonym: tent master*) The person in charge of getting tents erected. The boss canvasman chooses sites for the tents and oversees the workers who set them up.

see also: top

BOSS CLOWN: The chief clown, in charge of all of the clowns in the show. This is an important position in the circus, not a role played by a clown in a performance.

BULL: An elephant (whether male or female).

(!) BUMP A NOSE: A clown phrase meaning "good luck"!

This phrase is widespread, but looked on with disfavor among some more traditionalist clowns. The Web site www.bigtop.com (defunct as of this writing) described "bump a nose" as "cutsie-poo amateur clown club jargon," and says a real circus clown would be more likely to say something like "go #$%& yourself."

BUTCHER: A vendor who walks through the audience selling candy, popcorn, balloons, etc.

CALLIOPE: (pronounced "CAL-ee-ope,") A steam-driven organ. Closely associated with circuses and carnivals but not in as widespread use as it once was.

CARPET CLOWN: Any clown who works between acts or among the audience.

CATCHER: A trapeze artist who catches other trapeze artists (as opposed to a flyer).

see also: flyer

CENTER POLE: (*synonym: king pole*) The tallest pole in the big top and the first pole raised.

see also: top, big top

CHARACTER CLOWN: A clown who portrays any type of character, particularly a hobo, but conceivably anything from a cop to a cowboy to a celebrity.

see also: hobo clown, tramp clown

CHERRY PIE: Extra jobs around the circus done by circus folk for extra money.

CLOUD SWING: A loop of rope used in some aerial acts.

CLOWN ALLEY: 1) Clown dressing rooms. 2) The area closest to the back door, behind the big top, where clown props are stored and where clowns wait when not performing.

CLOWN STOP: A very brief clown performance, usually between other circus acts as props are changed or equipment set up.

COME-IN OR COME IN: The time just prior to the performance, when the crowd comes into the tent. During the come-in, rides or games may be offered outside the big top, and pre-show clowns may perform.

COMP: *(synonyms: Annie Oakley, ducat or ducket)* A free pass.

COOK SHACK: *(synonyms: pie car or pie-car, cookhouse)* The place where circus people eat.

COOKHOUSE: *(synonyms: pie car or pie-car, cook shack)* The place where circus people eat.

DISASTER MARCH: "The Stars and Stripes Forever" march, by John Philip Sousa, played by a circus band during a performance to signal to all circus personnel if something has gone horribly wrong.

see also: windjammer

DONIKER: Toilet or restroom.

DOORS!: A call used to signal to other circus people that the big top is open for the public to enter.

DRESS THE HOUSE: When selling tickets, to distribute seating so that no section of the stands looks empty.

"The 'protected seats' mean that the center (near the aisle) will be filled first, unless a patron asks for ten seats, in which case they would get the seats with '#' in them. Its just another way to **dress the house**."

DUCAT OR DUCKET: *(synonyms: Annie Oakley, comp)* A free pass.

DUKEY RUN OR DUKIE RUN: A relatively long distance; for example, more than one night's travel between show locations, or the walk to an inconveniently placed pie car.

EQUESTRIAN DIRECTOR: *(synonym: ringmaster)* The person in charge of horse acts.

FANCY PANTS: *(synonyms: announcer, gaffer)* The person who announces the acts; a Master of Ceremonies. Not to be confused with the ringmaster, who is actually the person in charge of horse acts.

see also: ringmaster

FIRST OF MAY: A circus hand or circus performer in his or her first season.

> "In the last few years a lot of people have gone to work for the circus who will always be **first of Mays** no matter how long they are around."

FLYER: An artiste in an aerial act who jumps from swings to be caught by a catcher.

see also: catcher

FUNAMBULIST: *(synonyms: high wire walker, tightrope walker)* An aerial artiste who walks on a rope or cable suspended high in the big top.

GAFFER: *(synonyms: fancy pants, announcer)* The Master of Ceremonies.

GAG: A brief clown skit, often collected with other gags into a full act.

GILLY: *(synonyms: townie or towner, native)* A member of the public; someone not part of the circus.

GILLY WAGON: An equipment cart for use on circus grounds.

GRANDSTANDS: The better seats, which directly face the center ring.

see also: blues, stalls

GREASE JOINT: A food concession cart for the public (instead of for the circus performers and hands).

see also: pie car

GUY: A rope, cable, or wire used to hold up or stabilize part of the show, especially a tent. Also "guy line," "guy cable," "guy wire," "guy rope."

see also: top, big top

HERALD: A flyer handed out or sometimes pasted up in advance of the circus coming into town.

see also: bill, hit, paper

HEY, RUBE!: A call for help from other circus people, especially in a fight with locals. Widely understood, but waning in use.

HIGH WIRE WALKER: *(synonyms: funambulist, tightrope walker)* A high wire performer.

HIPPODROME: The horse track around a circus ring.

> "You now enter the big top, and it is bigger than you thought, and you walk down the **hippodrome** track and all you can see are the wires for all the aerial acts."

HIT: Any surface on which circus advertising is posted.

see also: bill, herald, paper

HOBO CLOWN: A happy, energetic version of a hobo/tramp clown.

see also: *tramp clown, character clown*

HOOFSTOCK: Any hoofed animal: a horse, zebra, etc.

see also: *painted pony*

HOUSE: The audience.

HUMP: A camel.

IRON JAW ACT OR IRON JAW TRICK: A stunt performed by an aerial artiste, hanging in the air by the strength of his or her bite from a specialized apparatus.

JACKPOT: A personal true story or tall tale told by a circus performer or circus hand about circus life.

JOEY: (as a noun) A clown, especially a more experienced clown. (as a verb) To perform as a clown.

JUMP: The trip between show locations.

KID SHOW: A sideshow that travels with the circus; an attraction that's not part of the main performance.

KIESTER: (pronounced "KEE-stur") 1) A circus person's trunk or luggage. 2) A display case used by a pitchman. 3) A person's backside. This usage may come from a misunderstanding of the expression "sitting on your kiester," which meant sitting on your luggage. 4) Jail.

KING POLE: (*synonym: center pole*) The tallest pole in the circus tent.

KINKER: Any circus performer.

KIP: A bed, or any other sleeping place.

LARRY: Anything broken or useless.

LIBERTY OR LIBERTY HORSE: A horse trained to perform without a rider; this performance is called a "liberty act."

> "These are circus **liberty horse** routines which, as far as I know, you could teach a horse to do while sitting."

LOT: The circus grounds.

LUNGE ROPE: A rope attached to a harness on an aerial artiste during practice and held taut as a safety measure; the person holding the rope can prevent the performer from falling.

see also: *mechanic*

MECHANIC: A safety harness worn by aerial artistes while practicing.

see also: *lunge rope*

MENAGE: (pronounced "men-AHGE," to rhyme with "garage") A performance that displays a number of trained animals, usually horses.

MIDWAY: The area where side-shows and concessions are located, outside the main circus tent. A carnival (see page 55) is a midway without a circus connected to it.

(!) MUD SHOW: While this term is sometimes used by circus out-siders to refer to a small circus, it is not currently in use among circus folk and may have only ever referred to circuses that traveled in horse-drawn carts.

NATIVE: *(synonyms: gilly, townie or towner)* A member of the public.

ON THE SHOW: Part of the circus. Terms like "with the show" are not used.

"Most people live on the train. Your status **on the show** will dictate what kind of room you live in and in which train car."

PAINTED PONY: A zebra.

see also: hoofstock

PAPER: Posters for the circus.

see also: bill, herald, paper

PIE CAR OR PIE-CAR: *(synonyms: cookhouse, cook shack)* The place on the circus site where food is prepared for and eaten by circus people. The pie car is not open to the public.

see also: grease joint

PITCHMAN: Anyone who talks to an audience at a circus to sell merchandise. A pitchman might work on the midway or might use the loudspeaker between acts to encourage patrons to buy from vendors (butchers) moving through the crowd.

POSSUM BELLY: A storage box hanging under a wagon or rail-road car.

RED WAGON: The circus' main of-fice, regardless of whether or not it is actually red or a wagon.

RIGGER: A circus hand who sets up ropes, wires, and apparatus used in aerial acts.

see also: rigging

RIGGING: The ropes, wires, and apparatus used in aerial perfor-mances such as tightrope walking and trapeze acts.

see also: rigger

RING: A circular performance area in the big top. Some circuses have one ring, others three. The term refers to the area enclosed by the ring curbs, not to the ring curbs themselves.

see also: ring curb

RING CURB: A wooden section used to create a circular area (a ring) for circus performances.

see also: ring

RINGER: 1) A substitute person or animal passed off as the real thing, for instance, an understudy going on when a famous performer is ill. 2) A guest performer.

(!) RINGMASTER: *(synonym: equestrian director)* The person in charge of horse acts at a circus. The term is often incorrectly used to refer to the fancy pants (also called the gaffer or announcer).

ROSINBACK: A horse used for bareback riding performances.

ROUSTABOUT: A general laborer.

"The most intelligent, best read and in some ways the happiest man I ever met spent his life as a circus **roustabout**. That suited him, and he made the most of the life he had picked for himself."

SIDEWALL: The canvas wall of a tent. A top held up by poles, together with sidewalls, makes a complete tent.

see also: top

SPEC: A parade or production number that shows off the performers as colorfully as possible. Short for "spectacle."

SPOOL TRUCK OR SPOOL WAGON: The truck that carries the tent canvas.

STALLS: The medium-priced seats.

see also: blues, grandstands

STAND: The set of performances at one location over a period of time (a day, a week, several weeks, etc.).

STRAW HOUSE: A sold-out performance.

see also: turnaway

"When Culpepper played a string of small farm towns in the Salinas Valley this season, they played **straw house** after **straw house** to crowds of farm workers."

STRINGERS: *(synonym: blues)* The cheapest seats.

STRIPE: A tiger.

TENT MASTER: *(synonym: boss canvasman)* The person in charge of tents.

TIGHTROPE WALKER: *(synonyms: funambulist, high wire walker)* A high wire performer.

TOP: 1) The top of a tent (not including the sidewalls). 2) More broadly, an entire tent (e.g., the "big top").

see also: big top, sidewall

TOWNIE OR TOWNER: *(synonyms: gilly, native)* A member of the public.

TRAMP CLOWN: A depressed hobo/tramp-type clown.

see also: character clown, hobo clown

TROUPE: Any group of artistes who perform an act together.

TROUPER: A person who has worked with the circus for at least one season.

TURNAWAY: A show that is not only sold out, but actively turning patrons away.

see also: straw house

TWENTY-FOUR HOUR MAN: A circus employee who travels a day ahead of the circus, planning the route to the lot and sometimes marking it for the circus to follow.

WAGON: Anything used to carry circus equipment, animals, or personnel (e.g., trucks, trailers, etc.).

WALKAROUND OR WALK-AROUND: A clown performance in which the clown interacts with the audience.

> "Look close when the clowns are doing their **walkaround** stuff. Normally there should be at least one juggler in there."

WEB: Ropes or canvas tubes that hang from above and that aerial artistes hang on to in certain kinds of performances.

WHITEFACE CLOWN: A type of clown that is played more seriously than other types and whose makeup includes covering all exposed skin with white.

WINDJAMMER: A circus musician.

WINTER QUARTERS: The location for a particular circus over the winter; performances are given at that location until the next traveling tour.

ZANY OR ZANIE: A clown.

Coin and Money Collectors

Coin collecting and paper money collecting ("numismatics" and "notaphily," respectively) include a wide and precise vocabulary for describing types of dies, metals, conditions, features on particular coins, specific kinds of damage and discoloration, and grades of condition, jargon too detailed to cover properly here.

In addition, collectors have names for a variety of specific coins: the Buffalo Nickel, Teddy's Coin, the Little Princess, the Bellybutton Dollar, the Little Orphan Annie, the Fat Head, and many others.

While many of the special terms used among coin and paper money collectors seem formal, names of coins and coin features are the exception.

Some collectors collect coins as an investment, which is understandable given that an individual piece can sell for as much as three million dollars, as a 1907 gold eagle (a ten dollar coin) did. Others may value the history that each coin embodies or the sensation of possessing a collection of small, beautiful objects or the challenge of finding coins and properly determining their value despite complicated grading criteria, damage, discoloration, wear, and even alteration and counterfeiting.

In the past there have been a variety of coin grading systems. The main one in use today

was assembled from two other systems by the Professional Coin Grading Service (PGCS), one of the two major coin appraisal companies. Under the PGCS system, coin grades have both an abbreviation and a number. The numbers range from 1 to 70, mostly in increments of 5.1 represents "nearly destroyed," while 70 means "marvelous beyond all description." The abbreviations stand for the terms used to refer to the coin's grade, and each abbreviation matches one or more numeric ratings. The word "choice" indicates better condition than the corresponding term without the word, e.g., "choice very fine" is a step up from "very fine."

Those grade abbreviations, with their corresponding numeric grades, are MS *or* Unc. (mint state or uncirculated: grade 60–70), AU (about uncirculated: 50, 53, 55, 58), XF *or* EF (extremely fine: 40, 45), VF (very fine *and* choice very fine: 20, 25, 30), F (fine: 12, 15), VG (very good: 8, 10), G (good: 4, 6), AG (about good: 3), Fr (fair: 2), and PO (poor or "basal state:" 1).

Some of these terms are counter-intuitive. For instance, "good" condition means that a coin has heavy wear or noticeable damage. So, good is bad (but "about good" is worse).

RELATED SUBCULTURE:

Stamp Collectors (Philatelists)

ACCUMULATION: A group of coins that is not organized or intentional enough to be called a collection. Not a derogatory term.

BLAZER: *(synonyms: monster, moose, wonder coin)* A coin in incredibly good condition that immediately attracts the eye.

BODY BAG: A plastic sleeve in which a coin is returned from a grading service when the service could not grade the coin; for instance, because it is damaged or may not be authentic.

see also: no-grade, cull

BOURSE: A coin show.

CONTEMPORARY COUNTERFEIT: A copy of a coin or note made during the period the currency was legal tender; that is, a counterfeit meant to be spent instead of to fool a collector. Contemporary counterfeit coins are generally made of cheaper metals than the real coins.

CULL: A coin in such bad condition, it's essentially of no interest to collectors.

see also: *no-grade, body bag*

> "Looks like it could be new, but I'm not sure. It's certainly not a rag (or a **cull**)!"

DESIGN TYPE: A single image or design used on multiple coins or notes.

DEVICE: *(synonym: emblem)* Any lettering or other decoration marked on the surface of a coin.

see also: *field*

DIP: To clean a coin in a solution of soap, acid, or other agents. Many kinds of dipping can strip off thin layers of metal, devaluing the coin.

see also: *over-dipped*

DOCTORED: In reference to a coin, inappropriately altered to attempt to improve appearance or increase value.

ELECTROTYPE: A counterfeit coin made from the cast of a legitimate coin.

EMBLEM: *(synonym: device)* A marking on a coin.

EYE APPEAL: The aesthetic impact of a coin; its beauty or visual interest.

> "I think the best and most affordable collection would be high **eye appeal** XF to AU's."

FANTASY NOTE: An invented piece of paper currency, often created as a novelty.

see also: *fantasy piece*

FANTASY PIECE: An invented coin, created either as a novelty or (occasionally) as a fraud.

see also: *fantasy note*

FIELD: The flat background areas of a coin.

see also: *device*

FINGER: *(synonym: thumb)* To rub a finger over a coin to hide flaws.

FLIP: (as a noun) A clear, plastic pocket for holding coins from

a collection. (as a verb) To sell a coin soon after buying, for a quick profit.

"Give each attendee a collectable coin in a 2x2-inch **flip** with numismatic information and the A.N.A. Web address on the insert."

- FROM AN AMERICAN NUMISMATIC ASSOCIATION PRESS RELEASE

FRESH: In reference to a coin, made available for sale soon after being bought from an old collection.

GRADE: (as a noun) The condition and rating of a particular coin. More specifically, the condition specified by one of the main professional grading services. See the introduction for specifics about grades. (as a verb) To assign a grade to a coin.

HOARD: A large quantity of a single type of coin, held either as an investment or because the collector likes that coin.

see also: hoarder

HOARDER: A person who amasses a large number of a particular coin. For instance, a Nevada farmer named Lavere Redfield distrusted banks after the Depression and regularly turned his savings over for newly minted silver dollars, of which he eventually amassed 600,000.

see also: hoard

KEY: In reference to a coin, the most difficult-to-obtain of a set. Used in expressions like "key coin," "key date," and "key to the set."

"I started out collecting Lincoln cents from circulation. Usually it's necessary to buy the **key** coins."

MELT OR MELT VALUE: The value of the raw precious metals in a particular coin.

"The same holds true of spot market values: Buy below '**melt**' and quickly dispose of the stuff at a convenient smelter."

MONSTER: *(synonyms: blazer, moose, wonder coin)* An incredibly fine coin.

MOOSE: *(synonyms: blazer, monster, wonder coin)* An incredibly fine coin.

NO-GRADE: A coin that a grading service refused to grade (i.e., give an official certification of condition for); for example, because the coin

has been cleaned (because cleaning a coin can damage it over time).

see also: body bag, cull

NOTE: A piece of paper currency.

OVER-DIPPED: In reference to a coin, chemically cleaned (dipped) so frequently that it has become dull.

see also: dip

(!) PEDIGREE: The history of ownership of a particular coin or note. The term "provenance" is usually preferred, and some collectors consider the word "pedigree" inappropriate for coins.

see also: provenance

PLUGGED: In reference to a coin, having had a hole that was later filled in. Plugged coins are significantly less valuable than coins that have not been altered.

POP OR POPULATION: The number of individual coins or notes known to exist of a particular issue.

PROOF: 1) In reference to coins, a version of a coin manufactured especially for collectors rather than for circulation. 2) In reference to paper money, a final or nearly-final design for a note.

PROVENANCE: The ownership history of a particular coin or note.

see also: pedigree

RAW: In reference to a coin, not yet graded by one of the major, recognized coin grading services.

REMAINDER: A piece of paper money never put into circulation and that may be missing some finishing touches (e.g., a signature).

RIP: A coin purchased for significantly less than its actual value.

> "But the coin collecting fraternity, those with similar interests, those with similar experiences, those who really appreciate the **rip** you just made or just how deeply you are buried in a bad purchase, in short, your cohorts in this addiction, these connections are what make this such a marvelous hobby."

SCRIPOPHILY: Study of and interest in securities certificates, such as stock certificates and bonds.

SERIES: A set of coins, one for each year of a particular issue.

SHELDON SCALE: The 1-to-70 numerical grading system for coin condition.

SLAB: (as a noun) A clear, plastic holder with a coin encased in it. (as a verb) To encase a coin in such a holder. Grading services generally slab coins once they are graded.

SLABLAND: A general term for the professional grading services.

"A few more are at **slabland**, but these should do for now."

SLIDER: A coin that isn't quite in uncirculated condition but is close enough that it might be sold as uncirculated by a dishonest dealer.

THUMB: *(synonym: finger)* To rub the thumb over a coin, allowing oil from the skin to prevent flaws from gleaming and giving themselves away. Coin grading services never clean or polish coins since this can damage them, so the oil isn't removed when the coin is examined for grading (see grade).

see also: tongue

TONGUE: To dab saliva on a coin to prevent flaws from gleaming and attempt to fool a grading service into assigning the coin a higher grade than its actual condition warrants.

see also: thumb

TONING: Natural discoloration over time. Toning isn't always undesirable; for instance, some collectors favor silver dollars that have an attractive rainbow toning to them.

TYPE: A specific design and set of issues for a particular coin.

"When the dies are hand-cut, it is hard to maintain a standard '**type.**'"

VEST POCKET DEALER: A collector who sells coins part-time.

(!) WEENIE: A derogatory term for a collector obsessed with a particular type of coin.

WHIZ: To mechanically or chemically alter a coin (often by using a wire brush) to make it appear more lustrous than it naturally would and attempt to deceive collectors or graders.

"Most services will not slab coins that have been altered, **whizzed** or cleaned."

- FROM THE COIN COLLECTING FAQ ON REC.COLLECTING.COINS

WONDER COIN: *(synonyms: blazer, monster, moose)* An incredibly fine coin.

Con Artists and Scammers

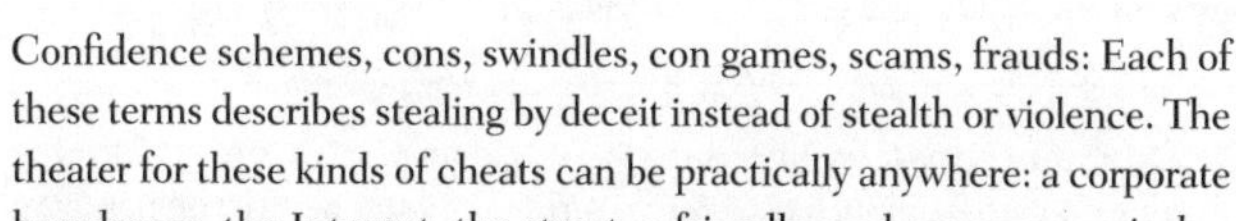

Confidence schemes, cons, swindles, con games, scams, frauds: Each of these terms describes stealing by deceit instead of stealth or violence. The theater for these kinds of cheats can be practically anywhere: a corporate boardroom, the Internet, the street, a friendly card game, a carnival, a telephone call, the train station, or even an elaborately-designed fake store or brokerage house filled with fake workers and fake customers.

One of the odd things about con game slang is that fiction and movies often use con artist slang from the first half of the twentieth century as though it were still current. Possibly that's because of the wide exposure older con slang has gotten in movies like *The Sting* (released in 1973, about 1930s con artists) and in books like David Maurer's popular non-fiction work *The Big Con* (1940).

And in part, it may be because the slang con artists used at the time was so colorful. Yet the modern version of con artist slang is just as entertaining and a good deal more disturbing, crowded with references to ways to take advantage of people, from the evergreen swindle called the "Pigeon Drop" to the "Badger Game," "curbstoning," and the nefarious "Salami Attack."

Perhaps because of movies like *The Sting, Matchstick Men*, and the recent remake of *Ocean's Eleven*, fictional con artists also have an appealing notoriety. Real-life scammers are less dashing, their ranks being populated with methodical criminals who specialize in defrauding senior citizens together with 419 scammers who spam barely-coherent e-mails to tens of thousands of people at a time.

With that in mind, it seems more appropriate to use the unflattering term "scammer" instead of the more elegant "con artist" or "confidence man." The definitions that follow use these terms more or less interchangeably.

419: *(synonym: Nigerian letter fraud or Nigerian money transfer fraud)* A common scam in which the scammer sends an e-mail or letter claiming to need assistance in getting a large amount of money out of a foreign country, especially Nigeria. There is no such money; the scammer is actually trying to get the intended victim's bank account information.

In Nigeria, this kind of fraud is a violation of section 419 of the criminal code.

see also: Advance Fee Scheme

ADDICT: A person who falls for multiple confidence schemes and still won't wise up.

see also: mark, reloader

ADVANCE FEE SCHEME: 1) A scheme targeting people who need loans or mortgages by claiming that the intended victim has been approved for financing. The scam requires an "advance fee" or payment for a bogus service connected with the loan. 2) Sometimes used to refer to a 419 scam.

see also: 419

AUTOGRAPH SCAM: *(synonym: signature fraud)* A scam in which the scammer claims to be collecting autographs and wants yours (to forge checks with).

BADGER GAME: A scam in which an attractive woman entices the intended victim—ideally a married man—to spend some intimate time with her, then exploits the situation for money. For instance, a hidden partner may take photographs to use as blackmail, or the

woman may threaten to file rape or sexual harassment charges, or a partner may burst in, pretending to be the jealous husband.

BANK EXAMINER SCHEME: A con in which a con artist pretends to be a bank official or law enforcement officer trying to catch a crooked teller. The intended victim is asked to hand over their money for "marking."

BEEF: *(synonym: squawk)* To complain to the authorities or others about a scam. A mark (victim) who beefs or squawks is bad for business and may need to be cooled down—that is, calmed and made to stop complaining (generally without the use or threat of violence).

see also: come through

BIG CON: *(synonym: long con)* A large-scale swindle.

BLACK DOLLAR SCAM: A con game in which black paper is passed off as currency that has been taken out of circulation by covering it with black ink. The scammer offers to sell the intended victim supplies for removing the ink along with the "currency" itself.

BLOCK HUSTLE: A scheme in which a scammer sells a reputedly valuable item cheaply, disclosing that it's cheap because it's stolen. The item is actually a cheap substitute or a Rock-in-a-Box, but the victim generally won't go to the police because he or she knowingly offered to purchase stolen goods.

see also: Rock-in-a-Box

BOILER ROOM: A location where a group of scammers telephone people from a list to pressure investors into buying worthless stocks. Victims are often promised very high returns and told that the scammers possess inside information.

The intention of the scam is usually to temporarily drive up the price of worthless stock owned by the scammers.

The Internet version of this kind of operation is called a "boiler-net room."

BONNETEAU: *(synonyms: Three-Card Monte, The Three-Card Trick or Three-Card Molly, Monte, The Broads, Find the Lady or Follow the Lady)* A rigged card betting game.

BOOSTER: A type of shill (con artist who works with one or more other con artists but pretends not to know them). A "booster" can mean either a shill who initally pretends to be a skeptic, or a shill who claims to be a satisfied customer.

see also: *shill*

BROAD TOSSER: *(synonyms: operator, card tosser, springer, tosser, dealer)* A con artist working a rigged betting game called Three Card Monte.

THE BROADS: *(synonyms: Three-Card Monte, The Three-Card Trick or Three-Card Molly, Bonneteau, Monte, Find the Lady or Follow the Lady)* A rigged card betting game.

BUNCO: *(synonyms: confidence scheme, scam, confidence game, confidence trick, dodge)* Any use of trickery for personal gain.

BUNCO ARTIST: *(synonyms: confidence man, confidence trickster, con artist or con man, scam artist or scammer, flimflam artist or flimflam man, grifter, hustler)* A person who steals through deception.

BUNCO SQUAD: Policemen whose job it is to catch confidence men.

COD SCAM: A scam in which the scammer pretends to be delivering a COD item addressed to a recently deceased person in order to get the COD payment amount from a relative of the deceased. The item is actually a Rock-in-a-Box.

see also: *Rock-in-a-Box*

CACKLE BLADDER: A rubber pocket full of fake blood, used to act out a convincing "murder;" designed to scare away the victim of a confidence scheme once the con is over. The term is antiquated, but still in use.

CAPPER: One of a team of con artists who pretends not to know the others; he or she bets or bids alongside the intended victim of a con.

see also: *shill*

CARD TOSSER: *(synonyms: operator, springer, tosser, dealer, broad tosser)* A con artist working a rigged betting game called Three Card Monte.

CARDING: *(synonyms: phishing, spoofing)* Sending fraudulent e-mails to convince recipients to send personal financial information.

CHILL: In reference to an intended victim, to lose interest in a con game and back out.

COME THROUGH: To go after a con artist after having been cheated. A victim who comes through is one who doesn't view the worldly wis-

dom gained through being fleeced as a fair trade for whatever money or goods were taken.

see also: beef

COME-ON: The portion of a scam in which the con artist gets the intended victim interested. Can also mean a special enticement or supposedly-helpful information that makes a con game or rigged gamble look more appealing.

COMMITMENT HOLDER: *(synonyms: inside man, trustee, trader, funder)* A con artist passed off as a financial VIP.

CON: (as a noun) Any use of trickery for personal gain. (as a verb) To steal by use of deceit.

see also: confidence scheme

CON ARTIST OR CON MAN: *(synonyms: confidence man, confidence trickster, scam artist or scammer, bunco artist, flimflam artist or flimflam man, grifter, hustler)* A person who steals through deception.

CONFIDENCE GAME: *(synonyms: confidence scheme, scam, bunco, confidence trick, dodge)* Any use of trickery for personal gain.

CONFIDENCE MAN: *(synonyms: confidence trickster, con artist or con man, scam artist or scammer, bunco artist, flimflam artist or flimflam man, grifter, hustler)* A person who steals (or attempts to steal) using trickery instead of burglary or violence. A confidence man may operate in the open (as with operators of rigged betting games); or approach the intended victim with an offer (fake goods for sale, financial opportunities); or act as part of a group; or work behind the scenes.

see also: confidence scheme

CONFIDENCE SCHEME: *(synonyms: scam, bunco, confidence game, confidence trick, dodge)* An attempt to get money or goods by misleading another person.

see also: confidence man

CONFIDENCE TRICK: *(synonyms: confidence scheme, scam, bunco, confidence game, dodge)* Any use of trickery for personal gain.

CONFIDENCE TRICKSTER: *(synonyms: confidence man, con artist or con man, scam artist or scammer, bunco artist, flimflam artist or flimflam man, grifter, hustler)* A person who steals through deception.

CONVINCER: Money paid to the intended victim (the mark) early in the course of a scam to make it appear legitimate. More broadly, any action that gets the mark to believe the scam is legitimate.

CRAM: To add products or services to an order without authorization, or to bill for non-existent products or services along with legitimate charges.

CREDIT CARD GENERATOR: A Web site maintained by scammers who have stolen credit card information. The information is made available to other scammers for a fee.

CURBSTONER: A person who makes a used car appear to be in better condition than it is (e.g., by hiding evidence of an accident, rolling back the odometer, etc.) and sells it. Refers to the practice of showing the vehicle at the victim's location to avoid revealing the scammer's own workplace or home.

CUTTING HOUSE: A made-up term for a location where fresh securities are minted; used in con games aimed at people unfamiliar with financial markets.

see also: fresh-cut security, secondary market

DEALER: *(synonyms: operator, card tosser, springer, tosser, broad tosser)* A con artist working a rigged betting game called Three-Card Monte.

DODGE: *(synonyms: confidence scheme, scam, bunco, confidence game, confidence trick)* Any use of trickery for personal gain.

EVERGREEN: In reference to a confidence scheme, reliably producing profit year after year, always attracting new suckers.

FIDDLE GAME: A venerable, two-person con in which one scammer poses as a poor fiddle player and the other pretends to be a wealthy man willing to pay a huge amount of money for the poor man's violin. For the con to succeed, the intended victim buys the violin, which is actually a cheap knock-off, from the "poor fiddler" in order to turn around and sell it to the "rich man," who has conveniently disappeared. End result: The victim has paid a lot of money for a cheap violin.

FIND THE LADY OR FOLLOW THE LADY: *(synonyms: Three-Card Monte, The Three-Card Trick or Three-Card Molly, Bonneteau, Monte, The Broads)* A rigged card betting game.

FISH: *(synonyms: mark, pigeon, rube, sucker)* A victim or potential victim of a confidence scheme.

FLIMFLAM ARTIST OR FLIMFLAM MAN: *(synonyms: confidence man, confidence trickster, con artist or con man, scam artist or scammer, bunco artist, grifter, hustler)* A person who steals through deception.

FLOAT: The time between the cashing of a bad check and the arrival of that check at its final destination, where it is discovered to be no good.

FORECASTER SCAM: A scam in which the con artist makes different stock predictions to different groups of people and continues to contact only that increasingly smaller group of people who by chance received accurate predictions. By this means, the con artist can appear to have special knowledge of the market and can exploit the situation to sell or promote dubious investments.

FRESH-CUT SECURITY: A made-up type of financial instrument. The scammer explains that a fresh-cut security has just been issued, and that a great deal of money can be made by selling these instruments to regular investors who don't have direct access to them.

see also: cutting house, secondary market

FUNDER: *(synonyms: inside man, trustee, trader, commitment holder)* A con artist passed off as a financial VIP.

GAFFED: Rigged in favor of a scammer. For instance, a gaffed roulette wheel might be set to land on a specific number when the scammer operates a hidden control.

GIFTING CIRCLE: *(synonyms: gifting club, giving club)* A pyramid scheme disguised as a charitable and social organization.

GIFTING CLUB: *(synonyms: gifting circle, giving club)* A Ponzi scheme disguised to look like charity and friendship. People (usually women) in need of a lot of money are invited into the group. At set intervals, they give significant amounts of money to more senior members of the group (who are also, supposedly, in financial need). The idea is that newer members will continue to come in and give monetary gifts to veteran members, so that by giving these gifts yourself and staying in the organization, a victim is as-

sured she will eventually receive much more money than she has paid out. The problem is that of course all that money is just coming out of the pockets of other gifting circle members in need, and sooner or later the available pool of new members will be tapped out, meaning everyone at the lower levels will be left with no chance of recouping their money.

see also: Ponzi scheme

GIVING CLUB: *(synonyms: gifting club, gifting circle)* A pyramid scheme disguised as a charitable and social organization.

GRIFTER: *(synonyms: confidence man, confidence trickster, con artist or con man, scam artist or scammer, bunco artist, flimflam artist or flimflam man, hustler)* A person who steals through deception.

HEAVY RACKET: A crime that involves violence or the threat of violence. By definition, a confidence scheme is not violent, although some con games can be combined with the threat of violence (for instance in a badger game scam).

HEP: *(synonym: wise)* Aware of a scam or fraud.

HOT CHECK: An actual check drawn on a bank account that has been closed or has insufficient funds. One of a variety of scams used by check forgers (paperhangers).

see also: paperhanger

HUSTLER: *(synonyms: confidence man, confidence trickster, con artist or con man, scam artist or scammer, bunco artist, flimflam artist or flimflam man, grifter)* A person who steals through deception.

IMPERSONATOR SCAM: A scam in which the con artist pretends to be a utility worker, police officer, etc., in order to gain access to a home or secure a person's confidence.

INSIDE MAN: *(synonyms: trustee, trader, commitment holder, funder)* In investment scams, the scammer who plays the role of a financial VIP. When the intended victim reaches a certain stage in the scam, the inside man is introduced in an environment that makes the meeting seem like a great privilege. From there, it's the inside man's job to charm the victim into going on to the next stage of being scammed.

JAMAICAN SWITCH: *(synonym: Pigeon Drop)* An intended victim

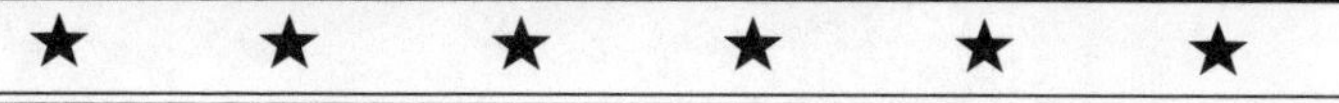

is asked to hold money or other valuables while his or her own money is requested as a deposit to prove honesty.

LAPPING: A means of making a con game appear legitimate. As new "investors" come in, the scammer gives some of their money to earlier participants, and in this way it appears for a short time that the investment really pays off.

LEAK: To accidentally show an intended victim a crooked move in a con or a rigged game.

LESS-CASH DEPOSIT SCHEME: *(synonym: Split Deposit)* A scam in which a bogus check is deposited to a bank account for the purpose of receiving cash. For instance, the scammer deposits a bad check for $500 and asks for $100 back in cash. Because a deposit is being made, bank personnel may pay the cash without asking for credentials. The scammer thus gets $100 for a worthless check.

LONG CON: *(synonym: big con)* A large, complicated, high-stakes con game.

MANAGED EARNINGS SCAM: Making corporate earnings look better than they actually are for the purpose of artificially inflating one's own stock. The scammers generally own the stock. After running this scam, they sell it at the inflated price.

MARK: *(synonyms: pigeon, rube, sucker, fish)* A past or potential victim of a confidence scheme. *see also:* addict

MICHIGAN ROLL: A bundle of low-denomination bills, or plain paper with a high-denomination bill on the outside; masquerades as a roll of high-denomination bills. Used in scams like the Pigeon Drop.

see also: Pigeon Drop

MONTE: *(synonyms: Three-Card Monte, The Three-Card Trick or Three-Card Molly, Bonneteau, The Broads, Find the Lady or Follow the Lady)* A rigged card betting game.

MOOCH LIST: *(synonym: sucker list)* In telemarketing scams, a list of the telephone numbers of potential victims.

MULTI-LEVEL MARKETING OR MLM: *(synonyms: Ponzi Scheme, pyramid scheme)* A scam in which newer participants pay veteran participants on the assurance that they will be paid in a similar fashion later on.

MUSTARD SQUIRTER: A street scam in which the scammer squirts the intended victim with mustard (or anything similarly messy), and then cleans it off while removing the victim's wallet.

NIGERIAN LETTER FRAUD OR NIGERIAN MONEY TRANSFER FRAUD: *(synonym: 419)* A scam used to get bank account information by promising a share of a foreign fortune.

NUT: 1) The money or other proceeds from a successful scam. 2) The money a con artist needs to run a scam.

ON THE SEND: Sending the intended victim to get additional money from friends, relatives, or saved assets.

OPERATOR: *(synonyms: card tosser, springer, tosser, dealer, broad tosser)* A person who operates a game of Three-Card Monte. Three-Card Monte is a betting scam in which the game operator shows three cards, one of which is a queen. He then shuffles the cards; the bettor must indicate which is the queen. Operators use a variety of shuffling tricks—the hype, the overthrow, the toss, the Mexican turnover, and others—to make the queen appear displaced. Three-Card Monte is a scam, not a "legitimate" gamble.

The term "operator" can also be used to refer to any confidence trickster.

see also: Three Card Monte

OUTSIDE MAN: *(synonym: roper)* A type of shill who identifies a likely victim, gains that person's confidence, and sets him or her up as the victim of a confidence scheme.

PAPER PLAYER: A gambler who uses marked cards.

PAPERHANGER: Someone who purposely passes bad checks. The checks might be written against a closed or empty account, forged, or altered.

PHISHING: *(synonyms: carding, spoofing)* Sending e-mails requesting or demanding personal information in the guise of a legitimate, well-known business. If the recipient provides the information requested, the scammer uses the data to steal from the victim.

PIGEON: *(synonyms: mark, rube, sucker, fish)* A victim or potential victim of a confidence scheme.

PIGEON DROP: *(synonym: Jamaican Switch)* A term that covers several versions of a time-honored con game. The intended victim (the mark) is asked to hold onto a large amount of money or something else of value, and is promised payment when it's time for the scammer to take the money or valuables back. To seal the deal and prove good faith, the mark is asked to give the scammer a sum of money that amounts to much less than the supposed value of whatever the mark is holding. Never mind that this makes no sense; people fall for this one on a regular basis.

PIG-IN-A-POKE: *(synonym: Rock-in-a-Box)* A rock packaged and sold as valuable merchandise.

POKE: 1) An intended victim's wallet. 2) A gambler's bankroll.

PONZI SCHEME: *(synonyms: pyramid scheme, multi-level marketing or MLM)* A scam that involves recruiting multiple "levels" of participants, all of whom pay fees to those who have been involved longer and who recruit more participants to pay their own money into the scheme. Once the pool of suckers is exhausted, all of the later arrivals—most of the participants—are out of luck.

see also: gifting club

PRIME BANK: *(synonym: top world bank)* A scammer's made-up term for a bank that's supposedly legitimate and very stable. In one common prime bank scam, the scammer sells bogus financial instruments that they say are guaranteed by the prime bank.

PUT THE MARK UP: To bring in a potential victim for a con game.

PYRAMID SCHEME: *(synonyms: Ponzi Scheme, multi-level marketing or MLM)* A scam in which newer participants pay veteran participants on the assurance that they will be paid in a similar fashion later on.

RELOADER: A scammer, usually using telemarketing, who returns to the victim of a scam and tries to deceive them again; sometimes the scammer promises a means of recouping money lost on the earlier scam.

see also: addict

ROCK-IN-A-BOX: *(synonym: Pig-in-a-Poke)* A scam in which valuable goods, usually electronics or

watches, are offered for sale on the street, cheap. Bargain hunters buy the goods and go home to find out that they've purchased rocks, although the box itself is often genuine. The scammer uses discarded packaging from trash heaps and similar sources and re-shrink wraps it. Sometimes a generic box with a picture of the item is substituted for genuine packaging.

see also: Block Hustle

ROPER: *(synonym: outside man)* A type of shill who identifies a likely victim, gains that person's confidence, and sets him or her up as the victim of a confidence scheme.

see also: shill

RUBE: *(synonyms: mark, pigeon, sucker, fish)* A victim or potential victim of a confidence scheme.

RUBE ACT: Acting the part of an ignorant stranger in order to further a con game.

see also: shill

SALAMI ATTACK: A type of theft in which tiny amounts are stolen from a large number of transactions or accounts. Because the transactions may never be viewed together and are inconsequential individually, they are difficult to detect. The real victim of a Salami Attack is usually the bank or other entity processing the transactions.

SALTING: Any of several scam-related practices, including two types of fraud and one anti-fraud technique:

1) Offering several individuals a legitimately wonderful deal on merchandise, then using these individuals as references for a much larger group who are enticed to pay for the same kind of merchandise, but who never receive it. 2) A manufacturer's or wholesaler's anti-fraud technique, in which coupons worth cash are planted in a shipment of merchandise so the merchandise can be found if illegally diverted to another destination. The contact information coupon redeemers supply tells the manufacturer or wholesaler where the goods ended up. 3) Adding valuable minerals to a mine or mineral sample in order to convey the false impression that the mine contains a good deal of that type of mineral.

In senses 1 and 3, the word is often used in the phrase "salting the mine."

SCAM: *(synonyms: confidence scheme, bunco, confidence game, confidence trick, dodge)* Any use of trickery for personal gain.(as a verb) To steal by use of deceit. (as a noun) A confidence scheme; theft by scamming.

SCAM ARTIST OR SCAMMER: *(synonyms: confidence man, confidence trickster, con artist or con man, bunco artist, flimflam artist or flimflam man, grifter, hustler)* A person who steals through deception.

SCAM BAITING: Pretending to play along as the victim of a con while actually being wise to it, either for the purpose of stealing from or humiliating the scammer. Scam baiting has become a popular Internet sport.

SCORE: *(synonyms: touch, take)* Money gained from a confidence scheme.

SECONDARY MARKET: A made-up securities market that will supposedly buy "seasoned" securities that are sold to the intended victim as "fresh-cut." Selling these fresh-cut securities to people who don't have first-hand access to them, the scammer claims, can make a large amount of money. (This is, of course, a lie.)

see also: fresh-cut security, cutting house

SELF-LIQUIDATING LOAN: There's a legitimate thing called a self-liquidating loan, but the scam version is a loan that can be used to procure assets that will pay the loan back, with some money left over for the borrower, but the methods scammers describe to make a loan "self-liquidating" don't actually work. Scammers make money by offering to sell information on such loans or by accepting application fees for them.

SHILL: A con artist who pretends to be a stranger to the people running the con. Shills are often used to "win" at crooked games like Three-Card Monte; to drive up prices in online auctions; to preempt bettors who might otherwise have won a bet; to pretend to offer inside information; and for other purposes.

see also: Three-Card Monte, booster, roper, capper

SHORT CON: Any confidence scheme designed to pay off immedi-

ately. Contrasted with the long con, which requires time to pay off.

see also: big con, shill, Three-Card Monte

SHOULDER SURFING: The practice of looking over someone's shoulder as they write a check, use an ATM machine, enter their credit card number into a telephone, etc. The information is used to steal money or services, or is sold to another thief.

SIGNATURE FRAUD: *(synonym: Autograph Scam)* A scam intended to obtain signatures for forging checks.

SKIMMER: A device used to record information from a credit or debit card in order to use or sell the information. Some people who use skimmers work the register at legitimate businesses and will surreptitiously skim cards customers use to pay for their purchases.

SLAMMING: The illegal practice of switching a person's long distance phone service provider without permission.

SPLIT DEPOSIT: *(synonym: Less-Cash Deposit Scheme)* A scam in which the goal is to get cash back when depositing a bogus check.

SPOOFING: *(synonyms: phishing, carding)* Sending fraudulent e-mails to try to get personal financial information.

SPRINGER: *(synonyms: operator, card tosser, tosser, dealer, broad tosser)* A con artist working a rigged betting game called Three-Card Monte.

SQUAWK: *(synonym: beef)* To complain publicly or to authorities about a scam.

STORE: Used in phrases like "big store" and "dollar store" to mean a location established to facilitate a con game.

SUCKER: *(synonyms: mark, pigeon, rube, fish)* A victim or potential victim of a confidence scheme.

SUCKER LIST: *(synonym: mooch list)* A list of potential victims for a telemarketing scam.

TAKE: *(synonyms: touch, score)* Money gained from a confidence scheme.

THREE-CARD MONTE: *(synonyms: The Three-Card Trick or Three Card-Molly, Bonneteau, Monte, The Broads, Find the Lady or Follow the Lady)* A con masquerading

as a game. The victim is shown three cards, one of which is the "money card," usually a queen. The dealer, or operator, shuffles the cards in an intricate pattern, and the victim tries to say which of the cards is the money card. The game is sometimes played by the operator alone and sometimes with an entire cast of con men, including shills, who pretend to be actual players and to win a lot of money, or who act as lookouts or muscle. Shills can be used in various ways to avoid actually paying a winner.

Three-Card Monte is just a playing card version of a scam that can be perpetrated with any number of props, especially with a ball under a shell in the age-old Shell Game.

THE THREE-CARD TRICK OR THREE-CARD MOLLY: *(synonyms: Three-Card Monte, Bonneteau, Monte, The Broads, Find the Lady or Follow the Lady)* A rigged card betting game.

TOP WORLD BANK: *(synonym: prime bank)* A fictitious bank that is meant to sound legitimate and stable.

TOSSER: *(synonyms: operator, card tosser, springer, tosser, dealer, broad tosser)* A con artist working a rigged betting game called Three Card Monte.

TOUCH: *(synonyms: score, take)* The money or other proceeds from a successful confidence scheme. This is occasionally called the "nut." Can also mean the money a con artist needs to accomplish a job.

TRADER: *(synonyms: inside man, trustee, commitment holder, funder)* A con artist passed off as a financial VIP.

TRUSTEE: *(synonyms: inside man, trader, commitment holder, funder)* A con artist passed off as a financial VIP.

WASH: To remove all handwritten information from a check or other document by submerging it in a solution (for example, acetone). New information such as a new payee and amount can be written in. Newer, more secure checks cannot be washed in this way.

WISE: *(synonym: hep)* Aware of a confidence scheme. An intended victim who is hep is of no use to the con artist.

YAK: A telemarketing scammer.

Cowboys and Rodeo Riders

There are three main remnants of traditional cowboy talk in modern times. First are modern cattle ranches, where modernization has simplified and eliminated much of what went into making a cowboy a cowboy. Second are rodeos, where cowboy skills are still valued. And last are the tourist attractions: dude ranches, cattle drives, and cowboy museums. These institutions preserve a version of historical cowboy slang.

Modern cowboy slang still includes some of the historical lingo even away from tourist locations, and much of that historical cowboy talk comes from Spanish. Both historical and modern cowboys have been known to speak some Spanish, and cowboy slang includes a number of Spanish words that have been transformed into English. For instance, both the Spanish word for "cowboy," *vaquero*, and its English derivative, "buckaroo" are used in cowboy talk. The term "dally" (to wrap a rope around a saddlehorn) is said to come from the Spanish *da le vuelta*, which means "give it a turn."

Cowboy slang has always varied a bit from one area to another; for instance, in one region a cowboy may be referred to as a "cowboy," while in another he may be called a "cowpoke," "puncher," "buckaroo," or "vaquero."

AVERAGE: In a rodeo, the cumulative score for an event based on the total of the tries a contestant has taken; some prize money is awarded based on the average.

see also: *go-round*

"He has dominated the **average** for the week, and I expect him to rope very smart over the next five days."

BEDROLL: Rolled-up bedding: a sleeping bag, blankets, or quilts wrapped in a tarp for sleeping under the stars.

BROKE: In reference to a horse, trained; accustomed to carrying a rider.

see also: *bronc buster*

BRONC BUSTER OR BRONCO BUSTER: *(synonym: peeler or bronc peeler)* A person skilled in training wild horses.

see also: *broke*

BRONCO: A wild horse.

(!) BUCKAROO: A cowboy; sometimes used more specifically to refer to a cowboy from the Great Basin Desert area in and around Nevada. Not all cowboys like this term, so use it with care.

(!) BUCKLE BUNNY: A rodeo groupie (usually used in reference to a girl or a woman).

"I don't recall rodeo ever having to rely on a rodeo queen, much less a **buckle bunny**, to get fans."

CATTLE DRIVE: Herding cattle down a trail from a ranch to a distant railroad or market. Today this is an activity for tourists, although it once was an essential part of ranching. Modern ranchers, except those who run dude ranches or similar operations, generally ship their cattle to market on trains or trucks.

see also: *trail*

CHAPARRAL: (pronounced "SHAP-uh-ral") Thick underbrush made up of plants typical to the western plains.

CHAPS: *(synonym: leggings)* (pronounced "shaps," *not* "chaps") Protective leather leg coverings that usually go from about thigh to ankle. Chaps ward off underbrush, cacti, etc.

see also: *chinks*

CHINKS: Fringed leather leg protection that usually goes down to just below the knee. Chinks are easy to pack and carry as well as more comfortable in hot weather than full-length chaps.

see also: chaps

CHUCK: Food; provisions.

CHUTE OR BUCKING CHUTE: A small pen in which a steer, bull, or wild horse is held just prior to being in an event.

"Normally if the animal breaks the **chute** and shows any buck at all, and then locks up, the option of a reride will not be given."

CINCH: (as a noun) A strap that goes under a horse's belly to hold a saddle in place. (as a verb) To put a cinch on a horse.

COVER: In rodeo competition, to stay on a wild horse or bull long enough to earn a score.

"Myron was also the only bull rider to **cover** all four bulls."

COW HORSE: A horse trained to work around cattle.

COW PUNCHER: *(synonyms: cowboy, cowpoke, puncher, vaquero)* A cowboy.

COWBOY: *(synonyms: cowpoke, cow puncher, puncher, vaquero)* A person who makes a living working with cattle on a ranch or who is skilled in rodeo events; refers to both men and women. Different terms for "cowboy" are preferred in different areas. For instance, "buckaroo" is used more in the Great Basin area in and around Nevada but may be considered a little insulting to a Texan.

see also: buckaroo

(!) COWGIRL: A word generally *not* used for a female cowboy. The recommended term is cowboy, cowpoke, or whatever other word happens to be preferred locally.

COWPOKE: *(synonyms: cowboy, cow puncher, puncher, vaquero)* A cowboy.

CROW HOP: In reference to a horse, to make wimpy, little, stiff-legged jumps instead of really trying to throw the rider.

"Once saddle trained, the first couple of minutes of every day's ride was punctuated by the occasional buck or **crow-hop**."

CUT: To ride a horse with the intent to separate specific cows from the herd.

DALLY: To wrap a rope around a saddle horn.

DAY MONEY: In a rodeo, prize money won for the best rider in an event on a particular day; contrast with average. Not all rodeos still pay day money.

see also: average

"I know the main awards are figured on the average, but I don't recall if they pay **day money**."

DOGIE: (pronounced "DOE-ghee") A motherless calf.

GO-ROUND: One attempt at a particular event in a rodeo.

"Corn roped his final calf in 11.8 seconds, winning fourth in the **go round** and fifth in the average."

HACKAMORE: A halter for a horse's head that has no bit for the mouth.

HEAD: One cow (or other animal). Used when talking about a number of animals.

HOBBLE: (as a noun) Restraints around a horse's lower legs, used to prevent it from wandering off. (as a verb) To put a hobble on a horse.

LARIAT: (*synonym: lasso*) A rope used to catch and tie up livestock. It used to be that a "lasso" meant specifically a rope made out of grass or other plant fibers, while "lariat" (from the Spanish "la riata") meant a rawhide rope, but these days the terms are used interchangeably.

LASSO: (*synonym: lariat*) A rope used to tie livestock.

LEGGINGS: (*synonym: chaps*) Protective leather coverings for the legs.

MAVERICK: A cow, bull, or steer roaming wild, with no brand.

MUSTANG: Any wild horse.

OUTLAW: A horse that can't be trained (broke).

see also: broke

PEELER OR BRONC PEELER: (*synonym: bronc buster or bronco buster*) A person skilled in training wild horses.

PICKUP MAN: A rodeo worker who helps riders off bucking horses.

PUNCHER: (*synonyms:* *cowboy, cowpoke, cow puncher, puncher, vaquero*) A cowboy.

REMUDA: The group of saddle horses used during a roundup.

> "The drive consists of four to six horse-drawn wagons driven by experienced teamsters; a small herd of longhorn cattle trailed by drovers; as well as a **remuda** of extra horses trailed by the horse wranglers."

ROUNDUP: The bringing together of cattle.

SEEING DAYLIGHT: In reference to a rodeo rider, lifted so high above the animal's back that a gap appears between animal and rider. Can mean that the rider is about to be thrown, or just that he or she is using a looser riding technique.

TENDERFOOT: A person new to cowboy skills and lifestyle. This word is not used as widely as it once was.

TRAIL: To bring cattle from one place to another.

see also: cattle drive

VAQUERO: (*synonyms:* *cowboy, cowpoke, cow puncher, puncher*) A cowboy.

WADDY OR WADDIE: A ranch hand or cowboy hired to fill in temporarily.

WRANGLER: A ranch hand who works with horses.

see also: cowboy

Drug Pushers and Users

"Necessity," they say, "is the mother of invention," and while that may or may not be true across the board, it's dead on target in terms of drug slang. Users and sellers of illegal substances often speak about them in roundabout ways, constantly developing new drug slang terms.

Soon, however, these terms become common enough that they no longer serve the purpose of secrecy, and newer ones have to be created. As a result, the total number of terms in the drug vocabulary is mind-boggling, especially when taking into account local and regional drug slang, which is not documented here.

"Discussions about drugs, over the telephone particularly, almost always occur in code," says Judson Roberts, a former organized crime investigator and prosecutor. "The codes are constantly changing and very localized. They pretty much always involve some mention of an amount of something, though, and a cost. Amounts could be described as almost anything—a pint of milk, or quart or gallon—with respective prices representing the price to be charged."

One complication in drug slang is that the same term is sometimes used to refer to several different substances. For instance, "beans" can

mean cocaine, depressants, mescaline, or amphetamine. To make matters worse, one drug may have literally hundreds of different names.

Drug slang encompasses a huge number of words and phrases related to specific drugs: terms for the drug itself, for different ways of taking the drug, for mixtures of that drug and another, for different levels of quality, and so on.

Despite the number of terms drug users generate, the meanings of those terms are very limited, the great majority having to do with specific drugs, drug quality, purchasing drugs, ingesting or inhaling or injecting the drugs, and the feelings associated with the process. If you read them straight through, the listings below quickly begin to feel repetitive.

Throughout this book, definitions are written as an outsider would define the terms, not in the language of the subculture itself. That's especially true for this particular section: For instance, a marijuana user would generally *not* refer to a roach as "the remainder of a marijuana cigarette" (unless perhaps in a funny voice, just prior to laughing until weak).

ACID HEAD: An LSD user.

ARTILLERY: *(synonyms: gimmick, works, tools, kit, rig, business)* Equipment used to inject drugs.

AUTHOR: A doctor who sells prescriptions to drug users.

BABY HABIT: *(synonym: ice cream habit)* A small-scale drug habit.

see also: chip

BACK UP: *(synonyms: bring up, bridge up)* To get a vein ready for an injection.

BAD TRIP: An experience with a drug that panics or horrifies the user. Used most often in reference to LSD use.

BAG BRIDE: *(synonym: skeezer)* A female prostitute addicted to crack, or one who will offer sexual favors in exchange for crack.

BAKED: Under the influence of marijuana.

BALLOON: *(synonym: paperboy)* A heroin dealer.

BAMMER: (*synonyms:* *ditch weed, downtown brown*) Poor-quality marijuana.

BANG: (*synonyms:* *shoot up, boost, crank up, boot, draw up, fire, gun, hit the needle, jack up, miss, slam, spike, track, mainline, jab, laugh and scratch*) To inject a drug (into oneself).

BASE: (*synonyms:* *freebase, chase, ghostbust*) To smoke cocaine.

BATT: (*synonyms:* *gaffus, glass gun*) A hypodermic needle.

BEAMER: (*synonyms:* *buffer, crack head, chaser, cluck, crackerjack, pipero, puffer, thirst monster*) A crack addict.

BEAT ARTIST: (*synonym:* *zoomer*) A dealer who sells fake drugs.

see also: bump, gaffel, burn, blank

BEDBUG: An addict (used mainly by addicts to refer to other addicts).

BING: The amount of a drug needed for one injection.

BLANK: Fake or very low-quality drugs.

see also: burn, beat artist

BLAST: (*synonyms:* *blaze, blow a stick, blast a joint/stick/roach, fire up, hit the hay, mow the grass, toke up*) To smoke marijuana.

BLAST A JOINT/STICK/ROACH: (*synonyms:* *blaze, blow a stick, blast, fire up, hit the hay, mow the grass, toke up*) To smoke marijuana.

BLASTED: (*synonyms:* *lit up or all lit up, turned on, charged up, hopped up, flying, on a trip, tripping, stoned, wasted, high, wired, lifted, loaded*) Under the influence of a drug.

BLAZE: (*synonyms:* *blow a stick, blast, blast a joint/stick/roach, fire up, hit the hay, mow the grass, toke up*) To smoke marijuana.

BLOW: (*synonyms:* *snort, do a line, horn, one and one, pop, sniff, toke*) To inhale cocaine into the nose.

BLOW A FIX: (*synonym:* *blow a shot*) To miss the vein and waste the injection.

BLOW A SHOT: (*synonym:* *blow a fix*) To miss the vein and waste the injection.

BLOW A STICK: (*synonyms:* *blaze, blast, blast a joint/stick/roach, fire up, hit the hay, mow the grass, toke up*) To smoke marijuana.

BLUNT: A hollowed-out cigar that has been filled with marijuana.

BOOST: *(synonyms: shoot up, bang, crank up, boot, draw up, fire, gun, hit the needle, jack up, miss, slam, spike, track, mainline, jab, laugh and scratch)* To inject a drug (into oneself).

BOOT: *(synonyms: shoot up, bang, boost, crank up, draw up, fire, gun, hit the needle, jack up, miss, slam, spike, track, mainline, jab, laugh and scratch)* To inject a drug (into oneself).

BOXED: *(synonym: on ice)* In jail.

BREWERY: A place where drugs are made, prepared, or packaged.

BRIDGE UP: *(synonyms: bring up, back up)* To get a vein ready for an injection.

BRING UP: *(synonyms: back up, bridge up)* To get a vein ready for an injection.

BROKER: A middleman in a drug deal.

BUFFER: *(synonyms: beamer, crack head, chaser, cluck, crackerjack, pipero, puffer, thirst monster)* A crack user.

BUMP: *(synonyms: gank, flex, perp, fleece)* Fake pelletized (crack) cocaine.

see also: gaffel, beat artist, burn

BUNK: *(synonym: gaffel)* Fake cocaine.

BURN: To sell fake drugs.

see also: bump, gaffel, beat artist, blank, push

BUSINESS: *(synonyms: artillery, gimmick, works, tools, kit, rig)* Equipment used to inject drugs.

C JOINT: A place where cocaine is sold.

see also: crack gallery

CANDYMAN OR CANDY MAN: A drug dealer.

CARPET PATROL: *(synonym: chicken scratch)* A hands-and-knees search for dropped crack.

CASHED: In reference to a marijuana pipe or water pipe, empty.

CHANNEL: *(synonyms: gutter, sewer, pipe)* The vein into which a drug is injected.

CHANNEL SWIMMER: *(synonyms: hype, schmecker, sleepwalker)* A heroin addict.

CHARGED UP: *(synonyms: lit up or all lit up, turned on, blasted,*

hopped up, flying, on a trip, tripping, stoned, wasted, high, wired, lifted, loaded) Under the influence of a drug.

CHASE: *(synonyms: freebase, base, ghostbust)* To smoke cocaine.

CHASE THE TIGER: To smoke heroin.

CHASER: *(synonyms: beamer, buffer, crack head, cluck, crackerjack, pipero, puffer, thirst monster)* A crack user.

CHECK: A personal supply of drugs.

CHICKEN SCRATCH: *(synonym: carpet patrol)* A hands-and-knees search for dropped crack.

CHIP: To use drugs occasionally.

see also: baby habit

CLOCKER: A crack dealer who will sell at any time of the day or night.

CLUCK: *(synonyms: beamer, buffer, crack head, chaser, crackerjack, pipero, puffer, thirst monster)* A crack user.

COLD BUST: A drug-related arrest that occurs when police come to a location to investigate a non-drug-related problem, such as a domestic dispute.

COME DOWN: *(synonym: come home)* To emerge from a drug experience, especially in reference to LSD usage (an acid trip).

COME HOME: *(synonym: come down)* To reach the end of a drug experience.

COP: *(synonym: get through)* To acquire drugs.

CRACK GALLERY: *(synonyms: rock house, crack spot)* A place where crack is sold.

see also: C joint

CRACK HEAD: *(synonyms: beamer, buffer, chaser, cluck, crackerjack, pipero, puffer, thirst monster)* A crack user.

CRACK HOUSE: *(synonym: house piece)* A place where addicts smoke crack.

see also: crack gallery, shooting gallery

CRACK SPOT: *(synonyms: crack gallery, rock house)* A place where crack is sold.

CRACKERJACK: *(synonyms: beamer, buffer, crack head, chaser, cluck, pipero, puffer, thirst monster)* A crack user.

CRANK UP: *(synonyms: shoot up, bang, boost, boot, draw up, fire, gun, hit the needle, jack up, miss, slam, spike, track, mainline, jab, laugh and scratch)* To inject a drug (into oneself).

CRASH: 1) To emerge from a drugged state. 2) To go to sleep.

DEAL: *(synonyms: push, slang)* To sell drugs.

DIME BAG: Ten dollars worth of drugs.

DIME'S WORTH: Enough heroin to kill a person.

DITCH WEED: *(synonyms: downtown brown, bammer)* Poor-quality marijuana.

DO A LINE: *(synonyms: snort, horn, one and one, pop, sniff, toke, blow)* To inhale cocaine into the nose.

DOWNTOWN BROWN: *(synonyms: ditch weed, bammer)* Poor-quality marijuana.

DRAW UP: *(synonyms: shoot up, bang, boost, crank up, boot, fire, gun, hit the needle, jack up, miss, slam, spike, track, mainline, jab, laugh and scratch)* To inject a drug (into oneself).

DROP: To take a drug in pill or tab form.

ELBOW: One pound of a drug.

EMERGENCY GUN: An improvised substitute for a hypodermic needle and syringe.

FACTORY: 1) A place where drugs are made, prepared, or packaged. 2) A syringe.

see also: brewery

FIRE: *(synonyms: shoot up, bang, boost, crank up, boot, draw up, gun, hit the needle, jack up, miss, slam, spike, track, mainline, jab, laugh and scratch)* To inject a drug (into oneself).

FIRE UP: *(synonyms: blaze, blow a stick, blast, blast a joint/stick/roach, hit the hay, mow the grass, toke up)* To smoke marijuana.

FIX: (as a noun) A dose of a drug. (as a verb) To inject a drug.

FLEECE: *(synonyms: bump, gank, flex, perp)* Fake cocaine.

FLEX: *(synonyms: bump, gank, perp, fleece)* Fake cocaine.

FLYING: *(synonyms: lit up or all lit up, turned on, blasted, charged up, hopped up, on a trip, tripping, stoned, wasted, high, wired, lifted,*

loaded) Under the influence of a drug.

FREEBASE: *(synonyms: base, chase, ghostbust)* To smoke cocaine.

GAFFEL: *(synonym: bunk)* Fake cocaine.

see also: bump, beat artist, burn

GAFFUS: *(synonyms: glass gun, batt)* A hypodermic needle.

GANK: *(synonyms: bump, flex, perp, fleece)* Fake cocaine.

GET THROUGH: *(synonym: cop)* To acquire drugs.

GHOSTBUST: *(synonyms: freebase, base, chase)* To smoke cocaine.

GIMMICK: *(synonyms: artillery, works, tools, kit, rig, business)* Equipment used to inject drugs.

GIVE WINGS TO: To teach a person to inject heroin.

GLASS GUN: *(synonyms: gaffus, batt)* A hypodermic needle.

GROUND MAN OR GROUND CONTROL: Someone who watches over a friend who is using a drug.

GUN: *(synonyms: shoot up, bang, boost, crank up, boot, draw up, fire, hit the needle, jack up, miss, slam, spike, track, mainline, jab, laugh and scratch)* To inject a drug (into oneself).

GUTTER: *(synonyms: sewer, pipe, channel)* The vein into which a drug is injected.

HAND-TO-HAND: In reference to a drug sale, in a small quantity and direct to the customer.

HAND-TO-HAND MAN: A dealer who sells small amounts of crack.

HEAD SHOP: A store that sells drug paraphernalia, especially for marijuana use.

HIGH: *(synonyms: lit up or all lit up, turned on, blasted, charged up, hopped up, flying, on a trip, tripping, stoned, wasted, wired, lifted, loaded)* Under the influence of a drug.

HIT HOUSE: *(synonym: shooting gallery)* A building where addicts go to use drugs.

HIT THE HAY: *(synonyms: blaze, blow a stick, blast, blast a joint/stick/roach, fire up, mow the grass, toke up)* To smoke marijuana.

HIT THE NEEDLE: *(synonyms: shoot up, bang, boost, crank up, boot, draw up, fire, gun, jack up, miss, slam, spike, track, mainline, jab, *laugh and scratch)* To inject a drug (into oneself).

HOOK (A PERSON) UP: To make contact with someone who can provide drugs.

HOPPED UP: *(synonyms: lit up or all lit up, turned on, blasted, charged up, flying, on a trip, tripping, stoned, wasted, high, wired, lifted, loaded)* Under the influence of a drug.

HORN: *(synonyms: snort, do a line, one and one, pop, sniff, toke, blow)* To inhale cocaine into the nose.

HOUSE FEE: Money paid to get into a shooting gallery or crack house (a building set aside as a place to use drugs).

HOUSE PIECE: *(synonym: crack house)* A place where addicts smoke crack.

HYPE: *(synonyms: channel swimmer, schmecker, sleepwalker)* A heroin addict.

ICE CREAM HABIT: *(synonym: baby habit)* A small-scale drug habit.

JAB: *(synonyms: shoot up, bang, boost, crank up, boot, draw up, fire, gun, hit the needle, jack up, miss, slam, spike, track, mainline, laugh and scratch)* To inject a drug (into oneself).

JACK UP: *(synonyms: shoot up, bang, boost, crank up, boot, draw up, fire, gun, hit the needle, miss, slam, spike, track, mainline, jab, laugh and scratch)* To inject a drug (into oneself).

JAG: An extended period under the influence of drugs, continuously taking more as the effects wear off.

JOINT: A marijuana cigarette.

see also: pin or pinner

JOLLY POP: A person who uses heroin occasionally.

JONES: To crave a drug.

JUNK: *(synonyms: merchandise, stuff)* Drugs.

KEY: One kilogram of a drug.

KICK: To stop using a drug.

KIT: *(synonyms: artillery, gimmick, works, tools, rig, business)* Equipment used to inject drugs.

LAUGH AND SCRATCH: *(synonyms: shoot up, bang, boost, crank up, boot, draw up, fire, gun, hit the needle, jack up, miss, slam, spike,*

track, mainline, jab) To inject a drug (into oneself).

LIFTED: *(synonyms: lit up or all lit up, turned on, blasted, charged up, hopped up, flying, on a trip, tripping, stoned, wasted, high, wired, loaded)* Under the influence of a drug.

LIT UP OR ALL LIT UP: *(synonyms: turned on, blasted, charged up, hopped up, flying, on a trip, tripping, stoned, wasted, high, wired, lifted, loaded)* Under the influence of a drug.

LOADED: *(synonyms: lit up or all lit up, turned on, blasted, charged up, hopped up, flying, on a trip, tripping, stoned, wasted, high, wired, lifted)* Under the influence of a drug.

MAINLINE: *(synonyms: shoot up, bang, boost, crank up, boot, draw up, fire, gun, hit the needle, jack up, miss, slam, spike, track, jab, laugh and scratch)* To inject a drug (into oneself).

MERCHANDISE: *(synonyms: junk, stuff)* Drugs.

MISS: *(synonyms: shoot up, bang, boost, crank up, boot, draw up, fire, gun, hit the needle, jack up, slam, spike, track, mainline, jab, laugh and scratch)* To inject a drug (into oneself).

MOW THE GRASS: *(synonyms: blaze, blow a stick, blast, blast a joint/stick/roach, fire up, hit the hay, toke up)*: To smoke marijuana.

MULE: A person who transports drugs.

NARC: 1) A narcotics officer. 2) A person who tells the police about a drug user or dealer.

see also: uncle

ON A MISSION: Looking for crack.

ON A TRIP: *(synonyms: lit up or all lit up, turned on, blasted, charged up, hopped up, flying, tripping, stoned, wasted, high, wired, lifted, loaded)* Under the influence of a drug.

ON ICE: *(synonym: boxed)* In jail.

ONE AND ONE: *(synonyms: snort, do a line, horn, pop, sniff, toke, blow)* To inhale cocaine into the nose.

PANIC: A situation in which drugs are scarce.

PAPERBOY: *(synonym: balloon)* A heroin dealer.

PEAKING: Experiencing the most intense part of an LSD trip.

PERP: *(synonyms: bump, gank, flex, fleece)* Fake cocaine.

PIN OR PINNER: A very thin marijuana cigarette.

see also: joint

PIPE: *(synonyms: gutter, sewer, channel)* The vein into which a drug is injected.

PIPERO: *(synonyms: beamer, buffer, crack head, chaser, cluck, crackerjack, puffer, thirst monster)* A crack user.

POP: *(synonyms: snort, do a line, horn, one and one, sniff, toke, blow)* To inhale cocaine into the nose.

PUFFER: *(synonyms: beamer, buffer, crack head, chaser, cluck, crackerjack, pipero, thirst monster)* A crack user.

PUMP: To sell crack.

PUSH: *(synonyms: deal, slang)* To sell drugs.

see also: burn

RAVE: An all-night dance party, usually one where hallucinogens or other mood-altering substances are used.

see also: trip

RIG: *(synonyms: artillery, gimmick, works, tools, kit, business)* Equipment used to inject drugs.

ROACH: The almost-too-small-to-smoke remainder of a marijuana cigarette.

ROCK HOUSE: *(synonyms: crack gallery, crack spot)* A place where crack is sold.

SCHMECKER: *(synonyms: channel swimmer, hype, sleepwalker)* A heroin addict.

SCORE: (as a noun) A drug purchase. (as a verb) To acquire drugs.

SERVER: A crack dealer.

SET: A place where drugs are sold.

SEWER: *(synonyms: gutter, pipe, channel)* The vein into which a drug is injected.

SHOOT UP: *(synonyms: bang, boost, crank up, boot, draw up, fire, gun, hit the needle, jack up, miss, slam, spike, track, mainline, jab, laugh and scratch)* To inject a drug (into oneself).

SHOOTING GALLERY: *(synonym: hit house)* A building where addicts go to use drugs.

SHOTGUN: In reference to smoking marijuana: 1) To exhale smoke into another person's mouth to give that person some of the effect. 2) To uncover a hole in a water pipe in order to suck up the smoke in it.

The term can also refer to several other ways to inhale marijuana.

SKEEZER: *(synonym: bag bride)* A woman who trades sex for crack.

SLAM: *(synonyms: shoot up, bang, boost, crank up, boot, draw up, fire, gun, hit the needle, jack up, miss, spike, track, mainline, jab, laugh and scratch)*: To inject a drug (into oneself).

SLANG: *(synonyms: push, deal)* To sell drugs.

SLEEPWALKER: *(synonyms: channel swimmer, hype, schmecker)* A heroin addict.

SNIFF: *(synonyms: snort, do a line, horn, one and one, pop, toke, blow)* To inhale cocaine into the nose.

SNORT: *(synonyms: do a line, horn, one and one, pop, sniff, toke, blow)* To inhale cocaine into the nose.

SPIKE: *(synonyms: shoot up, bang, boost, crank up, boot, draw up, fire, gun, hit the needle, jack up, miss, slam, track, mainline, jab, laugh and scratch)* To inject a drug (into oneself).

STASH: 1) A personal supply of drugs. 2) A place to hide drugs.

STEP ON: To cut a drug with other substances; to dilute a drug. The resulting, less potent drug is said to have been "stepped on."

STONED: *(synonyms: lit up or all lit up, turned on, blasted, charged up, hopped up, flying, on a trip, tripping, wasted, high, wired, lifted, loaded)* Under the influence of a drug.

STRUNG OUT: Addicted.

STUFF: *(synonyms: junk, merchandise)* Drugs.

THIRST MONSTER: *(synonyms: beamer, buffer, crack head, chaser, cluck, crackerjack, pipero, puffer)* A crack user.

THOROUGHBRED: A dealer who sells pure product. Many drug dealers mix their products with less expensive substances to make more money, using anything from a lower-quality version of the same drug to household chemicals.

TOKE: *(synonyms: snort, do a line, horn, one and one, pop, sniff, blow)* To inhale cocaine into the nose.

TOKE UP: *(synonyms: blaze, blow a stick, blast, blast a joint/stick/roach, fire up, hit the hay, mow the grass)* To smoke marijuana.

TOOLS: *(synonyms: artillery, gimmick, works, kit, rig, business)* Equipment used to inject drugs.

TRACK: *(synonyms: shoot up, bang, boost, crank up, boot, draw up, fire, gun, hit the needle, jack up, miss, slam, spike, mainline, jab, laugh and scratch)* To inject a drug (into oneself).

TRACKS: Injection scars.

TRAVEL AGENT: LSD dealer.

TRIP: A hallucinogenic drug use experience.

see also: rave

TRIPPING: *(synonyms: lit up or all lit up, turned on, blasted, charged up, hopped up, flying, on a trip, stoned, wasted, high, wired, lifted, loaded)* Under the influence of a drug.

TURNED ON: *(synonyms: lit up or all lit up, blasted, charged up, hopped up, flying, on a trip, tripping, stoned, wasted, high, wired, lifted, loaded)* Under the influence of a drug.

UNCLE: A federal narcotics officer.

see also: narc

WASTED: *(synonyms: lit up or all lit up, turned on, blasted, charged up, hopped up, flying, on a trip, tripping, stoned, high, wired, lifted, loaded)* Under the influence of a drug.

WIRED: *(synonyms: lit up or all lit up, turned on, blasted, charged up, hopped up, flying, on a trip, tripping, stoned, wasted, high, lifted, loaded)* Under the influence of a drug.

WORKS: *(synonyms: artillery, gimmick, tools, kit, rig, business)* Equipment used to inject drugs.

ZOOMER: *(synonym: beat artist)* A dealer who sells fake drugs.

Flyfishers and Sport Fishermen

★ ★ ★ ★ ★ ★

The most popular types of sport fishing are fly fishing (attracting fish by making an artificial insect sit or dance on the surface of stream), ice fishing, and angling (traditional, baited rod-and-reel fishing). Depending on the fisherman (this term encompasses both men and women) the main goal of fishing may be relaxation, a chance to spend time in nature, socialization, the challenge of catching and fighting large fish, an opportunity to bring in food, and/or some time to drink beer in a rowboat.

About three times as many U.S. sport fishermen fish in fresh water as in salt water. The most popular types of freshwater fish are bass, panfish (sunfish, perch, and bluegill), trout, catfish, and crappie. The most popular fish among saltwater sport fishermen are flatfish (halibut and flounder), followed by striped bass, sea trout, bluefish, salmon, and mackerel.

In addition to the fishing itself, many flyfishers make a hobby of fly tying, the craft of creating effective flyfishing lures out of hooks, feathers, thread, and other materials.

RELATED SUBCULTURE:

Hunters

★ ★ ★ ★ ★ ★

BARNEY: A person who is unskilled, incompetent, or new at fishing.

BREEZERS: Fish that are travelling by and that may not go for bait.

> "It is here that I will see the late spring **breezers**, big yellowtail feeding at the surface."

BUG: A fly-fishing fly.

CANDY: The type of bait a particular type of fish prefers.

CATCH AND RELEASE: A type of fishing in which fish are released back into the water.

> "Almost all Everglades bass fishing is **catch-and-release** because of mercury contamination in the bass."

CATTLE BOAT: A crowded sport fishing boat.

> "If I don't have better luck soon, I may have to squeeze myself onto a **cattle boat** and catch some real fish."

CHICKEN OR SEA CHICKEN: A seagull.

CHUMMER: A person who vomits over the side of a boat.

> "I was seasick almost the whole time, and yes I took Dramamine the night before as well as before leaving ... oh well, I guess I just have to live with being the **chummer**."

DINK: A little fish.

> "I'd be more concerned with a lake that has only a handful of really big bass and an outrageous number of **dinks**."

DROWN SOME WORMS: To go fishing and not catch anything.

FARMER: Someone who regularly loses fish that strike his or her line.

GET HUNG: To catch a fish.

HIT: *(synonym: strike)* A bite from a fish.

LUNKER: A large fish.

NERVOUS WATER: A place in a body of water that is stirred up by a lot of small fish.

> "Try to find some **nervous water** with bait fish jumping, then fling the surface walker into the middle."

PUT DOWN: To scare (fish).

> "You could yell all day when standing in a sandy bottom river and not **put** the fish **down**."

RIP: For a fish, to get free of a line after an initial hit.

> "We got **ripped** a couple of times, and the boat captain said that it was tuna, but we never got a chance to see what it was."

SALAD: Any aquatic plant that gets entangled with a fishing line.

SLAMMED: To get many bites from fish.

> "I was fishing sencos and was getting **slammed**. The only problem was, they were all pickerels."

STRIKE: *(synonym: hit)* A bite on a line from a fish.

> "I didn't catch anything (fished for an hour and a half), but did get one **strike**."

Furries

Furry fandom—enthusiasm for and identification with anthropomorphic animal characters—is a subculture marked by surprisingly deep divisions.

Both the characters and the members of the subculture are called "furries." Some furry characters combine human features with the those of mammals like horses, cats, or skunks; others are anthropomorphized non-mammals like dragons and sharks; and still others are wholely imaginary creatures. This last category includes such beasts as centaurs and chakats, creatures with the lower body of a large feline and a human or mixed human and feline upper body.

The most divisive issue in furry fandom is sex. Many furries consider furrydom as innocent fun and wouldn't see a meaningful distinction between cartoon characters like Tom and Jerry and their own favorite furry characters.

Other furries are interested in yiff, the subculture of furry sex. Yiff encompasses erotic anthropomorphic art, virtual sex, real-life sexual encounters (sometimes in costume), and even sexual attraction to stuffed toys.

Not surprisingly, many non-yiff furries don't consider yiff furries part of furrydom at all, and they

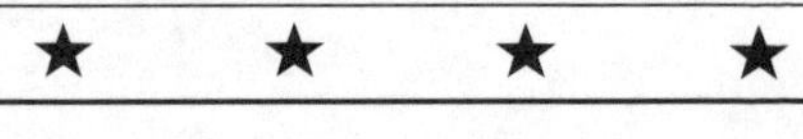

sometimes resent the attention yiff receives from the general public, fearing that yiff gives the impression that all furry activity is erotic.

In addition to furry slang, furries use a variety of zoological terms, such as "mustelid" to refer to any mammal in the weasel family, or "digitigrade" to refer to those mammals that walk on their toes (a group which, surprisingly, includes cats, dogs, and horses).

Furry characters are categorized by the type of animal on which the character is based. Popular categories include bovine (cow, bull, buffalo, etc.), canine (dog), equine (horse, zebra), feline (house cat, lion, leopard, etc.), lupine (wolf), murine (mouse, rat), musteline (weasel, skunk, otter, wolverine, mink, etc.), ursine (bear), and vulpine (fox).

Typical furry activity includes online chat or discussion groups, conventions, and drawing. A large number of furries spend time socializing with other furries on the Web, in character. Brief descriptions of actions, such as waving goodbye with one's tail or cuddlicking (simultaneously cuddling and licking another furry, not necessarily with any implication of yiff) are common in these discussions.

RELATED SUBCULTURES:

Sci-Fi and Fantasy Fans, Anime and Manga Fans

ANTHRO: Short for "anthropomorphic;" (as a noun) A character based on an animal that also has some human characteristics. (as an adjective) Having to do with an anthro character.

see also: furry

ANYFUR: In in the context of furry fandom, anyone.

see also: everyfur

CON: *(synonym: furcon)* A convention for furries, usually taking place in a city over a weekend, with costumes, art shows, dealers of furry-related

items, presentations, etc. A given con might be specifically for furries, or it might be a science fiction convention that includes some furry events. See the "Sci-Fi and fantasy fans" section for more information on science fiction conventions.

EVERYFUR: In the context of furry fandom, everyone.

see also: anyfur

FLOOF: 1) (verb) To fluff up one's fur as much as possible. 2) (noun) A great fluffing up of fur. 3) (noun) Substantial fluffiness. 4) (interjection) An exclamation indicating that a character has floofed. 5) (various) A general-use euphemism and replacement word.

see also: floofy

"I would worry about my family, but the rest of society can go **floof** themselves."

FLOOFY: In reference to a furry character, having fluffed-up fur.

see also: floof

FUR: *(synonym: furson)* 1) A person involved in furrydom. 2) A furry character.

see also: furry

FURCON: *(synonym: con)* A convention of furry fans.

FURRY: 1) A person who identifies with a particular animal or with animals in general, and who usually creates an alter ego anthropomorphic character. 2) A furry character. 3) Having to do with furrydom. 4) A furry lifestyler: a person whose connection with a particular type of animal is central to how she or he lives.

FURRYDOM OR FURRIDOM: Furry fans as a whole.

FURSON: *(synonym: fur)* A person involved in furrydom.

FURSUIT: A full-body costume of a furry character.

see also: fursuiter

FURSUITER: A person who regularly wears a furry character costume.

see also: fursuit

(!) FURVERT: A person who associates furries with sex. The term can be considered either neutral or derogatory.

see also: yiff

(!) GREYMUZZLE: (occasionally "graymuzzle") (as a noun) An older furry who has been involved with furrydom for some time; greymuzzles are usually at least forty to fifty years old. (as an adjective) Having to do with greymuzzles.

"Greymuzzle" can be neutral, complimentary, or slightly insulting, depending on the situation and how the individual feels about being called a greymuzzle.

> "Try to get a **greymuzzle** to answer that, since they may have been around that long."

LIFESTYLER: A person who identifies spiritually, psychologically, or in other ways with a certain type of animal. Lifestylers sometimes adopt characteristics of the animal in their appearance or mannerisms. Regardless of how the connection is expressed, a lifestyler is a furry who considers it central to his or her identity.

see also: therianthropy

MACROFURRY: A very large furry character.

MORPH: (as a verb) To change from a human into a furry character. Used especially in chat rooms, stories, and other virtual or fictional contexts. (as a suffix or noun) A furry character based on a type of animal. For instance, a bat-morph (or "batmorph" or "bat morph") is a furry character based on a bat.

see also: non-morphic

(!) MUNDANE: (as an adjective) Not part of the furry subculture. (as a noun) A person who is not part of furrydom. Can be derogatory or neutral.

Furry fandom shares this word with some other subcultures, such as science fiction and fantasy fans (see separate section).

> "Just keep minors, unsuspecting **mundanes** and the press off the NC-17 and X stuff."

NON-MORPHIC: Having the full appearance of an animal rather than combined animal and human characteristics.

see also: morph

PLUSHOPHILE: A person who is sexually aroused by furry animal toys.

This term is much less often used to refer to people who are simply plush toy enthusiasts.

see also: yiff

TAUR OR 'TAUR: Any furry character that is human in one section of its body and animal in another; for example, a centaur or minotaur character.

THERIANTHROPY: A spiritual or psychological connection with a particular type of animal. People who use this term often prefer to differentiate themselves from furry fandom (a.k.a. furrydom).

see also: lifestyler

WHELPED: Born, usually in reference to a furry character.

"It's not like anyone I don't know really cares when I was **whelped**."

YIFF: (as a verb) To have sex (virtually or otherwise) in a context that involves furries. (as a noun) Sex involving furries.

see also: yiffy, plushophile

YIFFY: Sexy, erotic, or aroused in the context of furries.

see also: yiff

"I'm genuinely unsure whether I *want* to know what a **yiffy** roach looks like."

Gamblers and Poker Players

Gambling slang is easy to learn—a welcoming kind of slang—because everybody in the gambling world loves to teach a newbie, usually by taking his or her money.

The most popular types of gambling are card games (poker, blackjack, baccarat), games in which players bet on which numbers will appear or hope for certain numbers to be picked (roulette, craps, bingo, keno, lotteries), slot machines, and wagers on events (horse racing, sporting events, proposition bets, and so on). Most of these types of betting can be done in casinos, where odds or fees are arranged so that the casino generally receives a portion of the money wagered.

This section covers the slang of gambling, but not the terms used in specific games. Knowing the difference between a flush and a full house is part of learning how to play poker, and believe me, I'm not the person you want to have teaching you to play poker. On the other hand, the following is rich in general gambling slang information, like the difference between being the fish and being the shark. (Hint: if you're not sure, you're the fish.)

RELATED SUBCULTURE:

Con Artists and Scammers

ACTION: The amount of money a player has wagered on one hand or game.

ACTIVE: Still playing the hand. A player who is active in the hand hasn't folded.

see also: fold

ALL IN: In reference to a player, having bet all of one's chips or money.

see also: pot, raise

ANTE: (pronounced "AN-tee") The chips a player must put in the pot in order to participate in a hand of Poker.

APPLE: *(synonyms: fish, sucker, mark)* A player likely to lose money.

BANKROLL: *(synonyms: roll, wad)* The total amount of money a player has available to bet. Can mean the amount set aside for one game, for a gambling session, or for a gambling trip.

> "The fish is dumping his whole **bankroll** before his 'experiment' ends, at this rate."

BASIC STRATEGY: In blackjack, playing exactly the way the odds dictate for the cards in one's hand. For a player to use basic strategy he or she must memorize all of the odds involved. Unlike card counting, basic strategy is allowed in casinos.

BLIND BET: In certain kinds of poker, a bet made before seeing any cards.

BOOKMAKER OR BOOKIE: A person who sets odds for betting on events and accepts wagers on them. In places where running a book is legal, "bookmaker" is the preferred term for someone who runs a legal betting operation.

BUMP: *(synonym: raise)* To bet an additional amount in a poker game.

BUST: 1) To receive a total hand of more than twenty-one in a game of blackjack and therefore lose. 2) To lose all of one's money.

see also: down to the felt

> "So if he has a 12, then there's a possibility that he'll **bust**."

BUTTON: A round marker in poker that indicates the current dealer.

CALL: 1) In poker, to match the current bet amount without increasing it. 2) In keno and bingo, to read out the numbers being chosen.

"At that point I realized that if I was willing to **call** his reraise, I should have just gone all in on the flop."

CARD COUNTING: Memorizing and analyzing statistics regarding cards that have been played so far in a hand so as to gain an advantage in predicting what will happen in the game. Not cheating, but prohibited in casinos.

Card counting is more involved than basic strategy. To use card counting, the player must keep track of which cards have been played so far and consider that with other factors. By contrast, basic strategy relies on simply comparing one's hand to the card the dealer is showing.

CARPET JOINT: A luxurious place to gamble.

CASE MONEY: Emergency or reserve betting money.

CATCH: 1) In keno, for a number you've marked to be drawn. 2) In card games, to receive the cards you need.

CHECK: 1) (noun) A chip; used to stand in for money in a game. 2) (verb) In a poker game, to stay in the game but not offer a bet.

CHIP: A disc used to stand in for money during a game so that no actual money sits on the table.

see also: check

COLD: 1) In reference to a gambler, losing. 2) In reference to a deck of cards, arranged beforehand and then snuck into play after the shuffle (a form of cheating).

COLOR UP: To exchange one's chips for a smaller number of chips with higher values, in order to keep one's winnings under control as they grow.

"I was fortunate to participate in one or two hot rolls, and after playing about fifty minutes, I **colored up** with $388, up $188."

COMP: Any free amenity offered by a casino to encourage gamblers.

COWBOY: In card games, a king.

see also: lady, paint

CUT: To split a deck of cards and put the bottom group on the top.

CUT CARD: A blank, plastic card used to cut a deck and then placed on the bottom to prevent dealing from the bottom of the deck.

DOWN TO THE FELT: Out of money.

"If he's got nothing he'll fold if you come back over on the flop or turn, unless he's **down to the felt**, in which case he'll call with his last few chips."

DROP: 1) To give up on a hand of a card game and forfeit any money wagered so far. 2) To lose money.

see also: *fold*

EVEN MONEY: A bet that pays off the same amount wagered.

FISH: *(synonyms: sucker, apple, mark)* A player likely to lose money.

FOLD: *(synonym: pass)* To give up on a hand of a card game and forfeit money wagered on that hand.

see also: *drop*

GEORGE: Anyone likely to be a good source of money, e.g., a person who tips well, or a poor player.

see also: *Tom, fish*

GRINDER: *(synonym: rounder)* A poker player who earns a living at the game.

HIGH ROLLER: A person who bets large amounts of money.

see also: *whale*

HIT: 1) To deal another card to a blackjack player. 2) To call for another card in a game of blackjack.

"Before you know it, I was dealt a 13 versus a dealer 6, which I **hit** because I was convinced it was a safe card."

HOLE CARD: A face-down card that is revealed at the end of the hand.

HOUSE: The casino or other establishment in which one is gambling.

HOUSE EDGE: The extent to which odds are in favor of the casino, so that on average gamblers will tend to lose more money than they win. The house edge provides a large portion of the casino's income.

see also: *juice, rake*

JUICE: 1) The money the casino takes out of each pot in a game as their percentage. 2) A particular, advanced card marking system. 3) Any card marking system.

see also: *rake, house edge*

"I guess they have a higher overhead than an online casino, but it seems like a lot of **juice**."

LADY: In card games, a queen.

see also: *cowboy, paint*

LET IT RIDE: *(synonym: press)* To leave winnings on the table as a new wager.

LONG ODDS: A low probability of winning.

see also: short odds

LOOSE: In reference to a slot machine: 1) Taking only a small percentage for the establishment that owns the machine and therefore tending to offer comparatively good payouts. 2) Considered likely to pay off.

see also: tight

"I've never had any luck in finding a **loose** slot machine."

MARK: *(synonyms: fish, sucker, apple)* A player likely to lose money.

MARKER: An IOU or bank check a player writes to the gambling establishment for credit to make further wagers.

MECHANIC: A cheater. The term can refer to a player or to a house dealer, and is most often used in reference to card games.

ON TILT: To react to losses by making bad gambling decisions; to gamble recklessly after bad luck.

PAINT: In card games, one or more face cards.

see also: lady, cowboy

PAPER PLAYER: A player who uses marked cards.

PASS: *(synonym: fold)* To drop out of a hand of a card game.

PIT: An area with playing tables arranged around a central area for dealers where players come to the outside of the tables to play.

see also: pit boss

PIT BOSS: The supervisor of multiple games at a gambling establishment.

see also: pit

POT: All of the money (or chips) bet by the players so far in one hand of a card game.

PRESS: *(synonym: let it ride)* To leave money one has just won on the table as a wager for the next round of betting.

"I played and won, played and won, **pressed** and won, **pressed** to three chips and won."

PROPOSITION BET: A wager on an outcome that is not usually the subject of betting, such as how far a person can throw a ball, or which of two words will come up next in a political speech.

Proposition bets are also sometimes offered by small-time con artists. For more information on con artists, see the con artists section on page 87.

PUSH: In a card game, a tie between a player and the dealer.

QUADS: Four cards in one's hand with the same value.

RAISE: *(synonym: bump)* To bet an additional amount in Poker, so that other players must meet the new bet to remain in the game.

RAKE: The money the casino keeps as a fee out of all player bets at a card game.

see also: vig

ROLL: *(synonyms:* bankroll*, wad)* The total amount of money a player has available to bet.

ROUNDER: *(synonym: grinder)* A person who earns a living at Poker.

RUN A BOOK: To offer odds and accept bets on an event.

see also: bookmaker

SHARP OR SHARK: 1) A person who is expert at card games. 2) A skilled cheater at card games.

SHILL: A casino employee who plays with house money to earn winnings for the casino or to encourage players and fill out games. The word doesn't have as negative a connotation here as it does among con artists (see page 99).

SHORT ODDS: Odds where the likelihood of winning is comparatively high (and the payoff usually that much lower). If the odds on a particular event improve, they are said to shorten.

see also: long odds

"If you're betting a horse with long odds and a horse or horses with **short odds** to finish in the top three, you'll get a very small payoff."

SPOOK: In reference to a spectator, to stand behind a player and communicate (as discreetly as possible, of course) information about that player's hidden card to an associate who is playing in that game.

STACK: 1) (noun) A pile of chips, usually twenty per stack. 2) (noun) All of the chips in front of a particular player. 3) (verb) To arrange a deck with the intention of using it to cheat.

SUCKER: *(synonyms:* fish*, apple, mark)* A player likely to lose money.

TELL: A habit or gesture that unintentionally communicates information about a player's hand to one or more of the other players.

"You don't think they are using their peripheral vision to pick up a **tell**: No, they're probably working out the math."

THREE-CARD MONTE: A betting scam in which the game operator shows three cards, one of which is a queen. He then shuffles the cards, and the bettor must indicate which is the queen.

Monte is a scam because it can so easily be manipulated, and is not a casino game. (See the section on con artists on page 87 for more information.)

TIGHT: In reference to a slot machine, keeping a fairly high percentage of money wagered for the owner of the machine and therefore tending to pay out poorly.

see also: loose

TOKE: A monetary tip from a player to a dealer, usually in the form of one or more chips.

TOM: Any gambler who doesn't tip well.

TRIPS: In poker, three cards of the same value in one player's hand.

TRUE ODDS: An accurate prediction of the likelihood of an event. True odds are usually more favorable than the odds bookmakers offer for bets; the difference between the real odds and the bookmaker's odds yield the bookmaker's profit.

see also: house edge, bookmaker

VIG OR VIGORISH: The fee or percentage of money wagered that is paid to the gambling establishment.

"The **vigorish** is not returned even if the bet wins, which is the fly in the ointment."

WAD: (*synonyms:* bankroll, *roll*) The total amount of money a player has available to bet.

WHALE: A person who bets enormous amounts of money, making high rollers look timid.

see also: high roller

WHITE MEAT: A gambling establishment's profit.

Gardeners

★ ★ ★ ★ ★ ★

The most useful words in a gardener's vocabulary are plant names because if you don't know if your plant is a begonia or a bougainvillea, how are you going to find out anything about taking care of it?

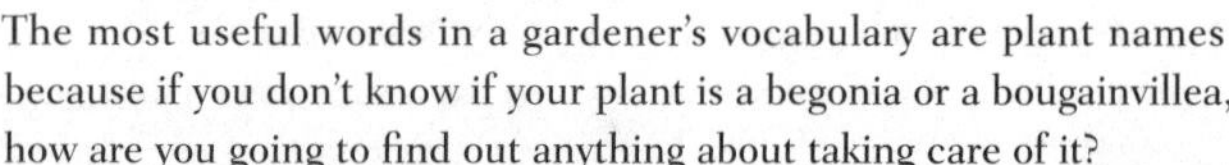

Gardeners also tend to have a healthy list of agricultural and botanical terms covering issues like climate, soil, fertilizers, seeds, and growing methods. To round out the gardener's vocabulary, of course, there's gardening slang, which in some instances transforms what most people might think of as an object—a plant—into a thinking being with emotions and preferences. Plants invade or volunteer, taste soil and find it sweet or sour, and find themselves shocked at being transplanted (and who wouldn't?).

Gardeners cite a variety of motivations that bring them outside in their free time to do what many people would call hard work. These include a desire to be outside and interact with nature, the gratification of bringing an edible plant to maturity, the relaxation that gardening brings, and the ability to beautify their immediate surroundings.

★ ★ ★ ★ ★

AMENDMENT: Anything mixed into soil to improve conditions for plants; for instance, compost or bone meal.

"Why would the application of **amendment** too early (before soil has warmed) stunt plants?"

COLD FRAME: A boxy structure with a transparent lid used as a miniature greenhouse.

COMPANION PLANTING: Planting two or more kinds of plants together so that they can benefit one another. For instance, one type of plant might fix nitrogen into the soil that another plant needs, or one may shelter another from the wind.

"I started to do **companion planting** recently. Yesterday, I planted both beans and corns on the rows next to each other."

COMPOST TEA: Water run through compost and applied to a garden, to add nutrients to the soil.

DEAD-HEAD: To cut or break off spent blossoms to encourage the growth of new blossoms.

EXOTIC: Any plant not native to the area in which it grows.

see also: invasive exotic

"Many of us don't think twice before splashing some colorful plants (mostly **exotics**, or at least horticultural artifacts) into our gardens."

FORCE: To coax a plant to bloom in an artificial environment at a time or place where it would not normally flower.

HARDEN OFF: To accustom an indoor plant to the outdoors.

HEIRLOOM: In reference to plants or seeds, identical genetically to those grown fifty to a hundred years ago, or more. Heirloom plants are varieties cultivated prior to modern agricultural innovations and modern standardization of seed stock. They may be unusual in taste, texture, appearance, suitability to a particular region, or in other respects.

INVASIVE EXOTIC: Any plant not native to the area in which it's growing and that tends to spread and displace native species.

see also: exotic

LASAGNA BED: An area where plants are grown in soil that has been piled up on top of the existing ground in layers of different planting materials.

LEGGY: In reference to a whole plant or part of a plant, growing long and thin instead of thick and bushy.

"I read that lack of light will cause **leggy** plants, but I'm not short of light with my setup, am I?"

PASS-ALONG PLANT: A plant that is easily shared with other gardeners, e.g., through cuttings or seeds.

PINCH BACK OR PINCH OFF: To cut or pinch off the tip of new growth on a plant so that it will tend to fill out more.

ROOT-BOUND: In reference to a plant, being confined to too small a container so that roots become massed and tangled.

SOUR SOIL: Acidic soil.

see also: *sweet soil*

SUCCESSION PLANTING: Planting a particular type of plant at intervals so that the harvest will last longer.

SWEET SOIL: Soil that's more alkaline than acidic.

see also: *sour soil*

TRANSPLANT SHOCK: A negative, often temporary reaction from a plant when replanted in a new location.

VOLUNTEER OR VOLUNTEER PLANT: An interesting plant that springs up naturally, for instance, from seeds transported by birds.

"Last year I gave away dozens of **volunteer** plants, which I called 'Mystery Tomatoes' because I had no idea what they were."

WEED TREE: Any tree that decides to grow where it's not wanted, especially an undesirable species.

ZONE BENDING: Finding ways to grow a plant in a climate where it wouldn't usually thrive.

Gay, Lesbian, Transgendered, and Bisexual People

The many people who fall into categories like gay, lesbian, bisexual, and transgendered are hard to name as a group because that group is so diverse. The most inclusive way to talk about the subculture as a whole is to use the abbreviation GLTB (gay, lesbian, transgendered, bisexual), or one of its variants (GTLB, GLB, etc.).

At least three features encourage slang to flourish and expand in the GLTB community. First, it encompasses a very large group of people. Second, many members of this community go out of their way to differentiate themselves from the average straight person. Third, standard English isn't adequate to easily describe some of the subjects that come up in conversations about gay, lesbian, bisexual, and transgendered life.

At the same time, a large number of people in this community use little or no GLTB slang to avoid standing out from the rest of society because, in some cases, they don't want to be identified as part of the subculture.

A sizeable portion of GLTB vocabulary comprises slang for sexual acts, but I'll leave those out here because this isn't that kind of book. If you search on the Web or in book stores, though, you'll find thousands of these kinds of terms.

There are a variety of symbols for gays, lesbians, and the GLTB community in general, including the labrys (two-bladed axe), the rainbow, the pink triangle, the double male symbol, the double female symbol, etc. This is also the only subculture I know that can lay claim to an entire color (lavender).

Some of the most common terms used for GLTB people outside the GLTB subculture—"homosexual," "transvestite," and "hermaphrodite," for instance—are less popular inside the GLTB community. GLTB slang alternatives for these words are "gay" (or "lesbian"), "cross-dresser," and "intersex."

Many GLTB terms that seem derogatory, like "bone smuggler" or "bull dyke," are generally not derogatory at all when used within the subculture. Of course, *outside of* the subculture, there are people for whom any word associated with GLTB culture is considered derogatory, including otherwise neutral terms like "gay" itself.

Gender is a key issue in GLTB culture, and using non-slang terms to describe GLTB gender issues can be misleading. In the following definitions, words like "masculine," "feminine," "effeminate," etc., shouldn't be taken to mean literally having to do with one gender or another, but instead as having to do with characteristics usually associated with that gender.

ALLY: A straight person who is actively supportive of the GLTB community.

BABY BUTCH: A young lesbian who acts in a more masculine than traditionally feminine manner.

see also: butch

"You are just as bisexual as the woman who mostly has relationships with men but every couple of years picks up a cute **baby butch** down at the dyke bar."

BABY DYKE: 1) A lesbian in her teens or early twenties. 2) A woman who has only recently come to think of herself as a lesbian.

see also: dyke

(!) BASHER OR GAY BASHER: Anyone who harasses, publicly disparages, or assaults gays, lesbians, bisexuals, or transgendered people.

BEAR: A very hairy, gay man, especially if heavyset. Usually not derogatory.

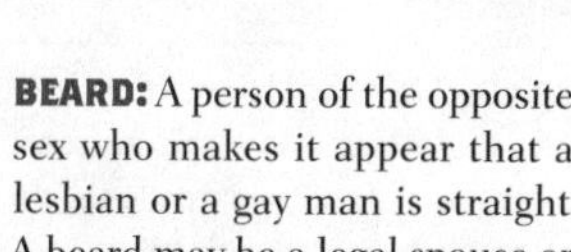

BEARD: A person of the opposite sex who makes it appear that a lesbian or a gay man is straight. A beard may be a legal spouse or simply a friend who will come to parties or family gatherings.

> "She will act as his **beard** when his parents come over and at office parties."

BI OR BISEXUAL: (as an adjective) Attracted to both males and females. (as a noun) A person who is attracted to both males and females. "Bisexual" is used as a noun more frequently than "bi."

A person can be bisexual without ever being physically involved with people of both genders; a person's mindset and identity are generally considered to be definitive, although opinions on the subject vary.

see also: monosexual

BONE SMUGGLER: *(synonym: drag queen)* A man dressed as a woman.

BOTTOM: *(synonym: catcher)* The more passive person in a sexual relationship or in a particular encounter. Used especially regarding gay men.

BOY: 1) (as a noun) The more passive man in a gay, male couple. 2) (as an adjective) For a male transvestite, having to do with presenting himself as a male, as in the phrase "my boy clothes." 3) (as a noun) A young lesbian whose appearance and behavior are somewhat masculine. See also baby butch.

see also: bottom, girl

(!) BREEDER: A heterosexual. Not universal among lesbians and gays, in part because it's derogatory.

> "Nobody suggested a *totally* gay cast. Just a mostly gay one (six gays, one, ahem, **breeder**)."

BULL DYKE OR BULLDYKE OR BULL: *(synonym: diesel dyke)* An assertive, tough, masculine lesbian.

see also: butch

BUTCH: Tough, masculine, assertive, or macho. Used especially regarding lesbians, but can also be applied to gay men, or in other situations.

This term is often preferred to words like "masculine," and can be considered complimentary in some situations.

Not all lesbians fall into the categories of butch and femme.

see also: bull dyke, baby butch, femme, stone butch

"[She] is a lesbian, a **butch** one, and that has been evident for years."

CAMP: Anything playfully exaggerated or satirical, especially effeminate affectations in gay men. Also, any experience or performance that lends itself to this kind of exaggeration, for instance, *The Wizard of Oz*.

see also: friend of Dorothy, flaming

CATCHER: *(synonym:* bottom*)* The more passive person in a sexual relationship.

CHAPSTICK LESBIAN: 1) An androgynous lesbian, one who is neither particularly butch nor particularly femme. 2) A lesbian who likes playing sports.

CHICKEN: 1) An underage male who is either gay or being pursued by an older gay man. 2) A very young gay man who is, however, above the age of consent.

see also: twink

CLOSET: A metaphorical hiding place for one's homosexuality. A lesbian or gay man who does not make her or his sexuality public is "in the closet"; a person who is publicly homosexual is "out of the closet."

see also: out, come out

"I guess I feel that the sort of 'f*** you' toughness one needs to assert a bisexual identity is not fostered by remaining in the **closet**."

COME OUT: 1) To reveal to others that one is lesbian, gay, bisexual, transgendered, etc. 2) In the phrase "come out to oneself," to come to the realization that one is gay, lesbian, or bisexual.

see also: closet, out

COMMITMENT CEREMONY: A ceremony for a gay or lesbian couple that's similar to a wedding, used in areas where gay marriage is illegal.

CROSSDRESSER OR CROSS-DRESSER OR CROSS DRESSER OR CD: *(synonym: transvestite)* A person who takes on an appearance associated with the opposite gender; a man who dresses as a woman or a woman who dresses as a man. Cross-dressing may involve clothing, cosmetics, hairstyle, gestures, voice, and other characteristics.

The term "cross-dresser" is often preferred to "transvestite." Cross-dressers may be gay, straight, bisexual, or other. ("Other" is beyond the scope of this book, and cross-dressing is confusing enough without getting into that whole thing.)

Some people regarded as cross-dressers by others may not consider themselves cross-dressers, identifying more with the gender they present than their anatomical gender.

see also: male-to-female, female-to-male, transgendered, identify as, pass, read, drag, drag queen, drag king

DE-DYKE: To remove all evidence of lesbianism from one's house in preparation for visitors to whom one isn't out.

see also: re-dyke, out

"I have heard a couple of closeted friends of mine discuss the need to '**de-dyke**' their apartment before one of their mothers came to visit."

DIESEL DYKE: *(synonym: bull dyke or bulldyke or bull)* A lesbian who presents herself in a manly, tough way.

DRAG: The appearance of the opposite gender. Both men and women can be in drag. The term is reputed to be an acronym for "dressed resembling a girl."

see also: cross-dresser

DRAG KING: A woman dressed as a man.

see also: female-to-male, cross-dresser, drag

(!) DRAG QUEEN: *(synonym: bone smuggler)* A man, usually gay, dressed as a woman, especially when dressed flamboyantly or for a drag performance. Usually neutral or even complimentary, but can occasionally be derogatory; for instance, if the person is not actively trying to look like the opposite gender.

see also: male-to-female, cross-dresser, drag, flaming

"When a straight man puts on a dress and goes on a sexual kick, he is a transvestite. When a man is a woman trapped in a man's body and has a little operation, he is a transsexual. When a gay man has way too much fashion sense for one gender he is a **drag queen**. And when a tired little Latin boy puts on a dress, he is simply a boy in a dress!"

- FROM THE MOVIE *To Wong Foo Thanks for Everything, Julie Newmar*, WRITTEN BY DOUGLAS CARTER BEANE

(!) DYKE: A lesbian, especially one who is masculine in appearance or who acts assertively. This term used to be derogatory and now can still be taken that way, especially when used by a non-lesbian, but has largely been reclaimed as an appropriate, informal synonym for "lesbian."

Terms within the GLTB community that incorporate the word "dyke" (such as "bulldyke") are generally not derogatory, as they may be when used by outsiders.

see also: butch, bull dyke, baby dyke, fag

DYKON: A lesbian icon; a lesbian celebrity.

see also: dyke

(!) FAG OR FAGGOT: A gay man. Can be harshly derogatory, but is also used by gay men as a neutral way to refer to other gay men, especially effeminate or swishy ones.

"Faggot" is more likely to be used insultingly than "fag."

see also: dyke, swish

(!) FAG HAG: A woman with close friends who are gay men. Can be derogatory or neutral.

FAIRY: An effeminate, gay man.

see also: fag, swish

FAMILY: Gays and lesbians. A person who is lesbian, gay, or bi is "family." Sometimes capitalized.

see also: friend of Dorothy

> "Is he **family**? Did he achieve gay-icondom while I wasn't looking ... ?"

FEMALE-TO-MALE: Born female but now presenting as a male, whether through surgery or cross-dressing.

see also: male-to-female, drag king, cross-dresser, transgendered, transsexual

FEMME: Behaving in a manner traditionally associated with females. Applies especially to lesbians, but can also be used for an effeminate or submissive gay man.

see also: butch, bottom

(!) FISH: A straight woman. This is a mildly derogatory term used by some gay men.

FLAMING: In reference to a gay man, flamboyantly effeminate.

see also: drag queen, camp

FRIEND OF DOROTHY: A gay man or a lesbian.

see also: camp, family

> "However, I do intend to meet a friend who is a '**friend of Dorothy**' while I'm there."

GAY: (as an adjective) Attracted to people of the same gender; homosexual. While this term can be taken to include both men and woman and sometimes to include bisexuals (especially in set phrases like "gay pride" and "gay marriage"), it refers most often to gay men.

Some people identify as gay based on their mindset, even if they have not been physically involved with a person of the same gender. Other people use the term to refer only to people who become romantically involved with someone of the same gender. (as a noun) A homosexual man.

see also: LesBiGay, lesbian, bi, queer

GAYDAR: Awareness of potentially gay or lesbian people nearby. Straight people can sometimes possess gaydar. Sometimes used to ask whether someone nearby is gay or to assert that that person is, as in "my gaydar is going off."

GENDER F*CK: Mixing elements of both genders in one person's appearance, usually with the intention of shaking up traditional gender ideas.

GENDER IDENTITY: A person's own beliefs about his or her gender, not necessarily linked with appearance, anatomy, or birth sex.

GENDERQUEER: (as an adjective) Not fitting easily into lesbian, bisexual, gay, or straight sexuality. (as a noun) A person who doesn't fit easily into one of these categories.

see also: queer

"Actually, your multiple gender claim is just pandering to [people who say] that transsexuals should not 'try to be women,' but should simply be some sort of **gender queer**."

(!) GIRL: A feminine or submissive gay man or lesbian. Because the term "girl" can be used condescendingly, it can come across as an insult in some situations.

see also: boy

HANKY CODE: A somewhat dated way for gay men (and sometimes lesbians) to signal the kind of encounter they are interested in by wearing a handkerchief of a particular color on a particular side of the body.

HASBIAN: A woman who formerly thought of herself as a lesbian but has come to consider herself straight.

see also: identify as

HET: (*synonym: straight*) Heterosexual.

HETEROSEXISM: The belief that heterosexuality is the only proper type of sexuality.

HIR: A gender-neutral substitute for "him" or "her" used by some transgendered people.

see also: sie

IDENTIFY AS: To think of oneself as part of a particular gender or group. For example, a male cross-dresser who identifies as a lesbian considers him/herself to actually be a lesbian who has a male anatomy.

Often used in situations where the role identified with is not universally accepted by others.

> "I'm saying that if an individual **identifies as** male and is physically male, they should use the men's room."

(!) IN THE LIFE: Openly gay, lesbian, bisexual, or transgendered, and involved in the GLTB community.

Caution is advisable when using this term; it has different meanings in other subcultures, for instance, it can mean being a prostitute.

INTERSEX: (as a noun) A hermaphrodite; a person with genitalia that are both male and female. (as an adjective) Having the characteristics of an intersex.

LESBIAN: (as a noun) A woman who is sexually or romantically attracted to other women. (as an adjective) Attracted to other women.

see also: *gay, dyke, bi, LesBiGay*

LESBIGAY: (pronounced "LEZ-bye-gay") Lesbian, bisexual, or gay. This term is more inclusive than "gay" and more consistent and pronounceable than "GLTB" and its variants.

> "I'll assume that many of them are **lesbigay**, and some of them announce their sexual preferences, but no one is asked to do so."

(!) LIPSTICK LESBIAN: A lesbian who presents herself in a traditionally feminine manner, e.g., wearing cosmetics and dresses. Often appears straight to casual observers. Can be considered derogatory.

see also: *lesbian, femme*

MAKE: (synonym: read) To detect a cross-dresser's anatomical gender.

MALE-TO-FEMALE: Born male but now presenting as a female, whether through surgery or cross-dressing.

see also: *female-to-male, drag queen, cross-dresser, transgendered, transsexual*

MARY: A form of address between gay men; a substitute for a gay man's actual name.

see also: *Nelly*

MISS THING OR MISS THANG: 1) A drag queen. 2) A sometimes ironic term for a flamboyant gay man.

> "One look at **Miss Thing** up there on stage and he shouts, 'That's a *man*!'"

MONOSEXISM: The belief that both homosexuality and heterosexuality are proper and appropriate sexual orientations, but that bisexuality is not.

MONOSEXUAL: (as a noun) A person who is attracted to people of one gender only. Lesbians, straight people, and gays are all monosexual. (as an adjective) Attracted to people of only one gender; not bisexual.

NELLY: A swishy name used between gay men to refer to one another.

see also: Mary, swish, flaming

OUT OR OUT OF THE CLOSET: (as an adjective) Openly gay or bisexual. A person may be out in one situation and not in another, for instance, out to him- or herself but not to the rest of the world, or out at work but not to family. (*out* as a verb) To disclose that someone is gay or bisexual. A person can out her- or himself, or can be outed by another person.

PASS: To successfully hide one's anatomical gender; to be perceived to be of the opposite gender.

see also: cross-dresser, read

> "I know at least one person who cross-dresses who is not trying to **pass** for female (the guy wears a full beard, skirts and high heel pumps), and gets an amazing amount of stares."

PITCHER: (*synonym: top*) The more active partner in a gay relationship.

POST-OP: Having completed sexual reassignment (sex change) surgery.

see also: pre-op, transsexual, transgendered

PRE-OP: Intending to go through gender reassignment surgery (a sex change operation).

see also: transsexual, post-op, transgendered

> "My last employer wanted a **pre-op** transsexual as a receptionist."

QUEEN: 1) An effeminate or campy gay man 2) A drag queen.

(!) QUEER: (as an adjective) Lesbian, bisexual, gay, or transgendered. (as a noun) A person who is queer.

This term is generally considered neutral or positive within the GLTB community, but can be derogatory when used by an outsider.

see also: gay, lesbian, LesBiGay

READ: *(synonym: make)* To notice the anatomical gender of a cross-dresser without being told or shown. The cross-dresser is said to have "been read."

see also: pass, cross-dresser

RE-DYKE: To replace evidence of lesbianism in one's home after a visitor has left.

see also: de-dyke, out

SIE: A gender-neutral form of "he or she" used by some transgendered people.

see also: hir

STONE BUTCH: A masculine lesbian who is physically unresponsive or who doesn't like to be touched sexually.

see also: butch

"Before I knew you were a guy, I thought you were a **stone butch**."

STRAIGHT: *(synonym: het)* Heterosexual. Sometimes implies being conservative in terms of sex, drugs, etc., but this is not a standard part of the meaning when talking about sexuality.

SWISH: (as a noun) A flamboyantly effeminate gay man. (as an adjective) In reference to a gay man, flamboyantly effeminate.

see also: fag, fairy, Nelly

"I'm recognizable as gay by my jewelry and my build, possibly by the all-black attire. But I'm not **swish,** and I don't do the 'accent.'"

TOP: *(synonym: pitcher)* The more active partner in a lesbian or especially a gay relationship.

TRANSGENDERED OR TRANS: Crossing traditional gender boundaries; for instance, by cross-dressing or gender reassignment surgery.

see also: cross-dresser, transsexual, intersex

TRANSSEXUAL: A person who intends to have (pre-op) or has already had (post-op) a sex change surgery.

see also: transgendered, pre-op, post-op

TRANSVESTITE: *(synonym: cross-dresser or crossdresser or cross dresser or CD)* A person who takes on the appearance of the opposite gender.

TWINK: An attractive, young gay man.

see also: chicken

Goths

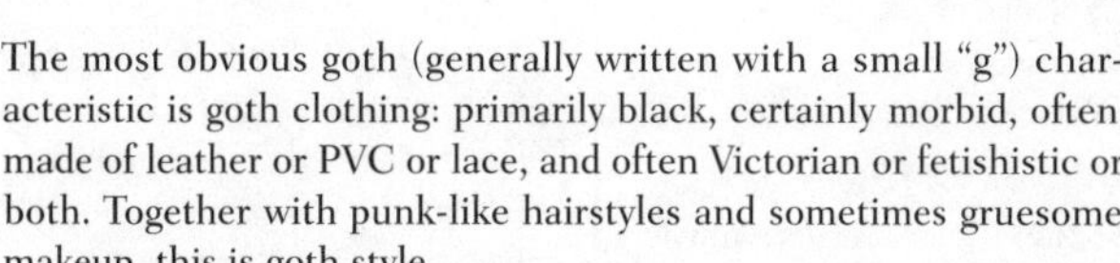

The most obvious goth (generally written with a small "g") characteristic is goth clothing: primarily black, certainly morbid, often made of leather or PVC or lace, and often Victorian or fetishistic or both. Together with punk-like hairstyles and sometimes gruesome makeup, this is goth style.

But the clothes don't make the goth: A number of groups flirt with gothdom, but aren't consistently accepted as gothic. Chief among these are the Mansonites (Marilyn Manson fans) and Nine Inch Nails fans (sometimes called, uncharitably, "NINnies"), whom goths usually exclude from gothdom because they don't listen to what most goths consider gothic music. Then there are the varieties of people who dress like goths but don't listen to goth music and are therefore often consigned by goths to pseudo-gothic categories like "doom cookie," "bleep," and "instagoth."

Goth music is one of the three pillars of goth culture and arguably the strongest thing uniting goths. The second key element of goth culture is, of course, appearance. The third is a preoccupation with death and all things grave, since although goths aren't required to be morbid, it's certainly a popular choice.

(!) BABY BAT: *(synonym: babygoth)* A person who has only recently become a goth; alternatively, a young goth. Can be derogatory.

see also: spooky kid, kindergoth

"... and I don't care how uber you are, dressing like a teeny bopper (or **baby bat**) at a certain age makes you look like an idiot."

BABYGOTH: *(synonym: baby bat)* A young or novice goth.

(!) BLEEP: Electronic goth music. Can be a neutral or a derogatory term. This kind of music is sometimes described as "bleepy," and this same term can be used as a noun to refer to its fans.

BLOWFISH: A term used to describe spiky, gothic jewelry. Often associated with the kinkier aspects of the gothic scene.

CANDY GOTH: A (usually) female goth who listens to goth music and by and large dresses goth, but who displays ungothlike tendencies, such as an affection for glitter. Can be a synonym for perkygoth.

see also: perkygoth

CORPGOTH OR CORPORATE GOTH: A goth who works a day job that is not compatible with a gothic lifestyle. The job may not necessarily be at a corporation.

see also: weekender

"What would be some appropriate male corpgoth attire?"

(!) CROW MAKEUP: Make-up applied in a goth-like fashion but taken to an extreme, named after the main character in the movie *The Crow*. Usually derogatory.

CYBERGOTH: A goth sub-subculture devoted to electronic music, luminescence, and a cyberpunk attitude.

(!) DOOM COOKIE: A usually derogatory term for a girl or woman who looks goth but is not a goth; a female goth wannabe.

FIRST GENERATION: The gothic subculture that emerged in the late seventies and early eighties based on an interest in bands like Bauhaus and Siouxsie and the Banshees. Contrast with second generation.

see also: second generation

"I'm going out with someone old enough to be my father—he's **first generation** goth and I'm a baby. It's kind of funny, but we couldn't help it!"

(!) **GLAMGOTH:** A flashy or fashion-conscious style of goth dress (not derogatory). Also used to label a band or person as someone who works hard to look goth without embracing the goth subculture.

GOFF: (adjective) An uncommon, alternate spelling of "goth."

GOTH AS FK:** Very, very gothic: a compliment. Can be abbreviated as "GAF."

GOTH CARD: An unofficial and usually figurative goth membership card.

see also: goth points

"If the Nephs represent the roots of goth culture I shall formally hand back my **goth card**!"

GOTH CODE: Also "goth.code," "gothcode." A string of apparently random characters that describes the attributes of a particular goth, including appearance, preferences, location, age, sexuality, etc. Goth codes are used on Web sites and as signatures in posts on the Web.

Goth coding appears to be a trend that is on its way out.

GOTH POINTS: A fictitious scoring system used for registering gothic look and behavior.

see also: goth card

"I deserve **goth points** because until recently, even when I was smiling people told me to cheer up!"

GOTH TEST: Though it's said to have started as a joke, this one isn't like goth points and the goth card: There really is a goth test—or rather, there are a number of goth tests. By answering questions about lifestyle, the test-taker is rated from 0–100 percent for gothic qualities.

One of the definitions of net.goth is a person who scores 80 percent or better on a goth test.

see also: net.goth

GOTHIC OR GOTH: Related to gothdom.

GOTHIC ROCK: A music genre, loosely related to punk, that began with bands like Bauhaus and Siouxsie and the Banshees in the late 1970s.

GOTHIC SLIDE: A gothic dance move in which the dancer's feet don't leave the floor.

GRAVER: A goth raver. Rave scene is a subculture traditionally associated with wild dance parties and heavy use of drugs like MDMA (Ecstasy) and LSD (Acid).

> "In my mind, the one good goth night in the area (well, industrial) took on a logo a few weeks back, it was undeniably a drawing of a **graver** chick."

IN THE SCENE: Actively and socially gothic, or involved in goth pursuits.

> "They are also burnt out on this concept that 'change is bad' that is perpetuated by many people **in the scene**."

(!) INSTAGOTH: Also "insta-goth." A person who suddenly begins to dress goth and calls him- or herself a goth. Not a compliment.

(!) KINDERGOTH: 1) A young goth (not derogatory). 2) A young teen or preteen who calls him- or herself goth but isn't very familiar with the gothic subculture (derogatory). 3) A comic strip about a group of black-clothed, sarcastic kindergarteners.

see also: baby bat, spooky kid

> "The first **kindergoth** I encountered this year entranced me with his ability to speak and write in Middle English."

(!) MANSONITE: A devoted fan of Marilyn Manson. Mansonites generally dress somewhat like Manson.

Most goths do not consider Mansonites gothic, and the term can be considered derogatory. Presumably whether or not it's an insult depends on what you think of Marilyn Manson.

see also: NINny, spooky kid

(!) MOPEYGOTH: Also "mopey goth." A mildly derogatory term for a goth who acts solemn or depressed.

see also: perkygoth

NET.GOTH: A goth who uses the Internet heavily, especially if involved in goth discussion groups.

(!) NINNY: A derogatory term for a devotee of the band Nine Inch Nails (NIN). Fans of NIN often look gothic, but are considered non-gothic by many goths.

see also: Mansonite

PERKYGOTH OR PERKY GOTH: Strange as it sounds, an upbeat goth. Since the two main requirements for being a goth are an interest in gothic music and a gothic wardrobe, there's nothing inherent in gothdom that requires that a person be morbid or preoccupied with death and pain.

Perky goths tend to be playful and fun-loving. This term is not generally considered derogatory.

see also: mopeygoth

> "If I were a goth, even a **perkygoth**, I would not own John Denver CDs and I would not wear a pinkish leotard."

SECOND GENERATION: A gothic subculture that arose in the late eighties around bands who, unlike their first generation forebears, called themselves "gothic."

see also: first generation

SPOOKY KID: A teen or younger fan of Marilyn Manson and related bands. Most goths do not consider spooky kids goths, but outsiders often don't make this distinction. Not specifically derogatory.

While there is not complete agreement on the matter, Marilyn Manson's music is generally not considered to be part of the goth scene.

see also: baby bat, kindergoth, Mansonite

(!) ULTRAGOTH: 1) A goth who lives, breathes, and exudes gothness; 2) A derogatory term for a goth who takes him- or herself too seriously and scoffs at others' attempts at gothness.

(!) WEEKENDER OR WEEKEND GOTH: A person who dresses goth only on weekends or in his or her spare time. Can sometimes refer to a person who is only playing at being a goth. Can be derogatory, but usually isn't.

The term "weekender" is used in England to mean a weekend event, and a number of goth weekenders occur there each year.

> "In short, I'm tired of goth being trendy. Damnit ... don't be a **weekender**."

Graffiti Writers

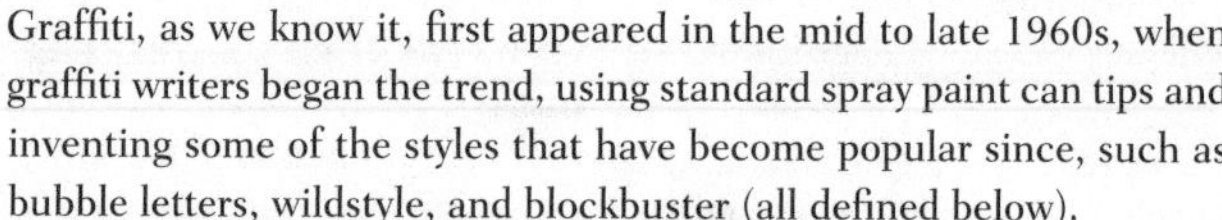

Graffiti, as we know it, first appeared in the mid to late 1960s, when graffiti writers began the trend, using standard spray paint can tips and inventing some of the styles that have become popular since, such as bubble letters, wildstyle, and blockbuster (all defined below).

Being primarily an urban subculture, graffiti writers share a good deal of slang with the hip hop subculture. For more information on that group, please see the appendix on the language of hip hop.

Graffiti writing occurs primarily on structures and railroad cars. Railroad cars particularly are a subject of graffiti slang terms, as the different types of surfaces they offer the graffiti writer are suited to different types of graffiti and different methods of writing.

Technically, the word "graffiti" is the plural of "graffito," but like "criteria" (plural of "criterion") and "data" (plural of "datum"), many people use it as a singular noun.

Many people outside the graffiti subculture refer to writers as "graffiti artists," but this term is not popular among graffiti writers themselves.

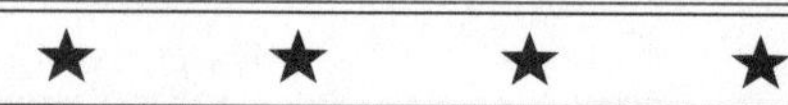

ALL-CITY: In reference to a particular graffiti writer's work, present in many locations; locally famous.

see also: up, bomb

BACK-TO-BACK: In reference to graffiti, covering an entire wall.

BATTLE: (as a noun) A contest between rival graffiti writers or crews to either write a lot of graffiti in an area or to create the best piece in a given period of time. (as a verb) To have a graffiti battle.

BITE: To copy another graffiti writer's work.

"Actually, I didn't **bite** off of you."

BLACK BOOK: *(synonym: piece book)* A graffiti writer's sketchbook.

BLOCKBUSTER: Graffiti writing that uses capital letters in wide block print, covering a large area with each letter.

BOMB: To write graffiti in many locations within a particular area.

see also: kill

BUFF: (as a verb) To remove graffiti; e.g., by sandblasting. (as a noun) The process of removing graffiti.

BURN: 1) To outdo other graffiti writers in terms of style. 2) In reference to a piece of graffiti, to be very stylish or impressive.

BURNER: A stylistically impressive, brilliantly-colored piece of graffiti, usually written in a complex pattern of interlocking letters and other visual elements (wildstyle).

"Now it means to hit up anything, anywhere, with any form of graffiti, from a tag all the way up to a wildstyle **burner**."

CAP: *(synonym: tip)* A nozzle that can be fitted onto a spray paint can to achieve a specific distribution of paint; used as a painter would use different brushes.

CREW: A group of affiliated graffiti writers.

CROSS OUT: *(synonym: go over)* To paint over someone else's graffiti.

DING-DONG: A type of stainless steel subway car. The abundance of flat surfaces on these cars makes them a desirable target, except that paint is easily removed from ding-dongs.

see also: flat, ridgie

FILL OR FILL-IN: The solid colors inside letters or shapes. Outlines are normally painted over the fill.

FLAT: A subway or train car with flat sides.

see also: *ding-dong, ridgie*

GO OVER: *(synonym: cross out)* To paint over someone else's graffiti. Considered a mark of disrespect.

> "I remember when people had to **go over** each other's pieces on the 101 in Hollywood."

HIT: (as a noun) A graffito; any graffiti writing or piece. (as a verb) To write graffiti.

INSIDES: The interior of any mass transit vehicle (as a place to write graffiti).

KILL: To write graffiti all over; to saturate an area with one's graffiti.

see also: *bomb*

KING: The most skilled person at a particular graffiti-writing activity; e.g., throwups, insides, etc.

LAY UP: In reference to a train or subway car, to stay in one place for a period of time, making a much easier target for graffiti.

see also: *layup*

LAYUP: A side track where trains and subway cars are sometimes parked when not in use.

see also: *lay up*

MOTION TAGGING OR MOTIONING: Writing graffiti on train or subway cars while they're moving.

> "Once in '79, a cop had me step out of a train for **motion-tagging**, and then he made me stand against a wall."

OLD SCHOOL: The graffiti scene from its beginnings through the early 1980s, although there are different opinions on the exact years that should be considered "old school."

PIECE: (as a noun) A graffiti painting; something more involved than a simple tag or throwup, with multiple colors. (as a verb) To create a piece.

PIECE BOOK: *(synonym: black book)* A graffiti writer's sketchbook.

RACK: To steal. Most often used in reference to cans of spray paint.

RIDGIE OR RIDGY: A subway car with a rippled texture on its side, undesirable for more involved graffiti pieces.

see also: *flat, ding-dong*

TAG: (as a noun) A graffiti writer's graffiti signature or logo. (as a verb) To spray paint one's graffiti signature or logo. Also "tag up."

see also: tagger

TAGGER: A person who generally writes only his or her signature, not more complex pieces.

see also: writer, tag

THROWUP OR THROW-UP OR THROWIE: A piece of graffiti writing that is written quickly, usually with no more than two colors.

see also: piece, tag

"The whole culture of graffiti developed in the subways. The first **throw-up**, the first piece, the use of crew names, the numbers after the names ..."

TIP: (*synonym:* cap) A spray paint nozzle.

TOP TO BOTTOM OR TOP-TO-BOTTOM: A graffiti piece that covers the entire height of a subway car, train car, or wall.

TOY: An inexperienced or unskilled graffiti writer.

UP: In reference to a graffiti writer, having one's work in a variety of locations.

see also: all-city, bomb

WILDSTYLE OR WILD STYLE: A graffiti style characterized by a complex pattern of interlocking letters and shapes.

see also: burner

WRITER: A person who creates graffiti.

see also: tagger

"In my videos only **writers** speak. They are the voices of the LA graffiti art community, period!"

Gun Enthusiasts

Gun enthusiasts comprise a variety of overlapping groups, such as hunters (see page 185), survivalists, advocates of firearms as a personal defense, historical re-enactors (see page 176), people interested in military history, and firing-range patrons. Hunting slang and military slang are therefore part of the language of gun enthusiasts, as are terms for types of guns, ammunition, and parts of a gun.

Many gun enthusiasts collect or shoot specific types of guns, for instance, fully automatic weapons, revolvers, or Civil War-era weapons. Some accumulate as many guns as they can without regard to type, while others are not collectors.

The most influential U.S. gun enthusiast organization is the National Rifle Association (NRA), which is active in firearms-related political issues and also sponsors competitions and gun safety educational programs. As a group, gun enthusiasts tend to strongly support education to promote safer use of guns.

RELATED SUBCULTURES:

Hunters, Historical Reenactors

BOOMER: A loud, high-powered rifle.

> "Your lifestyle, budget, physical makeup, or a number of other reasons might preclude carrying a big **boomer**."

BRASS: Spent shell casings; metal shells cast off when certain kinds of ammunition are fired.

BUCKSKINNER: A person interested in learning and recreating mountain-man-type survival techniques from the eighteenth, nineteenth, and early twentieth centuries. Many of the skills of a buckskinner relate to guns and shooting.

> "Even better, find ya a dedicated **buckskinner** who's also of the flinter persuasion."

BULLET HOSE: A dependable gun that fires rapidly but that may not be particularly accurate.

CAN: A sound suppressor for a gun; a silencer.

> "First off, good **cans** are expensive ... mine was almost $400."

DOWN RANGE: The direction in which guns are fired on a gun range.

EARS: Ear protection for a person firing a gun, normally used on a range.

EYES: Eye protection for a person using a gun on a range; goggles.

GRAIN: An otherwise rare unit of weight used to measure bullets and gunpowder, equal to about 1/450 of an ounce.

GREASE GUN: Any unsophisticated machine gun, especially the U.S. military model called the M3; it resembles a mechanic's grease gun, i.e., a tool used to squirt grease.

GROUP: Several shots fired in succession at the same target.

JUNK GUN: A cheap, low-quality handgun. Has the same meaning as the general slang term "Saturday night special," but without the implication that the gun is for criminal use; "Saturday night special" is not specifically a gun enthusiast term.

SPEED RIG: Any holster that makes it easy to draw and fire a gun quickly.

SPOTTER: One who helps to direct a shooter to hit a target, for instance, by reporting on where previous shots have hit.

SURVIVALIST: A person who expects or is seriously concerned about the possibility of bad times to come and who devotes substantial effort to preparing for such a time. Survivalists may store long-lasting food, precious metals, firearms, and agricultural materials. They also often prepare a specific shelter or refuge.

Survivalists' may prepare for situations like civil war, famine, natural disaster, nuclear war, and invasion. Many focus on preparations to resist an oppressive government. Most survivalists consider it important to have firearms and be familiar with them.

Not all survivalists concern themselves with weapons, but those that draw the most media attention tend to be militaristic.

see also: buckskinner

WIND DOPING: Anticipating the effects of wind on the path of a bullet, a skill usually gained with practice.

see also: windage

"Watching where the bullet strikes and comparing it to where the shot was called will tell you if your **wind doping** was good or otherwise."

WINDAGE: (pronounced "WIHN-daj") Adjustments to a gunsight to account for wind pushing a shot to the left or right.

see also: wind doping

Hackers and Programmers

Hackers and computer programmers as a group tend to enjoy word play and have come up with a disproportionately large amount of slang. Much of this body of slang, however, is used only in particular technical circumstances. For instance, a particular slang word for a lazy programmer may only apply to a programmer who works with a particular language and is lazy about one technique in that language. In this book, we'll steer clear of terms like this and stick to more general hacker and programmer slang.

One important characteristic of computer slang is the convention of speaking to a piece of computer hardware or software as though it were a human being. Perhaps you've done this yourself: "Hello? Hello?" "Give me my file, or I swear I'll smash you in with this stapler!" "No, it is *not* OK!").

People who are deeply involved in this subculture, whether they crack systems or simply are excited about programming, are often called hackers. People who are highly skilled but less absorbed in hackerish concerns are often called coders. People who just type the instructions into the

computer and go home are called programmers, although that term can be neutrally applied to coders and hackers as well.

Computer slang contains a bewildering variety of abbreviations and acronyms, many of which are used in conversation. Some abbreviations are spelled out when they're pronounced (for instance, FTP is pronounced "eff tee PEE"); others are pronounced as a word (GUI is pronounced "GOO-ee"); and yet others can be treated either way (SQL is pronounced "ess kyoo ELL" or "SEE-kwul"). Some are pronounced as a word but have more than one pronunciation; for instance, PDL can be pronounced "PIH-dul" or "PUH-dul."

RELATED SUBCULTURES:

Sci-Fi and Fantasy Fans, Online Gamers

AUTOMAGICALLY: Accomplished through programming without manual intervention and by means that are not immediately apparent.

BELLS AND WHISTLES: Flashy or attractive features that are not essential in a particular program.

BRUTE FORCE (AND IGNORANCE): An approach to programming or hacking that relies on large amounts of code or excessive use of processing power to solve a problem rather than on a clear understanding of the situation.

BUG: An error in programming code.

see also: crufty, workaround

CODE: Programming instructions; the material that programmers (coders) write.

see also: source or source code

CODE MONKEY: A programmer who is not particularly sophisticated or self-directed, but who can churn out programming under guidance.

"One curious trend: a shop will carefully plan their logic layer, then throw a **code monkey** at the GUI."

CRACK: 1) (verb) To break through security measures into a computer or network. 2) (verb) To circumvent or disable security measures in a piece of software. 3) (noun) Programming or a software tool that allows people to circumvent software security measures. 4) (noun) A successful attempt to break through software security measures.

see also: cracker, hacker, hack

CRACKER: A person who attempts to break through computer security measures.

see also: crack, hacker

CRIPPLEWARE: Software that is made available with significant features disabled, for example, as a demo or trial.

CRUFTY: In reference to programming, poorly conceived or poorly executed, especially if the coding is more complex than necessary.

see also: bug

"I would just add that sometimes old crufty software depends on old **crufty** libraries."

DEMOSCENE: A programming subculture concerned with creating computer-generated visual experiences, generally using a relatively small file to do so.

DIE: In reference to a computer, piece of software, process, piece of hardware, etc., to fail in such a way that it can't be brought back up.

see also: hang

EASTER EGG: A hidden animation, message, or feature that requires an unlikely series of commands or steps to bring out.

ELEGANT: In reference to a piece of programming, efficient, effective, and unusually well-conceived.

FOO AND BAR: Nonsense syllables used to stand in for programming objects or variables. Perhaps not coincidentally, when put together these syllables make the same sound as the acronym "FUBAR" ("f*cked up beyond all recognition").

HACK: 1) (verb) To break into a system. 2) (verb) To circumvent security on a software product. 3) (verb) To write a program. 4) (noun) Programming that provides a means of getting around software security

measures. 5) (noun) A quick and dirty piece of programming.

see also: crack, hacker, kludge

HACKER: 1) A person who tries to circumvent software and system security measures. 2) A programmer, especially one who programs enthusiastically or recreationally.

see also: cracker, hack

THE HACKER ETHIC: The philosophy that all information, including programming and computer systems, should be free and available to all. The Hacker Ethic is sometimes used as justification for cracking.

see also: open source

HANG: In reference to computer hardware or software, to lock up and stop responding. A hung computer or process may respond to a restart.

see also: die

HELLO WORLD: The archetype of a simple test program, either as a first exercise for a programmer learning a new language or as a test of a programming system installation. A "hello world" program simply displays the message, "Hello, world!"

HOSE: To cause a system to slow down, choke, hang, or die.

> "*Some* network adapter drivers will **hose** themselves up so that when you're done with the install and exit back to DOS, the machine will hang."

KILLER APP: A program so useful that it encourages widespread adoption of the system it runs on.

KLUDGE OR KLUGE: (pronounced "klooj") A piece of programming or a programming fix that is: a) cleverly executed but poorly conceived, b) quick and dirty, or c) much more complex than necessary.

> "The 'best' I've been able to do so far is to use the following **kludge** instead of SetForegroundWindow."

LIVE: (pronounced "laeev" like "live wire," not "liv" like "live and let live") In reference to data, comprising real-life information instead of information made up for testing.

In reference to a system, available to its intended users instead of in development or testing.

"The following does not show **live** data, but works when running the app."

MASSAGE: In reference to data, to make changes for compatibility or consistency.

OPEN SOURCE: In reference to software, available for free use, including source code. Open source software can be modified by anyone who wants to work with it.

see also: the Hacker Ethic

PHASE OF THE MOON: A facetious factor blamed for determining whether or not a system will work properly.

"Of course, your success depends a lot upon your abilities, luck, shoe size, the **phase of the moon**, etc."

PHREAK: To break into a phone network in order to explore or steal services.

RTFM: "Read the f***ing manual." One of the first recommendations that leaps to mind for computer support personnel when a user has trouble that could be addressed by a better understanding of the system.

(!) SECURITY THROUGH OBSCURITY: A more or less derogatory assessment of a lack of precautions on a system, when the people responsible for the system don't consider it to be at risk because it seems unlikely anyone will guess enough of the system's particulars to be able to attack it.

see also: hack, crack

SOURCE OR SOURCE CODE: The actual programming that went into a system, rather than the series of instructions that programming is translated into. Lines of programming are converted into "object code," which is the language the computer (rather than the programmer) understands. A programmer reads and writes source code, and a computer executes object code.

SPAGHETTI CODE: Programming that is poorly written and messy.

SPOOF: To attempt to circumvent security by diverting and/or impersonating an authorized stream of data.

"What makes you think you can't **spoof** the user-agent header?"

"I believe this to be **user error**. Modutils is doing exactly what it should."

SUPER USER OR SUPERUSER: A person who is not a programmer but who is skilled enough with computers to use fairly technical features.

THREE-FINGER SALUTE: *(synonym: Vulcan nerve pinch)* Any three-key combination that forces a computer to restart.

TROJAN OR TROJAN HORSE: A malicious program designed to enter a system in disguise so as to wreak havoc from the inside, rather than attacking the system from the outside.

USER OR END USER: A person for whom a particular program is a tool, as distinct from programmers and other technical personnel, for whom the program is a project.

see also: user error

USER ERROR: A problem that technical personnel identify as stemming from someone using the software the wrong way.

see also: user

VAPORWARE: A piece of software that is announced but never released.

VULCAN NERVE PINCH: *(synonym: three-finger salute)* Any three-key combination that forces a computer to restart.

WYSIWYG: (pronounced "WIZ-zee-wig") "What you see is what you get." Describes a system that allows a person to edit information in the same format as the one used in its final presentation.

WAREZ: (pronounced "wayrz") Software products that have been stripped of their copy protections and made available in violation of copyright.

see also: warez d00dz

WAREZ DOODZ: (pronounced "wayrz doodz") Crackers who remove copy protection from software and use it or make it available to others.

see also: warez

WEBIFY: To make preexisting information or software available on the World Wide Web.

WELL-BEHAVED: In reference to programming, interacting in desirable ways with other components and using resources modestly.

"Even people who had been trying to write **well-behaved** software didn't know if they'd gotten it right until it was run on larger memory machines."

WETWARE: Humans, or human brains. Contrasted with hardware (computer components) and software (programming).

WORKAROUND: Any means of getting a malfunctioning program or system to work without fixing the problem.

see also: <u>*bug*</u>

"I can see how this might be used as a successful **workaround**, but I'd really like to know why this is occurring in the first place."

YOYO MODE: A state in which a system alternates between being available (up) and unavailable (down) due to persistent problems.

"Testing is incomplete because the POS API has been in **yoyo mode** for most of the two weeks it has been accessible."

Ham Radio Operators

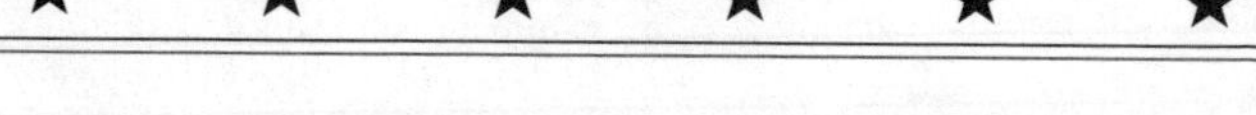

Ham radio operators, also called amateur radio operators, are licensed amateurs trained in shortwave radio transmission and reception. Operating a radio might not seem a particularly technical task, but ham radio operators often know a great deal about their radio equipment, can pick out individual signals from locations around the world, and know how to get a signal to travel much farther than an untrained person could manage.

One challenge to transmitting over long distances is the curvature of the earth. Since radio signals usually travel in a straight line, a direct transmission from Boston to London would be blocked by a huge amount of ocean water. Ham radio operators get around these limitations by techniques like using a repeater or bouncing the signal off the ionosphere (a layer of charged particles in the earth's atmosphere), a satellite, or every once in a while even off the Moon.

In addition to the ham radio slang here, ham radio operators generally are familiar with various kinds of radio equipment, with Morse Code, and with the technical jargon of radio operation.

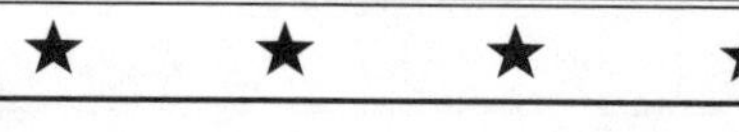

73: Morse code shorthand for "best regards."

88: Morse code shorthand for "love and kisses." Usually reserved for close relatives.

ALLIGATOR: A repeater (device that boosts radio signals) that can transmit over greater distances than it can receive. Thus it has small "ears" but a big "mouth," like an alligator.

"The alligator got you" is the usual translation of the code received back from a repeater if an operator has been using it longer than permitted and was cut off.

see also: elephant

AMATEUR RADIO: *(synonym: ham radio)* Two-way radio transmission at amateur radio frequencies.

BIRD: A satellite.

"In addition, *all* of these **birds** could respond to a standard DCS tone, to accommodate wilderness users and priority health and welfare traffic."

BIRDIE: Any apparent signal that is really just a problem with a receiver.

BOOTLEGGER: An unlicensed person who uses a ham radio.

see also: pirate

(!) BROADCAST: *Not* used to refer to sending out amateur radio signals; the proper word is "transmit." To broadcast is to send a signal to everyone; by contrast, amateur radio is usually transmitted between specific stations.

BUNNY HUNT: *(synonyms: foxhunt or fox hunt, T-hunt)* A contest to find a hidden transmitter.

BUSTED CALL: A mistake in logging an operator's call sign.

"If they don't know much English, it's a bit rough on them to use nonstandard words, and even if they do, it increases the chance of a **busted call** in the log."

CALL SIGN OR CALLSIGN: A unique license code assigned to an operator.

COPY: (as a verb) To be able to hear a transmission clearly, or to listen to a transmission. (as a noun) A signal that comes through clearly.

DX: (as a verb) To contact a distant location by amateur radio. (as a noun) A distant amateur radio station.

see also: DXer

> "But I've noticed something strange: each time I **DX**ed and got a QSL, the country disappeared!"

DXER: A ham radio operator who works to communicate with distant or unusual stations.

see also: DX

DEAD ZONE: A place that can't be reached by radio signals from a particular location.

ELEPHANT: A repeater (device that boosts radio signals) that receives signals at greater distances than it can transmit, so that it's said to have a small "mouth" compared to its big "ears."

see also: alligator

ELMER: A skilled ham radio operator who helps operators with less experience.

> "I went from N.C.T. to General in less than a month, my **elmer** had me so excited about ham radio."

EYEBALL: A meeting of two ham radio operators in person rather than over the airwaves.

FIRE BOTTLE: A vacuum tube. Older ham radio rigs use these.

FIRST PERSONAL: *(synonym: personal)* First name.

FOXHUNT OR FOX HUNT: *(synonyms: T-hunt, bunny hunt)* A contest for ham radio operators and other radio hobbyists to physically track down a hidden radio transmitter.

GALLON OR FULL GALLON: The maximum amount of transmission power allowed for ham radio operators.

HAM: *(synonym: operator)* A person licensed to transmit on amateur radio bands; a radio hobbyist with the ability to operate a ham radio rig.

HAM RADIO: *(synonym: amateur radio)* Operation of two-way radios by licensed hobbyists within those radio frequencies designated for amateur radio use. Ham radio operators transmit voice, Morse Code, digital teletype signals, and even video.

HAMFEST: A gathering for ham radio operators.

HARMONIC: A child (of a ham radio operator).

"Keep in mind that the majority of 'young people' who become successfully involved in amateur radio are usually the '**harmonics**' of parents who happen to be hams."

HI HI: Morse code laughter. "Hi hi" transmitted in Morse code sounds a bit like someone with a high voice laughing. The phrase is sometimes used to mean laughter even when Morse code isn't being used.

HOP: A signal sent into the atmosphere and bounced back to a distant location on Earth.

KEY UP: To start transmitting.

"Under United States law, those people have as much right to get on amateur radio frequencies and swear up a storm as another person does to **key up** and talk about her doll collection or stamp collection."

LID: A ham radio operator who doesn't follow proper procedures or who makes a lot of mistakes.

MOTORBOATING: Undesirable feedback in low frequency reception. It sounds something like a motorboat.

NET: A group of ham radio operators who contact each other on a particular frequency at a particular time.

OPERATOR: *(synonym: ham)* A person licensed to use amateur radio.

OVER: "I finished what I was saying; you go ahead now." Used when reception is not ideal and a ham wants to ensure the other person has heard everything.

PADDLE: The key one presses to send Morse Code.

PERSONAL: *(synonym: first personal)* First name.

PILEUP: Multiple operators trying to transmit to the same station.

PIRATE: A person who transmits illegally using another person's call sign.

see also: bootlegger

Q SIGNAL: Three-letter codes representing short messages when transmitting Morse code. For instance, QRX means roughly "hang on a second," and QRS means "send more slowly."

QSL: A postcard sent to confirm a radio contact. Taken from the Q signal system, in which QSL means "understood."

RAGCHEWING: Ham operators talking informally via radio.

"There are two things I love more than anything else in ham radio. One is DXing, and the other is **ragchewing**."

RETTYSNITCH: *(synonym: wouff hong)* An imaginary instrument of torture used to threaten bad ham operators.

RIG: A ham radio set used to send and/or receive.

SILENT KEY: A ham radio operator who has died.

SKYHOOK: An antenna.

SPUR: Noise or an unwanted signal in a transmission.

T-HUNT: *(synonyms: foxhunt or fox hunt, bunny hunt)* A contest to find a hidden transmitter.

TICKET: A ham radio license.

TRAFFIC: Messages transmitted over amateur radio.

WORK: To transmit to another station.

"This station has **worked** all the voice/CW birds, completed many aurora contacts, and even copied VE3ONT's moonbounce downlink during an EME contest."

WOUFF HONG: *(synonym: rettysnitch)* An imaginary instrument of torture used to threaten bad ham operators.

Hikers and Backpackers

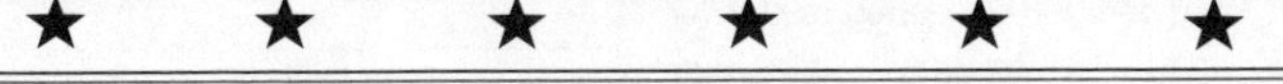

Hikers often follow a few common rules of hiking etiquette, such as downward-hiking groups yielding to uphill-hiking ones when the path is narrow, putting the slowest hiker in front to set the pace so as not to leave stragglers, carrying out trash after stopping in wild areas to rest or camp, and making a minimal amount of noise when hiking in order not to disturb wildlife or other hikers. The exception to this last rule is that hikers often make a lot of noise in territory where they might otherwise accidentally surprise a dangerous animal.

Water sources take on special importance to a hiker, and hikers will often refer to them in ways that make it clear how much water can be had: some common terms of this kind are "gusher"—water that pours out in substantial amounts; "dripper"—water that must be caught drop by drop; and "dipper"—water deep enough to scoop out with a cup.

The two longest trails in the United States are the Appalachian Trail, which wanders through more than 2,000 miles of mountainous terrain from Maine to Georgia (or vice versa), and the even longer Pacific Coast Trail, which stretches for about 3,000 miles along the Pacific coast.

RELATED SUBCULTURES:

Bicyclists and Mountain Bikers, Cavers and Spelunkers, Rock Climbers

2,000-MILER: *(synonym: end-to-ender)* A hiker who has hiked the entire Appalachian Trail.

BEAR BAG: A sack in which hikers put food before hoisting it into the air with a rope that has been run over a tree branch or similar object. This technique sometimes successfully keeps the food out of reach of bears.

see also: mouse hanger

BIG UPS: Long, upward slopes.

"Then I had a **big up** and a big down to get up and over Pond Flat, and came down to Watango Lake where I took a monkey shower and laid on the swimming area for a bit."

BLAZE: A paint mark that indicates a hiking trail.

BLUE-BLAZER: An Appalachian Trail hiker who doesn't mind hiking off the main trail (marked with white blazes) onto side trails (marked with blue blazes).

BOUNCE BOX: A box of supplies a hiker sends ahead to use further down the trail.

see also: mail drop

BRUSHING: Clearing the trail of branches and other obstacles.

CAMELING OR CAMELING UP: Drinking as much water as possible at a water source to supplement the water one will be carrying.

"It was another hot, humid day when any exertion caused me to sweat buckets. I carried extra water and '**cameled up**' at every stream crossing."

DOUBLE BLAZE: Two blazes together in one place, which usually signals a turn in the trail.

DUCK: A cairn; a pile of rocks used as a marker.

END-TO-ENDER: *(synonym: 2,000-miler)* A person who has hiked the entire length of the Appalachian Trail.

see also: through-hiker

FLIP-FLOP: To hike from point A to point B, drive from point B to point C, and hike back from point C to point B; to hike a continuous section of trail out of order.

GREEN TUNNEL: Sections of trail where trees, bending in from both sides, form a kind of roof.

"The beauty of the Pacific Crest Trail and its many faces cannot be compared to the Appalachian Trail and its endless days of **green tunnel**."

HANDRAIL: Any feature that runs alongside an intended route and therefore serves as an easy way to ensure one isn't getting off the trail.

HAZARD TREE: *(synonym: widow-maker)* A tree that is in danger of falling onto hikers.

HIKER BOX: A box at a place frequented by hikers, where items one hiker doesn't need or want are left for potential use by other hikers.

MAIL DROP: A package of supplies sent to a particular point on a trail. The package may be sent by the hiker himself, or by a friend providing support.

see also: bounce box

MAINTAINER: A volunteer who helps keep a trail in good condition.

MOUNTAIN MONEY: Toilet paper.

MOUSE HANGER OR MOUSE TRAPEZE: A tin can lid threaded on a string, used to hang a food bag; the lid prevents mice from climbing down to the food (sometimes).

see also: bear bag

NOBO: A north-bound hiker on the Appalachian Trail.

PUDS: "Pointless ups and downs;" climbs and drops in the trail, as seen by a person who has gotten tired of them.

see also: roller coaster

PEAK BAGGING: The practice of climbing and making log entries of as many mountain peaks as possible; hiking for conquest.

"I have done some **peak-bagging** in the Sierras in the summer and do know the basics of snow travel and have used (and own) crampons."

POSTHOLE: To hike through deep snow so that each footstep makes a deep hole.

PURIST: A hiker who resolves to hike a particular route and then does it exactly as planned.

RIDGERUNNER: A person hired to hike and watch over a trail, offering information to hikers, monitoring trail usage, etc.

ROCK SCRAMBLE: A steep, rocky incline on a trail.

ROLLER COASTER: Any section of trail characterized by hills and dips.

see also: PUDs

RUCK: A gathering of hikers.

> "So if you want to spend a weekend meeting and talking and eating and watching slides and videos and playing with gear and, for the very bold, weighing your pack ... in public ... and hiking and talking and eating and not getting near enough sleep, you should come to the **ruck**!"

SOBO: A southbound hiker on the Appalachian Trail.

SECTION HIKER: A person who is trying to hike all of a long trail by traversing different sections of it on separate occasions.

SLAB: To maintain a fairly constant elevation or a modest grade by avoiding steeper parts of the terrain. For example, taking a longer route winding up a mountain instead of going straight up, or keeping to the most level sections of a ridgeline. Both hikers and trails can be said to slab.

SLACKPACK: To hike without a backpack, for instance by sending it ahead.

STEALTH CAMPING: Camping in a manner that leaves no damage or litter at the campsite.

THROUGH-HIKER: A person attempting to hike the entire length of the Appalachian Trail.

see also: end-to-ender

TOURON: A person who has gotten to the same amazing place the hiker has with much less effort, for instance by driving to a scenic spot on a trail.

TOWN CLOTHES: Clothes carried for use only in populated areas, in order to be able to dress presentably.

> "I have talked to a fellow who hiked the PCT with an initial eighty pound pack load because he carried his '**town clothes**,' etc. with him."

TRAIL ANGEL: Anyone who gives unexpected help to a hiker.

TRAIL MAGIC: Any unusually gratifying or unexpectedly helpful incident on the trail.

TRAIL NAME: A nickname a hiker uses on the trail.

TRUDGE MODE: A state of exhaustion or trail-weariness that results in dull-eyed plodding.

"So we strike camp and hit the trail. Terry quickly enters heads-down **trudge mode**. Too much weight (eighteen pounds) and too little sleep."

TURTLE: To fall over on one's back, pack underneath, and have trouble getting back up.

WIDOWMAKER: *(synonym: hazard tree)* A tree or tree limb that is in danger of falling on hikers.

YOGI: For a hiker, to get a person to offer something needed without explicitly having to ask for it.

YO-YO: To hike from one end of a trail to the other, then turn around and hike back.

ZERO DAY: A day in which a hiker doesn't travel any farther down the trail (this is, travels zero miles).

Historical Reenactors

People who reenact historical events or scenes, such as Civil War battles or Colonial towns, may be drawn by a fascination with history, the fun of immersing themselves in a different world, an interest in an outdated skill or craft, or just the innocent pleasure of shooting a damn Yankee.

In almost any large reenactment, the issue of participants' historical accuracy in terms of such things as clothing materials and uniforms is a major preoccupation. It's usually far more difficult to be entirely true to the period than to be just *mostly* true to the period, so many participants make do with an approximation of historical accuracy and simply set out to enjoy themselves. Others are committed to detailed authenticity.

Along with better-known types of historical reenactments like the ones mentioned above, events can be found that simulate periods and events from other world cultures, such as ancient Roman battles and Scottish Highland games.

RELATED SUBCULTURES:

Society for Creative Anachronism Members, Renaissance Fairegoers, Gun Enthusiasts

ACW: The American Civil War (a.k.a. The War Between the States, The War of Northern Aggression).

BOOSHWAY: The person who organizes a reenactment.

see also: dog soldier

(!) BUTTON PISSER: A person fanatically devoted to authenticity. Usually derogatory.

Reputedly refers to a reenactor so devoted, he'd urinate on metal buttons he intends to use for his uniform so as to discolor them properly (although it's not clear that anyone actually does this).

see also: hard core, soap eater, thread counter or thread Nazi

"I am by no means a **button pisser** ... nor do I condone farb bashing."

DEFARB: To get rid of or hide anything modern in preparation for a reenactment. Can refer to a site, an object, a person, etc.

see also: farb

"He has a lot of the original marking dyes from the U.S. armory and will **defarb** the gun so it really looks original."

DOCUMENTARY INTERPRETATION: Dressing and acting the part of an actual historical person.

see also: representative interpretation, first person interpretation

DOG SOLDIER: A volunteer who handles security or other tasks at a reenactment.

see also: booshway

(!) DUMB PATRON STORY: A joking answer to a question commonly asked of reenactors by the public. An example from www.historicgames.com: A reenactor was told by a patron that they didn't have nails in the 18th century. He replied, "No ma'am, they didn't; they put Christ on the cross with duct tape."

(!) FARB: (as a noun) A person who strays far from historical accuracy; for instance, by wearing polyester or carrying a twentieth century gun in a Civil War reenactment. (as an adjective) Inauthentic and inappropriate.

Said to come from statements that begin "Far be it from me to criticize ..."

FIRST PERSON INTERPRETATION: A portrayal of a character from a particular historical time and place in which the reenactor avoids any

reference to the present, speaking as much as possible from the point of view of the time period instead of simply about the time period.

see also: representative interpretation, documentary interpretation, my time and your time

(!) FLATLANDER: Visitors to a reenactment who aren't participating in the reenactment itself. Can be mildly derogatory.

see also: dumb patron story

FUR TRADE RENDEZVOUS: A reenactment event that showcases a variety of American frontier skills and trades.

HARD CORE: In reference to a reenactor, seeking as much authenticity as possible.

see also: button pisser, mainstream

MAINSTREAM: In reference to a reenactor, casual about authenticity and unlikely to go to great lengths to stay historically correct.

see also: hard core, motel militia

> "The next morning, the 'general' of a **mainstream** battalion called us over and asked that we not do any more 'racist' songs, as it was detrimental to our reputation and the hobby."

(!) MOTEL MILITIA: *(synonym: Ramada rangers)* Reenactors who sleep in hotels and are otherwise not trying to achieve a 24/7 depiction of the historical period.

see also: tin teepee

MY TIME AND YOUR TIME: Phrases used when playing a character from a historical setting to act out a character without having to pretend modern things don't exist.

see also: first person interpretation

PERIOD-CORRECT: Appropriate to the time and place being reenacted.

RAMADA RANGERS: *(synonym: motel militia)* Reenactors who stay in hotels and go to restaurants instead of camping out in period style.

REPRESENTATIVE INTERPRETATION: Any portrayal of a typical type of person from a given historical period, but not of an actual, historical individual.

see also: documentary interpretation, first person interpretation

(!) SOAP EATER: A joking term used to imply that a person is so obsessed with authenticity that he would eat soap, as starving

soldiers are said to have done in the Civil War.

see also: <u>*hard core, button pisser, thread counter or thread Nazi*</u>

(!) THREAD COUNTER OR THREAD NAZI: A person so obsessed with authenticity in a reenactment that he or she will criticize the weave of the cloth in a costume or uniform. Sometimes derogatory.

see also: <u>*hard core, soap eater, button pisser*</u>

> "I am, however, a bit of a **thread counter** and authenticity nut."

TIN TEEPEE: A trailer or RV used as sleeping quarters at a reenactment event.

see also: <u>*motel militia*</u>

(!) TOURON: An obnoxious or ignorant tourist. Derogatory.

This term is sometimes used by other subcultures, such as hikers.

> "Judy is *much* too polite to actually call a **touron** a **touron** to his face."

(!) YUPPIE LARVA: A child who has come to watch (but not participate in) a reenactment, especially if noisy or disrespectful. Usually derogatory. Sometimes used as a plural, although technically the plural should be "yuppie larvae."

Hot Rodders

If you don't mind using it loosely, the term "hot rodder" can encompass at least four kinds of car enthusiasts:

- Street rodders, who modify cars (usually older models) to make them faster and more powerful—and so that the result will turn heads.
- Rat rodders, who also make engines more powerful but tend not to go in for the flashy exteriors.
- Lowriders, who modify cars to sit low to the ground and install hydraulic systems that allow them to raise parts of the car. Lowriders can also be considered to be part of the street rod scene, and may customize their cars' appearance.
- Import scene car enthusiasts, who alter modern (usually Japanese) cars with eye-catching customizations and who sometimes make engine modifications. These cars are sometimes looked down on by other kinds of car enthusiasts, many of whom refer to them by the derogatory term "rice burners."

ANTIQUE: (noun) A car that is at least twenty-five years old. (adjective) In reference to a car, at least twenty-five years old. A relatively newer "antique" car may not be called antique if it isn't a good model or isn't in good condition.

see also: vintage

BINDERS: Brakes.

BOX: A transmission.

CHANNELED: In reference to a car, having a body that has been dropped lower on its frame to ride closer to the ground.

see also: lowboy, lowrider, chopped, sectioned

"I've always kind of liked the 1978 242 Bertone coupe, the one that looks like it was chopped and **channelled**."

CHOPPED: In reference to a car, having a lowered roof and shorter windows for a streamlined look.

see also: channeled, sectioned

CUSTOM: Significantly modified. Cars may be customized in terms of engines, appearance, or both.

Restoring a car to its original condition isn't considered customization.

see also: customize

CUSTOMIZE: To make significant alterations to a car.

see also: custom

DECKED: In reference to a car, customized to remove trim from the trunk.

see also: frenched, shaved

FILL: To cover up seams in a car's body with body filler or lead so the car will look smooth and molded.

see also: molded

FLAME THROWER OR FLAMETHROWER: A car customization that turns the unburned gases in the car's exhaust into flames as they come out of the tailpipe.

"Based on what I heard and saw, the working **flame throwers** were on older cars that were running rich."

FRENCHED: In reference to a car accessory, especially headlights or tail lights, modified so that it's sunken into the car body instead of sticking out.

see also: decked, shaved

"The headlights were **frenched**, and he'd installed tail lights from a 1953 Pontiac, also frenched."

GHOST FLAMES: A flame pattern painted onto a car in a shade slightly different than the body so that the flames are barely visible.

GLASS OR 'GLASS: Fiberglass.

GROCERY GETTER: A hot rod driven around for daily use.

see also: street rod

"But for your typical '**grocery getter**,' the tranny can make a *huge* difference."

HANDLER: A hot rod that reacts precisely and smoothly when driven.

"Many who own them cannot drive ... and believe the myth that their car is the greatest **handler** of all time."

HIDES: Tires.

HOT ROD: *(synonym: rod)* (occasionally "hotrod") A car modified to be faster and/or to turn heads. "Hot rod" originated as a derogatory term, but is considered neutral or complimentary these days.

see also: custom, street rod

IMPORT SCENE: The subculture that modifies recent-model, imported cars (usually Japanese) for appearance and sometimes performance.

see also: ricer, rice burner, rice boy, rice rocket

"I've spent way too much money on the Civic and fell in love with the **import scene**. Now I'm a fanatic."

LOUD PEDAL: A car's accelerator pedal.

LOWBOY: A car that's been modified so that it sits lower on its frame.

see also: channeled, lowrider, slammed

LOWRIDER: 1) A car, often a classic model, that's been modified to sit low to the ground, usually on a hydraulic system that allows the driver to raise and lower different parts of the car. Some of these cars can practically dance in place. 2) A person who drives or works on such cars.

see also: channeled, lowboy, slammed

"If you don't like the cars or the systems in them, that's fine, but being a **lowrider** goes much deeper than owning a car with hydraulics on it."

MILL: An engine.

MOLDED: In reference to a car, having had the tiny gaps between its body panels filled with body filler or lead for a smooth look.

see also: fill

MUSCLE CAR: *(synonym: pony car)* Any gas-guzzling, American car with a massively powerful engine manufactured between the mid-1960s and the early 1970s.

NEW OLD STOCK: Left over, never-used car parts that are no longer being manufactured.

> "I just want to let you know that you all got opportunities to upgrade the wheels on your cars with these **new old stock** wheels that this eBay seller has to offer."

PONY CAR: *(synonym: muscle car)* Any powerful car made between the mid-1960s to early 1970s.

RAT ROD: A car that has been modified for speed and often for minimalist appearance. Rat rods may look stylish, but generally aren't flamboyant except mechanically. They are often painted dull colors, and sometimes have an exposed engine. Not a derogatory term.

> "Flat black is more authentic for a real '**rat rod**,' from what I've seen."

(!) RICE BOY: A derogatory term for someone who drives or works on flashy, recent-model cars, usually imported, that have no meaningful performance improvements.

see also: import scene, ricer, rice burner, rice rocket

(!) RICE BURNER: An imported, usually Asian car that looks flashy but has nothing special under the hood. Derogatory.

see also: import scene, ricer, rice boy, rice rocket

(!) RICE ROCKET: 1) A legitimately fast, recent-model, imported car. Not derogatory. 2) A flashy, recent-model, imported car with much customization but no significant performance improvements. Derogatory.

see also: import scene, ricer, rice burner, rice boy

> "This morning I saw a **rice rocket** that was really woeful!"

(!) RICER: 1) A recent-model car, usually imported and especially Japanese, that has been modified to appear powerful or eye-catching, but that lacks meaningful performance improvements. 2) A person who drives or works on such cars.

"Ricer" is a derogatory term, coined by other car enthusiasts and not used in the import scene itself.

see also: rice burner, rice rocket, rice boy

ROD: *(synonym: hot rod)* Short for hot rod. A car that has been modified for performance and/or appearance.

SECTIONED: In reference to a car, having a horizontal section of the body cut out for a lowered, streamlined look.

see also: channeled, chopped

"For the record, the rear bumpers were not 'bent' to fit the front, but were **sectioned** and welded on the right and left portions to end up narrower."

SHAVED: *(synonym: smoothed)* In reference to a car, modified with removal of trim, door handles, and other parts that otherwise wouldn't sit flush with the body panels. The lines where body panels join are also often filled with body filler or lead.

see also: decked, frenched

SLAMMED: In reference to a car, modified to sit as close to the ground as possible while still allowing the car to move.

see also: lowboy, lowrider, channeled

"The coolest car at the Portland Swap Meet last year was a chopped and **slammed** Checker."

SLEEPER: A car that has been modified for speed and power but that looks like it's just an old beater.

"But what amazes me most is the potential **sleeper** this car could be."

SMOOTHED: *(synonym: shaved)* In reference to a car, made to look more streamlined by removing anything that doesn't lie flush with the body panels.

STREET ROD: A car with many modifications, usually for both performance and appearance, that is legal to drive on the street.

see also: grocery getter, hot rod

SUICIDE DOOR: A car door hinged in the rear instead of the front. Suicide doors were standard features on some older cars, but are also sometimes added as modifications.

"Over the years I have owned many of the 4-door 'stump jumpers' with **suicide doors**."

VINTAGE: A particularly old car.

see also: antique

Hunters

Hunters can be categorized by the types of game they hunt (turkey, duck, deer, etc.), by the weapons they use (bow, rifle, flintlock), and sometimes by the animals they hunt with (hunting on horseback, hunting with dogs). A number of hunters are also gun enthusiasts; see the section on gun enthusiasts (page 156) for more information.

Not surprisingly, hunter slang includes informal names for a wide variety of game animals, including some birds that are referred to the same way birders refer to them (see page 41 for birding slang). A number of these game animal terms are included in the listings here.

Deer hunting is by far the most popular type of hunting in the U.S., with more than ten million hunters participating each year according to a 2001 U.S. Government survey. Wild turkey is the second most popular game animal, with 2.5 million hunters, followed by squirrel (2.1 million), rabbit/hare (2.1 million), pheasant (1.7 million), duck (1.6 million), and dove (1.5 million).

RELATED SUBCULTURES:

Birders, Flyfishers and Sport Fishermen, Gun Enthusiasts

BALDIE: *(synonyms: skinhead, slickhead)* A fawn or doe.

BIRDY: In reference to a hunting dog, excited when it picks up a scent.

BOMBER: A Sage Grouse.

BOSS: In reference to a game animal, a male that's especially large or dominant in its group.

BRUISER: *(synonym: wall-hanger)* A large buck.

BUCK FEVER: A sense of awe or paralyzed amazement at the sudden appearance of a buck.

BUSHYTAIL: *(synonym: tree rat)* A squirrel.

BUST OR BUST UP: To purposely or inadvertently scare game birds out from cover.

CALL-SHY: A game bird that doesn't emerge in response to calls.

> "We use less decoys early in the year (mostly bigfoots) but also shells and add to the spread as the geese get more educated and **call-shy**."

COMEBACK CALL: A series of forlorn honking or quacking noises used to call after waterfowl that have flown off.

> "It is a single reed and gives a good **comeback call** the harder you blow."

CONFIDENCE DECOY: A decoy of a species of bird not being hunted, used to assure a game bird that the setting is safe (which of course, it isn't).

> "Over the past year I've gone from my first effort at a wooden bird to completion of about 2 dozen decoys, including mallards in various poses, five bluebills, one drake bufflehead, a couple of scoters, one drake Barrow's goldeneye (an 'ornamental' working decoy made as a present) and, just for fun, a full-sized blue heron **confidence decoy**."

COURTESY GOBBLE: A single gobble from a turkey in response to a hunter's call, after which the turkey is quiet.

DITCH PARROT: A pheasant.

FISH COP: A game warden. This generally isn't meant to be derogatory.

FLARE: For a group of waterfowl, to veer away from possible danger while flying.

> "A few of these flocks headed our way, and some came in for a close look but **flared** at the last minute."

FLOAT HUNT: To hunt out of a small boat.

FLOCK SHOOTER: A hunter who shoots into a flock of birds instead of taking aim at a single bird.

FOOL HEN: A Spruce Grouse.

GLASS: To search for game through binoculars or a spotting scope.

GOBBLER: A wild turkey.

GREENHEAD: A male Mallard Duck.

GRINNER: An opossum.

GROUND SHRINKAGE: The apparent reduction in size of a deer or other game animal that seems to occur after it's shot and the hunter gets to where it is; i.e., the effect of a realizing she or he has imagined an animal was larger than its actual size.

"There was no **ground shrinkage** with this buck—instead, it was a case of ground *growth*!"

HONKER: A Canada Goose.

see also: wavy

JAKE: An immature, male turkey.

see also: longbeard

JUMPER: A Whitetail Deer.

LONGBEARD: A mature, male turkey.

see also: jake

MAGNUMITIS: A compulsion to buy really big guns.

MAKE GAME: For a hunting dog, to catch a scent.

PARTY HUNTING: Hunting in a group. Some kinds of party hunting are illegal in some states, for instance, if a group of hunters share a single hunter's legal permission to hunt for a particular kind of game.

PUDDLE DUCK: Any duck that dabbles (tips over) to feed rather than diving.

RACK: Antlers.

SHOE-POLISHER: A hunting dog that stays near a hunter's feet instead of chasing scents.

"She is basically a **shoe-polisher**, and if you saw her point you would probably laugh at her, but she's my baby, and she is used strictly for hunting, and she does her job well enough."

SHOOTER: A sizable game animal; one large enough to shoot.

SKINHEAD: *(synonyms: baldie, slickhead)* A fawn or doe.

SKY BUSTING OR SKYBUSTING: Shooting at game birds that are too high to hit easily.

SLICKHEAD: *(synonyms: baldie, skinhead)* A fawn or doe.

SLING A STICK: To shoot an arrow.

SLING LEAD: To shoot a gun.

SPECKLEBELLY: A White-Fronted Goose.

SPEED GOAT: A Pronghorn Antelope.

SWAMP DONKEY: A moose.

TARGET PANIC: Becoming jittery or unable to hold the gun or bow steady just as one aims at an animal.

"I've shot in leagues and tournaments and love bow hunting, but in the last few years I've developed **target panic**."

TIMBERDOODLE: An American Woodcock.

TREE RAT: *(synonym: bushytail)* A squirrel.

WALL-HANGER: *(synonym: bruiser)* A large buck.

WAVY: A Snow Goose.

see also: honker

Kayakers, Canoers, and Rafters

The slang of kayakers, canoers, and rafters conveys a gung ho attitude much like that of mountain bikers or snowboarders. It incorporates general nautical terms (stern, painter, amidships), an array of terms for parts of boats and paddles (blade, throat, thwart), and terms for water conditions, such as water churning in different directions or different kinds of rough water.

One important kind of information paddlers need when planning a trip is knowledge of how tricky a section of river is to navigate. For this purpose there's a standardized system of whitewater classifications, from Class I to Class VI.

Class I is too calm to even be considered whitewater: At most, there may be a few small waves or some shallows. Class II rapids are easy to navigate, but require a little work. Class III rapids are tricky, with opportunities to swamp or capsize, or to hit obstacles. Class IV rapids are difficult, turbulent, and dangerous; they require scouting and planning. Class V rapids are extremely difficult; even rescuing someone from parts of such an area may be hard to manage. Class VI rapids are the aquatic equivalent of a meat grinder.

BANK SCOUT: To get out of a boat and walk downriver to assess conditions.

see also: *boat scout*

BEAR OFF: To push away from a rock, log, bank, etc.

BELOW: Downriver; in the direction of the current.

BOAT SCOUT: To examine a section of river without getting out of the boat.

see also: *bank scout*

> "Heath slid in downstream of the hole, ferried across the stream, and caught the eddy below to **boat scout** the next drop."

BOIL: In reference to river water, to churn up at a particular point, usually indicating a submerged obstacle or tricky current.

BONY: In reference to rapids, having a lot of rock in comparison to water.

BOOF: (as a verb) To paddle a kayak so that it jumps off a rock or ledge and (if all goes well) lands safely beyond it. (as a noun) A jump off a rock or ledge in a kayak.

> "He made a beautiful **boof** off the pourover just to the left of center."

BROACH: To catch against an obstacle, sideways to the current. Very undesirable; similar to parking a car perpendicular to oncoming traffic.

> "It doesn't matter how long the boat may be; it'll still **broach** if the conditions are right (i.e., wrong)."

C-1: A one-person canoe with a deck instead of an open interior.

see also: *C-2, K-1*

C-2: A two-person canoe with decking.

see also: *C-1, K-2*

CARNAGE: Unwelcome events such as capsizing and damage to boats.

CHUTE: A place where a river offers a narrow passage with rapidly flowing water and no obstacles.

CLOSED BOAT: Any canoe or kayak with permanent decking on the top, as opposed to one with an open design. Canoes of this type are called C-1's (with an opening for only one person) or C-2's (with openings for two people).

COCKPIT: The place where the kayaker sits in a kayak.

CURLER: A wave that curves back on itself. Usually created by a rock or other object underwater.

DROP: Any steep descent on a river, including falls and rapids.

DRY BAG: A waterproof bag used to hold all the items in a boat that should not get wet.

"Normally, I lash a large **dry-bag** to the canoe so that if I turtle, the bag won't disappear downstream."

EDDY FENCE: *(synonym: eddy wall)* The boundary between the river's main current and a counter-current that is lower or higher.

see also: eddy line

EDDY HOP: To negotiate a series of rapids by stopping periodically in eddies to scout ahead.

EDDY LINE: The boundary between the main current and an eddy, where the current moves in a different direction.

see also: eddy fence

EDDY WALL: *(synonym: eddy fence)* The boundary between the river's main current and a counter-current that is lower or higher.

ENDER: A showy maneuver in which the front of the boat goes down into the water and the rear comes up until the boat is temporarily vertical. If the move is done in a kayak and the paddler makes the boat spin, it's called a "pirouette."

"You can do an **ender** or pirouette with the stern of your boat instead of the bow, although they are harder."

ESKIMO ROLL: A maneuver that brings a capsized kayak upright with the kayaker staying in place inside the boat.

"A kayak can survive breaking surf and can **Eskimo roll** for the ultimate self-rescue."

FERRY: To move the boat from one side of a river to the other without getting pushed downstream by the current.

"Finally we got a break in the crowd, so I told Jean, who was down-eddy (up-river) from me to **ferry** on across to the staging eddy."

FLAT WATER: Any body of water that has neither current nor waves.

GREEN WATER: The water pouring over a ledge or rock.

see also: hole

HEADWALL: A cliff or steep bank that is hit head-on by the current.

HOLE: *(synonym: reversal)* A place where water has poured over a ledge or rock and churns back against the main current. Some holes are suitable places for recreation, e.g., tipping the boat vertically into an ender.

see also: green water, hydraulic

HUNG UP: In reference to a boat, caught on a rock.

HYDRAULIC: A place in a river where water churning back under a rock or ledge is dangerously strong.

see also: hole

K-1: A one-person kayak.

see also: C-1, K-2

K-2: A two-person kayak.

see also: K-1, C-2

KEEPER: A place where water circulates back upriver and holds or spins a boat.

see also: hole

MAYTAGGED: Thrashed around in a churning part of the river as though in a washing machine.

"Checking over my shoulder, I found the rock wall and its accompanying monster wave only a few meters behind me. I just had time to return the guide's horrified look before I was sucked under and **Maytagged**."

MYSTERY MOVE: The disappearance of a boat under the water, followed by its reappearance somewhere downriver. Usually done to the paddler by the river rather than the paddler doing it on purpose.

"Nunez, paddling the Riot Disco, tried to emulate one of Paul's tricks by performing a **mystery move** at the top of the Falls of Leny. Onlookers were amazed when the Disco went vertical, then totally submerged, only to resurface at the bottom of the falls with Nunez clinging onto half a paddle."

OFF SIDE: The side of the boat opposite the one on which the paddler is paddling.

see also: on side

ON SIDE: The side of the boat on which the paddler is paddling.

see also: off side

PFD OR PERSONAL FLOTATION DEVICE: A lifejacket or life vest.

PILLOW: A place where water bulges around an obstacle.

"The sensation of lift was incredible as I ramped up the face of the colossal green **pillow** that loomed out of the sea in front of me."

PORTAGE: (as a verb) To carry boats and gear overland from one body of water to another. (as a noun) A trip across land from one body of water to another, carrying boats and gear.

PUNCH: To paddle hard through a place where the river churns up.

PUT-IN: The place where the boat is put in the water and the trip starts.

see also: take-out

READ THE WATER: To examine rapids, eddies, holes, etc., and infer what obstacles and possibilities a section of river presents.

REVERSAL: (*synonym:* hole) A spot under a rock or ledge where water churns backwards.

RIFFLES: A shallow section of river where the water appears rippled due to rocks just beneath the surface.

ROCK GARDEN: A section of river that is navigable but full of rocks.

SHUTTLE BUNNY: A person who moves vehicles from the place where the boats are launched to a designated pick-up location.

see also: put-in

SPRAY SKIRT: A piece of material that stretches from a kayaker's hips to the edge of the kayak cockpit, designed to keep water out of the kayak.

SQUIRT BOAT: A small, specially-designed kayak that submerges easily and allows the kayaker to execute tricks.

STANDING WAVE: A permanent wave in a river, sometimes caused by faster water meeting slower and deeper water.

STRAINER: Any obstacle in a river that allows water through but traps paddlers and boats.

TAKE-OUT: The place down river where the trip ends and the boats are taken out of the water.

see also: put-in

TECHNICAL: In reference to a section of river, rapids, a rock garden, or other obstacles that require substantial skill to successfully navigate.

> "I've never built a boat before, but would like to build a canoe or kayak suitable for use on lakes and non-**technical** rivers."

TONGUE: An angle of smooth water that indicates safe passage through a rough section.

TURTLED: In reference to a boat, upside-down in the water.

WAR CANOE: A large canoe, built to accommodate a large number of canoers.

WET EXIT: Getting out of a capsized kayak rather than rolling it upright.

WRAP: To slam a canoe sideways into a rock, striking hard enough to bend the canoe around the obstruction.

Magicians

★ ★ ★ ★ ★ ★

Important: If you'd like to retain a sense of wonder when you see magic tricks, you might not want to read this section. It's not intended specifically to show how tricks are done, but learning some of the vocabulary of magicians does give away secrets. If you wish to retain your childlike awe, please turn to a different section *now*.

Still with me? That's what I figured. On to the secrets!

First, the essence of magic: misdirection. A good magician is generally doing at least two tricks at once: the one that produces the "magical" effect, and the one he wants the audience to see. For instance, a magician might have a specially built table that enables her to pull a rabbit out of a top hat. While a hidden assistant loads the rabbit into the table, the magician may be showing the hat to the audience and talking about how innocent the hat is, which of course makes the audience study the hat more closely while ignoring the table. The first trick

★ ★ ★ ★

is to make the rabbit appear, and the second trick is to make the audience focus on the hat instead of the table.

Traditionally, American magicians have tried to incorporate a sense of the luxurious and exotic in their work, which is why the old standby magic words tend to imitate or derive from languages like Latin ("hocus pocus"), Italian ("presto"), and Hebrew ("abracadabra"). In recent years, however, this Old World flavor has disappeared from the routines of many stage magicians.

And now I'll make the words of this section magically appear, if you'll just—hey, look! Reindeer!

And voila! Here they are.

BREAK: A gap in a deck of cards, not visible to onlookers, that helps the magician locate a particular card.

BROKEN WAND CEREMONY: An observance in memory of a deceased magician, in which a wand (not always one that belonged to the deceased) is broken, and a fellow magician makes a brief speech.

> "It may be possible that a family member will request that the **Broken Wand Ceremony** be conducted by the Ring."
>
> - FROM THE WEB SITE OF THE INTERNATIONAL BROTHERHOOD OF MAGICIANS

CARDICIAN: A magician who performs with playing cards.

> "You are obviously not a skilled **cardician**, as any skilled **cardician** knows that the classic force is far superior to the slip force."

CLOSE-UP MAGIC: Magic performed among an audience, most often with small, everyday objects.

see also: illusion

DISAPPEARANCE: (*synonym: vanishing*) Any magic trick in which the magician makes someone or something disappear.

see also: vanish, sleeve

DITCH: To discard something so that the audience won't see it later in the trick.

EFFECT: The magical thing that appears to happen when a magician performs a trick, as opposed to the mundane thing that is actually happening.

ESCAPE: Any performance in which the magician miraculously escapes from imprisonment or restraints.

FALSE CUT: A movement that appears to cut a deck of cards but in actuality leaves the sequence of cards unchanged.

FLOURISH: A showy, skillful movement.

> "I'm not actually asserting that this was a magic trick—just a **flourish**."

FORCE: In reference to a specific card, to cause a member of the audience to choose that card while giving the impression that he or she chose freely.

GIMMICKED: In reference to an object, altered or rigged to produce a magical effect. A gimmicked object may be in view of the audience (for instance, a two-faced card where the audience sees only one face at a time), or hidden from view (for instance, a magnet under a table).

> "I believe there is a version which uses only one **gimmicked** card."

GOSPEL MAGIC: A branch of performance magic that specializes in using magic tricks to emphasize Christian teachings.

HAT PRODUCTION: A magic trick in which the magician produces a series of objects from a hat.

see also: production

ILLUSION: A magic trick that presents a large-scale spectacle, as opposed to a smaller-scale or brief trick.

see also: close-up magic

JOG: (as a verb) To make a card stick out a little so as to more easily locate it during a trick. (as a noun) A card that is sticking out a little.

PALM: To hold something with one hand while making the hand appear empty. Palming an item can aid in appearances, disappearances, and other effects.

"When I need something to do with my hands, I will still practice **palming** the coin."

PAPER: *(synonym: readers)* Marked cards.

PARLOR MAGIC: *(synonym: stand-up magic)* Magic performed standing in front of an audience.

see also: illusion, close-up magic

"It is an old **parlor magic** trick. My dad learned it from a 'Doctor Backwards,' a stage mentalist."

PRODUCTION: Any trick in which something magically appears.

see also: hat production

PROFONDE: Deep pockets in the tails of a magician's tailcoat into which objects can disappear. Coats with tails are not nearly as common among magicians today as they used to be, however, so profondes are becoming rare.

see also: servante, sleeve, topit

READERS: *(synonym: paper)* Playing cards marked so that it's possible for the magician to know what each one is by viewing the back.

SERVANTE: A hidden shelf, compartment, or pocket into which things can disappear.

see also: profonde, topit

"I could use a variation of the classic napkin over the salt shaker, with a **servante**."

SLEEVE: To send something up a sleeve in order to make it vanish.

see also: profonde, disappearance, topit

SLIDE: A hidden tube that puts an object in an unlikely place.

STACK: Cards that have been arranged in a particular order to facilitate a magic trick.

STAND-UP MAGIC: *(synonym: parlor magic)* Magic performed standing in front of an audience.

STEAL: To remove an object without the audience realizing it has been taken away.

SUCKER EFFECT: A magic trick that leads audience members to believe they know how it works, then proves them wrong.

"Magic for Sale—*very* reasonable, slightly used 'Rabbit Hotel' (good **sucker effect**) $40.00."

SVENGALI DECK: A special deck of playing cards in which half the cards are duplicates of each other and shorter than usual.

TALKING: Unwanted noises made by magical props; for instance, cooing from hidden doves.

TOPIT: 1) A jacket with hidden pockets. 2) The hidden pockets themselves.

see also: profonde, servante, sleeve

VANISH: To make a person or object disappear.

see also: disappearance

> "This shell allows you to **vanish** the whole thing into a thumb tip, then reproduce the real one from somewhere else."

VANISHING: (*synonym: disappearance*) A magic trick in which something disappears.

ZOMBIE GIMMICK: A hidden rod that makes an object look as though it's floating in mid-air.

Mediums, Channelers, and Spiritualists

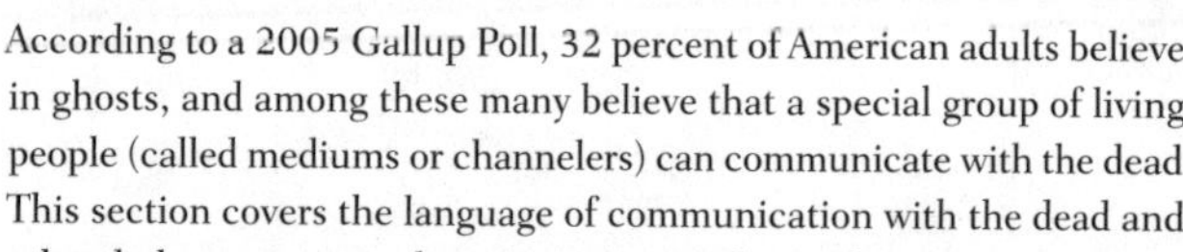

According to a 2005 Gallup Poll, 32 percent of American adults believe in ghosts, and among these many believe that a special group of living people (called mediums or channelers) can communicate with the dead. This section covers the language of communication with the dead and related phenomena, such as possession and ectoplasm.

Spiritualism as it is known today became popular in the 1840s, when mediums began to conduct séances in which they would contact or appear to contact spirits on behalf of clients who were present at the event to hear any messages.

Methods of communication attributed to spirits of the dead and other spirits include apparition (a visual projection of a deceased person or other spirit), automatism (a live individual doing a task, such as writing or drawing, under the control of a spirit), communication directly with the mind of the medium, sounds or voices coming from the air, and moving objects within the room where the séance is being held.

Spiritualism, séances, and ghost hunting differ from parapsychology (see page 230) in that spiritualist phenomena are attributed to spirits, usually spirits of the dead, whereas parapsychology generally deals with hidden powers believed to come from the human mind.

AGENT: A person or other entity at the focus of psychic activity. For example, a spirit involved in a haunting or a person around whom poltergeist activity occurs.

APPARITION: A projected vision of an entity not physically present, such as a dead person; or a person far away who is in the midst of a crisis (a "crisis apparition"). Apparitions are sometimes said to be accompanied by other sensory experiences, such as strange smells, or a sudden sense of cold.

APPORT: An object that appears in a closed room or container, having passed through solid matter to arrive there. Apports may materialize during a seance or due to a poltergeist.

see also: asport

> "The **apport** was a black onyx cross, two and a half inches by two inches, surmounted with gold filigree, a beautiful piece of work."
>
> - A. E. Perriman

ASPORT: An object that disappears from one location and appears in another, passing through solid matter on the way.

see also: apport

AUTOMATIC DRAWING/PAINTING/SPEAKING/WRITING: (*synonym: automatism*) Complex activities performed by an individual that are not under his or her conscious control.

AUTOMATISM: (*synonym: automatic drawing/painting/speaking/writing*) Any complex activity carried out without the conscious control of the individual performing it; a situation in which a spirit or other entity controls the body of an individual. Includes automatic writing, automatic drawing, automatic painting, and automatic speaking. Even music and surgery are said to have been performed through automatism, though rarely.

BILLET READING: An activity, usually performed publicly, in which a medium is handed a question written on a folded piece of paper. The medium attempts to contact a deceased person and tell the audience the answer to the question.

BOOK TEST: 1) A means of attempting to rule out telepathy of verifying that a spiritual entity is communicating with a medium. Conducted by naming a specific page of a particular book and asking the entity to relay the contents

of that page to the medium. Can be used as a noun or a verb. 2) A communication from a spiritual entity that indicates a meaningful message may be found on a specific page of a particular book.

CABINET: An enclosed space used by a medium during a seance to attempt to focus psychic energy.

CARTOMANCY: Predicting the future or determining facts about an individual through cards, usually the Tarot.

CHANNELER: *(synonym: medium)* A person who acts as a deliverer of messages for other entities.

CHANNELING: *(synonyms: spirit communication, mediumship)* A means of communication with spirits of the dead or other entities, in which the medium goes into trance and relays messages or serves as a vessel for the entity.

see also: medium

COMMUNICATOR: 1) An entity from whom a medium receives messages. 2) A medium.

CONTROL: *(synonym: guide)* An entity who takes over a medium during a seance and uses her to deliver messages. Not the same as a communicator, who gives messages directly to the medium instead of taking over the medium and simply using the medium's voice to communicate with others at the seance.

CRYPTOMNESIA: Information that a person has learned but forgotten the source of, so that when the information emerges, it may falsely appear to have been delivered through some paranormal means.

DAIMON OR DAEMON: A type of spirit that provides information and advice. Some mediums believe all daimons to be guardian spirits; others believe there to be both good and evil daimons.

DEATHBED VISIONS OR DEATHBED EXPERIENCE: Visions of dead loved ones who appear just before death to escort the dying person to the next world.

see also: near-death experience, apparition

DERMOGRAPHY: Writing that appears temporarily on the skin, usually as the result of demonic possession.

DIRECT DRAWING AND DIRECT PAINTING: Drawings or paintings that are made by a spiritual entity directly, without making use of a human hand to create them.

see also: automatism, direct writing

DIRECT VOICE: A voice, not produced by any human present, that emanates directly from the air or through a conical tube intended for this purpose during a seance.

DIRECT WRITING: Writing that appears directly through the agency of a spiritual entity without the use of a medium's hands, and sometimes without the use of drawing materials.

see also: direct drawing and direct painting, automatism

DISCARNATE: Not possessed of a body; in the form of a spirit. The word may be used to refer to deceased people or to entities that have always existed only in spiritual form.

DISSOCIATION: The phenomenon of an activity being separated from the conscious awareness of the person performing it; for instance, when a medium speaks while in trance, or automatism.

ECTOPLASM: A substance said to emerge from the body of a medium during a seance and to produce physical effects; it then goes back into the medium. Ectoplasm is described as taking a variety of shapes and densities.

ELECTRONIC VOICE PHENOMENA OR EVP: (*synonym: Raudive voices*) Voices or other sounds from spirits, especially of the deceased, that appear directly on recordings without having been audible to recorder.

FAITH HEALING: Curing disease or disability through the faith of the afflicted. Distinct from spiritual healing, which is administered by a medium and comes from the power of spiritual entities.

see also: spiritual healing

GLOSSOLALIA: The phenomenon of a medium, in trance state, speaking in an unintelligible language. Along with xenoglossy, sometimes called "speaking in tongues."

see also: xenoglossy

GUARDIAN SPIRIT: (*synonyms: guide, guiding spirit*) A protective or helpful spirit.

GUIDE: (*synonyms: guiding spirit, guardian spirit*) A spirit who protects and guides an individual, such as a guardian angel.

Can also be used as a synonym for control, meaning an entity who takes over a medium during a seance and uses her or him to deliver messages.

> "If this **Guide** comes, how can we know that they are a good Spirit Guide and not some entity, maybe disguised to look good, that wants to abuse us?"

GUIDING SPIRIT: *(synonyms: guide, guardian spirit)* A protective or helpful spirit.

IMPERSONATION: A medium temporarily taking on physical characteristics of a spirit she or he is channeling.

see also: medium, transfiguration

MATERIALIZATION: The temporary appearance of physical things, generally thought to be formed of ectoplasm, during the course of a seance. Materialization is considered a very difficult feat for a medium to accomplish.

MEDIUM: *(synonym: channeler)* A person able to contact spirits of the dead or other entities and relay messages from those spirits. May occur through speech, automatic writing, or other means.

see also: channeling

MEDIUMSHIP: *(synonyms: channeling, spirit communication)* Receiving messages from the dead or other entities through a medium.

NEAR-DEATH EXPERIENCE OR NDE: Separation of the spirit and the physical body; apparitions or other psychic phenomena experienced when a person comes close to dying.

NECROMANCY: Conjuring and controlling the dead through psychic powers.

NEWSPAPER TEST: A means of ruling out telepathy as an explanation for spirit communication. Through a medium, a spirit specifies names or dates that will appear in a particular issue of a newspaper or magazine not yet published.

OVERSHADOWING: A spiritual entity partly taking over a medium's body, with the medium's permission. Overshadowing is a more subtle and less complete process than channeling.

POLTERGEIST: A spiritual entity who wreaks physical havoc on a small or large scale. Physical manifestations of poltergeists may include levitation, materializing objects, noises, small cuts or scratches, etc. Poltergeist activity is often associated with a particular individual (the agent), usually a child or a teenager, and is thought by many parapsychologists to be not a separate spiritual entity but rather an unconscious use of psychic power emanating from the agent. (See page 230 on parapsychologists.)

RAPS: Knocking sounds that occur during seances, often said to be made by rigid ectoplasm striking a hard surface. Raps are sometimes used by spirits to communicate.

RAUDIVE VOICES: *(synonym: electronic voice phenomena or EVP)* Voices that are recorded without ever being heard.

READING: A session in which the medium gives information from the spirit world. A "cold reading" is one in which the medium has no prior information about the subject. A "hot reading" is, therefore, a phrase often associated with fraudulent readings.

see also: medium

SEANCE OR SÉANCE: *(synonym: sitting)* An event in which a group of people gather, usually sitting around a table and usually with a medium to attempt to contact one or more spiritual entities. Seances are normally conducted in closed rooms and are most often done with the intention of communicating with spirits of the dead.

see also: medium

SITTER: A person who attends a seance or otherwise consults a medium.

see also: medium, seance

"The **sitter** given the message passed it on to Mrs. Houdini, who then checked it out with a message in a safety deposit box."

SITTING: *(synonym: seance or séance)* An event in which a group of people gather to try to contact spiritual entities.

SPIRIT COMMUNICATION: *(synonyms: channeling, mediumship)* Receiving messages from the dead or other entities through a medium.

SPIRITUAL HEALING: A type of healing achieved through the power of spiritual entities, who work through a human medium.

see also: medium, faith healing

SPIRITUALISM: The practice or belief in existence after death and the ability of the living to communicate with spirits of the dead. Sometimes practiced as a religion.

see also: *spiritualist, survival*

SPIRITUALIST: A person who believes in life after death and communication with the dead.

see also: *spiritualism, survival*

STIGMATA: Markings or wounds on a person that appear to have a psychic or spiritual cause. The term is sometimes used specifically to refer to unexplained wounds that mirror those described in the New Testament as having been inflicted on Jesus.

SURVIVAL: The continued existence of an individual's personality after death.

see also: *spiritualism, spiritualist*

> "She would only be able to provide evidence of a spirit's **survival** to a person intimate with the behavior and personality of the spirit."

TABLE TILTING OR TABLE TURNING: Movements of a table in a seance, caused by spirits and sometimes used as a crude form of communication.

THE TAROT: (pronounced "TARE-oh") A deck of special cards, each with a symbolic picture on it, used in fortune telling since the high Middle Ages.

> "The **Tarot** was and is my first tool, though for several years I've used the *I Ching* as a sort of supplement and cross-check."

TRANSFIGURATION: The phenomenon of a dead person's features appearing over those of the medium at a seance.

see also: *medium, seance, impersonation*

XENOGLOSSY: The phenomenon of a medium, in trance, speaking in a language she or he does not know. Along with glossolalia, sometimes called "speaking in tongues."

Model Builders and Radio-Controlled Model Enthusiasts

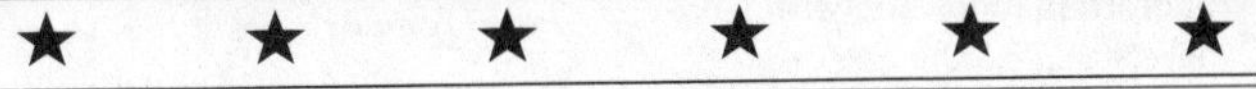

Apart from model railroads, the three most popular model-related hobbies are model rocketry, radio control airplanes, and vehicle scale models. Each of these hobbies has its own concerns and vocabulary, with very little crossover, so each is presented as a separate set of terms.

Model rocketry, being a hobby based on explosions, necessarily includes a bit of danger and destruction. Model rocketeers often enjoy and emphasize this aspect of the hobby. One sign of this is the naming of annual rocketry events, like the ones called "Fireballs" and "LDRS" (for "Large and Dangerous Rocket Ships"). Another sign is that rocketry slang is rich with terms for malfunctions and crashes.

People who fly radio control airplanes (also called "radio-controll*ed* airplanes;" there doesn't seem to be any consensus about which is the preferred term) use a number of terms from aviation, such as the names of maneuvers—"Immelmann," "flare," and "ground effect," for example—and the parts of a plane. Names for flying tricks comprise a large part of radio control airplane jargon and are too numerous to list here.

Scale model builders may work on anything from simple, inexpensive, out-of-the-box kits to unique conversion projects with photo-etched grills, real wiring, and working parts.

Model Rocketeers

AMATEUR ROCKETRY: *(synonym: experimental rocketry)* A type of model rocketry that is more complex, expensive, and high-powered than hobby rocketry. Deals with tricky fuel formulations and with large rockets that can fly miles up.

BAR: "Born again rocketeer." A person who used to work with model rockets, stopped for a while, and eventually came back to it.

BONUS DELAY: An unexpectedly long wait before a model rocket motor kicks in.

> "The motor had a **'bonus' delay** (about 7.5-8 seconds as verified on video and deployed while facing directly down), and the rocket somehow managed to fly directly into the chute."

CATO: Short for "catastrophic take-off" or "catastrophe at take-off:" a spectacular problem with a model rocket at launch that usually destroys the rocket itself.

CHAD: Short for "cheap and dirty." In model rocketry, any improvised fix that lacks grace, ingenuity, or perhaps a basic concern for safety.

CORE SAMPLE: *(synonym: lawn dart)* A model rocket failure that propels the rocket into the ground at high speed.

see also: power prang

CRUISE MISSILE: *(synonym: land shark)* A model rocket that veers off its planned vertical path and blasts along horizontally, terrorizing bystanders.

DEATH DIVE: *(synonym: power prang)* A malfunction in which a rocket turns and flies toward the ground under power.

DRAG RACE: An event at which a number of model rockets are launched at once.

EGG LOFTER: Any model rocket designed to carry an egg into the air and bring it back to earth without breaking it. Egg lofting competitions are a common model rocketry event.

ENGINE: *(synonym: motor)* The component that generates force to make a rocket fly.

EXPERIMENTAL ROCKETRY: *(synonym: amateur rocketry)* Building and flying very large-scale model rockets.

HOBBY ROCKETRY: The branch of model rocketry that deals with smaller-scale model rockets, including the relatively small "high-powered rockets."

KITBASH: To modify a kit so as to build a unique rocket, or to combine two rocket kits.

LCO: Launch Control Officer. The person in charge of launches on the rocketry range.

LAND SHARK: *(synonym: cruise missile)* A model rocket that veers off its intended path and flies horizontally.

THE LAUNDRY: Rocket components to be recovered after the rocket returns to earth, especially a rocket's parachute.

LAWN DART: *(synonym: core sample)* A model rocket failure in which the rocket flies straight down to the ground under power.

MOTOR: *(synonym: engine)* The component that propels a rocket, often comprising fuel plus a means to ignite it wrapped in a casing.

see also: whoosh generator

ODDROC: A weird-looking rocket, often resembling something unrelated to rocketry. Real-life examples include pink elephants, cacti, upside-down martini glasses, pyramids, and Bert from *Sesame Street*.

ORANGE BOOK: A book of regulations for using explosives, produced by the U.S. Bureau of Alcohol, Tobacco, and Firearms.

"The **Orange Book** does specifically exclude so-called model rocket propellant."

POWER PRANG: *(synonym: death dive)* A malfunction in which a rocket turns downward while still firing its engine.

see also: core sample, prang

"That way when you **power prang** or landshark and start a fire, the rocket will beat the fire out before you get there."

PRANG: In reference to a rocket, to fall ignominiously to the ground.

see also: power prang, core sample, cruise missile

RED BARON: A boost glider (rocket-assisted glider) that becomes entangled with its own parachute and tumbles out of the sky.

RE-KITTED: Crashed; in reference to a model rocket, broken into its component pieces in an accident.

"It flew reasonably well, but the ejection charge wasn't enough to pop the chute, and the rocket **re-kitted** itself on the ground."

ROCKETEER: A person who builds and flies model rockets.

SNI: "Slimy NAR Insider." The NAR is the National Association of Rocketry, and SNI's are people who have inside knowledge of the organization. Not particularly derogatory.

see also: SNP

SNP: "Slimy NAR Politician." A person who gets elected to the board of the National Association of Rocketry. Not particularly derogatory.

see also: SNI

SHRED: In reference to a rocket, to come apart in mid-air.

WHOOSH GENERATOR: The object that propels a rocket. This term arose from a long-standing debate about whether the propulsion component of a rocket should be called a "motor" or an "engine." The term "whoosh generator" conveniently makes the issue moot.

see also: motor

ZIPPERING: A situation in which a shock cord, which holds the nose onto the rest of the rocket, rips the rocket open in mid-air as the parachute or streamer deploys.

Radio-Controlled Airplane Operators

BORE HOLES IN THE SKY: To steer a radio-controlled airplane by whim, not using a flight plan.

"Part of the challenge of instruction is developing a syllabus that keeps the student too involved, excited, and busy to just **bore holes in the sky**."

BUDDY BOX: A double transmitter control box, with one set of controls for the student and one for the instructor. This instructor can override the student as needed.

CHICKEN STICK: Anything used to start the propeller of a model airplane while ensuring fingers are well clear.

FIGURE 9: A half-successful attempt at a figure-eight maneuver.

"At most three seconds later it completed its maiden flight, a graceful **figure 9**, and was upon completion of that maneuver transmogrified into styrofoam confetti."

FLIGHT BOX: A case used to transport equipment to and from the flying field.

HIT: To cause radio interference with a radio-controlled airplane.

see also: shot down

SHOT DOWN: In reference to a radio-controlled airplane, knocked out of the sky when radio interference makes it impossible to control.

see also: hit

Scale Model Builders

AFTER-MARKET: In reference to parts, obtained separately from the model kit.

CONVERSION: A combination of a kit with after-market parts or with parts improvised by the model builder to create a unique piece.

DETAILING: Making a model look more authentic; for instance, by painting, adding special after-market parts, adding wiring, etc.

FLASH: Extra bits of plastic on parts of a model that are artifacts of the manufacturing process.

RATTLE CAN: Spray paint.

SCALE: The size of a model compared to the size of the thing it's based on. Usually between 1/64 and 1/8.

SLAMMER: A simple model kit with little detail.

"That seems to be a good price for any kit, but is this a detailed kit on clearance or just a **slammer**?"

Model Railroaders and Railfans

Model railroaders share a good deal of their slang with railfans, people who have a strong hobby interest in real-life railroads, and of course there's some substantial overlap between the groups. In addition to terms covering model railroading, model railroaders and railfans often command a range of terminology about the railroading business, such as terms for railroad personnel and procedures, parts of a train, and types of engines and railroad cars.

Model railroads come in a variety of scales or gauges, each one representing a particular proportion of model size to real-world prototype size. The size of a scale is expressed as 1:*some number*, where "some number" is how many times larger than the model the real thing is. For instance, HO scale is 87.1 times smaller than real life, that is, 1:87.1. From smallest to largest, the most popular scales are N (1:152 or 1:160), HO (1:87.1), S (1:64), O (1:43.5, 1:45, or 1:48), and G (1:20.3 or 1:24).

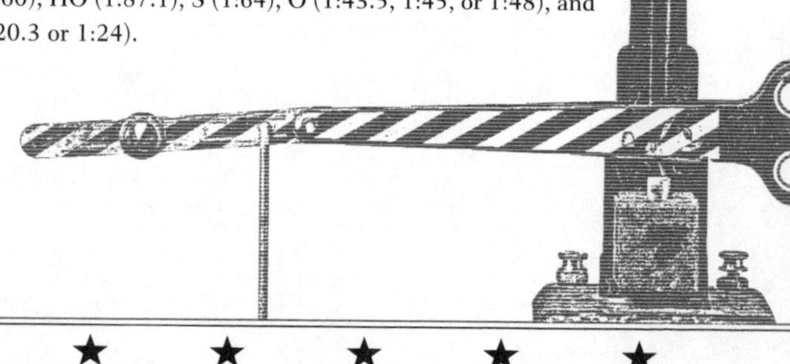

BENCHWORK: The frame or structure underlying a model railroad layout.

"I have used beam and girder construction throughout, so you could easily salvage the major **benchwork** and replace the top portion to create your own layout."

BLOCK: A section of track controlled by one electrical signal.

DEADHEAD: 1) An empty railroad car. 2) A train passenger who is allowed to travel without having purchased a ticket.

DUCKUNDER: Part of a model railroad <u>layout</u> that is large enough for a person to pass under it in order to get to another part of the layout.

DYNAMITER: A failed brake on a train.

FALLEN FLAG: A railroad that has gone out of business.

"The IHB is not a **fallen flag**; it is alive and well and should continue as such after the split-up on June first."

(!) FOAMER: A railfan. This is a mildly derogatory term usually used by railroad employees.

"In fact, I know of a couple of instances where a **'foamer'** has assisted the railroad by preventing a derailment and aided in the apprehension of real criminals."

FREELANCE: A model train layout that isn't based on a real-life railroad.

see also: <u>prototype</u>, <u>operation</u>

GAUGE: 1) The distance between rails on a particular type of real-life railroad track. 2) A particular size of model railroading track; synonymous with <u>scale</u> when used this way.

GOOFY GAUGE: The largest common size for model trains, more formally called "G-gauge."

see also: <u>gauge</u>, <u>scale</u>

HO SCALE: (pronounced "aitch-oh," never "hoe") The most popular size of model train, roughly half the size of O-scale trains (hence HO, short for "half-O").

KITBASHING: Combining parts from multiple model railroading

kits or layouts to create something unique.

LAYOUT: The tracks, scenery, framework, buildings, and decoration of a model railroad.

MAIN LINE: The most important tracks of a railroad normally used for travel, as opposed to sidings, spurs, yards, etc.

MASTER MODEL RAILROADER OR MMR: A person who has demonstrated mastery of at least seven areas of model railroading knowledge and skill as defined by the National Model Railroad Association.

"The one thing he has going for him is that he is a **MMR**."

OPERATION: A model railroad setup that mimics a section of a real-life railroad.

see also: freelance, prototype

PIKE: A model railroad setup.

PROTOTYPE: The actual train, railroad car, or railroad line on which a model train or its layout is based.

see also: operation, freelance

"The closer you follow **prototype** track plans, the better the operations."

SCALE: The size of a model railroad in comparison to its real-life prototype.

see also: gauge

SCENICKED: In reference to a model train layout, having had scenery applied.

"About 90 percent of track is laid with about 50 percent of the layout **scenicked**."

SCRATCH-BUILD: To build a model train or a layout from raw materials and basic parts rather than kits.

TEA KETTLE: An old steam engine.

Motorcyclists (Bikers)

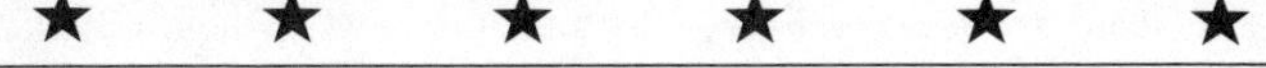

There's no single type of motorcycle rider: some are interested in on-road riding and others off-road riding; some ride sport bikes and others ride touring bikes; some ride crotch rockets or credit glides while others make do with rat bikes. And there's a particularly pronounced distinction between riders who own Harleys and riders who own a bike of any other brand. Still, among serious riders there's a shared language of motorcycle parts, makes and models, and of course, biker slang.

Many riders belong to local or national motorcycle clubs. Some of these clubs are affiliated with a particular make of motorcycle (for instance, Harley-Davidson or BMW), while others are not. Some have stable membership and dues, and others are essentially informal get-togethers. There are even biker churches, like Biker Haven church in Troy, Pennsylvania ("Loud pipes save lives … Jesus saves souls!"). The largest biker gatherings, however, are motorcycle rallies, such as Daytona Beach Bike Week and the Sturgis Motorcycle Rally, both of which draw more than half a million attendees each year.

APE HANGERS OR APES: Handlebars that are higher than the biker's shoulders, so that the biker grips them the way an ape might hang from a branch.

see also: clip-ons

"How about Harleys with **ape hangers**, straight-out exhausts, chain final drives with no guards?"

BAR HOPPER: An impressive-looking bike that isn't used for long trips because a) it's not very comfortable, and b) it might get dirty.

BARN QUEEN: A bike stored in an outbuilding for years that is in good shape for its age.

BASKET CASE: 1) A bike that's been taken apart and never reassembled, or a bunch of parts that together could comprise a full bike. 2) A bike assembled from a pile of parts.

"I am very interested in buying a Harley **basket case**."

BIKER: Someone who rides a motorcycle. This word sometimes implies a person who rides regularly and/or a rider who likes to raise a little hell.

see also: one percenter, rider

BOBBER: A motorcycle that's been stripped down to make it lighter and faster and to improve handling. Such a bike is said to have been "bobbed."

see also: chopper

BONEYARD: Any place that salvages and sells old bike parts.

BRAIN BUCKET: *(synonyms: lid, skid lid)* A helmet.

BURNOUT: Applying the front brake while spinning the back wheel in order to burn up the back tire and throw out a cloud of rubber smoke.

"I mean I wanted to fire up my bike right there and then with an open pipe and do a friggin' **burnout** in front of all of them."

CAFÉ RACER: A speedy little sport bike.

see also: sport bike

CAGE: A car, truck, van, bus, etc.: any closed-in, wheeled vehicle. The term "cage" refers to the fact that drivers and passengers are not in the open air.

see also: cager

"I seem to recall something from the Hurt study that the most common form of accident was a **cage** turning left and hitting a motorcycle."

CAGER: A person who drives anything other than a motorcycle.

see also: cage

CARVING: Riding a bike at high speed around tight curves, leaning first to one side, then the other.

CATWALK: Lifting the front wheel off the ground; a wheelie.

(!) CHICKEN STRIPS: Unworn tread on the sides of the tire of a sport bike. Chicken strips suggest that the biker rides conservatively, which can be embarrassing when among more adventurous types. Usually derogatory.

"Point two: **chicken strips** and dragging hardware do not make a superior rider."

CHOPPER: A motorcycle with an extended front fork so that the wheel protrudes a distance from the engine. Often choppers have been stripped down to necessities; hence the name.

see also: bobber

CLIP-ONS: Handlebars that are as low as the fuel tank.

see also: ape hangers

CLONE: A motorcycle designed to resemble a Harley-Davidson.

COLORS: A set of patches showing membership in a motorcycle club.

see also: rocker

"If a guy in motorcycle **colors** riding a Harley kicks out his leg at a banker in a Beemer, those twelve people would be much more likely to convict him."

COUPON: A traffic ticket.

CREDIT GLIDE: An expensive motorcycle owned by someone who doesn't ride regularly.

CROTCH ROCKET: A small, speedy bike with a big engine that is generally not comfortable for long rides.

CRUISER: A large motorcycle.

DRESSER: A motorcycle decked out with accessories (not necessarily to excess).

ENDO: *(synonym: stoppie)* A move in which the rear wheel comes well off the ground and the bike balances on its front tire. Can also refer to accidentally causing the rear wheel to fly up and sometimes tumble forward end over end after the bike hits an obstacle.

FAIRING: A covering and windshield on the front of a motorcycle, which sometimes wraps around to cover the front sides.

GET OFF: To crash.

HOG OR HOG: (pronounced "HAWG") An abbreviation for "Harley Owner's Group." Can refer to the group or to an individual Harley-Davidson motorcycle rider.

HIGH SIDE: A crash in which the bike flips, usually as result of a skid.

see also: low side, lay down

INDEPENDENT: A biker who is part of biker culture but not a member of a motorcycle club.

INK: A tattoo. (See tattoo slang on page 345 for more terms.)

see also: ink slinger

INK SLINGER: A tattoo artist.

see also: ink

IRON BUTT: An endurance ride; a long trip done at an ambitious pace.

JESUS CLIP: A fiddly little part on a motorcycle that holds handlebar switches in place. Named for what a person exclaims when it inevitably gets dropped.

JUG: An engine cylinder.

LANE SPLITTING: Riding between lanes of cars that are trapped in traffic.

LAY DOWN: To tip or crash a motorcycle.

see also: shiny side up, high side, low side

LEATHERS: Protective leather clothing for riding, e.g., jacket, gloves, etc.

LID: (*synonyms: brain bucket, skid lid*) A helmet.

LOW SIDE: A crash that occurs while leaning the bike hard to one side when it slides out from under the rider.

see also: high side, lay down

ONE PERCENTER: A biker who likes to raise hell. Not a derogatory term. The implication is that 99 percent of bikers are considerate and law-abiding.

> "I have always felt that under all of that painted plastic, fake-chrome plastic, and 'rubberized' plastic there was the beating heart of a **one percenter**."

PILLION: 1) (noun) The rear seat on a motorcycle (also called the pillion pad). 2) (noun) A motorcycle passenger riding on the rear seat. 3) (adverb) In reference to riding, on the rear seat of the bike.

see also: riding bitch, sissy bar

PIPES: The exhaust system of a motorcycle.

POKER RUN: A group ride during which each biker stops at a series of checkpoints to draw a playing card. The rider with the best hand at the end of the ride is the winner.

> "I decided that the **poker run** at the Meriden Motorcycle club was not something I was going to miss, despite the ¾ of an inch of rain that had only stopped falling the night before."

PUCKER FACTOR: The degree of panic felt during a near-accident.

(!) RUB: Rich urban biker." Implies an occasional rider who doesn't take the bike seriously.

RAKE: The extent to which the front fork of a motorcycle is at an angle to vertical. Choppers are more raked than most other bikes.

RAT BIKE: An ugly, cheap, or run-down motorcycle. Not generally derogatory.

(!) RICE BURNER: A Japanese motorcycle. This term can be considered derogatory.

RIDER: A person who rides a motorcycle. A more neutral term than biker.

see also: biker, one percenter

RIDING BITCH: Riding on the passenger seat, especially in reference to a male. Not specifically derogatory, but less refined than the classier-sounding "riding pillion."

see also: pillion, sissy bar

ROAD RASH: A skin condition caused by contact with asphalt at a high speed; a riding injury.

> "I fell off my motorcycle and ended up with **road rash** a foot wide from just below my bra to my waist."

ROCKER: A motorcycle club patch showing the town or geographical area where the club is based.

see also: colors

RUBBER: Tires.

RUBBER SIDE DOWN: (*synonym:* shiny side up) A reminder not to crash.

RUN: A motorcycle ride with a planned destination.

SCOOT OR SCOOTER: (*synonym: sled)* A motorcycle.

SHINY SIDE UP: (*synonym: rubber side down)* A sort of biker blessing meaning, "ride safe, don't crash."

see also: lay down

"Keep it **shiny side up** and on both wheels—what angle you choose is up to you."

SISSY BAR: A backrest for the passenger seat.

see also: pillion, riding bitch

SKID LID: *(synonyms: brain bucket, lid)* A helmet.

SLAB: (as a noun) A highway or other monotonous place to ride. (as a verb) Also "slab it." To ride on a highway.

SLED: *(synonym: scoot or scooter)* A motorcycle.

SPORT BIKE: A motorcycle built for speed rather than comfort.

see also: café racer, touring bike

(!) SQUID: An inexperienced biker who zooms around recklessly or without gear. Sometimes said to be short for "squirrelly kid," but may be named for the exhaust that squirts out when the squid speeds off.

STOPPIE: *(synonym: endo)* A move that lifts the rear wheel of the bike well off the ground.

TOURING BIKE OR TOURER: A bike built for comfort over long rides.

see also: sport bike

(!) TRAILER QUEEN: A motorcycle that is driven to locations in a trailer rather than used for long rides. Derogatory.

"Any **trailer queen** that slips past the judges is not eligible for a first place trophy. This is a ride-in show."

TRIKE: A three-wheeled motorcycle. Motorcycles with sidecars are not considered trikes, since in that case the third wheel is on the sidecar rather than the bike itself.

TWISTIES: A portion of a road that offers plenty of curves. Generally used only in the plural.

see also: twisty

"So the reason why you can smoke 600cc sportsbikes in the **twisties** has little to do with where your engine makes power."

TWISTY: In reference to a road, providing lots of satisfying bends and curves.

see also: twisties

WRENCH: (as a noun) A motorcycle mechanic. (as a verb) To work on a motorcycle.

YARD SHARK: A dog that races out to attack passing motorcycles.

Naturists and Nudists

"Naturism" and "nudism" are terms that are sometimes considered to mean exactly the same thing; however, some speakers use the term "naturism" to mean going without clothing in a relatively wild setting, and "nudism" to refer to going without clothing in a more social setting. Generally speaking, both terms encompass the attitude that nudity is natural and healthy.

Naturism and nudism crop up in national parks, public beaches, private clubs, resorts, and elsewhere.

The term "nudist colony" is not generally part of the language of naturists and nudists but instead is an outsider's term; "nudist club" is a fairly widely-used alternative term that is used within the subculture. Nudist or naturist organizations may be "landed" (i.e. they may own private property where they gather) or "non-landed" (i.e. they meet at private homes, resorts, and so forth).

In addition to socializing, popular nudist and naturist activities include swimming, sunbathing, canoeing, and group sports.

CANUDING: Canoeing nude.

CLOTHING OPTIONAL: In reference to a place or an event, allowing both nudity and clothing.

"My one concern is that I prefer a place that I go to be **clothing optional** and not mandatory nudity."

FREE BEACH: A public beach that includes an isolated section where clothing is not required.

LANDED NUDIST CLUB: A group that owns a naturist resort, campground, beach, or park.

NATURIST: 1) A person who spends some relaxation or recreation time nude. 2) More specifically a person who spends time nude and who enjoys and feels an affinity for natural settings.

see also: nudist

NUDIST: 1) A person who spends recreation or relaxation time nude. Some people who fit this description prefer the term naturist, while others have no preference. 2) More specifically, a person who enjoys nudity in social contexts, such as resorts and public places.

see also: naturist

(!) NUDIST COLONY: Not a term naturists and nudists typically use, but rather a term used by outsiders.

TEXTILE: (as a noun) A person who prefers to wear clothes in public places; i.e., someone who is not a nudist or naturist. (as an adjective) Having to do with clothed people.

"Closing a nude beach means banning nudity, while closing a **textile** beach means banning *access*."

TOPFREE: In reference to women, having a bare upper body. Also, a place or organization having to do with being topfree.

"Police have granted a permit but threatened to arrest any **topfree** women."

- FROM THE TOPFREE EQUAL RIGHTS ASSOCIATION WEB SITE

THE WORLD GUIDE: *Lee Baxandall's World Guide to Nude Beaches & Resorts*, a widely-known reference book among nudists and naturists.

Online Gamers

One of the unusual things about online gaming as a subculture is that online gamers usually don't meet in person; most contact occurs inside a game or through an instant messaging (IM) window. Another is that players interact, in part, in the personas of the characters they play. Because of this, computer gaming slang has a number of social terms for the way people play games, but hardly any vocabulary for real-world activities.

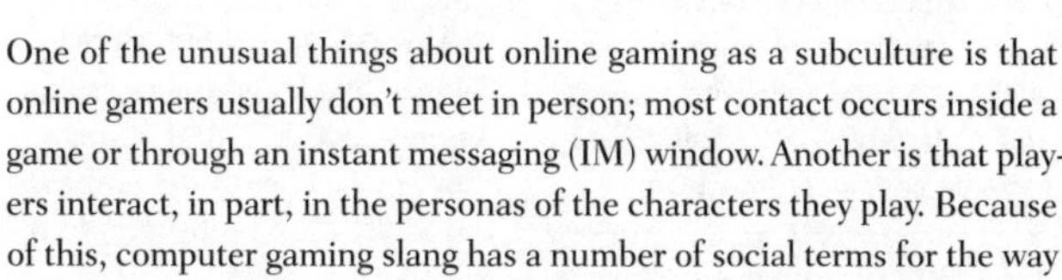

Like many other people who spend a lot of time on the Internet, many computer gamers use popular instant messaging symbols and abbreviations, like "lol" for "laughing out loud" or "k" for "OK." Instant messaging abbreviations, not being a subculture vocabulary, are beyond the scope of this book.

While there are computer games about more subjects than I can possibly list, most games fall into a small set of standard categories: "first-person shooter" games where a character wanders around shooting at people or things; fantasy games in which characters kill monsters and gather treasure; strategy games where the goal is to build up an army and defeat the armies of other players; and simulations of everything from one rickety airplane to the universe itself.

RELATED SUBCULTURES:

Hackers and Programmers, Role-Playing Gamers

ALPHA: An early version of a computer game (or any computer software) that has been only lightly tested. An alpha tester is a person who uses the game at that point and provides information about problems to the developers.

see also: beta

"LAN parties: been there, done that (back in the days when Doom was still in **alpha** and a 386 with a co-pro and 8 megs of RAM running Autocad was considered Da BomB!)."

AVATAR: An animated character that represents a player in a game.

BAN: *(synonym: kick)* To permanently expel a player from an online game, for instance, because of cheating or hacker mischief.

see also: booted

BETA: A version of a game (or any computer program) that is close to being ready to release but in need of a final round of testing. A game that is at this stage is said to be "in beta," and the company behind the game generally finds beta testers, who are allowed use the game for free in exchange for reporting problems.

BOOTED: In reference to a player, involuntarily thrown out of a game; for example, by an administrator for unfair play, or by a lost Internet connection, computer crash, etc.

see also: ban

BOSS OR BOSS MONSTER: A bigger, badder, stronger, meaner enemy at the end of a stage or level of a game. By defeating the boss, the player advances to the next level.

"If you're playing an open game, and everyone makes it to the **boss**, and everyone dies, *run as fast as you can to the transporter.*"

BOT: A computer-controlled character in a game, who may have limited conversational abilities; e.g., to give a clue to a puzzle, or to haggle with a player over the price of a weapon in the game. Bots may also be allies or inferiors of a player's character.

BUFF: (as a noun) An action or item that temporarily increases a character's abilities, for example,

a potion that makes a character less vulnerable. (as a verb) To do something to temporarily make one's character stronger.

"You also don't necessarily *need* to **buff** to hunt them."

CAMP: (as a verb) To take a position where many enemies emerge and ambush them there. (as a noun) A place where a player takes position to destroy enemies as they emerge.

Camping at a location where other players enter the game world and killing them is often allowed, but considered unsportsmanlike.

see also: spawn point

"I don't **camp** spawn points, or patrol spawn points looking for cheap kills."

CHEAT: Any means of getting an unfair advantage in a game.

see also: twink

CLAN: *(synonym: guild)* A group of players who regularly team up.

CONSOLE: A video gaming system that plays multiple games, normally using a TV set for a display. Arcade games, hand-held games, and devices that play games but aren't dedicated to the purpose (for instance mobile phones and computers) are not considered consoles.

DEATHMATCH OR DEATH MATCH: A type of multi-player game where the goal is to kill the other players' characters.

see also: player killing or PK

DEBUFF: (as a verb) To cause an enemy to become weaker or to lose abilities. (as a noun) A spell used to debuff.

"The only thing that gets better is that you'll get some 'resist **debuff**' spells."

EASTER EGG: A hidden animation, game location, or other bit of entertainment programmed into a game and accessed by a secret means. Unlike a cheat, an Easter egg doesn't usually give the player any special advantages.

EXPLOIT: Any means of gaining an advantage that the game designers did not intend. For example, a bug in the game software might make it possible for a player to earn unlimited amounts of money.

"Our **exploit** allows a player to calculate the exact deck being used for each hand in real time."

FIRST-PERSON SHOOTER OR FPS: A game in which the player sees through the eyes of a character whose job is to shoot things.

FPS also stands for "frames per second," which refers to how smooth an animation is, i.e., how many individual pictures make up each second of viewing.

FRAG: (as a verb) To kill an enemy in a game, especially if that enemy is another player (as opposed to a computer opponent). (as a noun) A kill.

see also: telefrag

"I wish that people who wanted to go around killing newbies and ruining the game for people who don't have fifteen hours a day to play the game would stick to action games like *Quake*, where they can **frag** to their heart's content."

GAMEPLAY: The general experience of playing a game. Often used in reviews.

"It maintains its reputation for gorgeous visuals, but has the **gameplay** caught up?"

- REVIEW BY MIKE SMITH ON HTTP://VIDEOGAMES.YAHOO.COM

GRIEFER: A player who makes a special effort to annoy or hamper other characters.

GUILD: (*synonym: clan*) A group of players who regularly team up.

KICK: (*synonym: ban*) To expel a player from an online game.

KITE: To attack an enemy or group of enemies, run away before they can respond, then repeat until the enemies are destroyed.

"That's exactly opposite my experience, where the **kiters** were yelled at because every direction they kited they overran a group camping something."

LAG: A delay in response from an Internet game.

see also: ping

(!) LLAMA: A derogatory word for an inexperienced player, especially an inept one.

MUD OR MULTI-USER DUNGEON: A text-based, multi-player, online game.

MOB: *(synonym: monster)* An entity in a game, operated by the computer, that exists to attack players.

"Join a group, and you get half the experience you would have gotten for killing the same **mob** solo."

MONSTER: *(synonym: mob)* A computer-controlled, antagonistic creature.

MULE: A secondary character added by a player mainly to carry things for the primary character.

"If your house hasn't been looted yet, it will be, so put everything you can in the bank and make **mule** characters carry the rest."

NERF: To make a power or weapon less potent or to fix a game bug or plug a loophole. Game developers nerf features that are throwing off the balance of elements in a game.

"Now all they have to do is add the code to **nerf** the Fame/Kill-Looter twinks, and I'll send them a check to cover my account for the next ten years."

NON-PLAYER CHARACTER OR NPC: A character controlled by the computer.

see also: player character or PC

PING: The speed with which a player's computer or console can communicate with the game server. "Low ping" indicates a rapid response from the server; "high ping" means a slow response, which can sometimes make it hard to play the game well.

see also: lag

"Trust me: when you get your cable modem and you experience just how much better online games are with a very low **ping**, you'll change your tune."

PLAYER CHARACTER OR PC: A character controlled by a human being (rather than by a computer).

see also: non-player character or NPC

PLAYER KILLING OR PK: Killing another player's character in a situation where that's not the object of the game.

see also: deathmatch or death match

REAL-TIME: In reference to a game, unfolding at the same rate as time passes in the real world, as opposed to allowing players to make decisions before game time proceeds.

see also: turn-based

"I haven't decided a lot yet, but it's basically a **real-time**, massively online, space war and commerce game."

SIM: A game designed to mimic conditions in real or imagined life; a simulation. Examples: a flight sim that presents an airplane cockpit, or an amusement park sim that requires business decisions.

SPAM: 1) To do or say something repeatedly, especially if it's annoying or lacking in imagination. 2) To distract other players with unwanted online chat during a game.

"Using it once or twice as a distraction is OK, but waypointing his base and **spamming** constantly is just sad."

SPAWN: (as a verb) For a game character or monster, to be created or emerge into the game. (as a noun) A monster that has recently emerged or that emerged as part of a group or stream of its type.

see also: spawn point

SPAWN POINT: A game location where characters or monsters regularly emerge.

see also: spawn, camp

TAUNT: 1) To send inflammatory messages to other players, especially during or just after a successful attack on that player. 2) To tease a monster in order to goad it into to attacking.

"The **taunt** message was 'your life sucked now your dead. your number #n' Why are teenagers so hopeless at grammar?"

TEAM KILL: To wound or kill an allied player's character in a game, whether accidentally or intentionally. Despite the use of the word "kill," the term does apply to nonfatal attacks.

TELEFRAG: To kill a character or monster in a game by teleporting into its location.

see also: frag

TRAIN: (as a noun) A group or series of monsters that is chasing a particular character in a game. (as a verb) To lead a group of monsters to another player's character in order to cause destruction.

"Well, all you could have done differently was shout '**train**!' to the zone. Hey, this is Everquest. Trains happen."

TURN-BASED: In reference to a game, waiting for a command from players before events proceed. The opposite of real-time.

see also: real-time

TWINK: (as a verb) To equip a new character in a game with help from a more powerful character. This makes the new character unusually powerful in comparison to the wimpy monsters she is likely to encounter at first. Twinking is more or less accepted in many games, although it's not standard practice. (as a noun) A character that has been twinked.

see also: cheat

"I want to buy gems with my high level toon and drop them to my **twink** so he can sell them."

Parapsychologists

★ ★ ★ ★ ★ ★

Parapsychologists study human abilities that aren't explained by conventional science, such as reading minds (telepathy), predicting the future (precognition), seeing things from a remote location (clairvoyance), hearing things at a remote location (clairaudience), and causing objects to move by thought alone (psychokinesis); these are often called "psi phenomena" or "psychic phenomena." Some parapsychologists also study life after death and spirits; terminology for those activities is covered in the section on mediums, channelers, and spiritualists on page 200.

According to a 1996 Gallup Poll, just under half of the general population in America believe that extrasensory perception (ESP) exists. While trained, reputable scientists who believe in ESP are not rare, there is a great deal of skepticism in the scientific community about the subject. This section doesn't address the validity of psychic phenomena, but simply documents the terms as parapsychologists use them.

RELATED SUBCULTURES:

Astrologers and Astrologists,
Mediums, Channelers,
and Spiritualists

★ ★ ★ ★ ★

ASTRAL BODY: *(synonyms: double, etheric body)* The spirit or soul of a person when separated and traveling away from the physical body, either in dreaming or during an out-of-body experience.

see also: out-of-body experience

> "Your **astral body** will start to take on the form, and that is your higher body, and you can move all over the world with it."

ASTRAL PROJECTION OR ASTRAL TRAVEL: *(synonym: out-of-body experience)* Travel by the spirit or soul outside the body.

AURA: A field of energy said to emanate from and surround a person, animal, or object. Auras display a variety of colors, varying from person to person, and are often interpreted by those said to have the ability to see them (usually considered clairvoyants) to reveal hidden information about the subject.

see also: Kirlian photography

BILOCATION: The state of being present or apparently present in two locations at once. One of the two copies of the person in question may be an apparition.

> "I have even been granted a unique level of **bilocation** ability, space-time bilocation, on Earth and other inhabited planets."

BIO-PSYCHOKINESIS OR BIO-PK: Use of psychic energy to affect a living thing directly.

see also: psychokinesis

CLAIRAUDIENCE: The phenomenon of hearing things not physically audible; receiving information paranormally in the form of perceived sound.

see also: clairvoyance

> "I am not restricted to a yes or no. If I choose to, I can open up my **clairaudience** enough to hear what [the visitor] says."

CLAIRVOYANCE: *(synonyms: remote viewing, second sight)* Perceiving people, things, or events through extrasensory means. Usually, but not always, implies that the clairvoyant receives a visual image or images.

see also: clairaudience, clairvoyant

CLAIRVOYANT: One who can perceive things by extrasensory

means. Can be used as a noun or an adjective.

see also: clairvoyance

CRYSTAL GAZING: *(synonym: scrying)* Looking into a crystal ball or reflective surface to perceive things by paranormal means.

DOUBLE: *(synonyms: astral body, etheric body)* A person's spirit or soul when it is temporarily traveling without the body.

DOWSING: An extrasensory means of locating things (often underground water sources or mineral deposits) through methods like holding a twig or rod and waiting for it to turn toward the ground, or by swinging a pendulum.

"I am a dowser, and as well as **dowsing** for water or metals I can dowse ley lines."

EMANATIONS: Types of radiation unknown to science that are said to come from the human body and to potentially be responsible for some psychic phenomena.

ETHERIC BODY: *(synonyms: astral body, double)* A person's spirit or soul when it is temporarily traveling without the body.

EXTRASENSORY PERCEPTION OR ESP: *(synonym: sixth sense)* Obtaining information about the past, present, or future with the use of psychic powers.

ESP is different from contact with the spirit world as performed by mediums in that no spiritual agent is involved. For more information on mediums, see the separate section on the subject.

KIRLIAN PHOTOGRAPHY: A photographic technology that uses electricity to capture an image that often includes an appearance of color or radiation around persons photographed. This effect is thought to be a visual record of a human aura.

"The stand on **Kirlian photography** is that it is coronal discharge. What I find interesting is that it reveals points of increased activity and 'upwellings' on the human body that exactly correspond with the acupuncture points."

MENTAL TELEPATHY: *(synonyms: telepathy, mind reading)* Direct, mind-to-mind communication.

MIND READING: *(synonyms: telepathy, mental telepathy)* Direct, mind-to-mind communication.

MUSCLE READING: Transfer of information from one mind to another through physical touch.

see also: *telepathy*

OUT-OF-BODY EXPERIENCE (OOBE OR OBE): *(synonym: astral projection or astral travel)* The phenomenon of the spirit or soul (the astral body) temporarily leaving the physical body. The astral and physical bodies are often said to be connected by a kind of spiritual tether called the "silver cord."

see also: *astral body*

> "I did once walk into the next room and view my brother playing a game of chess with a friend. This was an **OOBE** where I thought I was awake but was not."

PARAPSYCHOLOGY: The scientific study of psychic phenomena.

PRECOGNITION: A psychic knowledge of the future, a form of extrasensory perception.

PSI: A catch-all term for psychic phenomena, including abilities like extrasensory perception and telekinesis. Sometimes also considered to include channeling spirits; see the separate section on mediums, channelers, and spiritualists for more information on channeling.

PSYCHIC: (as an adjective) Having to do with paranormal phenomena, including extrasensory perception, bilocation, etc. (as a noun) A person with psychic abilities.

PSYCHOKINESIS OR PK: *(synonym: telekinesis)* Movement of objects solely through the use of the mind.

PSYCHOMETRY: The process of getting information from an object through psychic impressions.

REMOTE VIEWING: *(synonyms: clairvoyance, second sight)* Perception of visual information through psychic means.

RETROCOGNITION: Experience of a past event by a person who was not present at that event.

SCRYING: *(synonym: crystal gazing)* Looking into a crystal ball or a reflective surface (such as a mirror or pool of water) to receive images by extrasensory means. Scrying is a form of clairvoyance. Crystal balls and similar items are sometimes used as aids to focus a clairvoyant's energy.

see also: *clairvoyance*

"The techniques for **scrying** are many. My favorites (and the ones I have had some small measure of success with) are the bowl of black ink and the black crystal ball."

SECOND SIGHT: (*synonyms: clairvoyance, remote viewing*) Perception of visual information through psychic means.

SENSITIVE: A person with psychic abilities.

SIXTH SENSE: (*synonym: extrasensory perception or ESP*) An ability to gain information through psychic powers.

TELEKINESIS: (*synonyms: psychokinesis*) Movement of objects solely through the use of the mind.

TELEPATHY: (*synonyms: mental telepathy, mind reading*) Direct, mind-to-mind communication. Telepathy can either suggest a message broadcast to another person or information taken directly from another person's mind, with or without their involvement or consent.

Politicians and Politicos

Political slang is a heavily slanted set of terms, some of which pass into general use and become popular slang instead of terms used only by the politically astute. I've left well-known terms—"spin" and "think tank," for example—out of this section. Here you will find less widely embraced terms, as well as terms that are used within political organizations.

One type of terminology common in political campaigns—especially presidential campaigns—is that of categories for voters. While it may be simplistic to imagine that soccer moms share opinions on most issues, in recent years political campaigners and the media have created labels for an increasing number of these groups. Some currently in use include "angry white males," "the anxious class," "NASCAR dads," "security moms," "waitress moms," and "Wal-Mart clerks" (a broad term for religiously moderate, rural adults with limited education).

Because so many political terms are coined jokingly or to color a discussion, whether or not a particular term is derogatory is partly a matter of opinion. Yet it's clear that a lot of political terms are not very nice. Among the sixty-five subcultures in this book, politicians have a higher percentage of derogatory slang terms than any other group except the notoriously downbeat goths, beating out con men and incarcerated criminals. All things considered, almost any political slang term should be used with a certain amount of caution.

ACRONYM AGENCY: (*synonym: alphabet agency*) Any government agency known by its initials.

ACTORVIST: A politically active actor.

see also: politainer, raptivist

> "Clooney is an unreconstructed '**actorvist**' who'll defend any actor's right to make a political stink: 'I love anybody who sticks their neck out.'"

ADVANCE: Preparations for a visit by a political candidate.

ALPHABET AGENCY: (*synonym: acronym agency*) Any of the many government organizations known by a series of letters: the IRS, the CIA, the INS, etc.

AMEN CORNER: Any group of politicians that are consistent and predictable in their support of an issue or political figure.

(!) ASTROTURF: A political movement that is orchestrated by political players but intended to look like a spontaneous action by a large group of citizens.

see also: grass roots

> "Public relations firms are now warring with one another about who provides **AstroTurf** and who provides 'real' grass-roots organizing."

(!) ATTACK POLITICS: Day-to-day political operations or political campaigning that thrives on making accusations about political opponents. This is a derogatory term, not a political strategy per se.

BACK CHANNEL: A hidden or off-the-beaten-path approach to addressing a political problem.

> "**Back-channel** talks aim to clinch peace deal in two weeks."

(!) BAFFLEGAB: Speech or statements without clear meaning.

(!) BANANA: A derogatory term for someone opposed to a development project, or to development in general; it's an acronym for "build absolutely nothing anywhere near anyone."

(!) BARKING HEAD: A loud, opinionated political commentator.

"Bill's a triple-crown winner as a former bureaucrat, a propagandist, and a **barking head**."

BARNSTORM: To make a rapid series of brief campaign appearances in rural areas.

"He wasted no time after the election, hitting the road to **barnstorm** on the theme that there are too many lawsuits for too much money in too many courtrooms."

BEAUTY CONTEST: *(synonym: cattle show)* An appearance by multiple, competing candidates for one office.

(!) BIG GOVERNMENT: An implied accusation that a government is too expensive and/or obtrusive, or that its control is expanding. The term is usually used to characterize opponents in a political race.

BIG TENT: The basic elements of a political platform that attract and bind together different factions within the party.

BIGFOOT: (as a noun) A well-known media figure, usually an analyst or commentator, whose statements carry significant weight in politics. (as a verb) In reference to a media figure, to make an impact on a political campaign or other political process.

"You don't need to be a Big Politician, **Bigfoot** Journalist, Big Corporation or just plain Big Rich Guy to reach a salient number of your fellow citizens any more."

(!) BLEEDING HEART: A derogatory term for a person interested in social causes.

BOUNCE: (as a noun) A sudden increase in popular support for a political figure. (as a verb) To see such an increase in support.

(!) **BUBBA FACTOR:** The impact of blue-collar, white, Southern males on a given political issue.

BULLY PULPIT: A high political office that provides the opportunity to make public statements about a wide range of issues.

(!) **CAVE:** A joking, derogatory term for any group that opposes development or other changes in their area; an acronym for "Citizens Against Virtually Everything." Individuals may be called cave dwellers or cavies.

(!) **CATTLE SHOW:** (*synonym: beauty contest*) A campaign event where multiple candidates for a single office appear together.

> "I think the leadership conference will be the first major **cattle show** before the 2008 election, and it should be pretty much mandatory attendance for any candidate seeking election in 2008."

CLOTHESPIN VOTE: A vote made by citizens who see the candidate they're voting for as the least repugnant of a set of bad choices.

COATTAILS: The influence a popular political figure has in getting other politicians elected to office.

DARK HORSE: A candidate who unexpectedly emerges as the front runner in a field of candidates.

DEMICAN OR DEMOPUBLICRAT: (*synonym: Republicrat or Republocrat*) A Democrat said to be acting like a Republican, or vice-versa.

FENCE MENDING: For a politician, visiting one's home ground to shore up support after doing something unpopular.

(!) **FISHING EXPEDITION:** A political investigation with no clear goal except to unearth something damaging about a particular person or group.

(!) **GERRYMANDER:** To change the boundaries of voting districts so as to skew conditions in favor of a particular political party or group.

see also: kidnapping

> "A hardy perennial in Virginia politics is the ritualistic denunciation of **gerrymandering**. Sure, redistricting is unfair. But none of the alternatives looks any better."

GRASS ROOTS OR GRASSROOTS: 1) In reference to political action, driven by a group of citizens rather than by politicians, political candidates, or others in positions of power. 2) In reference to

a political campaign, appealing to people on a small scale and relying on supporters spread its message rather than using mass media or other highly public approaches.

see also: *AstroTurf*

HARD MONEY: Money donated to the campaign of a politician and limited by election law.

see also: *soft money.*

(!) HATCHET JOB: A carefully engineered attack that greatly damages the popularity or credibility of a political candidate. Can be derogatory.

INSIDE THE BELTWAY: Pertaining to the goings-on among Washington politicians. The Beltway is an interstate that encloses central Washington, D.C.

INVISIBLE PRIMARY: The period before an official primary, during which potential candidates raise money and garner support while jockeying for position.

JUNGLE PRIMARY: A type of primary election in which voters may cast a ballot in any primary they choose, regardless of their party affiliations.

KIDNAPPING: Changing voting district boundaries so that a politician's residence is moved outside his or her district.

see also: *gerrymander*

LAME DUCK: A politician who is still in office but who is either not eligible for another term or has already lost the election for the upcoming term.

LUNCH BUCKET: Having to do with working class issues.

> "It will take the intellectuals that debate the labor and societal issues to come down into reality and 'Joe **lunch bucket**' to quit worrying about only what is in his lunch bucket for there to be change."

MO: Momentum in a political campaign. "Big mo" is a large, beneficial effect for the campaign; "little mo" means a campaign that has bogged down.

(!) MOSSBACK: An old-fashioned, conservative politician.

(!) NIMBY: "Not In My Back Yard." Any political movement to keep a particular development or initiative out of the local area, for instance, to prevent a trash-burning plant from being built in a given neighborhood.

The term implies only opposition to the location of the project, not to the project in general. It is often derogatory.

PERSUADABLES: Potential voters who are not committed to any party or candidate and who may potentially be persuaded to support a different candidate at any time.

"The polls don't even agree on how many undecideds and '**persuadables**' there are in the country."

POLITAINER: A politician who originally became well-known as an entertainer. Not specifically derogatory.

see also: actorvist, raptivist

POLITICO: A person involved in politics or who spends a lot of time discussing politics.

PORK BARREL: In reference to legislation, not particularly in the interest of the public as a whole but benefiting a politician's voter base. Pork barrel legislation is intended to encourage support among the sponsoring politician's constituents.

PROTEST VOTE: A vote for a third-party candidate that stems not from enthusiasm for the candidate but from dissatisfaction with both the major parties.

see also: tactical voting

PUSH POLL: An activity that masquerades as a survey but is really intended to give survey-takers biased information about political candidates through slanted questions.

"This is obviously a '**push poll**,' where you call with a question such as, 'If Candidate X had once murdered someone, would it make you less likely to vote for her?' and thus plant a negative in the voter's mind."

RAPTIVIST: A politically active rap artist.

see also: politainer, actorvist

(!) RED-HEADED ESKIMO: 1) Legislation that benefits a very small group of people—in some cases, just one person. 2) A person benefiting from such legislation.

"There are very legitimate **red-headed Eskimos**, and they are few and far between."

- FORMER SPEAKER OF THE MARYLAND HOUSE CASPER R. TAYLOR, JR., QUOTED IN THE *Baltimore Sun*

(!) REPUBLICRAT OR REPUBLOCRAT: *(synonym: Demican or Demopublicrat)* 1) A politician of one of the two largest political parties who is said to act as though she or he were a member of the other party. Can be derogatory. 2) When used in the plural, can be an assertion that Democrats and Republicans are part of the same basic political mindset.

RUMP SESSION: A meeting on a subject not formally presented for discussion; for instance, to discuss issues within a faction of a political party.

"The nineteen-member opposition in the House protested loudly and held their own **rump session** just like what the new majority in the Senate did. They met in the lobby and used a rusty hammer for a gavel."

SLAPP: "Strategic Lawsuit Against Public Participation;" a lawsuit against a group or activist intended to scare off other groups or activists who might be interested in a particular issue.

(!) SHEEPLE: Any easily manipulated group of citizens.

"One of the keys to rebuilding public trust is to wake up the **sheeple** and convert them to critical thinkers."

SOFT MONEY: Money donated to a political party and not limited by election laws, but that can ultimately benefit specific candidates. The soft money loophole was theoretically closed in 2002, but some forms of soft money can still be said to exist.

see also: hard money

STRAW POLL: A simulated vote in which citizens are polled to predict the outcome of an election, or to gauge support for a political figure or initiative.

STUMP: To travel around campaigning personally in many localities.

TACTICAL VOTING: Voting for other reasons than to express a personal preference for the selected candidate. For example, a member of the Green Party might vote for a Democrat in hopes of preventing the Republican candidate from winning the election.

see also: protest vote

(!) TURKEY FARM: 1) A government organization or department filled with people hired because of their connections instead of their skills. 2) Any government organization that has more than its share of incompetent workers.

UGLY SEASON: The early stages of a political campaign, when multiple candidates from a single party may fight for a nomination or for popular support.

"Take cover; political **ugly season** is upon us, and the mud is being slung far and wide."

UNCONCEDE: To retract a concession speech; for example, if the final voters unexpectedly swing the election, or if a mistake is made in tallying the returns.

WASHINGTON READ: A quick look by a politician through a book or its index to find sections that refer to her- or himself.

WEDGE ISSUE: Any subject that causes a rift in an otherwise united group of voters, thereby lending strength to an opposing group.

WHIP: A politician appointed by a party to keep other party members united in support of the party's agenda.

WONK: An expert on a particular political subject, or a well-informed, studious person in general.

"He is a policy wonk generally devoid of the sort of Big Vision required to be a podium-pounding hectorer."

Prisoners

★ ★ ★ ★ ★ ★

One factor that differentiates prison slang is that prisoners live in an entirely separate world, one with different rules, roles, dynamics, economics, and physical barriers. While an adult in virtually any other subculture can decide to get a new job, or to travel, or to keep the light on for another hour, a prisoner's world is much more limited.

Prisoners use street slang, of course, but also have terms for people, experiences, and situations that don't occur in "the World" (as everything outside prison is called), such as drawing unwanted attention from guards, solitary confinement, and the manner in which a person lives out his or her sentence.

In the United States, over two million people are currently in state and federal prisons, more than in any other country in the world. The increasing number of incarcerations has led to serious prison overcrowding. Overcrowding has been blamed for a variety of problems in prisons, including an increased rate of suicide.

Many prison guards are wise to prison slang and sometimes speak it themselves.

★ ★ ★ ★ ★ ★

BE STOLE: To be hit by another prisoner without warning.

BEAN CHUTE OR BEAN SLOT: A slot in the door of a prison cell through which food can be passed and prisoners handcuffed.

BEEF: 1) A criminal charge. 2) A problem or complaint.

see also: bum beef

BIT: A short prison sentence.

see also: jolt

(!) BITCH UP: To act fearful or submissive.

see also: catch out, check in, turn out

BONE YARD: The place in a prison where prisoners have conjugal visits.

(!) BOSS: A correctional officer. Accepted as a respectful term; however, this word reputedly originated as a backwards acronym for "sorry son of a bitch."

BULL: *(synonym: five-oh)* A prison guard; a corrections officer.

see also: pig

BUM BEEF: An unfounded accusation or wrongful conviction.

see also: beef

CADILLAC: A job for prisoners that is considered desirable or easy.

CATCH OUT: To respond to fear by leaving the prison (in the case of a correctional officer) or going into protective custody (in the case of a prisoner).

see also: check in, bitch up

CELLIE: A cellmate.

CHAIN: (as a noun) A transfer to a different prison. (as a verb) To transfer to another prison.

CHECK IN: In reference to a prisoner, to go into protective custody.

see also: bitch up, catch out

CONVICT: *(synonym: lag)* This term has a specialized meaning among prisoners: A prisoner who can be relied on, has self-respect, and understands how to get along.

see also: inmate

D-SEG: *(synonyms: the hole, segregation or seg)* Disciplinary segregation; solitary confinement.

DECK: A pack of cigarettes, especially in the phrase "a deck of squares."

see also: square

(!) DING: A mentally ill prisoner.

DO YOUR OWN TIME: Serve your sentence with some dignity; stand up for yourself; don't get involved in anything stupid; don't disrespect other prisoners. "Do your own time" is standard advice to prisoners.

DOWN: In reference to a person, in prison.

DRY SNITCH: To draw attention to a fight or other illicit activity by being indiscrete, for instance, by talking where a corrections officer can hear or by gathering around a fight that might otherwise have gone unnoticed.

FISH: A newly incarcerated prisoner.

see also: inmate

FISHING LINE OR FISH LINE: A string or rope used to pull objects from one cell to another when guards aren't watching.

FIVE-OH: *(synonym:* bull*)* A corrections officer.

FIX UP: To give a prisoner extra food or special favors.

THE FREE WORLD: *(synonym: the World)* Normal life outside prison.

GATE: Release from prison.

see also: short

GATE MONEY: Money given to a prisoner on release, either from his own prison account or from the government if the prisoner doesn't have enough money. Usually a small amount.

GATE TIME: A point at which cell doors are opened for prisoners to come out or go back in.

(!) HACK: *(synonym:* pig*)* A corrections officer. Often derogatory.

HEAT WAVE: Constant attention from corrections officers toward a specific prisoner, making life difficult for other prisoners that associate with that person.

THE HOLE: *(synonyms:* D-seg*, segregation or seg)* Disciplinary segregation; solitary confinement.

HOME OR HOUSE: A prisoner's cell.

IN THE CAR: Part of a group, or involved in a plan or activity.

(!) INMATE: *(synonym: lop)* (This term has a specialized meaning among prisoners.) A prisoner who is unreliable or doesn't understand how to get along in prison.

see also: convict, fish

JACKET: 1) The file of information on a prisoner, including offenses, etc. 2) Information about or labeling of a particular prisoner by other prisoners.

JOHNNY OR JOHNNIE: A bag lunch.

JOLT: A long prison sentence.

see also: bit, lifer

JUMP OUT: To commit crimes.

KEISTER: (pronounced "KEE-stur") (as a verb) To hide something where the sun doesn't shine. (as a noun) The rectum.

KITE: 1) A message or letter sent between prisoners, often by fishing line. 2) A written request from a prisoner to prison officials.

LAG: *(synonym: convict)* An experienced prisoner.

LAY-IN: 1) Permission not to work on a particular day. 2) An appointment, for instance, with a prison dentist, which sometimes excuses the prisoner from working that day.

LIFER: A prisoner serving a life sentence.

see also: jolt

LOCKDOWN: A period of time during which prisoners are confined to their cells.

LOP: *(synonym: inmate)* A foolish or unreliable prisoner.

MULE: A person who smuggles contraband into a prison.

ON THE LEG: *(synonym: riding leg)* In reference to prisoners, friendly with correctional officers.

(!) PIG: *(synonym: hack)* A corrections officer. Often derogatory.

PRUNO: Alcohol made in a cell by fermenting juice in a hidden place.

(!) PUNK: 1) A homosexual. 2) A weak or vulnerable pisoner.

see also: turn out

RABBIT: A prisoner who plans an escape, or who has tried to escape already.

RACK: A prisoner's bunk.

RIDE: 1) To join in or be part of some activity. 2) To submit to another prisoner or provide favors in exchange for protection.

see also: turn out

RIDING LEG: *(synonym: on the leg)* Friendly with guards.

SALLYPORT: Any place where prison personnel enter the prison.

SEGREGATION OR SEG: (*synonyms: D-seg, the hole*) Disciplinary segregation; solitary confinement.

SHANK: An improvised, pointed weapon made by sharpening a hard object.

SHORT: In reference to a prisoner, getting close to his or her release date.

see also: gate

SLAM: 1) To forcibly restrain a prisoner. 2) To put a prisoner in segregation (solitary confinement).

see also: D-seg

SQUARE: A cigarette, especially in the phrase "a deck of squares."

see also: deck

STINGER: An electrical device used to heat water, sometimes improvised from lamp cords or similar items.

TACK: A tattoo.

TAILOR-MADE: A manufactured cigarette (as opposed to one the prisoner rolls).

TURN OUT: 1) To force another prisoner into a long-term submissive role. 2) To use anyone for one's own purposes.

see also: bitch up, punk, ride

WOLF TICKET: Aggression or shouting that is not backed up by a credible threat of force.

THE WORLD: (*synonym: the Free World*) Normal life outside prison.

Pro Wrestling Fans

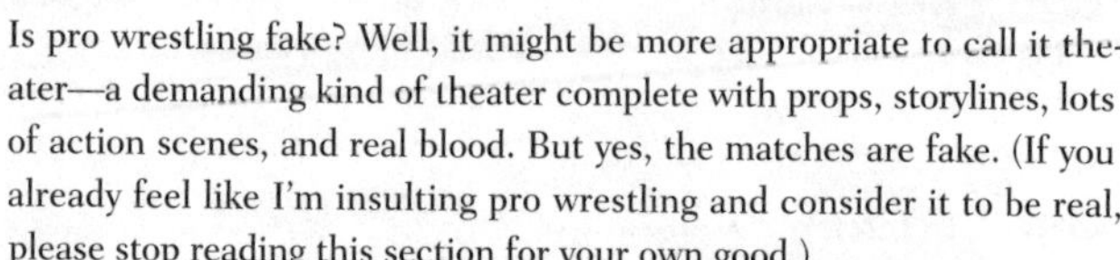

Is pro wrestling fake? Well, it might be more appropriate to call it theater—a demanding kind of theater complete with props, storylines, lots of action scenes, and real blood. But yes, the matches are fake. (If you already feel like I'm insulting pro wrestling and consider it to be real, please stop reading this section for your own good.)

Pro wrestling emerged in part from wrestling shows at carnivals, where presenting an exaggerated spectacle for the audience was the only intention, and deception was considered good showmanship. Some key terms used by pro wrestlers today come from the carnival; for instance, "mark" and (reputedly) "kayfabe."

Fights and rivalries between wrestlers, counterintuitively, require a good measure of cooperation. Since pro wrestling moves are not really intended to hurt or disable, the attacker and his or her opponent have to work together to give the appearance of a convincing blow. Many terms in pro wrestling slang (like "jobber," "feed," "do business," "sandbag," and "heavy") have to do with how well a person cooperates with an opponent in a fight.

Other pro wrestling terms have a lot to do with the trusty old story of good guy versus bad guy. Unlike team sports, for instance,

most of the audience is often on the side of one particular wrestler, the good guy: the babyface.

RELATED SUBCULTURES:

Carnival Workers

(!) ABORTION: A long-term storyline between wrestlers that is discontinued because it's not working. For instance, an energetic feud between two wrestlers may suddenly evaporate if fans aren't interested.

Because of the literal meaning of the word "abortion," some people find this term objectionable.

ANGLE: A storyline featuring wrestlers, often played out over a series of matches. Often two wrestlers are intent on causing each other's downfall.

see also: abortion, feud, turn, gimmick

A-SHOW: The wrestling match on a given night that involves the most popular wrestlers or that has the biggest draw.

see also: money match

BABYFACE: *(synonym: face)* A wrestler for whom the audience is intended to cheer; he or she comes across as a "good guy."

see also: tweener, heel, turn

> "If the past few weeks of WWE television are any indication, the WWE character that has portrayed a **babyface** for the longest consecutive period appears to be drifting toward the other side."

BLADE: *(synonym: geek)* For a wrestler to cut himself with a small, hidden blade in order to bleed during a match.

see also: color

> "I think enough people know they **blade** for it to be worthwhile, and even those who don't realize it's real blood will just act like the majority of fans and suspend disbelief."

BLOW OFF: (as a verb) To end a rivalry between two wrestlers. (as a noun) A big match during which long-term rivals fight, and one emerges the clear and final winner.

BLOW UP: To become exhausted during a match.

BOOKER: A person who handles a particular group of wrestlers, plans matches, scripts how feuds and other long-term storylines will play out, selects winners, and sets up events.

BOYS: Wrestlers.

BUMP: (as a verb) To fall after being hit or otherwise attacked and be out of action for a period of time. Both wrestlers and referees can bump. (as a noun) An instance of bumping.

> "Let's be honest, these **bumps** have a high 'gawk factor,' but is this really where you want wrestling to go in the future?"

BURY: To make a wrestler much less popular with fans, for instance, by requiring the wrestler to lose a series of matches.

see also: push

CANNED HEAT: Cheers, catcalls, chants, and other crowd noises that are piped into an arena or added to a taped match.

see also: heat

CARD: The series of matches planned during one night of wrestling.

CARRY: To put in extra work to make a match more exciting; to make a less skilled or less experienced opponent seem powerful.

see also: sandbag, do business, feed, sell, job

> "Anyone notice how Austin totally **carried** Benoit during their match on Smackdown?"

CHEAP HEAT: To generate angry enthusiasm from an audience by insulting or swearing at them.

see also: heat

> "Yeah, Lance Storm is all about the **cheap heat**, but it works and is entertaining, so what's the problem?"

CLOSET CHAMPION: A title-holding wrestler, generally one whom fans are intended to dislike, who is scripted to avoid fights and to do anything possible to prevent being defeated.

see also: the Deal

> "Mikey plays it to the hilt as he doesn't know what camera to look into and says how proud he is, will take on all comers, and won't be a **closet champion**."

COLOR: Blood during a match; the amount of blood that flows during a match.

see also: *blade, juice*

THE DEAL: *(synonym: strap)* A title belt.

DO BUSINESS: To cooperate with other wrestlers and with bookers to play out a storyline, no matter how that storyline makes the wrestler look; to act with professionalism.

see also: *sandbag, carry, feed, sell, good hand, job, jobber*

ENFORCER: A wrestler who will actually trounce other wrestlers if that is necessary to bring them into line for the booker or other person in charge. This pummeling is for real, not part of the show, and may not be apparent to fans as it's happening.

see also: *shoot, stretch*

FACE: *(synonym: babyface)* A wrestler who is a "good guy."

FEED: To make repeated attacks on one's opponent in order to be thrown down, with the intention of building fan enthusiasm for that opponent.

see also: *bump, carry, sandbag, do business, sell*

FEUD: *(synonyms: marriage, program)* A prolonged rivalry spanning multiple matches between individual wrestlers, or between two groups or teams of wrestlers. During the feud, both sides threaten and undermine each other repeatedly.

see also: *blow off, abortion, angle*

> "The longest **feud**, I think, is Carlos Colon and Abdullah the Butcher. It's gotta be over thirty years and *still* going."

GARBAGE WRESTLING: *(synonym: hardcore wrestling)* A type of pro wrestling in which weapons, props, foreign objects, interference, and blood are the primary draws.

see also: *gimmick*

GAS: Steroids.

see also: *juice*

GEEK: *(synonym: blade)* For a wrestler, to surreptitiously cut oneself during a match.

GIMMICK: 1) The character played by a wrestler, with specific, identifiable traits and persona. 2) An object brought into the ring to use as a weapon; for instance, a chair, especially if it has been specially

prepared to break easily. 3) To rig an object as a prop for a fight.

see also: garbage wrestling, turn

GO OVER: To win a fight or emerge looking good.

see also: put over

"Rumor has it he will start a feud with Vince McMahon to **go over**."

GOOD HAND: A wrestler who is easy to work with, including as an opponent.

see also: do business

HARDCORE WRESTLING: *(synonym: garbage wrestling)* A type of wrestling that uses props and interference instead of story to excite the audience.

HARD-WAY: In reference to a wound, accidental or inflicted by the other wrestler; not for show.

see also: blade, gimmick

HEAT: 1) A strong reaction from fans, whether positive or negative. 2) Real-world anger between wrestlers or others involved in wrestling.

see also: cheap heat, canned heat, pop

HEAVY: In reference to a wrestler, uncooperative in being lifted by his or her opponent.

see also: sandbag

HEEL: A "bad guy" wrestler.

see also: babyface, tweener, monster heel, turn

HOPE SPOT: A short period in a match when the "good guy" seems to finally be getting the better of the "bad guy." After the hope spot, the bad guy regains the upper hand.

see also: spot

"There was a **hope spot** here and there, but Roadie held the advantage for a few minutes."

JOB: (as a noun) Losing a match according to plan. (as a verb) To purposely lose a match.

see also: put over, do business, carry, jobber

JOBBER: A wrestler whose main purpose is to lose to other wrestlers, building their reputations.

see also: do business, carry, squash

"If he wrestles one more **jobber**, then I am going to denounce him for good!"

JUICE: 1) Blood. 2) Steroids.

see also: gas, color, blade

KAYFABE: (as a noun) The illusion that matches are real, especially

for fans who believe this. (as a verb) To make someone believe the matches are real.

see also: mark, smark

> "I've heard several guys reply along these lines: 'Well, we're really entertainers rather than competitors.' The interviewer is typically satisfied by this, and I think **kayfabe** basically has been broken."

LIGHT OR LIGHTLY: Giving the appearance of going easy on one's opponent.

see also: stiff

MANAGER: *(synonym: mouthpiece)* A performer who speaks for a wrestler who is not good with the public, and who acts the role of the wrestler's business manager. A manager may also interfere with fights or otherwise become involved in the wrestler's storyline, but usually does not make actual business decisions.

(!) MARK: A fan who believes that wrestling isn't staged and that matches are real contests where the participants genuinely strive to win. Neutral or mildly derogatory.

see also: mark out, smark, kayfabe, smart

> "While I'm not a Benoit **mark**, I do like him and respect what he can do in a ring."

MARK OUT: To know that a wrestling match is staged but to enjoy it as thought it were real.

see also: mark, smark, smart

MARRIAGE: *(synonyms: feud, program)* A long-term, staged rivalry between wrestlers.

MONEY MATCH: The non-title match on a particular night that provides the biggest draw for fans.

see also: A-show

MONSTER HEEL: A physically huge, seemingly unstoppable, "bad guy" wrestler, often scripted to lose in a final showdown with a "good guy" wrestler (babyface).

see also: heel

MOUTHPIECE: *(synonym: manager)* A performer who helps speak for a wrestler in public situations.

NO-SELL: A period during which a wrestler shrugs off attacks as though he or she has become invincible.

see also: sell, sandbag

OVER: Popular with fans.

PAPER: (as a noun) Free passes used to fill seats for a televised event. (as a verb) To give away free passes to an event.

POP: A sudden, loud reaction from the audience, whether positive or negative.

see also: *heat*

POPCORN MATCH: A low-excitement match immediately following intermission, used to give the audience more time to buy concessions and merchandise.

PROGRAM: (*synonyms: feud, marriage*) A long-term, staged rivalry between wrestlers.

PROMO: An interview with or speech by a wrestler or manager designed to get fans worked up about a feud, ongoing story (an angle), or an upcoming match.

PUSH: (as a verb) To promote a wrestler energetically at events, over television, etc. (as a noun) A promotional boost for a particular wrestler.

see also: *bury*

PUT OVER: To surreptitiously help one's opponent achieve a planned win in a fight.

see also: *go over, carry, do business, job*

> "He's **put over** Vader more than once; he's put over Flair; he's put over Jake Roberts; he's put over Rick Rude."

RECEIPT: Any act of staged revenge against a rival.

see also: *feud*

> "Early reports are that Meanie will return next week, so expect a **receipt** from JBL."

(!) RING RAT: 1) A woman who hangs around wrestling matches and does her best to hook up with wrestlers. 2) Any fan who hangs around and tries to befriend a wrestler.

RUN-IN: Interference in a match by a wrestler who's not supposed to be fighting in it, for instance, to help an allied wrestler.

SANDBAG: To shrug off a wrestling move from one's opponent when one is supposed to be playing along.

see also: *carry, do business, feed, sell, heavy*

SCREW JOB: A match won through cheating or interference, designed to make fans angry at the winner.

SELL: To act as though seriously affected by an opponent's staged wrestling move.

see also: no-sell, sandbag

SHOOT: (as a noun) A match or move in which a wrestler seriously attacks his or her opponent instead of sticking with staged moves. (as a verb) To do something real instead of something staged.

see also: stretch

SHOW LIGHT: To accidentally allow the audience to see the gap between a staged wrestling move and its intended target; for example, when a staged punch "lands" several inches away from an opponent's face.

see also: kayfabe

> "Abyss leveled Onyx with a high kick that **showed light**. Onyx sold it huge."

(!) SMARK: 1) A fan who believes he or she understands the truth of pro wrestling but who doesn't really know all of the facts. Can be derogatory in this sense. 2) A fan who understands that pro wrestling is staged but gets excited about it anyway, i.e., who marks out.

see also: smart, mark, mark out

SMART: Knowledgeable about how pro wrestling really works.

SPOT: A wrestling move, or several wrestling moves in a row.

see also: hope spot

SQUASH: A one-sided match, in which one wrestler completely dominates the other.

see also: jobber

STIFF: *(synonym: tight)* In reference to wrestling moves, unusually forceful; stronger than necessary. If done well, it can help the match appear more authentic. Also describes a wrestler with poor control over his or her moves who is hitting too forcefully.

see also: light

STRAP: *(synonym: the Deal)* A title belt.

STRETCH: To use legitimate wrestling holds to discipline or dominate an opponent.

see also: shoot, enforcer

SWERVE: 1) A public practical joke on a wrestler. 2) An unex-

pected turn of events in a wrestling storyline (an angle).

"Funny how no matter it looks like things will not change, someone always books a **swerve**, and I, the fan, end up getting screwed in the end."

TAP OUT: To concede by slapping the mat.

TIGHT: (*synonym: stiff*) With more force than usual.

TURN: For a wrestler, to change one's persona and gimmicks, often also changing from a "good guy" to a "bad guy" or vice-versa.

see also: babyface, heel, tweener

TWEENER: A wrestler whose persona straddles the line between a "good guy" and a "bad guy," either changing back and forth or combining elements of both types of characters.

see also: babyface, heel, turn

"Do you think he'll turn heel, or will he be a long term **tweener**?"

WORK: (as a noun) A staged outcome. (as a verb) To believably fight a staged match.

Prostitutes and Other Sex Workers

Sex workers are a group that includes prostitutes, exotic dancers, sex phone operators, strippers, and others. Since many of these services are illegal, sex workers are usually cautious about what they say in public, and many use slang terms for discussing services and pricing.

There is a movement among some sex workers to decriminalize prostitution, and those in this group often advocate more respectful language, for instance, using the word "client" instead of "John" (which can be considered derogatory), and "service" or "session" instead of "trick" (which can imply deceit). This group draws a distinction between the language they use and the terms law enforcement and outsiders may use when discussing prostitutes. Advocates of legalizing prostitution also tend to object to characterizing voluntary prostitution as victimization.

Other sex workers are neither politically active nor concerned about which prostitution-related terms they use.

A range of slang terms and online posting codes and abbreviations used by sex workers cover the gamut of sex acts. Those terms are readily available on the Internet and elsewhere but aren't detailed here, both because this book is not intended to be sexually explicit and because those terms are a kind of jargon, the sex worker equivalent of the names of different skydiving formations or stamp issues.

AGENCY: *(synonym: escort service)* A business that manages and books appointments for prostitutes.

BAR FINE: *(synonym: take-out fee)* Money paid up front to leave a location and have a session with a prostitute.

BAREBACK: *(synonyms: sunny, uncovered)* In reference to a sex act, performed without a condom.

BERET: *(synonyms: cover, raincoat, interpreter, glove, party hat, umbrella)* A condom.

BLUE PILL OR BLUE STEEL: Viagra, a drug used to encourage male arousal.

CALL GIRL OR CALL BOY: A prostitute whose services can be arranged through a phone call.
see also: hooker

CASH AND DASH: In reference to a dishonest prostitute, running off with the fee without providing a service.

CINDERELLA FELLA: A male prostitute.

(!) CLOCKWATCHER: A prostitute who rushes through the encounter and leaves as soon as possible. Often derogatory.

COMMERCIAL COMPANY: A prostitute, or time spent with a prostitute.

COVER: *(synonyms: beret, raincoat, interpreter, glove, party hat, umbrella)* A condom.

CUP OF COFFEE: *(synonym: shot on goal)* A sexual climax. The phrase is generally used in the context of an agreement with a sex worker, for example, when discussing how

many cups of coffee are included in a particular session.

DATE: 1) A period of time with a prostitute. 2) A client.

DONATION: Payment to a prostitute or other sex worker.

ESCORT: A prostitute. Although "escort" in the sex worker subculture means "prostitute," not all escorts are prostitutes.

see also: call girl, hooker

ESCORT SERVICE: *(synonym: agency)* A business that manages prostitutes.

FREELANCER: *(synonym: independent or indie)* A prostitute who books clients directly, that is, who isn't represented by a pimp or an agency.

FULL SERVICE OR FULL MEAL DEAL: A session that includes intercourse.

GIRLFRIEND EXPERIENCE: A session with a female sex worker that has something of the feeling of a non-commercial relationship.

see also: porn star experience

GLOVE: *(synonyms: cover, beret, raincoat, interpreter, party hat, umbrella)* A condom.

THE HOBBY: The practice of hiring prostitutes.

HOBBYIST: The client of a prostitute, especially someone who uses the services of prostitutes regularly.

see also: date

HOOKER: *(synonyms: pro, working girl)* A prostitute.

IN-CALL: Sexual services at the prostitute's location.

see also: out-call

INDEPENDENT OR INDIE: *(synonym: freelancer)* A prostitute who books his or her own clients.

INTERPRETER: *(synonyms: cover, beret, raincoat, glove, party hat, umbrella)* A condom.

JACK SHACK: An establishment where limited sexual services are provided; not full service.

(!) JOHN: A prostitute's male client. This term is sometimes considered derogatory.

(!) LOT LIZARD: A prostitute who offer services in parking lots at truck stops.

MILEAGE: Quality and quantity of service from a prostitute. To

say that a prostitute is "high mileage" is a compliment; it's a statement that she or he provides good service.

NOONER: 1) A lunchtime session with a prostitute. 2) A client who meets a prostitute at lunchtime.

OFF THE CLOCK: In reference to time or sex acts between a prostitute and a client, offered without expecting payment.

OUT-CALL: A session with a prostitute that takes place at a location provided by the client.

see also: in-call

PARTY HAT: *(synonyms: cover, beret, raincoat, interpreter, glove, umbrella)* A condom.

PORN STAR EXPERIENCE: A relatively impersonal session with a prostitute that is extremely gratifying for the client.

see also: girlfriend experience

PRO: *(synonyms: hooker, working girl)* A prostitute.

PROVIDER: *(synonym: sex worker)* Anyone who offers sexual services, including prostitutes, phone sex operators, exotic dancers, etc.

see also: hooker, call girl

RAINCOAT: *(synonyms: cover, beret, interpreter, glove, party hat, umbrella)* A condom.

SESSION: A period of time with a sex work provider.

SEX WORKER: *(synonym: provider)* A person who offers sexual services.

SHOT ON GOAL: *(synonym: cup of coffee)* A sexual climax.

STREET ACTION: Offering sexual services on the street, usually to potential clients who are driving by.

see also: stroll

STROLL: A place where a number of prostitutes offer their services on the street.

see also: street action

SUNNY: *(synonyms: bareback, uncovered)* In reference to a sex act, performed without a condom.

TAKE CARE OF BUSINESS: To pay a prostitute.

TAKE-OUT FEE: *(synonym: bar fine)* Money paid up front to leave a location and have a session with a prostitute.

(!) TRICK: 1) A sex act for hire. 2) A client of a prostitute. Sometimes considered derogatory.

TROLL: To walk through an area looking to hire a prostitute.

UMBRELLA: *(synonyms: cover, beret, raincoat, interpreter, glove, party hat)* A condom.

UNCOVERED: *(synonyms: bareback, sunny)* In reference to a sex act, performed without a condom.

(!) WHORE: A prostitute. This term is considered insulting by some prostitutes, but others seek to reclaim it and encourage its use, considering it a synonym for "courtesan" because it ultimately comes from a Proto-Indo-European word that meant something like "lover."

WORKING GIRL: *(synonyms: hooker, pro)* A prostitute.

Punk Rockers and Straight Edgers

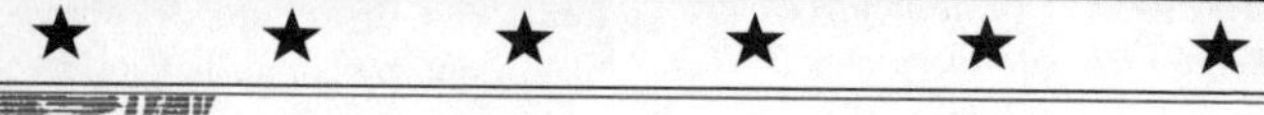

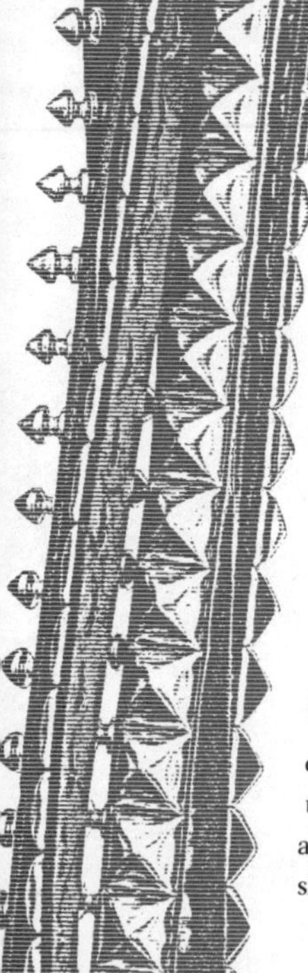

Punk rockers participate in a subculture based on rebellion and non-conformity, where emotional expression, often of anger, is considered appropriate and constructive. Punk culture places a high value on doing things for yourself; much of its literature and events are the work of fans. It may be this attitude of self-reliance that sometimes makes it unpleasant for punk rockers when a favorite band is signed to a major label and begins to be managed and commercialized like bands in other musical genres.

Within the punk scene, straight edgers unexpectedly combine the rebellion of punk with abstinence from drugs, alcohol, cigarettes, and casual sex. These guys are rebelling against society at the same time they're rebelling against rebellion.

The letter X looms large in straight edge culture. The first straight edgers who were of age to drink would voluntarily mark their hands with an X to mimic underage punk rockers who couldn't buy alcohol at shows, voluntarily removing their own ability to drink for the duration of the show. The letter is used in straight edge graphics and added to names of people and bands. Even the abbreviation of straight edge is not SE but sXe (pronounced "straight edge" or "ess ex ee").

CROWD SURF: To be lifted and passed around by the crowd at a punk show. Crowd surfers are sometimes accidentally dropped.

CRUST PUNK: A type of punk music that is loud, raw, and harsh.

DO IT YOURSELF OR DIY: A punk/rave habit of getting things done oneself. Applies to organizing events, putting out 'zines, and other activities, both having to do with music and with daily life.

While this term is common in mainstream culture, it has the special meaning here of a lifestyle or ethic.

EMO: Emotional punk rock, a type of punk music that varies in definition depending on whom you ask, but that is calmer or more melodic than most other types of punk music.

HARDCORE: A type of punk music that is loud, fast, and angry.

J-PUNK: Japanese punk rock.

MAINSTREAM: In reference to a punk band, having achieved widespread recognition and radio airplay. Going mainstream is sometimes viewed as a bad thing, if the original fans of the band find that the group has changed in becoming more popular.

> "They're like the most **mainstream** punk band I can think of and actually still consider punk."

MOSH PIT: An area at a punk show where punk rockers bang into each other (mosh), pogo, slam dance, etc.

see also: *moshing, pogo*

MOSHING: Banging into and shoving other members of the audience at a punk show.

see also: *pogo, mosh pit*

NEW SCHOOL: Newer types of punk music, as opposed to the original punk bands (old school bands). Punk rockers can become vehement in defense of either new school or old school.

see also: *old school*

OI!: 1) (interjection) An exclamation used to get a person's attention. 2) (noun) A working class style of punk music.

OLD SCHOOL: Punk rock in its original form.

see also: *new school*

"I don't like much **old school** hardcore punk anyway, so it's no surprise that I don't like NOFX old or new, for that matter."

POGO: A type of punk dance that mainly consists of bouncing up and down. It is related to slam dancing and other mosh pit activities.

see also: moshing, mosh pit

POP PUNK: Punk or punk-like music that appeals to teenagers and pop fans outside the punk realm.

PSYCHOBILLY: A type of music that combines punk rock with rockabilly. Draws some of its inspiration from low-budget horror movies.

PUNK: 1) A type of music that began in the 1970s as an emotionally loaded, energetic, loud, rebellious genre and has since evolved. 2) A mainly youth culture that listens to punk rock music and is based to some extent on a sense of discontent and non-conformity. Punk culture tends to be "in your face" in its styles and music, and in other respects.

RIOT GRRRL: A type of woman- and girl-oriented, hardcore punk music.

SKACORE OR SKA PUNK: A combination of ska—an upbeat, rhythmic type of music that originated in Jamaica in the 1950s—with punk rock music.

SKANKING: A type of ska and punk dancing in which arms and legs are thrown around rhythmically.

STAGE DIVE: To leap from the stage at a punk show into the audience, on the theory that people will catch you.

STRAIGHT EDGE OR SXE: A punk subculture; unlike most punk rockers, straight edgers avoid all drugs, alcohol, cigarettes, and casual sex.

TWEAK OR TWEAK OUT: To wildly express energy and excitement or anger.

"I'm just trying to play the devil's advocate here—don't **tweak out** on me."

Puppeteers

★ ★ ★ ★ ★ ★

Good puppeteers must master stagecraft, voice artistry, lip synch, and that strange combination of manipulation and acting that Jim Henson (of Muppet fame) called "wiggling the dollies:" That is, making puppets look like they're alive.

And if a puppeteer masters all of this, he or she can look forward to acclaimed performances, or, as one puppeteer put it, "a two-year-old's birthday party, when you're scheduled between the jumpy thing and the clown."

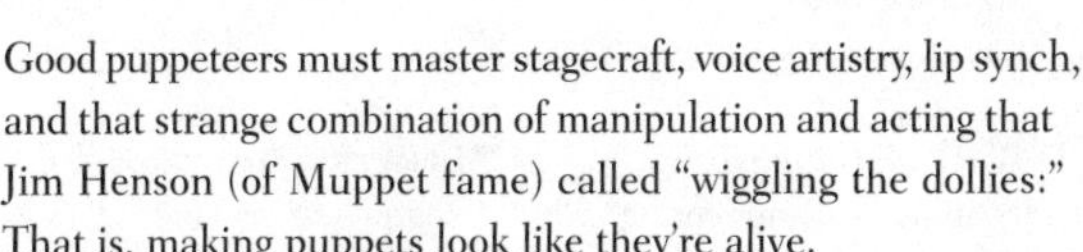

Puppeteers break the types of puppets down into five categories: rod, string, shadow, hand, and body. Rod puppets are moved by pushing or pulling rods, usually from below. String puppets are dangled from above; a common type of string puppet is the popular marionette. Shadow puppets are figures illuminated to throw larger shadows on a pale backdrop. Hand puppets are those that are operated by a hand inside the body of the puppet. Body puppets are puppets that are worn on the body.

Many puppets blur the lines between categories. For instance, shadow puppets may be articulated

★ ★ ★ ★ ★ ★

and operated with rods, and Jim Henson's famous Muppets combine hand and rod types.

Although in the United States puppet theater is popularly associated with children, many professional puppet plays have been produced specifically with adults in mind.

RELATED SUBCULTURE:

Thespians and Stage Crew

BLACKS: 1) Black clothing worn by puppeteers so as to disappear among the black cloth hangings around a puppet show stage. 2) Those selfsame black hangings.

> "Wearing our **blacks** out in public after performances sometimes engenders raised eyebrows and questioning looks. If asked why we're all wearing black, we'll often reply that we're either a) cat burglars, b) devil worshippers, or c) professional mourners."
>
> - PUPPETEER ANNE SCHAEFER

CONTROL OR CONTROLLER: The apparatus the puppeteer uses to control a puppet. The controller can be any of a wide variety of types, for instance rods or a wooden cross with strings.

CURTAIN OF LIGHT: *(synonym: light line)* A sharply-defined lighted area used in Czech black puppetry. The curtain of light prevents puppeteers (who are dressed head to toe in black velvet) from being seen even though there is no physical curtain to hide them.

see also: Czech black, Czech zone

CZECH BLACK: A form of puppetry in which no physical curtains are used to hide the puppeteers; rather, light is sharply focused on the puppetry stage and puppeteers lurk in the dark, wearing black clothing.

see also: curtain of light, Czech zone

CZECH ZONE: In Czech black puppetry, the dark area that hides the puppeteers.

see also: Czech black, curtain of light

DOLL: A puppet.

> "When he was boozed he used to start swearin' if he couldn't get the **dolls** up quick enough."

(!) DOLL WIGGLING: *(synonyms: dummy wagging, shaking the dollies, wiggling the dollies, wagging the dummies, shoving rubber)* A dismissive term puppeteers sometimes use to refer to puppeteering, either out of humility or in anticipation of a less-than-rewarding performance. Alternatively, can be derogatory.

> " After all, as [Jim Henson] was fond of saying, he had made a career out of '**wiggling the dollies**.'"
>
> - Chris Barry

(!) DUMMY WAGGING: *(synonyms: doll wiggling, shaking the dollies, wiggling the dollies, wagging the dummies, shoving rubber)* An unflattering term for puppeteering.

(!) FLAPPING: Doing a poor job of making the puppet lip sync, so that the illusion of talking fails.

see also: flip topping, fly catching, head bobbing

(!) FLIP TOPPING: Making a puppet talk by letting the top of the head go up rather than by letting the jaw go down; almost always considered bad puppetry.

see also: flapping, fly catching, head bobbing

(!) FLY CATCHING: Closing a puppet's mouth rather than opening it on each syllable, a practice that is considered amateurish.

see also: flapping, flip topping, head bobbing

FOCUS: The direction in which a puppet seems to be "looking."

see also: stargazing, magic triangle

HAND AND ROD: A type of puppet operated with a hand inside to work the mouth and rods outside to move the arms or other body parts. Most of Jim Henson's Muppets operate this way.

(!) HEAD BOBBING: Shaking the puppet's entire head on each syllable spoken.

see also: flapping, flip topping, fly catching

LIGHT LINE: *(synonym: curtain of light)* A sharply-defined, lighted area that helps hide puppeteers who are in the dark area surrounding it.

LIVE HANDS: *(synonym: practical hands)* A type of puppet that uses actual, human hands instead of remotely-operated puppet hands.

"I made a few **live hands** puppets like this over the years, and they were all done pretty much that way."

MAGIC TRIANGLE: The area defined by the puppet's eyes and nose as three corners of a triangle. The magic triangle determines where the puppet appears to be looking, i.e. its focus.

see also: focus

"It's important to remember that the so-called **'magic triangle'** is a three-dimensional one."

(!) MEAT ACTOR: A live actor. The term is used to contrast actors from puppeteers (who are sometimes known as "puppet actors") and is generally not meant to be derogatory, although it must be admitted that it's not necessarily popular with actors. Said to have originated with L. Frank Baum's *The Wizard of Oz*, in which the Cowardly Lion asks about Toto, "Is he made of tin, or stuffed?" and Dorothy answers that he's a "meat dog."

see also: meat theater

(!) MEAT THEATER: Live theater productions with live actors; used to differentiate from puppet theaters with puppeteers. While it's not generally meant to be a disparaging term, thespians tend to dislike it.

see also: meat actor

"Though we are a theatrical performance, there are certain things unique to our art form, which differentiate us from **'meat theater.'**"

MECH: (pronounced "MECK") Any device designed to help control a puppet.

see also: controller

PLAYBOARD: 1) A puppet stage 2) The shelf in front of a hand puppet or hand and rod puppet stage.

PRACTICAL HANDS: *(synonym: live hands)* A type of puppet that uses a puppeteer's hands as its own.

PUPPET ACTOR: A puppeteer.

see also: meat actor

SHAKE AND BAKE: Bad hand puppetry.

(!) SHAKING THE DOLLIES: *(synonyms: doll wiggling, dummy wagging, wiggling the dollies, wagging the dummies, shoving rubber)* An unflattering term for puppeteering.

SHOVING RUBBER: *(synonyms: doll wiggling, dummy wagging, shaking the dollies, wiggling the dollies, wagging the dummies)* An unflattering term for puppeteering.

STARGAZING: The impression given by a puppet whose gaze is directed too far up, either because the puppeteer is tired or because the puppet isn't well made.

see also: focus

TABLETOP: A type of performance in which the puppeteers are in full view but the audience focuses its attention on the puppet stage.

> "This is succinct but complete, and includes designs for several stages, ranging from a portable **tabletop** design to a full-size marionette stage with bridge and all."

TEA BAGGING: Dipping a marionette up and down across a stage so that it looks somewhat like it's walking.

(!) WAGGING THE DUMMIES: *(synonyms: doll wiggling, dummy wagging, shaking the dollies, wiggling the dollies, shoving rubber)* An unflattering term for puppeteering.

(!) WIGGLING THE DOLLIES: *(synonyms: doll wiggling, dummy wagging, shaking the dollies, wagging the dummies, shoving rubber)* An unflattering term for puppeteering.

Renaissance Fairegoers

Renaissance faires are creative re-creations, usually of Elizabethan English villages—or at least the fun parts. Elements of other nationalities and historical periods, especially the Middle Ages, often show up at faires as well, as does pure fantasy: hence fairy circles, the notorious privy monster, and the drinking of dragon piss.

Faire workers generally perform their duties in costume and use an approximation of period speech called Basic Faire Accent, or BFA. BFA incorporates some Elizabethan expressions, examples of which are included among the definitions below.

The Renaissance faire subculture overlaps with the Society for Creative Anachronism (SCA), whose vocabulary is on page 327. The main differences between a faire and an SCA event are: Faires are a rough re-creation of the Renaissance, whereas the SCA seeks to recreate elements of the Middle Ages; faires are done largely for patrons, while SCA events are primarily for members; and the SCA is much more heavily armed (period weapons are much more important at SCA events than at Renaissance faires).

RELATED SUBCULTURES:

Society for Creative Anachronism Members, Historical Reenactors

ACADEMY: A training session for performers before the faire.

ACTOR: *(synonyms: performer, participant)* A (usually costumed) faire employee or volunteer.

ANON: Goodbye, or later (Basic Faire Accent).

AROINT: Away (Basic Faire Accent).

AYE: *(synonym: yea)* Yes (Basic Faire Accent).

BACKSTAGE: Any area set aside for performers, where patrons aren't allowed. The backstage area is usually not behind an actual stage.

BASIC FAIRE ACCENT OR BFA: A rough approximation of Elizabethan English. This style of speech is widely used at Renaissance faires and more or less required of performers.

"What amazes me are the booths and vendors who don't do **BFA** at the small faires."

BAT SWEAT: *(synonym: dragon piss)* Lemonade or a similar drink mixed with salt. Drunk by performers during hot faires to prevent dehydration.

BELIKE: *(synonyms: perchance, mayhap)* Maybe (Basic Faire Accent).

BIT: *(synonym: gig)* A brief performance or sketch given by a performer to lend color to the faire.

"Some faires also use 'in sooth' to indicate that what I am saying really *is* true or important and not just part of a faire **bit**."

BOOTHIE: A person working at a faire in a booth selling merchandise, refreshments, etc.

see also: performer, hawker

BROADSHEET: A daily schedule of events at a faire.

see also: grid

CANNON: The cannon blast used to mark the beginning and end of the day at many faires. Events that occur after the faire has closed are said to happen "after cannon."

see also: opening gate, closing gate

CARBON CONDITION: An indication that something is on fire, intended to convey that information among faire workers without alarming the patrons.

"If you see a security problem—a drunk, a pickpocket, a **carbon condition**, etc.—find the nearest security person and report the situation."

CAST: Faire volunteers or employees who perform in entertainments.

see also: performer

CLOSING GATE: A show many faires hold outside the front gate at the end of each faire day.

see also: opening gate, cannon

DANE OR 'DANE: A visitor to the faire who is not in period clothing. Short for "mundane," but also, conveniently, a reference to a period-appropriate nationality.

see also: traveler, turkey

DRAGON PISS: (*synonym: bat sweat*) Lemonade with salt.

E'EN: Evening (Basic Faire Accent).

ENOW: Enough (Basic Faire Accent).

FAIRE BOOGERS: Nasal crud that accumulates over the course of a day of walking around raising dust at the faire.

> "The place tends to be rather dusty towards the end of summer (when it typically opens) so you end up with **faire boogers** if you spend more than about half a day there."

FAIRY RING: An attack by a group of people at a faire in which a couple is surrounded and must kiss each other to be released.

see also: hog tie

FESTIVAL: 1) The faire. 2) Faire management.

FIE: Darn! Dang! Rats! (Basic Faire Accent).

GARB: Period-appropriate (or at least period-inspired) Renaissance faire clothing.

GIG: (*synonym: bit*) A brief performance or sketch.

GRAMERCY: Thank you (Basic Faire Accent).

GRID: (as a noun) A daily, printed schedule for faire performers. (as a verb) To schedule a faire event.

see also: broadsheet

HAWKER: A faire worker who calls out to patrons to buy what he or she has to sell.

see also: boothie

HOG TIE: An event where a person is suddenly surrounded by a small group and must kiss each member to get out.

see also: fairy ring

IN SOOTH: (*synonym: verily*) Really (Basic Faire Accent).

IN VERY SOOTH: "I am really, really, completely serious." A statement made to distinguish real-life situations from faire performances, since faire performers generally stay in character at all times.

KISSING JOHN BARLEYCORN: Drunk.

MAYHAP: *(synonyms: belike, perchance)* Maybe (Basic Faire Accent).

MORROW: Day (Basic Faire Accent).

NAY: No (Basic Faire Accent).

OFT: Often (Basic Faire Accent).

OPENING GATE: A show given outside the front gate before the faire officially begins for the day.

see also: closing gate, cannon

PARTICIPANT: *(synonyms: performer, actor)* A (usually costumed) faire employee or volunteer.

PERCHANCE: *(synonyms: belike, mayhap)* Maybe (Basic Faire Accent).

PERFORMER: *(synonyms: actor, participant)* An employee or volunteer who plays a role, works a booth, or provides entertainment at the faire. The term applies as much to a ticket seller as to one who juggles in the street, since both are usually playing a role and wearing costumes.

see also: boothie, cast, playtron

PLAYTRON: A faire volunteer who uses faire garb and language.

see also: performer

PRAY OR PRITHEE: Please (Basic Faire Accent). Prithee is an abbreviated form of "I pray thee."

PRIVY: A bathroom or outhouse.

see also: privy monster

PRIVY MONSTER: An imaginary, horrible creature lurking in the privy at Renaissance faires. It gobbles up unwary children.

see also: privy

> "The **privy monster's** name is Harvey, and he's a real friendly sort at 3 A.M. after you've been drinking all night and stumbling around in the dark."

REN FAIRE: *(synonyms: Renaissance faire, ren fest)* A Renaissance faire.

REN FEST: *(synonyms: Renaissance faire, ren faire)* A Renaissance faire.

RENAISSANCE FAIRE: *(synonyms: ren fest, ren faire)* An event, usually held annually, that lasts for anything from one day to more

than a month; it re-creates a village inspired by life in the Renaissance, mainly by Elizabethan English towns. Its main goals are fun and entertainment rather than strict historical re-creation.

RENNIE OR RENNY: A person who works at one or more Renaissance faires, especially one who travels from faire to faire.

"When she found out that we were '**rennies**', she said 'but your hair is so clean!'"

SHIRE: A ren faire name for a real-life geographical area, used to avoid referring to modern cities, states, etc. For instance, the Newman College Renaissance Faire in Kansas occurs in the "Shire of Littlemore."

see also: village

STREET: Having to do with street performances at the faire.

TRAVELER: An uncostumed visitor to a faire; their modern clothing implies that they must be from a place far away.

see also: Dane

(!) TURKEY: A slightly derogatory term for a faire visitor, especially for one not in costume.

see also: Dane, traveler, turkey with dressing

(!) TURKEY WITH DRESSING: A slightly derogatory term for a costumed faire visitor.

see also: Dane, traveler, turkey

"I'm actually what is referred to as a '**turkey with dressing**.' I've never worked a faire, but I'm trying to build up an act."

VERILY: *(synonym: in sooth)* Really (Basic Faire Accent).

VILLAGE: The site of the faire. A faire village sometimes has a specific name, sometimes not.

WENCH: A young woman, especially an unattached one. Not considered derogatory among regular Renaissance fairegoers.

"Alas, fair **wench**! Your blithe comment has caused me to soil my knickers!"

WHEREFORE: Why or because (Basic Faire Accent).

YEA: *(synonym: aye)* Yes (Basic Faire Accent).

Rock Climbers

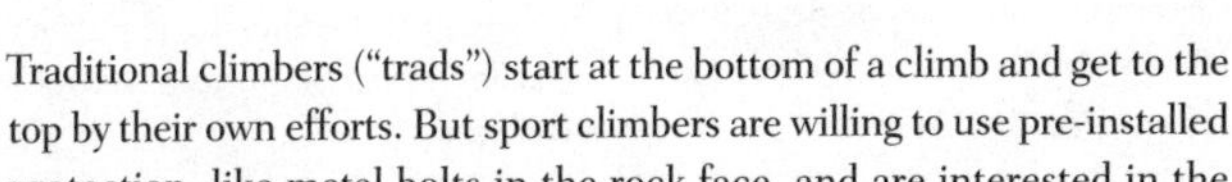

Traditional climbers ("trads") start at the bottom of a climb and get to the top by their own efforts. But sport climbers are willing to use pre-installed protection, like metal bolts in the rock face, and are interested in the style and energy of the ascent as much as in reaching the summit.

Trads sometimes look down on sport climbers because many sport climbers permanently alter the rock they're climbing, a practice that is not popular with many trads.

Among other types of rock climbing are bouldering, ice climbing, aid climbing (which includes most sport climbing), and indoor climbing.

The most common grading system for climbs in the U.S. is the Yosemite Decimal System (YDS), which always uses some species of a 5 for a "free climb." The number 5 in these ratings is followed by a period and a number. These numbers are whole numbers, so a 5.12 is much higher than a 5.2. The ratings are spoken as two separate numbers, for instance "five-twelve" for 5.12.

RELATED SUBCULTURES:

Cavers and Spelunkers, Hikers and Backpackers

ABSEIL: (pronounced "AB-syle") To walk or jump down a cliff face using a rope. This term is more common in Europe; rappel is used more frequently in the United States.

see also: rappel

> "We have just been out and spent a silly amount of money on new climbing and **abseil** ropes, as our old ones are now over five years old."

AID CLIMBING: *(synonym: artificial climbing)* Climbing with the help of pitons, bolts, or other hardware attached to the rock.

ALPINE START: A very early time for the start of a climb. Alpine starts are needed when climbers want to avoid dangerous melting of ice on high peaks and to return to camp by nightfall.

ANCHOR: (as a noun) A point where a climber's rope attaches securely. (as a verb) To fix a rope to an anchor.

see also: pro

APPROACH: The route taken to get to the climb; for instance, over flat terrain or easy slopes.

ARTIFICIAL CLIMBING: *(synonym: aid climbing)* Climbing with the help of hardware attached to the rock.

BARN DOOR: An accidental maneuver in which the climber's hold slips and the climber swings out from the face of the rock.

> "As I expect, laybacking is getting harder, and I begin to **barn-door** outwards."

BELAY: (as a verb) To hold the end of a safety rope for a climber in order to allow missed holds to be simply embarrassing rather than fatal. (as a noun) A safety rope setup.

A climber can be belayed from the ground or by another climber, making the ascent in turns.

BELAY MONKEY: *(synonym: belay slave)* A person who stays on the ground, anchoring the safety rope for a climber.

BELAY SLAVE: *(synonym: belay monkey)* Anyone who can be duped, bribed, coaxed, shamed, or flattered into staying on the ground to hold onto a safety rope while the climber makes the ascent and has a great time. Not particularly derogatory.

BETA: Advice or detailed data about a climb.

'BINER: (pronounced "BEE-nur") A carabiner, a clip used to attach a climber to a rope.

see also: carabiner

BOBPOINT: An ascent that never happened but that the climber believes she or he would have been able to do.

BOMBER: Anything of high quality; a fine specimen. Used especially in reference to an anchor.

BOMBPROOF: In reference to an anchor or other piece of protection, completely imperturbable.

see also: manky

BOOTY: Gear that is lost, forgotten, or abandoned by one climber, then found and appropriated by a different climber.

BOULDERING: Climbing over boulders, not usually high off the ground, without being belayed. Bouldering can be used as practice for roped climbs or as a sport in itself.

"I like the top roping there, but find the **bouldering** uninspiring."

BRAIN BUCKET: A helmet.

BUCKET: A generous handhold. This is a relative term: the easier the climb, the larger a hold would have to be to be considered a bucket.

see also: hold, jug

BUILDERING: Climbing a building.

BUMPER BELAY: 1) A distance between a parked vehicle and a climb that is so short, a safety rope for the climber could practically be run right from the vehicle. 2) Literally running a safety rope from a vehicle to a climber.

CAM: (as a noun) A metal device that can be collapsed and expanded at one end to wedge firmly into the rock; more broadly, anything that can be expanded into a crack. (as a verb) Inserting a foot sideways, then turning it flat to get a solid hold.

CARABINER: (pronounced "kare-uh-BEE-nur") A metal clip used by a climber to attach to safety ropes.

see also: 'biner

CHALK: Magnesium carbonate in a white powder, used to keep climbers' hands dry and aid in gripping the rock.

CHICKENHEAD: A knob of rock, usually found in granite.

CHIMNEY: (noun) A crack large enough to be climbed from the inside. (verb) To shimmy up a chimney.

CHOSS: Loose rock.

see also: choss pile

CHOSS PILE: A less-than-great climbing route; a route to be avoided.

see also: choss

CHUTE: A steep gully.

CLEAN: (as an adjective) In reference to climbing, done without use of gear. (as an adverb) Without use of gear. (as a verb) To remove gear from a climb as one passes, usually a job for the last climber.

CLIP IN: To connect to ropes, belays, or anchors with a carabiner.

CRANK: To pull hard on a hold or otherwise make a massive effort.

"So I'm seconding up and place my hand into this huge pipe hold and go to **crank** on it."

CRATER: *(synonym: deck)* To fall to the ground, usually from a great height.

see also: whipper, zipper, screamer

CRIMP: To get marks in one's skin from hanging off a rock.

see also: crimper

CRIMPER: A hold so small that using it leaves marks in the climber's fingers.

see also: crimp

"My head comes up and this 'ledge' was sloped at 45–50 degrees and the best hold I could feel was a super rounded **crimper**."

CRUX: The hardest part of a climb, whether the climber actually ascends it or not.

DEADPOINT: (as a noun) An upward lunge to a new hold, done while hanging on to other holds. (as a verb) To perform a deadpoint.

see also: dyno

DECK: *(synonym: crater)* To fall.

DIRT ME: A request to be lowered to the ground.

DOWNCLIMB: To climb down a cliff without hanging from a rope (because with a rope it would be rappelling).

see also: rappel

DYNO: An upward leap to a new hold.

see also: deadpoint

ELVIS: (as a noun) Uncontrolled shaking in the legs, from exhaustion, fear, or both. Also called Elvis leg. (as a verb) To experience an Elvis.

see also: sewing machine leg

"I've been **Elvissing** like crazy, got in a bit of gear, relaxed, and the shaking stopped like magic. My mental state affects how much I strain in a given position."

EXPOSURE: The situation of being located high off the ground with no real shelter to make one's position feel safe.

FIXED LINE OR FIXED ROPE: A rope left in place on a climb, temporarily or permanently, to allow the original climber to get easily up and down or to aid other climbers.

FLAMED: In a state of muscle exhaustion and unable to climb farther.

FLAPPER: A section of skin damaged in a climb and partly torn off.

see also: gobi

"Try your full weight on a match edge foothold in bare feet and you'll tear off a big **flapper**."

FLASH: To succeed in leading a climb one has never attempted before, with no embarrassing slip-ups, using information gained from scouting or other climbers.

see also: beta, onsight

FREE CLIMB: To climb without the help of ropes or other aids except as protection in case of a fall.

see also: free solo

FREE SOLO: To climb without any ropes or aids, even for protection.

see also: free climb

GLISSADE: (pronounced "glih-SAWD," "glee-SAWD," or "glih-SADE") A slide down an icy slope using an ice axe to slow, steer, and brake.

"I've talked to several people who've done it. One climbing ranger did the whole thing in a standing **glissade**!"

GOBI: (pronounced "GO-bee") A wound to the hand, sustained while climbing.

see also: flapper

GRIPPED: Frightened, tired, or both.

(!) GUMBY: A novice climber.

HAUL BAG: A big, heavy sack full of gear and supplies, carried on a climb.

HOLD: Any feature that can support a climber's hand or foot.

see also: bucket, jug

JAM: To cram a part of the body into a crack in the rock for use as a hold.

JUG: (as a noun) A generous hold. (as a verb) To use a specially designed device to climb a rope.

see also: hold, bucket

LEAD: (as a noun) The person who climbs first, setting anchors and finding the way. (as an adjective) The person in a group who climbs before the others and places protection along the way.

MANKY: Badly done, of poor quality, or nearly worthless. Used especially for poor protection on a cliff face.

see also: bombproof

"I looked down, realized that I was twenty-five feet off the ground and had forgotten to clip into the first piece—nothing stood between me and the deck but a single **manky** old piton sitting in the Zion sandstone."

OFF BELAY: A signal called out by a climber to a belayer to indicate that the climber is no longer depending on the safety rope.

see also: on belay

ON BELAY: A signal called out by the climber to the belayer to ensure the belayer is ready to handle the safety rope.

see also: off belay

ONSIGHT: (as a verb) To lead a climb successfully, without falling and without previous knowledge or experience of the climb. (Can also be used as a noun or adjective.)

see also: flash

PRO OR PROTECTION: Hardware placed on the rock face to hold ropes.

see also: anchor

PUMPED: In reference to parts of the body, especially the forearms, severely fatigued from climbing and not good for much until they recover.

RACK: The array of anchors and other protection carried by a climber.

RAPPEL: To descend a rock face with the use of a rope by walking or leaping.

see also: abseil

REDPOINT: (as a verb) To climb a rock face without aids, placing protection on the way for other climbers to use. (as a noun) A climb made without aids, placing protection on the way.

ROCK!: Exclamation. A warning, called out to inform people below that something—a piece of gear, a stone, etc.—is falling toward them at high speed.

RUNOUT: A section of a climb where no protection is in place.

SANDBAG: (as a noun) A climb described as being easier than it is. (as a verb) To describe a climb in terms that make it sound easier than it is.

SCREAMER: A long, horrifying fall. Generally used to refer to falls that were avoided.

see also: crater, whipper, zipper

"Oh, and there is nothing like taking a sevnty-five-foot **screamer** on marginal pro. It brings you closer to your maker."

SCUM OR SCUZ: To get a grip on the rock with a part of the body other than the hands or feet.

SEWING MACHINE LEG: *(synonym: Elvis)* Uncontrolled, shaking legs in a tired or panicked climber.

SLAB: A big, slanted rock surface that offers no decent holds.

SLOPER: A slanted place in the rock that can be called a hold only in the loosest sense.

SMEAR: To use friction against the bottom of a shoe in place of a proper hold.

SPORT CLIMBING: A type of climbing that combines energetic, athletic

movement with protection enabled by bolts mounted in the rock face.

TAKE!: *(synonym: tension!)* Exclamation meaning "Hold the rope tight!"

TENSION!: *(synonym: take!)* Exclamation. Called by a climber to a belayer to ask for the safety line to be pulled taut.

TRADITIONAL CLIMBING OR TRAD CLIMBING: A type of climbing in which the lead climber places nonpermanent protection as she or he proceeds rather than relying on permanent protection placed beforehand.

WHIPPER: A fall by the lead climber that results in being jerked in an arc by the safety rope.

see also: screamer, crater

"Bernie did take a huge **whipper**, which I unfortunately missed, breaking his leg. A few weeks later he hitchhiked to Mt. Whitney and made it up the mountaineer's route, leg cast and all."

WIRED: In reference to a climb, so well known that the climber can climb it perfectly.

ZIPPER: (as a noun) Protection that proves insufficient, popping out in sequence when a climber falls. (as a verb) For protection to pop out in sequence as a climber falls.

see also: whipper, screamer, crater

Role-Playing Gamers

Role-playing gamers gather to play out scenarios in worlds defined by various gaming systems, where typically all but one gamer play the part of one particular character each, and the remaining player (often called the game master) runs the event.

Much gaming plays out in present-tense narrative. "You come to the town. There's a tavern, an inn, a market, and an armorer's shop. What do you want to do?" the game master might ask.

"Let's go to the tavern and look for another fighter," a player would reply.

The amount of time and attention spent on role-playing proportionate to combat depends on the interests of the players. Some put great effort into playing meaningful characters, while others skip the touchy-feeling parts as much as possible and are interested only in fighting.

The game master dictates what is and is not allowed (generally, but not always adhering to the published rules of the game system), determines the outcomes of events, and plays the parts of any characters not associated with players.

Many role-playing games (RPGs) use multi-sided (polyhedral) dice that produce random numbers in a variety of ranges to help determine outcomes of combat, spells, encounters, etc. To refer to these types of dice, gamers usually use the letter "d" together with the highest number on the die. For instance, "d20" means a twenty-sided die, and

"2d6" means two six-sided dice rolled, their results then being added together. The most common dice are d4, d6 (the familiar cubic die), d8, d10, d12, d20, and less often, d100.

The RPG subculture arguably originated with a game called *Dungeons & Dragons* (often referred to as *D&D* or *AD&D*), which was first published in 1974. Several RPG slang terms originated with that game. For instance "save versus" is a *D&D* term used in situations like "save versus sleep spell" to describe an attempt to avoid being affected by something damaging (in this case, a sleep spell), but it has also come to be used in real life in phrases like "save versus having to go to Denise's piano recital."

A huge number of role-playing games have since been developed for a variety of subjects: space adventures, vampires, superheroes, sword and sorcery, and so on.

Many role-playing gamers also play related, non-role-playing games, such as collectible card games and wargames played with miniature metal figures.

RELATED SUBCULTURES:

Online Gamers, Sci-Fi and Fantasy Fans

BEER-AND-PRETZEL GAMING: Casual gaming, rather than intense and focused play.

> "Simple isn't always bad, though, because simple means **beer-and-pretzel gaming**, girls, and new blood."
>
> - FROM A REVIEW OF THE *Serenity* RPG ON TIMEWASTERSGUIDE.COM

BILBO THUMPER: A player obsessed with the work of J.R.R. Tolkien.

CAMPAIGN: A complete RPG storyline, generally with a particular goal for players to accomplish by the end.

> "I'm currently working on setting up a *Star Wars* RPG **campaign**, which I've decided to base on the *Aeneid*."

CAN I ROLL TO DISBELIEVE?: An expression of dismay when a favorite character is slaughtered, an important item destroyed, etc. From *Dungeons & Dragons*, in which characters can sometimes see through an illusion if they roll a high number on a die.

DUNGEON CRAWL: An episodic RPG adventure; a game that comprises a series of unrelated encounters with monsters, traps, or other dangers.

DUNGEON MASTER OR DM: *(synonym: game master, or GM)* The person who plans and referees an RPG.

FREE-FORM: A type of role-playing gaming that doesn't use a specific set of rules, sometimes played with dice and sometimes without.

GAME MASTER OR GM: *(synonym: dungeon master or DM)* The person in a role-playing game who plans the campaign, springs surprises, calculates outcomes, and plays all of the non-player parts.

GAMER: A person who plays role-playings games. Outside the RPG subculture, can mean computer gamers, etc.

see also: player

(!) GAMER CRACK: A derogatory (but at the same time oddly complimentary) term for the collectible card game *Magic, the Gathering*.

GAMING: Playing role-playing games. Outside the RPG subculture, this term can apply to other kinds of gaming.

GROGNARD: A veteran gamer, especially a wargamer, or a gamer who is meticulous, detail-oriented, and often critical of games other than his or her personal favorites.

> "They use the wrong size die for the superhuman roll. Any **grognard** knows it should be rolled with a d20, just like the strength itself."

HACK AND SLASH: A style of gaming that gets into bloody combat as soon as possible and doesn't spend much time on characters and setting.

HOUSE RULE: A rule made up or adopted by a game master, which trumps any official rule that may conflict with it.

LARP: "Live action role-playing." A style of gaming in which play-

ers act out parts of the game as it proceeds.

see also: tabletop gaming

MEAT SHIELD: *(synonym: sword sponge)* A strong character who is always the first into battle.

MIN-MAXER OR MINMAXER: *(synonym: munchkin)* A player who insists on playing unreasonably powerful characters.

MONTY HAULER: A game in which characters face weak opposition and gain disproportionate rewards; sometimes used to make characters more powerful quickly.

(!) MUNCHKIN: *(synonym: min-maxer or minmaxer)* A player who insists on having an unreasonably powerful character, or who builds a character that is very robust in some respects and very weak in others. This practice is frowned on by more serious gamers, and the term is derogatory.

PLAYER: A person who participates in a specific role-playing game. "Gamer" refers to someone who role-plays in general; "player" refers to a participant in a particular game.

see also: gamer

(!) RULES LAWYER: 1) A player who pushes the interpretations of rules to his or her own advantage. The term is derogatory in this context. 2) A player who knows the rules of the game in great detail. The phrase is usually not derogatory when used in this sense.

SAVE VERSUS: To try to avoid harm from a particular source. This term originated in *Dungeons & Dragons*, where a dangerous situation sometimes requires a die roll to see if a character is affected. It has grown to be real-world slang for real-world problems.

"Woohoo! I made my **save versus** Y2K!"

SPELLCASTER: In a fantasy role-playing game, any kind of character who can use magic.

SWORD SPONGE: *(synonym: meat shield)* A strong, robust character who wades into battle and absorbs most of the damage while more delicate characters use special powers in his or her wake.

"What sort of depth would you like to see with the henchman? Or is he just a **sword-sponge**, and you don't really care about him?"

TABLETOP GAMING: Any gaming that is done with dice, paper, and sometimes metal figures, as opposed to live action role playing (LARP).

TUNNEL OF FUN: An adventure in which the game master forces the characters into specific situations to follow a plot that she or he has planned.

(!) TWINK: To cheat or play counter to the spirit of a game in order to make one's character inappropriately powerful.

TWO-SIDED DIE: A coin, because it can be flipped to decide between two alternatives.

RV Owners

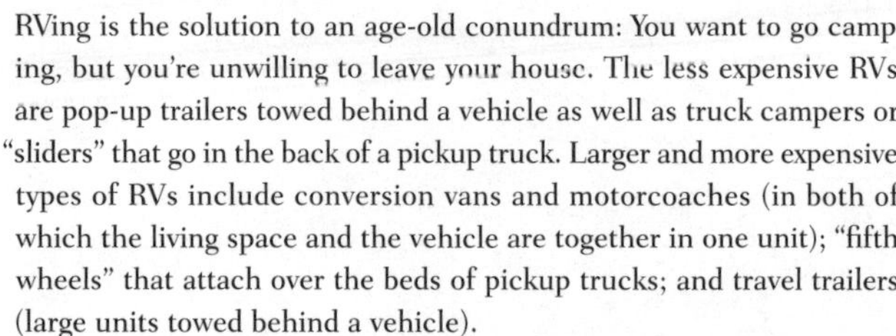

RVing is the solution to an age-old conundrum: You want to go camping, but you're unwilling to leave your house. The less expensive RVs are pop-up trailers towed behind a vehicle as well as truck campers or "sliders" that go in the back of a pickup truck. Larger and more expensive types of RVs include conversion vans and motorcoaches (in both of which the living space and the vehicle are together in one unit); "fifth wheels" that attach over the beds of pickup trucks; and travel trailers (large units towed behind a vehicle).

Some RVers travel only on weekends or vacations, but for others RVing is a lifestyle, whether that means settling down at an RV park for a full season or constantly traveling from one park to the next and living full-time in the vehicle.

RVs are usually called "caravans" in European English. In Australia, the term "RV" can mean what in America is called an "SUV" or "Sport Utility Vehicle."

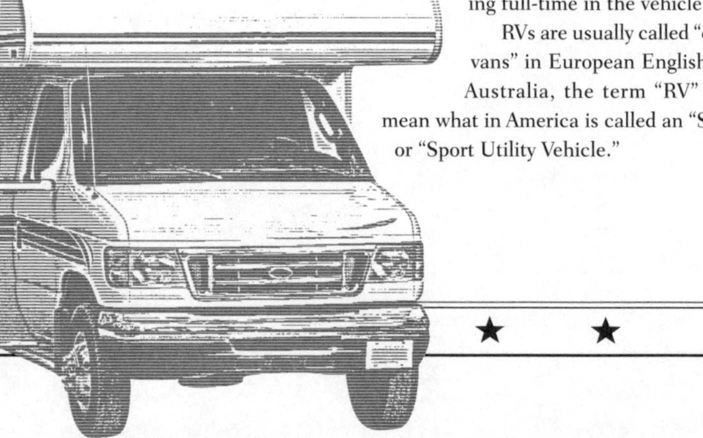

BASEMENT: A storage area beneath an RV's living space that is only accessible from outside the RV.

BLACK TANK: A tank that holds sewage (black water) until it can be emptied at a dump station.

see also: gray tank

BLACK WATER: Sewage from the RV's bathroom. Held in a black tank until emptied at an appropriate facility.

see also: gray water

> "I would also put heat tape all around the dump valve for the **black water** and keep it closed until over 3/4 full, then dump."

BOONDOCKING: *(synonyms: dry camping, primitive camping)* Camping with an RV in a place where there are no hookups for electricity, water, etc.

BUBBLE: A vague unit of measure describing how close to perfectly level an RV is; RVs are usually made to sit so that they aren't tilted when camping. Derived from carpenters' levels, which have a bubble that needs to line up in a particular position.

see also: leveling

CARAVAN: A group of RVs traveling together.

see also: tailgunner

CLASS A: A type of motorhome that consists of living space that's part of the vehicle itself. Larger than a van.

see also: class B, class C

CLASS B: A van that's been converted or customized into a motorhome.

see also: class A, class C

CLASS C: A motorhome where the living space is built onto the frame of a van.

see also: class A, class B

COACH: *(synonyms: motorhome, motorcoach)* A larger RV, especially a Class A.

DIESEL PULLER: A diesel RV with the engine in front.

see also: diesel pusher, puller

DIESEL PUSHER: A diesel RV with the engine in back.

see also: diesel puller, pusher

DINGHY: *(synonyms: toad or TOAD, towed)* A vehicle towed behind an RV.

DRY CAMPING: *(synonyms: boondocking, primitive camping)* RV camping without hookups.

DRY WEIGHT: The weight of an RV, not counting any passengers, cargo, fuel, water, waste, etc.

see also: wet weight

"I've seen several (Class A and C) where the **dry-weight** (measured at a scale, not what the builder said it was) exceeds the gross vehicle weight as specified by the frame's maker."

DUMP STATION: A place where wastewater tanks can be emptied, for a fee.

FROG: A towed vehicle. Short for "four rolling on ground."

see also: toad

FIFTH WHEEL OR FIFTH WHEEL TRAILER: *(synonym: fiver)* A large living space on wheels that fits over the back of a pickup or other truck.

see also: travel trailer

FIVER: *(synonym: fifth wheel or fifth wheel trailer)* A large living space trailer that fits over the back of a pickup truck.

FULL HOOKUP: 1) A campsite that offers water, sewer, and electricity hookups. Some campsites may use a less substantial definition of the term "full hookup" and not provide all three of these amenities, but this is a less common usage of the term. 2) An RV capable of using water, sewer, and electricity hookups.

"It will be forty **full hookups** to start with. Ten of them will be with good shade overlooking a forty-acre cove below the Tennessee river, four miles below Pickwick Dam."

FULL-TIMER: A person who lives primarily in an RV.

see also: part-timer

GENSET: An electric generator on an RV.

"I urge anyone thinking of using their RV **genset** for emergency house power to plan ahead and do what it takes to be *sure* you can't backfeed the incoming lines."

GRAY TANK: A tank that stores water used in sinks and showers until it can be emptied at a dump station.

see also: black tank, gray water

GRAY WATER: Used water from sinks and showers, stored in a gray tank.

see also: black water

LEVELING: Evening out the tilt of an RV so that the floor of the living space is level.

see also: bubble

MOTORCOACH: *(synonyms: motorhome, coach)* A larger RV, especially a Class A.

MOTORHOME: *(synonyms: motorcoach, coach)* An RV.

PARK MODEL: An RV that's meant to stay in one place for long periods of time, rather than to travel frequently.

"Or you can buy a lot with an established **park model**, maybe an Arizona room addition to expand the 400 square feet of a park model by another 200 to 300 square feet."

POP-OUT: *(synonym: slide-out)* Additional RV living space that pops out once the vehicle is parked.

PORPOISE: In an RV, to experience continuous up and down motion as the length of the RV goes over regular joints in a highway.

"Quietest engine of the three. 29.5 inch tires is the only option. Funny ... they call it a center console, but I blinked and missed it. **Porpoised** on rough roads."

PRIMITIVE CAMPING: *(synonyms: boondocking, dry camping)* RV camping without hookups.

PULLER: An RV with the engine in front.

see also: diesel puller, pusher

PULL-THROUGH: An RV campsite in which it's not necessary to back into a space, but instead it's possible to drive straight out when leaving.

PUSHER: An RV with the engine in back.

see also: puller, diesel pusher

SHORE POWER: Electricity delivered through wires, available to the RV through a plug. This is in contrast to the electricity an RV can generate with a generator, solar panels, etc.

SLIDE-IN: A living area that slides into the back of a pickup truck to transform the truck into a kind of small RV.

SLIDE-OUT: *(synonym: pop-out)* A section of an RV's living space that pops or slides out once the vehicle is parked.

see also: tip-out

TAILGUNNER: The RV at the end of a caravan of RVs, whose occupants are responsible for keeping an eye out for other RVs that might have dropped out or pulled over due to mechanical problems or other issues.

TIP-OUT: Extra living space that folds out from the RV when parked. These days, tip-outs have largely been replaced by slide-outs.

see also: slide-out

TOAD OR TOAD: *(synonyms: towed, dinghy)* A vehicle towed behind an RV. Sometimes said to stand for "towed on a dolly," but may simply be a whimsical spelling of "towed."

see also: FROG

TOWED: *(synonyms: toad or TOAD, dinghy)* A vehicle towed behind and RV.

TOY HAULER OR TOY BOX: Any large RV with substantial cargo space in back for small vehicles.

TRAVEL TRAILER: A living space that is towed entirely behind a truck.

see also: fifth wheel

WET WEIGHT: The weight of an RV when fuel, water, and waste tanks are full.

see also: dry weight

WORKAMPING: Performing services for an RV campground in exchange for a campsite and sometimes other benefits, such as cash payment.

Sci-Fi and Fantasy Fans

★ ★ ★ ★ ★ ★

Fans—or to use the preferred term, "fen"—of science fiction and fantasy television shows, books, and movies comprise an energetic and creative subculture that embraces strangeness. A given fan may have wide-ranging interests in all kinds of invented worlds, or an enthusiasm for—even an obsession with—a particular one.

Science fiction and fantasy subculture blurs into other subcultures at the edges. It's appropriate to call anime fans or furries or role-playing gamers separate subcultures, and each has a section in this book, but people from all of these subcultures can be found at the key social events of science fiction and fantasy fandom: conventions, or "cons."

Which is not to say that all fen attend cons. Other ways fen connect include fanzines (fan-produced magazines focusing on a particular area of interest), clubs and associations, and of course, the Internet.

RELATED SUBCULTURES:

Role-Playing Gamers, Furries, Anime and Manga Fans

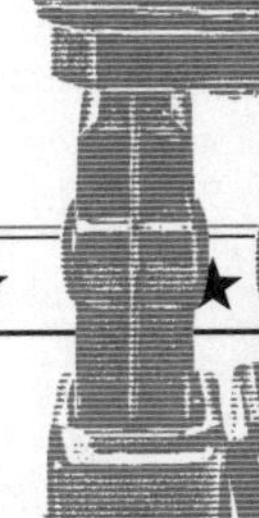

★ ★ ★ ★ ★ ★

APA: Amateur Press Alliance or Amateur Press Association 1) An organization where each person on a mailing list sends a contribution to the "Central Mailer," who collates and distributes the assembled material in an issue (or "ish"). 2) A publication produced by an APA; a collaborative fanzine.

"I ... was briefly in an **APA**, and I've had a couple of 'zines and contributed for others since then."

ANTHRO: *(synonym: furry)* People interested in anthropomorphic animal characters.

BADGE NAME: The name a con attendee is known by, shown on the attendee's badge. Often the wearer's real name; at other times, it may be an online handle, a nickname, the name of a character the wearer plays in a game, etc.

BETA: *(synonym: beta reader)* 1) (noun) A person who reads fan fiction to provide proofreading or critique. 2) (verb) To read an unfinished or unpolished fanfic. 3) (adjective) Unfinished; needing edits or feedback. 4. (noun) A fanfic that needs work.

"I need some **beta** readers for a new Batman fan fiction I'm working on."

BETA READER: *(synonym: beta)* A person who reads and responds to fan fiction.

BID PARTY: A party at a convention, hosted by a group that is lobbying to have its location chosen for a future con. This only applies to cons that move among cities from one year to the next, for instance, WorldCon, held in Toronto in 2003, Boston in 2004, and Glasgow in 2005.

CANON: Any information about a character from a movie, television show, book, etc., that comes directly from the original movie, show, or book, and is therefore indisputable. Contrast with fanon.

see also: fanon

"You'll be wasting your time trying to convince others that you possess the only true definition of Buffy **canon**."

CON: Short for "convention." A gathering of science fiction/fantasy/horror fans. These events are usually one weekend long and held annually. They may have a particular focus (anime, horror,

Star Trek), emphasize a particular medium (television and movies, literature, gaming), or include an annual awards ceremony for groups such as writers and fen. They may include contests, signings, dances, panel discussions, screenings, and other events. Con attendees are known as "members," except for those who are there to sign autographs, appear in panel discussions, etc., who are known as "guests."

see also: ConCom, ConOps, Relaxacon, Sercon

CON SUITE OR CONSUITE: *(synonym: hospitality suite)* A hotel suite where official parties for guests of a convention are held.

CONCOM: The "Convention Committee:" the group that organizes and presents a convention. Most ConCom members are responsible for some specific aspect of the con; for instance, the art show, or volunteering.

see also: ConOps

CONOPS: Administrative headquarters at a convention, where con members can go for information and where con security and other operations are administered.

CONREP: A con member's written report about the convention.

(!) CRETIN CON: A convention run for profit by non-fans. Tends to be commercial and to exclude most of the events that fen associate with fan-run cons.

CROSSOVER: *(synonyms: x/o, xover or x-over)* Fan fiction that uses characters from more than one source (television show, movie, book, etc.).

Notations like "slash" and "crossover" are generally added in a header to a fanfic, which may contain other kinds of information, spoilers, and warnings; for instance, whether the death of a major character is involved.

DEAD DOG PARTY: A party held after the official end of a convention.

DRABBLE: A very short element of a fanfic: a bit of dialog, a brief scene, etc. Usually one hundred words or less.

"You mean you've never read a **drabble**?"

EGOSCAN: (as a verb) To look through a publication for material by or about yourself. (as a noun) The act of egoscanning.

F/F (FEMALE/FEMALE): *(synonym: femslash)* Fan fiction with lesbian sexual content.

see also: M/M (male/male), M/F (male/female), slash

FIAWOL: Acronym (sometimes pronounced "FEE-a-wall") for "fandom is a way of life." A declaration of fannish enthusiasm.

see also: FIJAGH

FIJAGH: Acronym (sometimes pronounced "FEE-jog" or "FEE-jag") for "fandom is just a goddamn hobby" (or "fandom is just a ghoddamn hobby;" see the entry for 'h' for an explanation), meant as a direct rebuttal of FIAWOL ("fandom is a way of life").

see also: FIAWOL

(!) FAAN OR FAAAN: (pronounced as though spoken by a sheep) A fan who focuses on the politics and goings-on of fandom instead of on actual books, movies, television shows, etc. Generally derogatory.

FAFIATE: A word based on the acronym for "forced away from it all." A fafiated fan is one who has had to withdraw from fandom against his or her inclinations. The withdrawal is called "fafiation."

see also: gafiate

"She's been **fafiated** for medical reasons for far too long."

FAN: (Plural: "fen," or occasionally, "fans"). A devoted follower of one or more science fiction or fantasy books, movies, television shows, or worlds who is involved in activities like cons or fanzines.

see also: fanac, fannish

FAN FICTION OR FANFICTION: *(synonym: fanfic)* Amateur fiction that uses characters and settings from popular science fiction and fantasy shows, books, and movies.

FANAC: Short for "fannish activity;" activity that stems from enthusiasm for science fiction- or fantasy-related books, television shows, movies, etc. Can include contributing to or editing a fanzine, organizing or attending cons, participating in Internet discussion groups, etc.

"I was raised in a fandom where the running joke was 'anything two fans do is **fanac**.'"

(!) FANBOY: *(synonym: fangirl)* A derogatory term for a person obsessed with fannish activity. "Fangirl" is less insulting than "fanboy" among some fen, and is sometimes an acceptable term for an enthusiastic female fan.

FANDOM: The science fiction and fantasy fan subculture and all of its activities, such as cons and fanzines. More broadly, any subculture with a similar enthusiasm for its topic as SF/fantasy fandom.

see also: fan, fanac, fannish

> "I always thought the final stage of comics **fandom** was that you only buy cheap reading copies of silver age Jimmy Olsen comics."

FANED: (pronounced "FAN-ed") Anyone who edits or publishes a fanzine and typically does all of the work, sometimes up to and including writing all of the material.

FANFIC: *(synonym: fan fiction or fanfiction)* Amateur fiction written by a fan in the world of a movie, television show, book, comic book, etc. Occasionally used to mean any amateur fiction written by a fan even if it is not based in a well-known fantasy or science fiction world, although many fans do not consider such a story a "fanfic" in the proper sense.

see also: crossover, slash

> "They basically look like two barrels with eyes, but they play a major role later in the **fanfic**."

FANGIRL: *(synonym: fanboy)* A female fan who is obsessed with fannish activity.

FANNISH: Having to do with fandom; done in the way that fans would do it.

FANON: "Facts" about the characters or worlds of particular science fiction or fantasy television shows, books, or movies that are not part of the source material, but rather originate in fan fiction. Contrast with canon.

For instance, that Kirk and Spock in the original *Star Trek* series are friends is canon. That they are in love is fanon

see also: canon

FANTASY: Fiction that involves magic, mythical creatures, or other imaginary elements that aren't based on science and are not considered horrific.

Subgenres include dark fantasy (which is grim or horrific), epic fantasy, sword and sorcery, fairy tales, and urban fantasy. This last term is often applied to fantasy in a modern setting whether urban or not.

see also: *science fiction, speculative fiction*

> "If you have people do some magic, impossible thing by stroking a talisman or praying to a tree, it's **fantasy**; if they do the same thing by pressing a button or climbing inside a machine, it's science fiction."
>
> - SCIENCE FICTION AND FANTASY AUTHOR ORSON SCOTT CARD

FANZINE OR 'ZINE: A science fiction or fantasy publication written and distributed on a small scale by fans. A fanzine may consist of fan fiction; articles or commentaries about books, movies, television shows, or pieces about fandom itself.

see also: *fanac, faned, beta*

FEGHOOT: *(synonym: shaggy dog story)* A science fiction or fantasy short story written for the sole purpose of concluding with a horrible pun.

> "That's not a pun; that's a **feghoot**."

(!) FEMMEFAN: This term is archaic and is considered offensive by many fans. It was used to refer to a female fan, especially an unusually attractive one. The plural is "femmefen."

FEMSLASH: *(synonym: F/F [female/female])* Fan fiction with lesbian sexual content.

see also: *slash*

FEN: Preferred plural of fan. See fan.

FILK: *(synonym: filksong)* A song with science-related, science fictional, or fantasy-related lyrics, usually set to the tune of a well-known folk song, but sometimes set to other pre-existing tunes or to original music. Often a parody or otherwise humorous.

FILKSONG: *(synonym: filk)* A song about fan-related topics.

FLARE: The group of people at a con who handle security, minor emergencies, and related matters.

see also: *ConCom*

FURRY: *(synonym: anthro)* Anthropomorphic animal characters, or people who have a fan interest

in them. See page 122 for more information on furry slang.

GAFIATE: From an acronym for "get away from it all," to gafiate is to quit fandom. This is in contrast to fafiation, a forced removal from fandom.

see also: fafiate

GEN: Fan fiction that either has no sexual content ("for general audiences") or strictly heterosexual content. An alternative word for this latter is het.

see also: slash

GROK: To completely understand, integrate, encompass, or internalize. The word comes from Robert Heinlein's popular science fiction novel *Stranger in a Strange Land*.

> "The idea of a culture with no law but basic decency to one's fellows was appealing, but I didn't really **grok** it at the time."

H: The letter 'h' is sometimes added to a word to give it a fannish flavor. The two most common examples are "bheer" and "Ghod." Considered archaic in some corners of fandom.

H/C: *(synonym: hurt/comfort)* A type of fan fiction that focuses on a character in pain.

HALL COSTUME: A fan costume that can be worn comfortably for a long period of time. By contrast, some costumes at cons are elaborate, uncomfortable, difficult to remove, delicate, or pointy.

HEADER OR HEADER INFO: An introduction to a fanfic that specifies the show, movie, or book from which it originates and warns potential readers about elements that may be disturbing; e.g., sex, pain, etc.

see also: hurt/comfort, slash, crossover

HET: *(synonym: M/F [male/female])* Fan fiction that includes heterosexual erotica.

HOSPITALITY SUITE: *(synonym: con suite or consuite)* The location of official parties at a con.

HURT/COMFORT: *(synonym: h/c)* A popular type of fan fiction in which the pain of a major character is central to the story.

see also: fanfic

ILLO: An illustration.

"This is another preliminary sketch for a fanzine **illo**."

LETTER OF COMMENT: *(synonym: LoC)* A letter written to a fan magazine.

LETTERHACK: A fan who writes many letters of comment to fanzines.

LOC: *(synonym: letter of comment)* (sometimes spelled out; sometimes pronounced "LOCK.") A letter written to a fanzine about material printed in a previous issue. Many fanzines accept LoCs as payment for a subscription.

see also: letterhack

M/F (MALE/FEMALE): *(synonym: het)* Fan fiction that includes heterosexual erotica.

see also: M/M (male/male), F/F (female/female), slash

M/M (MALE/MALE): Fan fiction that includes male homosexual erotica.

see also: F/F (female/female), M/F (male/female), slash

(!) MARY SUE: A character who is meant to stand in fictionally for the author of a story, and who is often perfect and admirable. Usually female; there is not a widely-used male equivalent, although terms like "Marty Sue" and "Harry Sue" are sometimes used. Can be meant to disparage a character or author.

"Here is my **Mary Sue** test for ThunderCat fanfiction."

MEDIA CON: A convention dedicated to a particular book, movie, or television show.

see also: con

MEDIAFAN: A fan devoted to certain science fiction and fantasy movies or television shows, as contrasted with (for instance), gamers, fans of written SF and fantasy, comic fans, etc.

MINAC: The minimum amount required from a fan, usually in terms of number of pages of material written, to maintain membership in a fan group, especially an Amateur Press Association.

see also: fanac

"It didn't matter if you were more active in club or convention fandom as long as you kept up **minac** in fanzine fandom."

(!) MUNDANE: A person who is not a fan. As an adjective, having to do with things other than fandom. Can be considered insulting.

"A **mundane** hearing it wouldn't see any connection, even one who did know about fandom."

NEO: *(synonym: neofan)* A person who is new to fandom.

NEOFAN: *(synonym: neo)* A person who has only recently become a fan or who is attending a convention for the first time. As in other walks of life, sometimes called a "newbie."

PEACE BOND: To tie down or otherwise secure a potentially dangerous costume weapon, preventing others from drawing it.

see also: flare

"Weapons purchased on site will be **peace bonded** by the seller."

PERSONAL 'ZINE: *(synonym: perzine)* A one-person fan magazine.

PERZINE: *(synonym: personal 'zine)* A fanzine written entirely by a single person.

REAL PEOPLE FICTION: *(synonym: RL [real life] fiction)* Fan fiction about an actor or actress who plays a favorite character in a fantasy or science fiction TV show or film. May imply that the person is depicted taking part in sex acts (especially if called "real person slash" or "RPS"). Widely considered inappropriate, especially in its "slash" form.

see also: slash

REAL PERSON SLASH OR RPS: Fan fiction that is about an actor or actress who plays a favorite character on a science fiction or fantasy show and that involves sex.

see also: slash, real people fiction

"There's a lot of stuff that I'll consider slash that nevertheless doesn't interest me, such as **real person slash** or creating crossovers between TV shows just to get two attractive guys together, with no other plot necessity."

- Beth Friedman

RELAXACON OR RELAXICON: A party-centric convention for science fiction and fantasy fen, generally with few planned events.

see also: con

RL (REAL LIFE) FICTION: *(synonym: real people fiction)* Fan fiction about an actor or actress who plays a favorite character.

SMOF: Secret Master of Fandom. A person experienced and skilled in running science fiction conventions and/or in fan-related politics. Generally pronounced "smoff."

see also: con, ConCom

"You know, you could have your **SMOF** credentials revoked for revealing your secret plan."

SCIENCE FICTION OR SF: *(synonym: sci-fi or scifi)* When used in the narrow sense, "science fiction" refers to stories set in the future; in a scientifically-postulated, distant location (e.g., another planet, another universe); or in the present but including some scientific invention, discovery, or event.

More broadly, science fiction refers to futuristic or science-related fiction whether or not the setting has been extrapolated from science.

Even more broadly, any kind of speculative fiction, including fantasy, alternate history, and even sometimes horror.

Subgenres of science fiction include hard SF (with strong science elements), soft SF (either not strongly based on science or based on the so-called "soft" sciences, e.g. psychology), military SF, cyberpunk, steampunk, space opera, etc.

Variations of the term are sometimes used to denote more serious-minded ("SF") or less serious-minded ("sci-fi") science fiction. "SF/F" is short for "science fiction and/or fantasy," roughly equivalent to the term "speculative fiction." It is definitely not to be confused with F/F, which is something else entirely, although F/F is generally SF/F.

The variations on the term have spawned their own derivative words, such as "skiffy" (a phonetic pronunciation of "sci-fi" that is rarely written) and SFnal (pronounced "science fictional").

There is no universally-accepted definition of "science fiction": some camps emphasize marketing category; others emphasize content; others emphasize the feel or setting of the piece.

see also: speculative fiction

SCIENTIFICTION: An alternative, largely outdated term for science fiction.

SCI-FI OR SCIFI: (*synonym: science fiction or SF*) Fiction that involves science, new technology, space, or the future.

SECRET MASTER OF FANDOM: (*synonym: SMOF*) A person experienced in running fan-related events.

SERCON: A science fiction convention held to discuss speculative fiction as literature. Sercons generally don't include dances, masquerades, etc., but focus on discussions and panels.

see also: con, media con

SHAGGY DOG STORY: (*synonym: feghoot*) A story written to deliver a pun.

SKIFFY: A phonetic pronunciation of "SciFi," short for science fiction.

SLAN: A type of superbeing from the work of science fiction writer A. E. Van Vogt, from which comes a slogan: "fans are slans."

see also: slan shack

SLAN SHACK: A house shared by fen.

see also: slan

SLASH: Fanfic that contains or implies sex between two characters, usually homosexual. "F/F" means two females, "M/F" or "het" means a male and a female, and "M/M" means two males. Not always explicit. Sometimes lower-case letters are used to distinguish younger characters, and sometimes upper- and lower-case are used interchangeably.

Information like "slash" and "crossover" is generally added in a header to a fanfic. The header may contain spoilers, warnings, and other kinds of information; for instance, whether the death of major characters is involved.

see also: crossover, F/F (female/female), M/M (male/male), M/F (male/female)

(!) SPACE OPERA: A type of science fiction that features dashing heroes and highly dramatic situations. Can be derogatory. Much pulp era science fiction is considered space opera, as is some science fiction being published today.

SPECULATIVE FICTION: Any fiction that includes elements that are not realistic in our own world. Includes science fiction, fantasy,

alternate history, horror, magical realism, etc. Along with other non-mainstream types of fiction, such as romance and mystery, speculative fiction is a type of "genre fiction."

see also: science fiction

SQUICK: (as a noun) Anything in fan fiction that might offend or disturb some readers, including sexual content, excessive violence, death of a main character, etc. (as a verb) To disturb or put off a fan fiction reader.

see also: slash, header info

> "A lot of it I either don't believe or it makes me **squick**."

TREK: *Star Trek*, the popular television, movie, and book series. Different *Star Trek* series are referred to by their initials: TOS for the original series, ST:NG or TNG for *Star Trek: The Next Generation*, etc.

see also: Trekker

(!) TREKKER AND TREKKIE: A fan of *Star Trek* television shows, books, and movies. "Trekker" is usually considered more polite, whereas "Trekkie" is often considered derogatory. Some fans, however, consider "Trekker" pretentious and prefer the term "Trekkie."

Occasionally the terms are used to distinguish fans of the original *Star Trek* series from fans who prefer the later spin-off series; however, most fans don't recognize this to be the case, so it's probably useful to use this distinction only if you want to start an argument.

see also: Trek

TRUFAN: A person for whom fandom is a way of life and a principal concern.

see also: fan, mediafan, FIAWOL

TUCKERIZE: To name characters in a story after friends and acquaintances. Arises from the work of William Tucker, a venerable science fiction writer who was fond of this practice.

see also: fanfic

> "I may **Tuckerize** my mother-in-law."

XOVER OR X-OVER OR X/O: (*synonym: crossover*) Fan fiction that combines characters from different shows, books, or movies.

Scuba Divers

★ ★ ★ ★ ★ ★

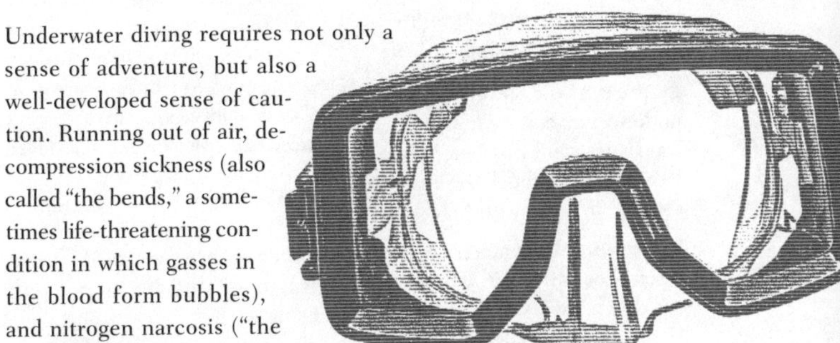

Underwater diving requires not only a sense of adventure, but also a well-developed sense of caution. Running out of air, decompression sickness (also called "the bends," a sometimes life-threatening condition in which gasses in the blood form bubbles), and nitrogen narcosis ("the wah-wahs") are only a few of the hazards of diving.

Not counting snorklers, there are two types of divers: Scuba divers, who use air tanks to stay underwater for long periods, and free divers, who stay under only for as long as they can hold their breath.

Scuba divers generally need to be trained to dive safely, since diving equipment is as dangerous as the underwater environment itself if not used properly. Diver training includes education about decompression and allowing the body to readjust to surface pressure, which is important to do properly to avoid the bends. Surfacing or decompressing too quickly, or even riding an airplane too soon after a dive, can cause the bends.

★ ★ ★ ★ ★ ★

AIR HOG: *(synonym: Hoover)* A diver who uses up his or her air supply quickly.

ARTIFICIAL SPIT: Little bottles of liquid used to keep scuba masks defogged; so called because real spit is often used for this purpose.

BACKSCATTER: Crud kicked up from the sea or lake floor by a diver, obscuring the view of other divers.

see also: silt-out, viz, Braille dive

BEAVER: A type of wetsuit jacket, no longer as common as it once was, with a tail-like flap in back that is pulled through the legs and secured in front with Velcro.

THE BENDS: Decompression sickness, a condition in which gasses that were dissolved in bodily tissues form bubbles in the body. Can be dangerous or fatal.

see also: bent

BENT: Having decompression sickness (the bends). Divers who surface too quickly can get bent. The bends can also occur when a diver flies in an airplane too soon after a dive.

see also: the bends

> "You can be in perfect condition, dive a perfect profile and you still have some risk of getting **bent**."

BOTTLE: *(synonym: cylinder)* An air tank for divers, generally called an air cylinder.

BOTTOM TIME: Time spent underwater (not necessarily at the bottom).

BOUNCE OR BOUNCE DIVE: A direct dive to maximum depth then a direct return to the surface; used to retrieve an item, assist a new diver, avoid having to go through decompression, or for recreation. Can be dangerous. Also can occur accidentally if a diver is not skilled at managing buoyancy.

> "It is my opinion that the only badge a deep **bounce dive** would earn me is one for stupidity, or one on a cemetery plot."

BRAILLE DIVE: A dive in murky conditions that blind the diver.

see also: viz, silt-out, backscatter

BUG: A lobster.

CALL A DIVE: To cancel a dive before it begins or to abort it early.

> "I **called the dive** and started the ascent with my 33 percent deco bottle."

CATTLE BOAT: A boat full of inexperienced divers.

C-CARD: A diver's certification card; proof of experience and training.

CHAMBER RIDE: A period of time in a decompression chamber, to avoid decompression sickness.

see also: bent

CHUM: *(synonym: feed the fish)* To vomit overboard. (Among commercial fishermen, chumming is throwing hacked-up fish and blood over the side to attract larger fishes.)

CYLINDER: *(synonym:* bottle*)* An air tank for divers.

DECO: (pronounced "DEE-co") Decompression.

see also: bent, chamber ride

DIVEMASTER: An experienced diver in charge of a dive.

DRIFT DIVE: A dive into an area with a current.

DRY SUIT: A watertight suit used in place of a wetsuit. Dry suits keep divers warm with a layer of air between skin and suit.

FEED THE FISH: *(synonym:* chum*)* To vomit overboard.

FREE DIVER: A diver who does not use an air cylinder, but instead holds her breath.

see also: bottle

GERRY LINE: *(synonym: granny line)* A line run underneath a boat.

GET WET: To go on a dive.

GRANNY LINE: *(synonym: gerry line)* A rope run beneath a boat for divers to follow to the anchor line.

"I've never seen anyone fin that fast either, and just getting to the down line would be tough without a **granny line** assist."

HOMEBREW: Gasses mixed and added to an air cylinder at home without professional equipment or training.

HOOVER: *(synonym: air hog)* A diver who uses up his air supply noticeably faster than other divers.

"After the first day, Michelle promised us we would be assigned a different group to avoid the **Hoover** and the lousy divemaster."

OFFGASSING OR OUTGASSING: For a diver, pausing during a return to the surface to let the body release nitrogen.

see also: bent, chamber ride, deco

PONY OR PONY CYLINDER: An extra, emergency air tank.

see also: bottle

RIDE THE HOOK: To jump from a boat while holding an anchor in order to descend easily.

SCUBA: "Self-contained, underwater breathing apparatus." The breathing equipment used by divers (except for free divers).

see also: bottle

SHOOT A BAG: To fill a specially designed bag with air from a tank while deep underwater in order to pull an object up to the surface.

SILT-OUT: A condition in which silt from the sea or lake floor is stirred up into an impenetrable murk, usually by a diver.

see also: backscatter, Braille dive, viz

SIX-PACK: A small boat that can carry up to six divers.

SKIN: A Lycra garment worn under a wetsuit to keep the diver warm.

SNOTTY: In reference to the weather at dive time, rough or problematic.

> "I dive a fair number of **snotty** days. 130 dives in Monterey last year. You can't do that and dive only the perfect days."

(!) STROKE: A diver who doesn't follow accepted safety practices for diving.

SURFACE INTERVAL: The time between two dive trips.

TOX: Oxygen toxicity; can occur, for instance, by diving deeper than appropriate based on the air mixture one is using.

> "This is a very good reason *not* to dive with different mixes. However, do not be overly concerned about being **toxed**."

UNDESERVED HIT: Decompression sickness striking a diver who followed all the usual safety procedures to avoid it.

see also: bent

> "There is always the risk of that **undeserved hit**. I met a student who flew three days after diving, and she ended up bent."

VIZ OR VIS: Underwater visibility.

see also: backscatter, Braille dive, silt-out

WAH-WAHS: Nitrogen narcosis, a state likened to the effect of being drunk; experienced by divers who go too deep.

> "Helium is *much* more forgiving than air. Why? If something goes wrong, you can fix it. If you are on air at deeper depths, you're too busy enjoying the **wah-wahs** and chasing mermaids."

Skateboarders

Skateboarding originated in the 1950s, primarily in California, and the earliest skateboarders were largely the same kinds of boys and young men who were interested in surfing. Although in recent years skateboarding has gained some popularity among people of different ages and backgrounds, the skating population still tends to be mostly male and white; according to *American Demographics,* only about a quarter of skateboarders are past their teen years.

There are four major types of skateboarding. Street skating is done in urban environments over terrain like streets, curbs, steps, and railings. Freestyle skating involves tricks performed on flat terrain. Vert skating takes place in skate parks and other locations where ramps, half pipes, and other obstacles are available, and is largely concerned with performing jumps and tricks. Downhill skateboarding is the sport of skating down steeply sloping streets.

Depending on background and other interests, skateboarders often use slang from other groups and subcultures, such as hip hop, snowboarding, and especially surfing.

RELATED SUBCULTURES:

Snowboarders, Surfers

AIR: 1) Time in which the skater is airborne after a jump. 2) The gap between a skateboard and the ground while it is airborne.

"Who were the goofy-footed doubles team that were known for their outrageous grinds and **air**?"

BANK: A smooth, sloped surface suitable for riding.

BOARD: *(synonym: deck)* The platform of a skateboard, not including the wheels and other hardware.

CARVE: To skate in curves.

"The skateboard I bought back in January has been a blast just to ride down the sidewalk and **carve** turns on."

DECK: *(synonym: board)* A skateboard platform.

DOWNHILL: A type of skateboarding done on steep hills.

see also: freestyle, vert skating, street

DROP IN: To push a skateboard over an edge and skate down a slanted surface.

FACE PLANT: A face-first crash.

FAKIE: In reference to riding a skateboard, backward. The skater faces in the normal direction, but the skateboard moves tail first.

"Once I got comfortable and busted out all my stock tricks, then busted them out again riding **fakie**, I proceeded to work on my hardest trick."

FOCUS: To break a skateboard deck in two.

FREESTYLE: A type of skateboarding involving tricks performed on flat ground.

see also: vert skating, downhill, street

(!) FRUIT BOOTER OR FRUIT-BOOTER: 1) A rollerblader. 2) A skateboarder who doesn't know what he or she is doing.

This is usually an insult, although it can occasionally be neutral when referring to a rollerblader.

see also: wood-pusher

GOOFY OR GOOFY FOOT: Riding a skateboard with the right foot forward, the opposite of regular.

see also: stance, switch stance

GRIND: To ride a skateboard on its trucks (the part on which the

wheels are mounted) along an edge or a narrow object.

> "Yeah, dude: **grind** in the middle of the mall. Everyone will think you're the most awesome guy on the planet."

(!) GROM: A beginning skateboarder. Mildly derogatory.

> "You're no better than some little twelve-year-old **grom** that can't see past the newer, technical side of skateboarding."

HALF PIPE: A ramp that curves up on both sides in a U-shape.

see also: vert skating, lip

HIP: A place where ramps join, or where an object comes to an edge.

see also: lip

JAM: A skateboarding gathering or contest. Often used for formal competitions.

see also: session

KICKER: A ramp designed to launch the skateboarder high into the air.

see also: air

KINK: A change in the angle of a handrail on a set of steps.

LIP: The top edge of a curved ramp.

see also: hip, half pipe

NOSE: The front of a skateboard.

see also: tail

REGULAR OR REGULAR FOOT: Riding a skateboard with the left foot forward.

see also: goofy, stance, switch stance

SESSION: A period of time spent skateboarding.

see also: jam

SET: A set of steps. Used with a number; e.g., "6-set" for six steps.

> "I would rather do things in a run, but I like big things, not technical: kickflip a gap, 360 flip after that, and then 180 a 6-**set**."

SKETCHY: In reference to a trick, poorly done.

SNAKE: To jump ahead in a queue; to preempt other skaters when using a particular object or area for skateboarding.

> "It's easy for [rollerbladers] to **snake** because they don't have to set up to drop in."

STANCE: The manner in which a skateboarder stands on a board: whether the left foot or the right foot is in front.

see also: regular, goofy, switch stance

STREET OR STREET SKATING: A style of skateboarding performed in an urban environment, in which skaters ride on streets, railings, steps, etc.

see also: freestyle, vert skating, downhill

SWITCH STANCE: For a skater, reversing his or her usual stance on the skateboard.

see also: goofy, regular, stance

TAIL: The back of a skateboard.

see also: nose

TECHNICAL: In reference to skateboarding or obstacles, complex and difficult.

TRANSITION: An incline or curve.

TWEAK: To change direction while riding a skateboard.

VERT SKATING: A type of skateboarding performed on ramps and other slanted, curved, and vertical surfaces.

see also: downhill, freestyle, street

WALL: A vertical or nearly-vertical bank in a curved skating environment, such as a half pipe.

(!) WOOD-PUSHER: A derogatory name for a skateboarder, used most often by rollerbladers. Not used much by skateboarders, but known in the skateboarding subculture.

see also: fruit booter

Skiers

The main varieties of snow skiing are alpine (also called downhill), which is the most popular type of slope skiing; cross-country, done on level or bumpy terrain; and Telemark, which is done primarily on slopes and incorporates some cross-country techniques into slope skiing. Telemark skis differ from alpine skis in that Telemark bindings leave the heel free to lift off the ski, as is the case with cross-country ski bindings. By contrast, alpine ski bindings hold the entire foot fast against the ski.

A newer type of skiing called skiboarding emerged in the mid-1990s. In it, short, wide skis are used without poles, creating an experience that is a cross between alpine skiing and snowboarding; it is also sometimes compared to rollerblading.

On ski slopes, a system of symbols tells skiers the level of difficulty of a slope. The standard set of symbols is green circle (easy), blue square (intermediate), black diamond (challenging), and double black diamond (expert).

RELATED SUBCULTURE:

Snowboarders

ALPINE SKIING: (*synonym: downhill skiing*) A type of slope skiing in which the ski boot is fixed to the binding so that the heel doesn't move. Alpine skiing is the most popular type of slope skiing.

see also: Telemark skiing, cross-country skiing

APRÈS-SKI: Night life that follows a day of skiing.

BASE: 1) The amount of stable snow on the ground. 2) The lodge at the bottom of a ski slope.

BREAKABLE CRUST: A type of snow characterized by a thin, icy layer over softer snow.

BUNNY SLOPE: A gentle slope for beginners.

CARVE: To turn sharply and neatly while skiing a slope.

> "Keep your weight in control so you're **carving** and not sliding the ski."

CATCH AIR: To jump off an obstacle and come entirely clear of the ground.

CROSS-COUNTRY SKIING OR XC SKIING: A type of skiing done on more or less level ground.

see also: alpine skiing, Telemark skiing

CRUD: Snow of mixed consistency.

CRUST: A partially melted, then re-frozen top layer of snow.

DOWNHILL SKIING: (*synonym: alpine skiing*) A type of slope skiing in which the heel is fixed in the ski binding.

DUST ON CRUST: A thin layer of snow over an icier crust.

> "The day started with **dust-on-crust** (or dust on very firm bumps), but by lunch it was just fresh, soft snow all around."

FALL LINE: The most direct path down a ski slope.

FREESTYLE SKIING: A variety of skiing that emphasizes tricks and jumps.

GAPER: 1) A skier who stops on a slope to take in the view. 2) An inexperienced or unskilled skier.

HELI-SKIING: A type of skiing in which the skiers are brought to the top of an otherwise inaccessible slope in a helicopter.

HUCKSTER: A skier who skis off cliffs.

LOUD POWDER: Icy conditions on ski slopes.

"I am sure he is desperate to ski eastern **loud powder**. You should press him with a really definite invitation."

MASHED POTATOES: Heavy, wet snow.

MOGUL: Snow bumps on a ski slope.

OFF-TRAILS: Places to ski that aren't official trails; often areas that are off-limits.

"True back country skiing is about skins, trekking **off-trails**, etc."

POWDER: Light, dry snow, usually very good for skiing.

SCHUSS: To shoot down a slope at top speed.

SCHUSS-BOOMER: A sudden, smartly executed stop by a skier.

SITZMARK: A mark in the snow made by a fallen skier.

"I believe I still am the holder of the record for the longest unbroken **sitzmark** at Alpine Meadows up in the Sierras."

SKI PORN: Pictures of expert skiing and ski equipment (because devoted skiers tend to lust after the slopes and/or the equipment).

SQUAD: A group of people who ski together often.

SUGAR SNOW: Soft snow in fine crystals.

TELEMARK SKIING: A type of slope skiing that differs from the more common alpine skiing in that the heel is free and the skis are designed somewhat differently to allow greater control. Telemark incorporates some aspects of alpine and others aspects of cross-country skiing.

see also: alpine skiing, cross-country skiing

YARD SALE: The aftermath of a spectacular skiing wipe-out that has scattered equipment all around.

Skinheads

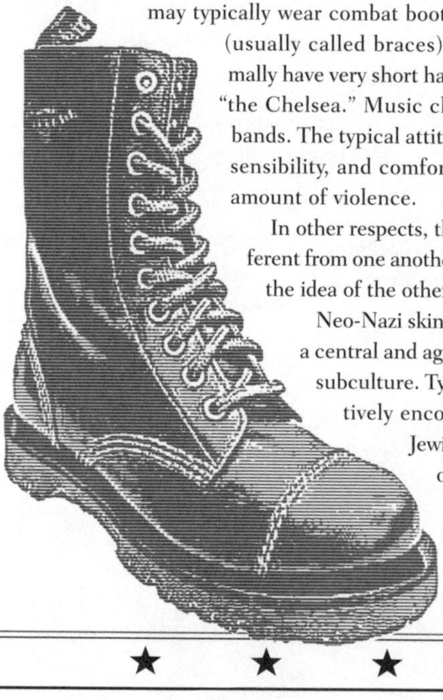

There are three main types of skinheads in America: neo-Nazi or racist skinheads, anti-racist skinheads, and traditional skinheads (trads). All three share similar taste in style, music, and attitude. A skinhead may typically wear combat boots; bomber jackets; and suspenders (usually called braces). Tattoos are common. Males normally have very short hair, while females wear hairstyles like "the Chelsea." Music choices often include Punk and Oi! bands. The typical attitude is of toughness, a working class sensibility, and comfort with or enthusiasm for a certain amount of violence.

In other respects, the three groups couldn't be more different from one another, and in many cases are disgusted at the idea of the other types being called skinheads at all.

Neo-Nazi skinheads and other racist skinheads are a central and aggressive part of the white supremacy subculture. Typically skinheads in this category actively encourage hate against people who are Jewish, black, gay, lesbian, or part of some other minority. Most are also rigidly nationalistic.

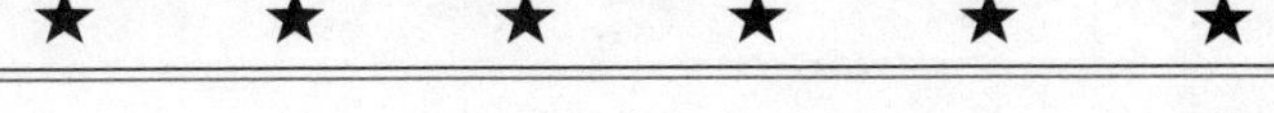

Anti-racist skinhead groups, by contrast, actively despise racism and often include members of multiple races; however, young white males still predominate. Some skinheads in this group consider themselves Communists or anarchists, while others don't declare any political affiliation.

The third type of skinheads, trads, has its roots in the original English skinhead movement that started in the late 1960s, a movement mainly of style and working class identity. They don't consider attitudes toward racism a part of what it means to be a skinhead.

88: Among neo-Nazis, code for "Heil Hitler;" said to be used because "H" is the eighth letter of the alphabet.

BEATDOWN: *(synonym: boot party)* An attack that involves a lot of kicking.

(!) BONEHEAD: A derogatory term used by anti-racist skinheads for neo-Nazi skinheads.

BOOT PARTY: *(synonym: beatdown)* An attack in which a group of skinheads jumps and knocks down an individual or small group, then repeatedly kicks the victim or victims.

"He was dragged from the car he was sleeping in, and again was the guest of honor at a **boot party**."

BRACES: Suspenders, a common article of clothing among skinheads. This is a mainstream British term, but it's used by American skinheads in preference to the more common American word "suspenders."

CHELSEA: 1) A skinhead girl. 2) A common haircut for skinhead girls.

"As cheesy as it may be, skinhead is something a lot deeper than a **Chelsea** or a number-two-with-sideburns."

CLAIM SKINHEAD: To declare oneself (in words or through clothing, haircut, etc.) to be a skinhead.

"I'm just honestly curious as to why you non-racists would want to **claim skinhead**, especially when you hate everything we very visible white power skins stand for."

CREW: An organized group of skinheads; skinheads who have pledged loyalty to each other and the group.

CURBSTOMPING: Stomping on a person's head as it lies against the edge of a curb.

(!) FENCE-WALKER: A skinhead who is not as enthusiastic or extreme in their beliefs as others around them. This is a derogatory term among skinheads.

FLIGHT: A flight jacket, a common piece of skinhead clothing.

FRESHCUT: Someone who has only recently become a skinhead.

"He is a pontificating **freshcut** who has spent the last three days telling us all how to be skinheads and calling anyone who disagrees with him a Nazi."

SUSS: (as a verb) Also "suss out." To check out, especially in reference to looking into the affiliations of an unfamiliar skinhead. (as a noun) Familiarity with skinhead customs.

SWAZI: 1) A swastika. 2) A neo-Nazi skinhead.

Skydivers and BASE Jumpers

Generally speaking, skydiving isn't about parachutes any more than waterskiing is about life preservers: The real fun in jumping out of an airplane, apart from the adrenaline rush, is in free fall. During free fall, skydivers can fly around at different speeds and in all directions, as though they were really floating in air and not plummeting toward the ground at a high rate of speed.

That said, the parachutes come in handy. Because of the potential for trouble, each skydiver has a main parachute and a reserve parachute, and strict regulations govern who may dive in what circumstances, who may maintain and repair parachutes, and so on.

Many skydivers participate in mid-air formations ("relative work" or "formation skydiving"), which take some practice to master, as each skydiver must control his or her rate of fall, direction, and speed of horizontal movement. Other skydivers concentrate on mid-air tricks with skyboards ("skysurfing"), aerial gymnastics ("freestyle" sky diving), or sit-flying.

BASE JUMPING: Jumping off stationary objects, which is not skydiving per se (because there's no airplane and no free fall) and which is illegal in most situations. BASE stands for "buildings, antennas, spans (bridges), and earth (cliffs)."

BACKSLIDE: To drift backward in free fall, usually by accident.

> "Though I seemed to be able to control my **backslide** a bit, I was sinking out relative to the student."

BAG LOCK: A skydiving malfunction in which the canopy of the parachute is stuck in the deployment bag.

see also: horseshoe, reserve

> "Is that little blurb telling me that the other jumpers saw him with the **bag lock**, ignored him, and continued on with the skydive, then ended up *on top of the guy* when he was trying to get his reserve out?"

BASE: The individual or small group around whom other skydivers gather when flying in formation.

see also: relative work

BOOGIE: A large group of skydivers gathered to have fun and try unusual jumping opportunities; for instance, record attempts.

BOUNCE: To land without opening a parachute, causing serious injury or death.

BREAK OFF: For skydivers in formation, to fly away from one another in to prepare to open parachutes.

see also: track

BREAKAWAY: *(synonym: cutaway)* Cutting off the main parachute during a malfunction in order to use the reserve chute.

BURBLE: The pocket of turbulence just above a skydiver in free fall, or above a deployed parachute when a skydiver isn't in free fall.

see also: funnel

CANOPY: The fabric and suspension lines of a parachute.

CANOPY RELATIVE WORK: Executing formations after parachutes have opened.

see also: relative work

> "Take this opportunity to learn or brush up on basic **canopy relative work** procedures."

CHUTE ASSIS: *(synonym: sit flying)* Free falling in a sitting position.

CORK: To flatten the body horizontally during free fall, slowing the rate of fall and making the skydiver appear to shoot upward relative to skydivers who are not flattened out.

CREEPER: A plastic board with wheels on which a skydiver can practice free fall techniques.

CUTAWAY: *(synonym: breakaway)* Cutting off the main parachute to use the reserve.

DIRT DIVE: A rehearsal of a skydive, performed on the ground.

DROP ZONE OR DZ: 1) A commercial skydiving center. 2) The area in which skydivers should to land.

FLARE: To pull down both sides of a parachute by using the steering toggles (brakes), converting some of the downward momentum into forward momentum.

"A **flare** performed too late has no effect. A flare performed too early can result in a stall in which the canopy loses forward speed and drops straight down. A correctly performed flare results in an exceptionally soft landing."

- FROM THE REC.SKYDIVING GROUP FAQ

FLOATER: A formation skydiver who jumps before the core formation group (the base) and who falls at as slow a rate as possible to be able to rendezvous with the rest of the group.

FORMATION SKYDIVING: *(synonym: relative work)* Multiple skydivers connecting in free fall to make a formation.

FREEFLYING: Any one of several unusual free fall techniques, such as skysurfing, sit flying, or freestyle.

FREESTYLE: A type of skydiving that involves choreographed gymnastic maneuvers in free fall.

see also: freeflying

FUNNEL: A problem that can occur when creating a formation in free fall. In a funnel, skydivers at the middle of the formation drop more quickly, making it look as though they are being sucked down out of the center and giving the formation the shape of a funnel.

HORSESHOE: A malfunction in which part of the parachute becomes entangled during deployment. A horseshoe malfunction usually makes it necessary to deploy the reserve parachute.

see also: bag lock

"I once flew for about 5,000 feet trying to communicate to a friend that he had a **horseshoe** malfunction ... bag and lines all dancing and spinning in the burble, and he was totally clueless."

JUMP RUN: The flight path of a plane dropping skydivers.

MAIN: The primary parachute.

see also: reserve

PACK: (as a noun) All of the parachute, except the harness that goes around the skydiver. (as a verb) To fold up and put away a parachute in preparation for a jump.

PUNCH A CLOUD: To skydive through a cloud. Illegal in the U.S. because low visibility makes it difficult to avoid accidents with other skydivers.

RELATIVE WORK: *(synonym: formation skydiving)* A group of skydivers connecting in free fall to form a geometric shape or other form.

RESERVE: The secondary parachute, for use in case of a problem with the main parachute.

see also: main

RIG: (as a noun) The entire parachute apparatus, including canopies, lines, container, and harness. (as a verb) To do maintenance or make repairs on a parachute.

To "rig up" is to put on a parachute.

"The Web page for Bridge Day has an article about converting your skydiver **rig** for BASE"

RIGGER: A certified technician who maintains and repairs parachutes.

SIT FLYING: *(synonym: chute assis)* Free falling in a seated position, which increases the speed of the fall compared to spreading out horizontally.

see also: freeflying

SKYBOARD: A rigid object similar to a snowboard that can be strapped to a skydiver's feet for the purpose of doing tricks in free fall.

see also: skysurfing

(!) SKYGOD: A skydiver overly impressed with his or her own abilities.

SKYSURFING: Performing tricks on a skyboard during free fall.

see also: freeflying, skyboard

SPOT: (as a noun) The point in the sky at which skydivers jump out of a plane. (as a verb) To plan the flight path and other details of a jump.

TRACK: To take a position during free fall that moves one forward at a good speed, either toward or away from other skydivers.

see also: break off

TURF SURF: To build up forward momentum and bleed off speed of descent just before landing so that the skydiver skims along the surface of the ground. Dangerous if not done correctly, since forward speed can get quite high.

WHUFFO: A non-skydiver, from the expression, "Whuffo you jump outta them planes?"

"Recently while landing on the beach at Ocean City, Maryland, I heard a **whuffo** who had joined the observing crowd comment to one of the other jumpers as we walked to the bus, 'We just wanted to see what you people looked like.'"

Snowboarders

Snowboarders draw liberally on slang from skiers, surfers, and skateboarders, and in return provide new slang to each of those subcultures. They share snow-related slang with skiers (see the skiers section on page 313 for snow-related terms). Snowboarders include those who primarily ride on obstacles in parks, as well as those who use trails or ski slopes.

Snowboarding tricks, of which there are many, involve combinations of grabs, body turns, board turns, jumps, flips, twists, and other moves. A number are named after the snowboarders who invented them or made them famous.

Turns in mid-air are named for the number of degrees the snowboarder turns: 360, 540, 720, 900, etc. Alternatively, they can be called by the first digit in the number of degrees: for instance, a 360 can be called a "3," a 540 a "5," etc. You can also call a 360 a "360 air," a 540 a "540 air," and so on.

If you have recently read the skateboarder section, you may experience déjà vu when reading some of the definitions here.

RELATED SUBCULTURES:

Skiers, Surfers, Skateboarders

AIRDOG: A snowboarder who spends as much time as possible in the air.

ALPINE SNOWBOARDING: Snowboarding down slopes rather than in terrain parks.

(!) BETTY: A female snowboarder. Can be derogatory.

BOMB: To snowboard down a slope at top speed.

see also: hammer

"I think within the next season or two the last things will click together, and I'll finally be confident in trees and be able to **bomb** steep and bumpy."

BONK: To run into an object while snowboarding.

CRATER: To crash, especially to crash spectacularly.

FACE PLANT: A face-first crash.

FAKIE: In reference to riding a snowboard, ridden so that the board (but not the snowboarder) is backwards.

FLAIL: To ride out of control.

FLOW: To give someone a product for free, especially a snowboarding-related product.

"They **flowed** me a couple pairs, and dude, they're hella strong."

FREERIDE: To snowboard at one's own pace on any natural terrain.

FREESTYLE: A kind of snowboarding that includes riding on constructed obstacles and executing tricks.

GAP: To jump an obstacle or a gap.

GOOFY FOOT: In reference to snowboard riding, putting the right foot forward instead of the left.

see also: regular foot, stance

(!) GROM OR GROMMET: A young or inexperienced snowboarder. Can be derogatory.

HALFPIPE OR HALF PIPE: A constructed obstacle shaped like half of a tube, cut lengthwise.

HAMMER: To ride at full speed.

see also: bomb

HUCKER: A snowboarder who likes to launch into the air, for example, over cliffs.

JIB: To snowboard on something other than snow; e.g., over trash cans or logs.

KICKER: A jump ramp.

(!) MUPPET: A fool; an idiot.

"A woman posts a message looking for valid advice, and some **muppet** comes out with a school yard gag."

PIPE DRAGON: A machine used to plow and rake half-pipes (curved snowboard terrain) into their proper shape after a snowfall.

POACH: To snowboard in an area that is closed or off-limits.

POW OR POW POW: Powder; light, dry snow. More generally, any kind of snow on which one can snowboard.

REGULAR FOOT: To ride with the left foot in front when snowboarding.

see also: goofy foot, stance

ROLL DOWN THE WINDOWS: To swing one's arms wildly around when out of control.

SESSION: A period of time spent snowboarding.

SHRED: To ride hard on any kind of terrain.

SKETCH: To ride awkwardly; to nearly fall while snowboarding.

SNAKE: To cut in front of someone in line; to take someone else's turn on an obstacle.

STANCE: How a snowboarder rides: right foot forward (goofy foot) or left foot forward (regular foot).

see also: regular foot, goofy foot

STICK: A snowboard.

"I want to wax my **stick** as soon as possible, and I'm wondering what the best way to get an even coat on my board would be."

STOMP: To make a good landing.

TERRAIN PARK: An area where constructed obstacles are available for snowboarders to ride.

TWO-PLANKER: A skier.

Society For Creative Anachronism Members (SCAdians)

The Society for Creative Anachronism (SCA) is a large organization dedicated to medieval-style events like feasting, having tourneys, fighting wars, and crowning royalty. While many SCA members—SCAdians—try for historical accuracy, others are more interested in the spirit of the thing than the historical specifics, so that SCA events may err on the side of entertainment rather than on the side of being historically informative.

The SCA is organized into nineteen kingdoms as of this writing, almost all of which are in the United States. A kingdom usually comprises a number of states, provinces or countries and has a king and queen, who are replaced periodically. Also, each kingdom has nobility: dukes and duchesses, counts and countesses, knights, and so on. Noble titles are bestowed by the king and queen based on virtue, skill, hard work, or royal whim.

SCAdians attend events in medieval (or sorta-medieval) costumes and try to speak in a manner evocative of the period—something that's called "speaking forsoothly." To avoid spoiling the effect, modern devices, when they are referred to at all, are sometimes given whimsical names, for instance, "dragons" (car), "elven torches" (flashlights), and "miniature Flemish painters" (cameras).

RELATED SUBCULTURES:

Renaissance Fairegoers, Historical Reenactors

ANNO SOCIETATIS OR AS: Year since the founding of the SCA, starting May 1; the second half of 2005 was the first half of AS 40.

"Given by our hands this day, the nineteenth day of February, **Anno Societatis** XVIII."

AUTHORIZED: Officially noted as having sufficient training to participate safely in SCA combat.

AUTOCRAT: (*synonym: steward*) The person who organizes an event.

see also: feastocrat, crashocrat

AWARD OF ARMS: Recognition from SCA royalty that gives a person the right to a coat of arms and to be called a Lord or Lady.

BABY HARP SEAL: A new and unskilled fighter who is about to be thrashed in combat.

BELTED FIGHTER: A knight; a member of the SCA's Order of Chivalry.

BOFFER: A foam weapon used for combat without armor.

CHATELAINE: An SCA officer who assists new members.

CHIRURGEON: A person who can offer first aid at SCA events.

CLEAR!: Warning that a weapon is about to be drawn.

see also: live steel

CORPORA: The real-world legal documents that define the SCA's mission, operating procedures, and other particulars.

CRASHOCRAT: An official in charge of finding places for people to sleep.

see also: feastocrat, autocrat

(!) CROWNIE: A woman (usually) who pursues fighters who look like they have a chance of winning their way into a royal title, in hopes of becoming royalty herself. Derogatory.

"**Crownies** have broken up many SCA marriages."

DAMP: In reference to an event, allowing wine, beer, and mead but not hard liquor.

see also: dry, wet

DRY: In reference to an event, not permitting alcohol.

see also: damp, wet

THE ERIC: *(synonym: list field)* 1) The markers around the combat field at an SCA event. 2) The combat field itself.

The term is said to derive from a battleground at a 1969 SCA event, which was marked off with pieces of red cloth. SCAdians began to refer to the markers as "the Eric" after the famous Viking Eric the Red, because of their color.

(!) FEASTOCRAT: The person in charge of food at an event, or of a feast. This term is sometimes frowned on as un-SCA-like; "Kitchener," "Head Cook," and "Chief Cook" are preferred.

see also: autocrat, crashocrat

FORSOOTHLY: A speech roughly approximating English as spoken centuries ago.

> "My one concession to speaking **forsoothly** is to try and eradicate 'O.K.' from my vocabulary."

GARB: Period costume, or a costume in the spirit of the event, even if not very historically accurate.

GUNCH: To fight with a heavy (rattan) weapon, especially when striking hard blows.

see also: rattan

HAT: 1) A fighter's helmet. 2) A crown or coronet. 3) Anyone who is entitled to wear a crown or coronet.

HEAVY WEAPONS: Weapons for SCA combat that are used only when the fighters are armored and trained properly in the weapons' use.

see also: rattan, light weapons

HOLD!: Warning to stop whatever one is doing and look for danger. Used especially by officials during combat.

KINGDOM: A branch of the SCA covering a particular geographical area. For instance, the Middle Kingdom covers Ohio, Kentucky, Indiana, Illinois, and parts of Michigan, Iowa, and Ontario.

LEG: In combat, to hit an opponent's leg or legs such that in actual battle, the limb would be unusable. Legged combatants are forced to continue on their knees until they are "killed" or combat ends.

LIGHT WEAPONS: Missile weapons, or weapons not as heavy as rattan ones. The rules for wielding light weapons are different from those for heavy weapons.

see also: heavy weapons

LIST FIELD: (*synonym:* the Eric) The combat area at an event.

LIVE STEEL: Any edged, metal weapon.

see also: clear!

MASHIE POW: Fighting with heavy weapons (e.g., swords, etc.).

see also: rattan

MUNDANE: Having to do with the modern world. This word is used in a variety of subcultures (e.g. furries, spelunkers, goths). In the SCA, generally not meant to be derogatory.

PAD BOY: A person who fights with the minimum allowable amount of armor.

PELL: 1) A stationary target for heavy weapons practice. 2) A fighter so unskilled that he or she is effectively a stationary target for heavy weapons practice.

PERIOD: (as a noun) The historical time ranging from about 600 to 1600 or 1650 C.E. (C.E. and A.D. are equivalent). (as an adjective) More or less historically accurate for some time and place between 600 and 1600 or 1650 C.E.

PERSONA: An individual's character or role at SCA events. A persona will have a period name and belong to a kingdom. It also sometimes involves a personal history, a household to which the character belongs, certain awards, and/or membership in a particular order.

> "Myself, I figure I'll remain 'Wade of Many Places' as I have been for the past twenty-six years. It's my general SCA **persona**."

POST-REVEL: A party after the SCA event for which most or all period detail is set aside.

RATTAN: The stem of a climbing palm plant, which is used to make weapons for armored SCA combat; it is heavy but safer than actual steel. To "fight rattan" is to participate in armored combat.

see also: gunch

RIG: A full set of armor.

SCADIAN OR SCADIAN: (pronounced "SKAY-dee-an" or less often, "SKAH-dee-an") A member of the Society for Creative Anachronism.

SMALLS: 1) Children. However, some people consider this term inappropriate for applying to children, because of its second definition. 2) Underwear.

"I am always looking for good ideas of activities for the **smalls** in my Barony."

STEWARD: *(synonym: autocrat)* The organizer of an event.

STICK: A fighter's sword (generally made of rattan).

(!) STICK JOCK: An SCA swordfighter who is obsessed with fighting. Can be mildly derogatory.

"If you're playing baseball and suddenly feel naked without a shield, you might be a **stick jock**."

- SCAdian Malachai Shel Ha Cheitz Shavar of Ealdormere (Ontario)

TROLL: A person who mans a table where fees are paid, directions dispensed, forms signed, etc.

TROLL GATE: A place where attendees at an event come to pay fees, sign forms, etc. Manned by trolls.

WET: In reference to an event, allowing liquor.

see also: dry, damp

(!) WIRE WEENIE: A person in the SCA who fights with a rapier. Can be derogatory or playful, depending on who says it to whom.

"I'm sure you're no more a **wire weenie** than I am a stick jock."

Stamp Collectors (Philatelists)

Stamp collecting, or philately (a term coined in 1835 from Greek words meaning roughly "lover of things that aren't taxed"), is a hugely popular hobby: The total number of collectors in the U.S. is estimated to be as high as 20 million. And while a number of local stamp clubs report declining or aging membership, worldwide clubs that don't meet in person and that are interested in a specific type or theme of stamp are on the rise, thanks to the Internet.

Stamp collecting offers glimpses into history. Special stamps have been printed for labor strikes, wars, scientific expeditions, and even to influence public opinion. For instance, the U.S. Office of Strategic Services once produced a "Hitler skull" stamp meant to mock a popular German stamp (and der Führer along with it).

Stamps also offer clues about things not shown on the stamp itself: They have been used as currency in times when no other currency was available; they bear witness to changes in government; and they've been recovered from mail on shipwrecks. Some small countries issue many more stamps than they need and create elaborate designs for them in order to realize extra income from sales to collectors.

Specialized terms in the stamp collecting vocabulary include types of paper used (for instance, laid or granite); printing processes; items used in stamp production (like the dandy roll and the doctor blade);

errors and malfunctions (like albinos); types of stamps; specialized stamp uses (such as commemoratives, air mail, Cinderellas, and scientific expedition stamps); how stamps are affixed, cancelled, and marked; damage to stamps (such as runs, hinging marks on the back from being mounted, creases, pinholes, etc.); and specific stamp issues, like the "brake shoe" or the 1856 one-cent British Guiana "Black on Magenta," which is worth a little under a million dollars. Stamp collectors who work with foreign stamps tend to learn some current and historical geography and a few words in other languages, especially words that have to do with postal practices.

Stamp condition is based on the original quality of manufacture, whether or not the stamp was ever used, how the stamp was cancelled, and the subsequent handling of the stamp. Grades range from "poor" to "superb." Even two stamps of the same issue that have been handled in exactly the same way may be considered to be different grades, for instance, if one was printed slightly off-center.

RELATED SUBCULTURE:

Coin and Money Collectors

AEROPHILATELY: Stamp collecting of airmail stamps.

ALBINO: A stamp printing mistake: a stamp that has no color and is only an impression, made by the die striking the paper without ink.

APPROVALS: Stamps or related items sent to a collector by a dealer to consider for purchase.

BOURSE: A stamp show; a gathering of stamp collectors and dealers where many stamps are shown for sale.

CANCELLED TO ORDER: In reference to a stamp, cancelled as a service by a postal authority but not actually used to mail anything.

CINDERELLA: Something that looks like a postal stamp but isn't; for instance a seal, bogus issue, or tax stamp.

see also: *fantasy stamp*

> "Secondly, our show has seen Arlene's exhibit on varieties of post-World War I German-area stamps, a postal history exhibit of covers from many countries showing different usages, and an exhibit on the Sage issue of France, none of which involves anything close to a **Cinderella**."

CLICHÉ: A metal die with the complete pattern for a stamp, grouped with many other identical dies to make a printing plate.

COMMEMORATIVE: A stamp issued to honor an individual or to mark a special occurrence.

COVER: The front of an envelope, paper from a package, or anything else that has a stamp affixed to it and was actually mailed.

> "It is a combo **cover** with six other stamps."

DISASTER MAIL: (*synonym: wreck mail*) Mail recovered from a wrecked plane, ship, or train.

DUMB CANCELLATION: A postmark that invalidates the stamp without including writing or other information.

ETIQUETTE: A sticker used in shipping or mailing that isn't a postage stamp; for instance, "priority mail" or "fragile" stickers.

EXCHANGE CLUB: A group of stamp collectors who send stamps that are available for purchase from one member of the group to the next.

FANCY CANCEL: A postmark with a picture.

FANTASY STAMP: A stamp that isn't a bona fide government postal issue, for instance, the "Skull Island" promotional stamp circulated when the original *King Kong* movie was released, or a bogus stamp intended to defraud collectors.

see also: *Cinderella*

FRANK: A stamped mark on a letter or package that serves in place of a postal stamp.

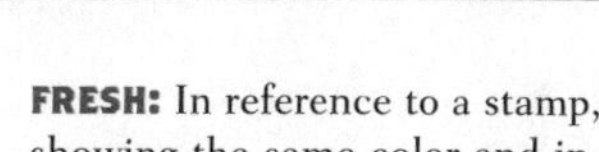

FRESH: In reference to a stamp, showing the same color and intensity it had when issued.

KILLER: A heavy, obliterating mark used by a postal authority to cancel a stamp to make sure nobody will try to use it again.

see also: obliterator

> "The postmark and **killer** look like the same ink."

KILOWARE: An assortment of stamps on paper (usually pieces of envelope) that have been used and are being sold as a lot.

LIFT: To unstick a stamp from an envelope or other item.

OBLITERATOR: Any mark used to cancel postage.

see also: killer

PHILATELY: 1) Stamp collecting. 2) Sometimes used to mean the study of stamps, although the word is from the Greek word for "love" and was not originally intended to imply study.

REMAINDER: 1) The stamps left in an album after someone has taken all the best specimens out. 2) Any stamps sold by a postal authority after that particular issue is no longer valid for postage.

> "This is a collection **remainder** similar to the British America I sold earlier."

SHORT SET: A set of related stamps that is missing at least one item, usually the most valuable stamp in the set.

SPACE-FILLER: A stamp in bad condition, used in a collection until a better specimen can be substituted.

THEMATIC COLLECTING: Collecting stamps and stamp-related items that have to do with a particular theme; for instance, World War II, or football.

WRECK MAIL: (*synonym: disaster mail*) Mail recovered from a wrecked ship.

Surfers

Surfers still use some terms that were popular in the 1960s, a period closely associated with the surfer subculture: terms like "gnarly," "bogus," and "bitchin'" are not outdated. But surfing has picked up a number of new terms over the last four decades and dropped some of the old ones.

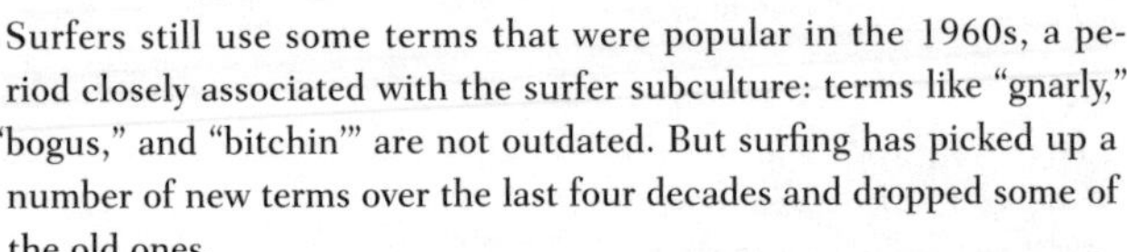

Among the new terms are some that have come over from skateboarding, as many surfers are also skateboarders. The slang from each subculture contributes to the other. Some hip hop slang has also been adopted by the surfer subculture, while additional surfer speak has been borrowed from surfing destinations around the world, such as Australia and Hawaii.

One of the great preoccupations of surfers is wave and surf conditions, so surfer slang incorporates a variety of terms for wave roughness, wave size, parts of a wave, and different stages of a wave's life cycle. Another substantial portion of surfer slang deals with attitude and emotional state, much of it directed toward nurturing a relaxed attitude that allows full appreciation of the sun, the cameraderie, and especially the ocean.

RELATED SUBCULTURES:

Skateboarders, Snowboarders

AGGRO: (as a verb) To become very angry; also "go aggro." (as an adjective) Belligerent.

see also: bent

"One of the best parts of my day yesterday was trying to catch a wave with this **aggro** jerk right behind me trying to grab my leash."

AXED: *(synonyms: stuffed, worked)* Smacked down by a wave.

"Then a huge set came. I went very late and got friggin' **axed** on the takeoff."

BAGGIES: Loose-fitting swim trunks often worn by surfers.

(!) BARNEY: A person who doesn't surf well, especially if that person seems to have a high opinion of his or her surfing.

BARREL: *(synonyms: tube, green room)* A tube-shaped wave.

BASHING: Body surfing.

see also: shark biscuit

(!) BENNY: A person who likes to act like a surfer or be involved in surfer culture but who rarely surfs. Can be derogatory.

BENT: Angry.

BLOWN OUT: In reference to waves, distorted by the wind so that they're not good for surfing.

"Not much greets my surf-starved gaze except for **blown out** slop."

BRAH OR BRO: Friend ("brother").

CHILLAX: To relax and not take things too seriously; to embrace the traditional surfer attitude.

CLEANUP WAVE: A large wave running perpendicular to other waves that smashes into and breaks up a group of surfers or sends them paddling away.

CLUCKED: Cowed by a wave.

CORE: In reference to a surfer, one who surfs in all kinds of weather and has developed substantial skill.

"You sound so ridiculous talking about how much of a '**core**' surfer you are because you just happen to vacation where there is surf a couple of times per year."

COVERED: *(synonyms: shacked, tubed, pitted)* To be within a tube-shaped wave, with water above, below, ahead, and behind.

see also: tube

CREW: A group of people who surf together regularly.

DA KINE: (pronounced "dah kyne") Top-notch; best of its kind. Widely used among surfers; borrowed from Hawai'ian.

see also: filth, nectar, rickt

> "He had a left-go-right move that discouraged snakes, then he assumed lotus position. He was "**da kine**" stylist, ya?"

DROP IN: To surf onto a wave that someone is already surfing, usually considered rude.

EAT IT: To wipe out; to be knocked off a surf board.

> "My confidence boost was soon taken away as I bogged on some lump around the next turn and **ate it** badly."

FILTH: Anything admirable or desirable. "Filthy" means "really good."

see also: da kine, nectar, rickt

> "Then further east along Vanua Levu's Coral Coast you can surf a **filth** beach break and river mouth setup!"

FRIG: *(synonym: snake)* To steal a wave by cutting off another surfer.

GLASS AXE: The lip of a wave, before it falls and breaks.

GO OFF: *(synonyms: rip, shralp, shred)* To perform at peak, whether in reference to a person or something inanimate.

> "... watching a kid who no one knew **go off** for six hours in fifteen-foot surf, alone, and stay out past dark, a quarter mile out to sea ...."

GREEN ROOM: *(synonyms: tube, barrel)* A tube-shaped wave.

GROM OR GROMMET: A young surfer. Not derogatory.

GUN: *(synonym: log)* A long, narrow surfboard for big waves.

see also: overgunned

HEMOED: (pronounced "HEE-mode") Destroyed.

(!) HODAD: 1) Any jerk on the beach, especially one who pretends to be a surfer but really isn't. The word is derogatory when used in this sense. 2) A beginning surfer. The word isn't necessarily derogatory when used this way.

see also: land shark

> "You gotta be a genuine Grade A **hodad** to think your sailboard will double as a quality surfboard."

JAG: A rest or retreat after a tiring surfing session.

(!) KOOK: An incompetent surfer. Derogatory.

(!) LAND SHARK: A person who claims to surf, but doesn't or can't.

see also: hodad

LOG: *(synonym: gun)* A long surfboard for big waves.

NECTAR: (as an adjective) Wonderful; beautiful. (as a noun) Anything top-shelf.

see also: da kine, filth, rickt

NEPTUNE COCKTAIL: A big gulp of sea water.

NOODLED: So exhausted that one has gone limp.

OVER THE FALLS: Wiped out on a breaking wave.

OVERGUNNED: Having too long a surfboard for the size of the wave.

see also: gun

OVERHEAD: A measure of wave height relative to the speaker. Waves can be overhead, double overhead, etc.

PITTED: *(synonyms: covered, shacked, tubed)* To be inside a tube-shaped wave.

POINT BREAK: A surfing condition in which waves come to a good peak due to a land form.

PUCKER FACTOR: The anxiety-inspiring appearance of an oncoming wave.

QUIVER: A surfer's collection of surfboards.

RICKT: *(synonym: shibby)* Great; marvelous.

see also: nectar, da kine, filth

RINSE CYCLE: The crash and suck of a wave after it breaks.

RIP: *(synonyms: go off, shralp, shred)* To surf at the height of one's ability.

SAND FACIAL: For a surfer, to be washed up by a wave and shoved face-first into the sand.

SCAB: A rock, reef, or other hard object in the water.

SHACKED: *(synonyms: covered, tubed, pitted)* To be inside a tube-shaped wave.

SHARK BISCUIT: *(synonym: sponge)* A body board.

see also: bashing

> "Hey, you guys! I ride a secondhand, beat-up, fifty dollar **shark biscuit**!"

SHIBBY: *(synonym: rickt)* Great; marvelous.

SHRALP: *(synonyms: go off, rip, shred)* To surf at the height of one's ability.

SHRED: *(synonyms: go off, rip, shralp)* To surf at the height of one's ability.

SNAKE: *(synonym: frig)* To cut off another surfer from a wave he or she is about to surf.

SPONGE: *(synonym: shark biscuit)* A body board.

(!) SQUID: An obnoxious surfer.

STICK: A surfboard.

STINK-EYE: A glare; a baleful look.

"I'm twenty-nine years old and want to be welcomed by the group, but all I get is **stink-eye** and rations from Eastcoasters and members of the GSA."

STUFFED: *(synonyms: axed, worked)* Driven under and pummeled by a wave.

SURFOLOGY: Careful attention to weather and ocean events as they relate to surfing. Not really a science, despite the "ology."

"Hey, as a foremost authority on **surfology**, hire me and I'll direct the Canary Island Extension program."

TAKEOFF: The start of a ride, once the surfer catches the wave.

TROLL: An impoverished, dedicated surfer who barely manages to eat and who sleeps anywhere available, as long as it's free. Not derogatory.

TUBE: *(synonyms: barrel, green room)* A long, cylindrical wave large enough for a person to surf inside; a very desirable phenomenon in the surfing world.

see also: covered

TUBED: *(synonyms: covered, shacked, pitted)* To be inside a tube-shaped wave.

WAHINE: (pronounced "wah-HEE-nay") A female surfer. (Hawai'ian for "woman.")

WORKED: *(synonyms: axed, stuffed)* Driven under and pummeled by a wave.

Sustainable Living Advocates

"Sustainable living advocates" is a clumsy and artificial phrase, but it's probably the most descriptive umbrella term for the various groups that make up this subculture: people who create alternative ways of living together, grassroots environmentalists, people who use local currencies, people interested in renewable fuels and building materials, and others who share these interests. The unifying thread is an interest in establishing systems that can be continued indefinitely without destroying anything.

Groups that fall into this category often find very unusual ways to meet everyday needs. Local currency users may buy groceries or carpentry services with currency based on the value of an hour of work rather than the dollar; communitarians may share lawns, meals, work space, and guest space; off-the-grid homeowners may get all of their electricity from solar panels, small-scale hydroelectric setups, or wind turbines.

Much of the language of sustainability sounds formal and even academic, perhaps because approaches like permaculture and intentional communities are complex and lend themselves to a lot of thinking. Yet the terms listed here are not specifically professional or academic; they are used in daily conversation within this subculture.

APPROPRIATE TECHNOLOGY: Methods of taking care of everyday tasks that can be sustained indefinitely; that is, that don't degrade the environment, cause social rifts, use up non-renewable resources, etc.

BIODIESEL: A diesel fuel made from vegetable oil instead of petroleum. Biodiesel exhaust smells like french fries.

BIOREGION: An area defined by common natural features, plants, animals, and soil types. Bioregions are not rigidly defined.

> "Of course, there are some areas where you have to truly wonder what they would be eating if they had to rely on their own **bioregion**."

CHARISMATIC LEADER: A leader and founder of an intentional community who holds that community together through one-person leadership. Charismatic leaders are generally found in religious or spiritual communities, although even in those they are not common.

CHICKEN TRACTOR: A portable fence enclosing a group of chickens. The fence can be moved around on a property so that the chickens consume weeds in first one area, then another.

COB: A building material consisting of mainly clay and straw, which can be made into walls by hand.

> "Gemma wants me to build a **cob** house, not to live in, but as a small sanctuary somewhere on the land we eventually intend to buy."

COHOUSING OR CO-HOUSING: A form of intentional community; a group of privately-owned (and sometimes rented) homes that are part of a larger, cooperative organization. Members of cohousing groups generally share some meals in a community dining room and tend to be physically designed to encourage social contact.

(!) COMMUNE: 1) An intentional community where residents share the ownership of most or all possessions, including housing, income, etc. 2) A very loosely-organized or anarchic intentional community. When used in this sense, can be derogatory when coming from a person who is not active in the intentional communities movement,

though it's usually not derogatory within the movement.

CONSENSUS: A decision-making approach that approves only proposals that all concerned accept. This is a more specific meaning then the one used by people outside the sustainability movement.

A consensus decision is not a unanimous vote; it's an agreement, sometimes one that has evolved during discussion, that each person is willing to support or allow even if not their first choice.

Some types of consensus are formalized and structured, often with a neutral facilitator helping keep things on track. Other approaches to consensus are more free-form. Consensus can be constructive and consistently successful, but when poorly managed it can be extremely unpleasant.

"We prefer facilitated **consensus**-seeking to shouting one another down."

COOPERATIVE: (as an adjective) In agreement on principles and working for mutual benefit. (as a noun) Any democratic organization owned by the participants, such as a food store owned by the people who shop there, a business owned by workers, etc.

ECOVILLAGE: An intentional community based on principles of benign environmental practices.

HOMESTEADERS: People who supply most or all daily needs from their own land; for instance, growing their own food, building their own home from materials they harvest from their land, etc.

INTENTIONAL COMMUNITY: A group of people who come together to live according to shared principles, values, or practices. May be spiritual or secular, communal or cooperative. Examples include monasteries, cohousing communities, ecovillages, communes, and kibbutzim.

"Originally our **intentional community** was in a rural area, but suburban sprawl has changed its character."

LETS: *(synonym: local currency)* "Local exchange trading system;" a means for trading goods and services locally without use of national currency.

LOCAL CURRENCY: *(synonym: LETS)* A currency minted in a local area and usable only with providers of goods and services who have opted into the system.

MONOCULTURE: The practice of devoting a large area of land to growing a single crop. Most large-scale American agriculture today is monoculture, but only people interested in ecological sustainability call it that.

PERMACULTURE: The philosophy or practice of designing agriculture to fit into the local ecology; maintain good soil quality; creating high yield without the use of petrochemicals; and otherwise promoting long-term, healthy food production practices.

> "To date, I've been more interested in the **permaculture** design of the site itself, rather than the resources and actions required to achieve the design."

SEEKER: A person looking for a cohousing group, ecovillage, commune, or other intentional community to join. This is a different usage than the New Age sense of someone on a spiritual journey.

STRAWBALE: A construction method that creates permanent, fireproof buildings out of bales of straw.

SUSTAINABLE: Only using processes and materials that can be renewed indefinitely. Systems can be ecologically sustainable, socially sustainable, economically sustainable, etc.

Tattoo Artists and Tattoo Enthusiasts

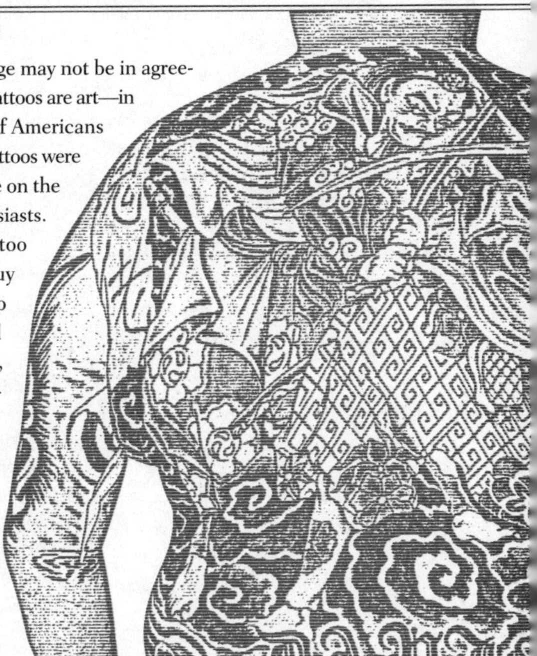

★ ★ ★ ★ ★ ★

While the population at large may not be in agreement about whether or not tattoos are art—in a recent poll, 40 percent of Americans surveyed said they thought tattoos were not art—there's little debate on the subject among tattoo enthusiasts. Aside from the kind of tattoo you get in prison from a guy named Bubba who uses two kinds of ballpoint pen and a contraband sewing needle, tattoos are widely considered art by those who get them, and looking at some of the work done by top tattoo artists, it's difficult to argue the point.

According to a 2003 Harris Poll, 16 percent of Americans have tattoos, and a higher percentage of the population on the west

★ ★ ★ ★ ★ ★

coast of the country is tattooed than in any other part of the country. Still 17 percent of people who had gotten tattoos said they regretted them: The most common reason being that they were tattooed with a name that they no longer want on their skin.

BACK PIECE: A tattoo that covers the entire back.

see also: sleeve, bodysuit

"I have a Haida sun and moon and tribal-style wings on my back and want to plan a full **back piece**."

BODYSUIT: Tattoos covering the entire body, often added progressively over time.

see also: sleeve, back piece

CANVAS: The skin of a person getting a tattoo.

"Get tattooed while your **canvas** is tight and show-off-able, and while you still enjoy cool things!"

COLLECTOR: A person who gets multiple, custom tattoos over a long period of time.

see also: meat

"Her excuse that she caught it from a dirty tattoo machine pisses me off, because I am a tattoo **collector** and think that it shines an ugly light on the tattoo community."

FLASH: Tattoos picked from a book; pre-designed tattoos.

GUN: A tattooing machine.

INK: *(synonym: tat)* A tattoo.

INK SLINGER: A tattoo artist.

"I'm sure every **ink-slinger** in here understands the joy I feel when someone has me draw something up for them that takes me hours to do, and then decides not to get it!"

JAILHOUSE TATTOO: A tattoo applied with crude methods, such as a sewing needle and ink.

see also: scratcher

"All I said about my **jailhouse tattoos** was that I've done them, not that I was incredibly ecstatic about them."

MEAT: Any tattoo customer who regularly comes in for new tattoos.

see also: collector

PIECE: A tattoo, especially a custom-designed one.

"This **piece**, on my left upper arm, was from a cover of a book."

SCRATCHER: A person who applies tattoos without training.

see also: jailhouse tattoo

"This especially happens when you get a tattoo from a scratcher, and if you don't know what a **scratcher** is you shouldn't get a tattoo in the first place."

SLEEVE: A tattoo that covers most or all of one arm.

see also: back piece, bodysuit

SLINGING INK: Tattooing.

TAT: *(synonym: ink)* A tattoo.

Thespians and Stage Crew

★ ★ ★ ★ ★ ★

Putting on a play is like operating an aircraft carrier: The people out on the deck are only the visible part of a much larger effort. In addition to the world the audience sees onstage, there's the improvisational and labor-intensive world of technicians and stagehands, flypeople and lampies, cans and flats.

Out of courtesy, most theater people observe the superstitions of the stage, but it's hard to know how many people actually believe in them. The two most common theatre superstitions are about saying the name of the play *Macbeth* and turning off the "ghost light," a light often left on outside the stage door through the full run of a play. Either action is rumored to bring bad luck down on the production.

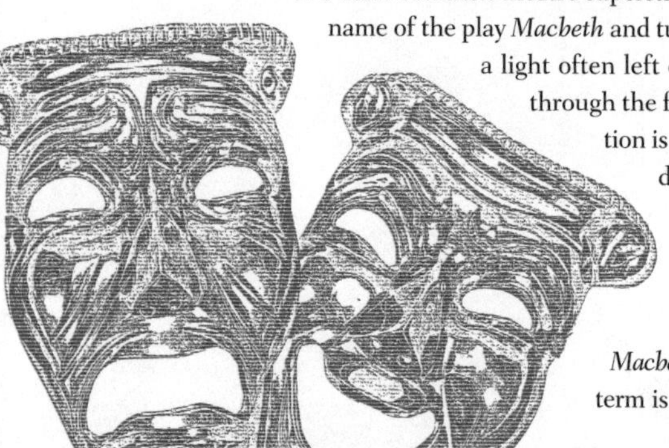

To avoid having to mention *Macbeth*—a particularly tricky proposition when *performing* the play *Macbeth*—the standard substitute term is "the Scottish Play."

RELATED SUBCULTURE:

Puppeteers

ACTOR: A person (whether male or female) who plays a part in a play. The term "actress" is also used, but "actor" is more common even for females.

BEAT: 1) A brief pause. 2) A small unit of time on stage. 3) A unit of the play's story. Each beat in this sense is one event, however long that takes and however many actors are involved.

"You don't throw away a cue line, wait a **beat**, and start singing."

BEGINNERS: The members of the company who must be in place at the beginning of an act. Most often used to summon them when the act is about to begin.

BELT VOICE: A strong voice for singing on stage. The same character can use a belt voice for some songs and a legit voice for others.

see also: legit voice

"I still am of the opinion that the role demands a big and aggressive **belt voice**; in other words, you can't act your way through Rose; you have to sing it."

THE BOOTH: The control room for lighting and sound.

"There's a special note in **the booth** telling visiting companies not to obstruct the panthers [a special kind of light used in this particular theater]."

BOX-PUSHER: A general purpose stage hand; a grunt.

BREAK A LEG: A traditional way to wish someone good luck before a play, since saying "good luck" is considered bad luck.

see also: The Scottish Play

BUSINESS: A bit of activity for an actor on stage, used to prevent the character from having to stand there like an idiot or for comic relief.

CANS: 1) Headphones. 2) A set of headphones equipped with a microphone for communication among techies during a performance.

CHEW THE SCENERY: To ham it up; to overact.

"Brian Blessed on film, in my experience, is a somewhat different proposition than Brian Blessed on stage, where, yes, he has a tendency to **chew the scenery**."

COME DOWN: In reference to a show, to come to the end of a particular performance. This is a reference to the curtain coming down.

see also: go up

COMPANY: Everyone who helps stage a production; e.g., actors, director, stage crew, and box office personnel.

DECK: The floor of the stage.

DOWNSTAGE: Toward the audience.

see also: upstage, stage right, stage left

"You don't just mark time until you get to go **downstage** and sing."

DRY: For an actor, to forget dialogue during a performance and stop speaking.

see also: fluff

ELECTRON HOSE: A good-sized electrical cable.

EQUITY: Actor's Equity Association, the U.S. union for actors, directors, and stage managers, which has rules about who can be cast in certain professional productions, payment arrangements, and other professional acting concerns.

FLAT: A wooden frame covered with canvas or muslin and painted as a part of a stage set.

FLUFF: To stumble, hesitate, or misspeak when delivering dialogue.

see also: dry

"A live performance is always imperfect: there are occasional noises off; a line or two may be **fluffed** ..."

FLYMAN: The person in charge of making actors or objects fly on stage. Theater flying includes such tasks as lowering backdrops between scenes and helping people ascend to heaven.

"I was enlisted as a **flyman** on the set-designer's assumption that some of the scenery could be flown during the show."

FOURTH WALL: The side of the stage facing the audience, where actors pretend there is a wall. A reference to the relationship between the cast and the audience.

GHOST LIGHT: A light on a stage or at a stage door left burning throughout a show's run and that is said to house the muse of theater.

GO UP: In reference to a show, to start.

see also: come down

"End result: show **went up** on schedule even though I hated the insensitive, inconsiderate @#*%! producer with a passion."

GREEN ROOM: A room, usually convenient to stage entrances, where actors gather before and (when not onstage) during a show.

HOUSE: 1) The audience. 2) The seating for the audience.

"In glancing at ticket sales for a local community theater for the past several years, I've come up with a theory as to what draws the largest **house**."

KILL: To deactivate or get rid of; for instance, to turn off a light or carry a prop off stage.

see also: strike

LAMPIE OR LAMPY: A lighting technician.

see also: techie

"I have been doing a lot of lighting myself over the last few months—I handle all the sound and all the light on board—and have been getting in touch with my inner **lampie**."

LEGIT VOICE: A pleasant, trained singing voice.

see also: belt voice

LINES: Dialogue to be memorized and spoken by the actors.

LUMASUCK OR LUMOSUCK: A mythical substance or object that makes unwanted light on or near a stage magically disappear.

"Buy a can of **lumosuck**. Just spray some on the cables and the light won't hit them!"

MR. SANDS: A code word some theaters use to refer to a fire in the building without causing a panic.

OFF BOOK: Performing on stage without a script. To get off book, an actor memorizes his or her lines.

see also: on book

ON BOOK: In reference to an actor rehearsing a play, not having memorized the lines yet and therefore reading from a script.

see also: off book

ROPE WRENCH: A knife.

THE SCOTTISH PLAY: Shakespeare's *Macbeth*. Many theater people will not mentioned it by name, because it's considered bad luck.

see also: break a leg

SKIN MONEY: Extra payment for actors whose parts require them to be naked onstage.

SPIKE: (as a verb) To mark a position on stage. (as a noun, also "spike mark") A piece of tape on the stage to mark the location of an object or where an effect needs to occur.

> "On the tour, we set a LeMaitre yellow smoke cartridge in the show deck at the **spike** mark where the Scarecrow fell after being 'hit' with the fireball."

SQUIB: A little explosive device installed on an actor, sometimes with fake blood, for use when the actor's character is shot.

STAGE LEFT: The left side of the stage from the point of view of someone facing the audience.

see also: <u>*stage right, upstage, downstage*</u>

STAGE RIGHT: The right side of the stage from the point of view of someone facing the audience.

see also: <u>*stage left, upstage, downstage*</u>

STRIKE: 1) To dismantle a show. 2) To remove an item from stage.

SWING: An actor who is able to take over any of several other minor roles at short notice. Differs from an understudy, who generally is available to fill in only for one major role.

> "For an emergency, the understudy (who is already at the theatre) would be used. (And a **swing**, who is also there, would cover her role.)"

TECHIE: A technician working on a play in areas like lighting, sound, costumes, props, etc.

see also: <u>*lampie*</u>

(!) UPSTAGE: (as an adjective, pronounced "UP-stayj") In reference to locations on the stage, away from the audience. (as a verb, pronounced "up-STAYJ") To draw attention to oneself at the expense of other actors. Usually pejorative among thespians.

see also: <u>*downstage, stage left, stage right*</u>

> "Now, had she picked *me*, I would have **upstaged** her in any way I could think of."

WALK-ON: In reference to a role, minor and usually not including any dialogue.

Truckers

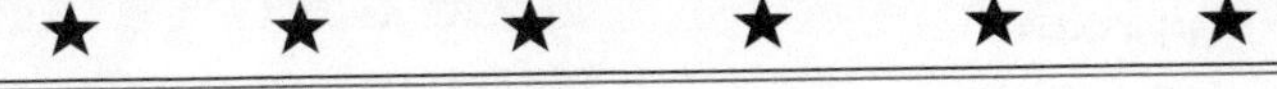

Truckers, in addition to constituting a profession, are a subculture in that they converse on CB ("citizen's band radio") and at truck stops and trucker-friendly restaurants to pass the time as they make their long trips. As CB users, they often use CB slang, some of which is particularly pertinent to truckers and is included here.

CB speak includes numeric codes beginning with a 10, such as 10-4 ("acknowledged; message received") and 10-20 ("my location is ...").

Trucker slang is particularly rich in terms for police officers and police activities, vehicles, traffic, and elements of a trucker's job. Because truckers travel widely, this slang tends to spread nationally rather than becoming localized.

According to U.S. Department of Labor Bureau of Labor Statistics, approximately 25 percent of truckers are self-employed owner-operators. The remainder are employed by trucking companies, manufacturing firms, wholesalers, and the like.

ALLIGATOR: A piece of tire lying by the side of the road.

AT YOUR BACK DOOR: Behind your truck.

BEAR: *(synonym: boy scout)* A police officer. "To feed the bears" is to get a ticket.

see also: *local yokel, picture taker, plain wrapper*

BOBTAIL: A truck cab that is not pulling a trailer.

BOY SCOUT: *(synonym: bear)* A police officer.

BRAKE CHECK: A traffic slowdown.

BUMPER STICKER: A vehicle following too close behind one's truck.

CASH REGISTER: A toll booth.

CHICKEN COOP: A weigh station.

CHICKEN LIGHTS: Unnecessary or decorative lights on an eighteen-wheeler.

COMIC BOOK: A truck driver's log book.

DARKTIME: Night.

DEADHEAD: (as a noun) A truck with an empty trailer or no trailer. A deadhead drive generally doesn't earn the driver any money. (as an adjective) Without cargo.

> "We took a load from Florida to Louisiana. Then one from Louisiana to New Mexico. Then **deadheaded** from New Mexico to Colorado."

FAT LOAD: A truck that is carrying more weight than allowed by law.

FLIP FLOP: 1) A return trip. 2) A U-turn.

FOG LIFTER: An interesting person who is talking on the CB.

FOUR-WHEELER: A car or small truck.

see also: *two-wheeler, roller skate*

HAMMER DOWN: Moving very quickly. To put the hammer down is to speed up; to have the hammer down is to drive fast.

> "I know a few truckers who drive the 400, and as they say, 'If it's spraying on the windshield, keep the **hammer down**. When it stops spraying, get off the road, 'cause it's freezing up.'"

INVITATION: A traffic ticket.

JACKKNIFE: A position in which the cab of the truck is turned at a right angle to the trailer. This can be done on purpose to maneuver the trailer into a tight spot, or accidentally, as may happen on ice.

> "When I touched my brakes, the trailer tried to **jackknife**. I ended up putting the truck into third or fourth gear and just lightly giving it fuel to keep the tires spinning."

LOCAL YOKEL: A town police officer.

see also: bear, picture taker, plain wrapper

MUD DUCK: 1) A person who isn't coming through clearly on the CB. 2) A CB that doesn't transmit well.

> "I have no idea what the transmit sounds like. The reports I get back are good and no one accuses me of being a **mud duck**."

PICTURE TAKER: A police officer who is tracking speed with radar.

see also: bear, local yokel, plain wrapper

PLAIN WRAPPER: An unmarked police car.

see also: bear, local yokel, picture taker

RATCHET JAW: *(synonym: windjammer)* A person who talks too much on the CB.

RIG: A tractor (the cab part of a tractor trailer; the actual truck).

ROLLER SKATE: A car, especially a small one.

see also: four-wheeler

SEAT COVER: An attractive woman in a car.

THERMOS BOTTLE: A tanker trailer.

TIN CAN: A CB radio.

TWO-WHEELER: A motorcycle.

see also: four-wheeler

WALK ON: To overpower a person's CB signal.

WILLY WEAVER: A drunk driver.

WINDJAMMER: *(synonym: ratchet jaw)* An over-talkative person on the CB.

YARDSTICK: A highway mile marker.

UFO Believers

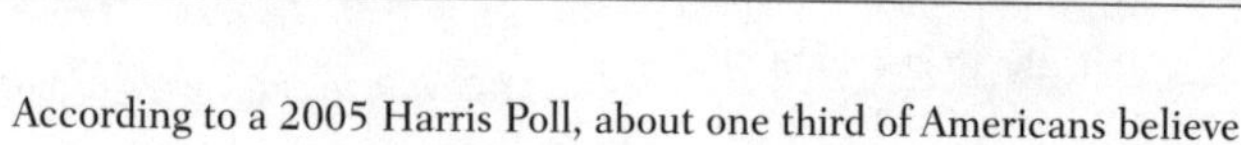

According to a 2005 Harris Poll, about one third of Americans believe in "UFOs." Technically a UFO ("unidentified flying object") is anything in the sky that can't be labeled with certainty, but in this context it's probably safe to say that those poll-takers believe alien spaceships have been sighted by humans.

Among people who study UFOs—called "ufologists"—there is a wide range of explanations for specific UFO sightings and a wide range of opinions on the implications of those sightings. Many people interested in UFOs maintain that the U.S. government has evidence of intelligent extraterrestrial life and is keeping it secret, perhaps to prevent widespread panic. They point to government installations (e.g., Area 51), documents, projects, and organizations that allegedly indicate government knowledge of extraterrestrial activity.

There's no widespread agreement in the community of people who follow UFO-related developments on which kinds of aliens exist, except that one race—often called Greys—is fairly common in UFO literature. Greys are humanoid aliens with large, black eyes and oversized heads; they're often depicted in entertainment media, such as the film *Close Encounters of the Third Kind*.

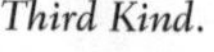

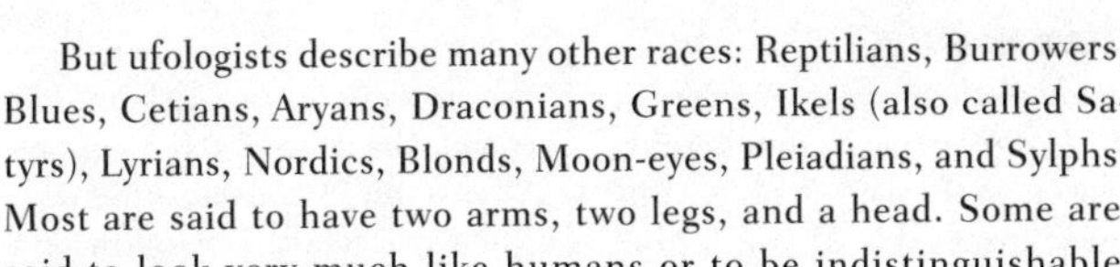

But ufologists describe many other races: Reptilians, Burrowers, Blues, Cetians, Aryans, Draconians, Greens, Ikels (also called Satyrs), Lyrians, Nordics, Blonds, Moon-eyes, Pleiadians, and Sylphs. Most are said to have two arms, two legs, and a head. Some are said to look very much like humans or to be indistinguishable from humans.

UFO-related sightings and documents range from almost universally acknowledged frauds to legitimate government findings that are made public through organizations like NASA and the FBI, although none of the government documents offers explicit evidence of alien visitors to Earth.

ALF: *(synonym: EBE)* An abbreviation for "alien life form."

see also: ET

ABDUCTEE: A person who has been taken aboard an alien spacecraft.

see also: abduction

ABDUCTION: Taking a human being onto an alien spacecraft against that person's will. Abductions may involve tests, biological samples, or surgical procedures (such as implanting a device in the brain).

Some UFO believers also speak of psychic abductions, such as forcing the spirit out of the body, or intrusion into dreams.

see also: abductee

"The more cooperative we are during our **abduction** experiences, the more they are willing to share with us."

AREA 51: *(synonyms: Dreamland, Groom Lake)* A tract of land in southern Nevada owned by the U.S. government, believed to be used for testing new military aircraft and said by some UFO believers to hide evidence of the existence of intelligent alien life.

BLACK PROJECT: Any Top Secret U.S. military project.

"To claim that these are government **black projects** insults my intelligence. The government does not test their secret experimental aircraft in people's backyards."

BLUE BOOK: A U.S. Air Force study of the possible dangers of UFOs (referring to unidentified objects in the air, not necessarily alien spaceships) that ran from 1952 to 1970. Available online from the FBI under the Freedom of Information Act. Some UFO believers allege that parts of the report that offer evidence of extraterrestrial life were taken out.

see also: Condon Report

BROOKINGS REPORT: A publicly available report from the Brookings Institution, commissioned by NASA and delivered in 1961. The report suggested that knowledge of extraterrestrial life might be disruptive to human affairs, although it made no specific recommendations of secrecy. Some UFO believers believe that this caused the U.S. government to adopt a policy of concealing any evidence of alien life.

CLOSE ENCOUNTER OR CE: Extraterrestrial sightings from close up (within 500 feet).

There are six kinds of CE's: A close encounter of the first kind (a CE-1) is a sighting of an unidentified flying object (UFO). The second kind is a sighting of physical evidence of aliens on earth, such as crop circles or cattle mutilations. The third kind is a sighting of extraterrestrials together with their spacecraft. The fourth kind is an abduction. The fifth kind is direct communication with an alien. The sixth kind is a sighting of a person or animal being killed by an extraterrestrial.

see also: Hynek Classification System, daylight disc, nocturnal light

CONDON REPORT: A 1968 study for the U.S. Air Force formally called the "Scientific Study of Unidentified Flying Objects" that concluded that all UFO sightings to date could be explained by conventional means. Some UFO believers consider the report to be a contrived, conscious attempt to discredit reports of extraterrestrials.

see also: *Blue Book*

CONTACTEE: A person who has received communications from extraterrestrials, sometimes through psychic means.

"He was a physical **contactee** with our Fleet. He has met many space brothers and sisters on the ground and aboard the spaceships, this *physically*."

DAYLIGHT DISC OR DAYLIGHT DISK: A UFO seen from a distance during the day.

see also: close encounter, nocturnal light

THE DRAKE EQUATION: An equation devised by Dr. Frank Drake in 1961 to determine the number of extraterrestrial intelligences in our galaxy with whom we might have contact, based on factors like the rate of star formation, the fraction of planets with life that go on to develop intelligent life, the expected lifetime of an intelligent alien species, etc.

The equation's result depends mainly on the assumptions made about these various factors, so in and of itself the equation isn't evidence in favor of the existence of extraterrestrial life.

see also: Fermi's Paradox

DREAMLAND: *(synonyms: Area 51, Groom Lake)* A government-owned tract of land in southern Nevada.

EBE: *(synonym: ALF)* An abbreviation for "extraterrestrial biological entity."

ET OR EXTRATERRESTRIAL: (as a noun) Any creature that comes from another planet. (as a verb) Coming from another planet.

see also: ALF

EXOGAMY: Sexual intercourse between humans and extraterrestrials.

FERMI'S PARADOX: A question posed by physicist Enrico Fermi: If the universe is so large and old, why haven't we been contacted by extraterrestrial life so far?

Some of the proposed answers to Fermi's Paradox are: "We have, but it's being covered up;" "Because there's no other intelligent life in the universe;" "Because we're being purposely shielded from contact by the extraterrestrials themselves;" and "Because we're looking for the wrong kinds of evidence of extraterrestrial life."

see also: The Drake Equation

FOO FIGHTER: A type of flaming or metallic, spherical UFO reported by American soldiers during World War II and thought at the time to be some kind of new enemy weapon.

"The mystery **foo fighters** were named as such because they were hostile to Allied aircraft and there was no mistaking the halo of fire surrounding each sphere."

GRAYS OR GREYS: One of the most commonly reported types of humanoid alien, having a large head; large, black eyes; and a small mouth. The aliens in the movie *Close Encounters of the Third Kind* fit the description of Greys.

Believers assert that multiple types of Greys exist, including a large-nosed variety and a variety who are seven to eight feet tall.

GROOM LAKE: *(synonyms: Area 51, Dreamland)* A government-owned tract of land in southern Nevada.

HYNEK CLASSIFICATION SYSTEM: A means of categorizing close-up sightings of or contact with extraterrestrials, devised by Dr. J. Allen Hynek.

see also: close encounters.

MJ-12: Allegedly, a very high secrecy rating used by the U.S. government for certain UFO-related documents. MJ is variously said to stand for "Majic," "Majestic," "Majesty" (in reference to the President), and "MAJI" or "Majority Agency for Joint Intelligence."

MEN IN BLACK OR MIBS: *(synonym: Men in Gray)* Alleged individuals who are said to visit UFO witnesses shortly after a sighting or visitation and identify themselves as government agents; they attempt to acquire any physical evidence of the alien contact and to convince or threaten the individual to pretend the incident never happened.

Some accounts of MIBs describe them as clearly human, whereas other accounts imply that they might be aliens who resemble or are impersonating humans.

"Then again, it is not the **men in black** you should worry about. Above them you have the men in grey ..."

MEN IN GRAY: *(synonym: Men in Black or MIBs)* Alleged agents who suppress information about alien encounters.

MISSING TIME: Time elapsed during some UFO sightings for which individuals involved cannot account.

"I can remember one instance of **missing time**. I had just woken up in the middle of the night from sleeping. Just for no reason, apparently. I looked at the clock and it was about 1:30. Just then my radio, which I keep on, became all staticky, and I looked at the clock and it was 3:45 and a different song was playing."

NOCTURNAL LIGHT: An unidentified light moving in the night sky.

see also: *daylight disc, close encounter*

PROJECT AQUARIUS: Allegedly, a U.S. government project organized to document alien presence on Earth and the interaction between human beings and aliens throughout human history.

PROJECT REDLIGHT: An alleged U.S. government project that test flies captured alien spacecraft.

ROSWELL: A town in New Mexico where a UFO is alleged to have crashed in 1947, and where the U.S. government is said to have performed alien autopsies.

UFO: "Unidentified flying object." The term technically means anything in the air that can't be readily identified, but it is often used to mean an alien spacecraft.

UFOLOGY: (pronounced "yoo-FAHL-oh-gee") The study of UFOs and extraterrestrial life.

"At the heart of popular **ufology** exist a few dedicated individuals. Some of them genuinely believe that aliens are visiting the Earth, based upon a personal experience."

UFONAUT: An extraterrestrial.

see also: *ET, ALF*

Wiccans, Witches, and Neo-Pagans

Neo-pagans, witches, Wiccans, and related groups are so diverse that even finding a single meaningful name for this subculture is problematic. The most widely-shared characteristic is following an earth religion (see below), yet some witches are not religious at all, instead being part of the pagan/witch subculture by virtue of their involvement with magick (often distinguished from stage magic by the "k"). Members of some of these various groups might argue that they have nothing meaningful in common with other members of the subculture.

Yet all of these groups share a certain vocabulary and sensibility. Most pagans and witches are young, enthusiastic about becoming part of an existing tradition (or establishing their own), and aware that a choice to become part of this subculture will marginalize them. For some, the shock value of calling themselves "witches" is a major benefit of involvement. For others, intolerance for paganism and earth religions is a painful downside to following their spiritual inclinations.

Wicca, a religious movement arguably established in the 1950s and nourished by pre-Christian Celtic practices, is the most cohesive group in the subculture, and many widespread terms originated with them. Other terms come from other earth religions, historical cultures (especially Celtic, to a lesser extent Norse, and interestingly, Jewish), and elsewhere.

Highly organized and ritualistic traditions anchor one end of a spectrum that stretches to the opposite extreme of eclectics, who piece together their religion from a variety of traditions and from personal inspiration, and solitaries, who worship alone. Solitaries may practice anything from Wicca to eclectic witchcraft to the worship of ancient Greek or other traditional gods and goddesses.

One practice that does not fall within this subculture, though it is sometimes associated with it by outsiders, is Satanism. By and large, earth religions and witchcraft don't even recognize the existence of an entity like Satan and are far more likely to emphasize balance or a unity of opposites than a concept of good versus evil. Individuals who identify themselves as Satanists or Satanic witches have little in common with members of earth religions, and neither group considers itself to have much to do with the other.

ASATRU: *(synonym: Odinism)* A modern earth religion based on pre-Christian, Norse paganism.

ATHAME: (pronounced "ath-UH-may" or "ATH-uh-may") A ceremonial dagger used in rituals. It is rarely used to physically cut anything; in many traditions, using an athame to cut a physical substance is expressly prohibited.

BALEFIRE: A bonfire used for magickal or ritual purposes.

BANE: Bad, evil, ill.

> "Either you can raise and direct power, or you can't. Your strength and skill can be used for blessing or for **bane**. The choice—and the karma—are yours."

BELTANE: A cross-quarter day sabbat, generally celebrated on May 1 or the evening of April 30. A fertility festival, usually involving balefires.

BESOM: A broom used to cleanse or purify a space, often in preparation for a religious or magickal ritual.

BLESSED BE: A greeting and farewell.

"Best wishes for a speedy and healthy return to better days. **Blessed Be**, A."

BOLINE OR BOLLINE: *(synonym: white-handled knife)* A ceremonial knife, usually curved and with a white handle. Unlike an athame, a boline is used to physically cut materials, such as to harvest herbs or engrave candles.

BOOK OF SHADOWS: *(synonym: grimoire)* (also "book of lights and shadows") A book recording spells and rituals for a particular tradition, coven, or witch.

BURNING TIMES: Those periods in the Middle Ages when accused witches were routinely burned, hanged, or drowned. While in the past this term was often accepted as describing a specific period in time, there is now some discussion in the witch and pagan community as to whether or not it's accurate to say there was such a period.

"In my opinion, the **Burning Times** had just as much to do with sexism as it had to do with religious bigotry."

CANDLEMAS: Imbolc, a festival marking the passing of winter. This name also refers to a Catholic holiday.

CHARGE: To ritually imbue a tool with magickal properties or a ceremonial purpose.

CIRCLE: 1) A magickal, pagan, or Wiccan ritual. 2) A place where a ritual is performed. 3) A group that performs a ritual.

see also: coven

CONE OF POWER: Magickal power raised in a circle and directed to a purpose.

CORRESPONDENCES: Materials used in magick that relate to the goal of the ritual or spell.

"Use magical **correspondences** of herbs, crystals, and stones to unlock the powers of the Sun, Moon, stars, and planets for your rituals."

- FROM A LISTING OF NEW HAMPSHIRE WITCHCRAFT CLASSES

COVEN: A gathering of witches, whether religious or otherwise. Usually a coven has a maximum of thirteen members.

COVENSTEAD: The place where a coven meets for rituals and, sometimes, spellcasting.

THE CRAFT: Another word for witchcraft; popular among non-religious witches, but also sometimes used in reference to witch religion.

> "In all that time I've only ever found one other wisened olde Witch who had the stature and presence of mind to engage me and who really understood **the Craft**."

CROSS QUARTERS OR CROSS-QUARTER DAYS: The four sabbats that don't fall on an equinox or solstice, namely Samhain, Imbolc (Candlemas), Beltane, and Lammas (Lughnassadh).

DARK PATH: *(synonym: Left-Hand Path)* Malign use of magick.

DEDICATION: A ceremony in which a witch pledges to be a true follower of a tradition.

DEGREE: A level of achievement in certain traditions.

> "The Cords are usually consecrated as part of the Second **Degree** Initiation."

DEOSIL: Clockwise; a direction normally associated with building, creating, or protecting.

DIANIC: Traditions that center on a goddess or the Goddess, sometimes the Roman goddess, Diana. There are both Wiccan and non-Wiccan Dianic traditions.

DRUIDISM: A neo-pagan tradition that attempts to reconstruct some elements of pre-Christian Celtic paganism.

EARTH RELIGION: Any of a number of nature-centric religions, often pagan. Earth religions often center on the worship of the Goddess alone or the Goddess and the God. Alternatively, an earth religion may be built around one or more historical or eclectic deities.

ECLECTIC: A witch, Wiccan, pagan, or practitioner of an earth religion who draws elements of rituals, beliefs, or spells from various sources, or who worships or follows deities from more than one tradition.

> "Can you take the course if you're an **eclectic** Pagan rather than a Druid in particular?"

ESBAT: A moon festival, held on each full moon.

FAERY OR FAERIE: *(synonym: Feri)* Either an ecstatic or a faery-related form of Wicca.

FERI: *(synonym: Faery or Faerie)* In pagan/witch culture, a sensual or ecstatic form of Wicca; alternatively, a form of Wicca combined with belief in faeries or other magical creatures.

(!) FLUFFY BUNNY OR FLUFFBUNNY: A derogatory term for a pagan, witch, or Wiccan who prefers the "sweetness and light" elements of the religion. Also used to describe someone new to the religion who may be considered naïve.

"You're a misguided **fluffbunny**, and I have no use for you."

GARDNERIAN WICCA: The Wiccan tradition founded by Gerald Gardner. Gardner, an Englishman, stated that he learned his practices from a group of people who had preserved traditional practice of witchcraft.

THE GOD: *(synonyms: the Horned God, the Green Man)* The primary male deity in some traditions.

THE GODDESS: The primary or sole female deity—and sometimes sole deity entirely—of many earth religions. The Goddess is variously considered not to have a name, to have a particular name, or to have many names (e.g., Isis, Astarte, Diana, Brigid, etc.).

GREAT RITE: A ritual symbolizing the union of the God and the Goddess, which involves either putting a ceremonial knife in a chalice or actual sexual intercourse, generally between a man and a woman.

THE GREEN MAN: *(synonyms: the Horned God, the God)* The primary male deity in some traditions.

GRIMOIRE: *(synonym: book of shadows)* A book of spells or rituals.

GUARDIANS OR GUARDIANS OF THE WATCHTOWERS: *(synonym: Watchers)* Spirits invoked at each of the four quarters to protect a circle during observance of a ritual or casting a spell.

"**Guardians of the watchtower** of the east, we do summon, stir, and call thee up to protect us in our rite."

- FROM A HARVEST RITUAL BY WICCAN MICHAEL FIX

HANDFASTING: A neo-pagan or Wiccan wedding; typically each of the two persons being married reaches out to the other with one hand, and the two hands are loosely bound with a ribbon.

> "In all likelihood, this will look very much like any other Wiccan or neopagan **handfasting** you've ever attended."

HEREDITARY WITCH: A witch raised in Wicca, paganism, or some other earth religion. Alternatively, a secular witch brought up in a magickal tradition.

HIGH MAGICK OR HIGH MAGIC: Ceremonial magick, or magick requiring study; alternatively, a structured system of magick that aims for spiritual improvement. Kaballah is an example of a discipline that is generally considered to be High Magick.

THE HORNED GOD: *(synonyms: the God, the Green Man)* The male deity or male aspect of deity in some Wiccan traditions and other earth religions.

IMBOLC: A cross-quarter day sabbat, generally celebrated on February 1 or 2, marking passing of winter. Sometimes a purification ceremony.

KABALAH OR QABALA OR CABALA: A Jewish mystic tradition or ceremonial magick that is incorporated into some forms of paganism and witchcraft.

LAMMAS: A cross-quarter day sabbat celebrated on August 1, the first of three harvest festivals.

LAW OF THREEFOLD RETURN: *(synonym: Threefold Law)* A belief that a person who does a good deed receives three times as much good in return.

LEFT-HAND PATH: *(synonym: Dark Path)* The practice of magick for selfish purposes or in opposition to nature.

LITHA: *(synonym: Midsummer)* The festival of the Summer Solstice, one of the eight sabbats.

LOW MAGICK OR LOW MAGIC: Folk, informal, or nature magick, often performed with natural materials and without great ceremony. The term is generally not meant to be derogatory.

LUGHNASSADH: (pronounced "LOO-nah-sah") The first harvest celebration of the year.

see also: *Lammas*.

MABON: The Autumnal Equinox, one of the eight sabbats, usually celebrated on or around September 21. The second harvest festival.

MAGIC: Often used to refer to stage magic or tricks, differentiating it from magick, which refers to witchcraft or spells as practiced by witches. Alternatively, has the same meaning as "magick."

see also: *magick*

MAGICK: A spell intended to effect some purpose. Magick may be considered an appeal to a deity or, for non-religious witches, a form of occult power.

MIDSUMMER: (*synonym: Litha*) The celebration of the beginning of summer.

NEO-PAGAN: A polytheist or follower of an earth religion. Interchangeable with "pagan," except that the latter can also be used to describe historical polytheist groups.

"I can think of a number of **neo-pagan** religions that do have various forms of clergy."

ODINISM: (*synonym: Asatru*) Paganism based on old Norse beliefs.

OLD RELIGION OR OLD PATH OR OLD WAYS: Another name for Wicca, earth religions, or witchcraft. These spiritualities often describe themselves as heirs to various pre-Christian religions. Some practitioners consider their religions to be a literal continuation of an ancient religious practice, although these are in the minority.

OSTARA: The Vernal Equinox, one of the eight sabbats, usually celebrated on or around March 21. Named for the Teutonic goddess Eostre; the pre-Christian version of this festival is the precursor to Easter.

PAGAN: See neo-pagan. Also used to refer to historical, polytheistic religions.

PENTACLE: A disk inscribed with a pentagram, used for ritual purposes.

PENTAGRAM: A five-pointed star, generally considered to represent the five elements: earth, air, water, fire, and spirit (although the number of elements in some traditions is four, omitting spirit).

The pentagram is usually drawn with the point facing up rather than down; a pentagram with a downward point is considered "inverted," and although used occasionally to represent the Horned God, the inverted pentagram is more commonly associated with Satanism, which is not part of this subculture.

PROJECTIVE ENERGY: Energy sent out by a witch to accomplish a specific goal, charge an object, or repel negative forces.

PROPER PERSON: An individual considered by a formal coven to have the appropriate qualifications to be initiated. These qualifications may include such elements as ethics, personal conduct, and knowledge of the coven's particular tradition.

"I will ever keep secret and never reveal the secrets of the Art, except it be to a **proper person**, properly prepared, within a circle such as I am now in."

- FROM A GARDNERIAN BOOK OF SHADOWS

QUARTERS: The four cardinal directions, each associated with one of the classical elements: north with earth, south with fire, east with air, and west with water.

QUERENT: A witch asking a question or making a request in the course of a ritual or spell.

RECEPTIVE ENERGY: Energy intended to attract something the witch desires, such as love.

"I've been in a women-only circle that was *very* balanced in terms of projective and **receptive energy**."

SABBAT: A solar festival. There are eight sabbats each year: the Summer and Winter Solstices (Midsummer and Yule), the Vernal and Autumnal Equinoxes (Ostara and Mabon), and the cross-quarter days (Samhain, Imbolc, Beltane, and Lammas).

"Basically, I observe the **Sabbats** and Esbats, and give thanks to the Goddess and God, with rituals that feel personal and comfortable for me."

SAMHAIN: (pronounced "SOW-in" or "SOW-ayn") A cross-quarter day sabbat, celebrated on October 31 or, occasionally, November 1. Samhain is the Celtic and Wiccan New Year, and is often considered a time to

remember the dead or celebrate the Crone aspect of the Goddess.

SKYCLAD: Naked for purposes of performing rituals, observing festivals (sabbats or esbats, initiations, etc.) or casting spells. In some traditions, certain rituals are meant to be performed skyclad.

> "My own coven works robed or **skyclad** depending on weather, location, and type of ritual. The nice thing about **skyclad** is that you don't have to worry about what to wear."

SOLITARY: A witch or pagan who worships alone, without a coven or worship group.

THREEFOLD LAW: *(synonym: Law of Threefold Return)* A Wiccan doctrine, also held by some other types of religious and nonreligious witchcraft and earth religions, that good deeds bring three times as much good back on the doer.

TRADITION: Any specific variety or practice of Wicca, witchcraft, or earth religion. For instance, Gardnerian Wicca is a Wiccan tradition.

UNCAST: In some traditions, to open or dispel a circle that was used to observe a ritual or cast a spell.

> "After the ritual, I **uncast** the circle going Widdershins."

(!) WARLOCK: This term is generally not used in witchcraft and earth religions except as an insult. The literal meaning is "traitor" or "oath-breaker." Male witches are *not* called "warlocks."

WATCHERS: *(synonym: Guardians or Guardians of the Watchtowers)* A type of protective spirit.

WHITE-HANDLED KNIFE: *(synonym: boline or bolline)* A ceremonial knife.

WICCA OR WICA: An earth religion that is also characterized as witchcraft. Wicca appears to have originated or (according to some sources) been repopularized in the mid-twentieth century. It incorporates aspects of pre-Christian European religions and is sometimes considered to be directly derived from such religions.

WICCAN REDE: A tenet of most Wiccan traditions: "An it harm none, do as thou wilt." (Sometimes phrased in a more modern way, as, "If it harm none, do what you will.")

WIDDERSHINS: Counterclockwise, a direction generally used to reverse, banish, or uncast.

"If your projective hand is your right hand and your receptive hand is your left hand, then if you face the center of a circle and charge the circle, it would be charged **widdershins** by projection to the right from your right hand and reception from the left with your left hand."

WITCH: 1) A practitioner of certain earth religions, especially Wicca. 2) A person who performs spells according to a non-religious, magickal tradition.

WITCHCRAFT: 1) Synonymous with Wicca or with certain other earth religions. 2) The practice of spellcasting by a non-religious witch.

YULE: Another name for the Winter Solstice, one of the eight sabbats, usually held on or near the 21 of December.

Appendix: The Language of Hip Hop

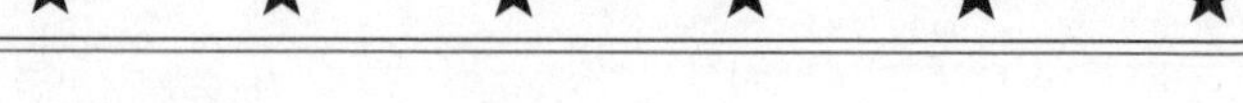

The slang associated with hip hop is used by millions of Americans. Entire books have been written to document hip hop slang (for instance, Alonzo Westbrook's *Hip Hoptionary*™ and Lois Stavsky's *A 2 Z : The Book of Rap and Hip-Hop Slang*). Both the number of people who use this slang and the number of terms it includes are far greater than is the case with the other subcultures in this book, and hip hop is more a worldwide phenomenon than simply a subculture. With all that in mind, this section is intended to be an introduction to and sampling of hip hop terms.

Before I begin, I should mention that hip hop slang routinely uses words that are considered offensive in "Standard English." These words generally have different and milder associations in hip hop slang, and they come up regularly. Because of this, the following contains a good deal of profanity, which I've tried to steer clear of in other sections.

The hip hop subculture includes two different groups: people interested in creating hip hop music, including rappers and DJs; and the enormous number of people who listen to hip hop.

As far as street slang is concerned, hip hop is really only a layer on top of the urban, black slang that preceded it. This dialect, which has been called Black English and Ebonics, includes not only a wide range

of terms not found in "Standard English," but slightly different grammar and pronunciation as well. But don't be fooled into thinking it's a separate language: It's a dialect, a variation on the English language like Australian, Scots English, or so-called "Standard English."

Spelling in hip hop slang isn't entirely fixed. Words that end in *er* may be written in hip hop slang with either an *er* or an *a*; for instance, *gangster/gangsta*. The letter *z* is sometimes substituted for *s*, and words ending in *-ing* are written to end with *in'* or *in*. Overall, the written form is less predictable and more phonetic than Standard English.

Additional unfamiliar terms come from some unusual word transformations. For instance, one type of hip hop slang places the syllable "iz" before the first vowel in some words (so that, for instance, "house" becomes "hizouse." A similar type uses only the first letter or two of a word and replaces the rest with "izzle", so that "fo' sure" or "fo' sho'" becomes "fo' shizzle" or even "fashizzle".

187: Murder. From Section 187 of the California Penal Code which covers homicide.

411: ("four one one," not "four eleven") Information.

5-0: (five-oh) A policeman; derived from the television series *Hawaii 5-0*, and/or because some police cars are 5.0 liter Ford Mustangs.

ALL THAT: Top shelf; high quality; very good of its kind. Often used to describe people.

ASS: Among other uses, "ass" can be added after an adjective for emphasis. It doesn't change the meaning of the word it modifies, but simply draws attention to it while changing the rhythm of the sentence, something that can come in handy for rappers.

When written, "ass" used in this way is often a separate word ("bad ass gangsta"), but can also, less often, be hyphenated ("bad-ass gangsta") or even connected to the end of the word ("badass gangsta").

"I really think this is and was a lame **ass** battle."

BALLER: A man who has money, respect, and attention from women.

BANGER: A dangerous gang member.

BANK: *(synonyms: cheese, chips, cream, duckets, ends, mail, paper, scrilla or scrillah)* Money.

see also: *flow*

BATTLE: (as a noun) A contest between rappers, who take turns rapping and trying to cut each other down and build themselves up. The winner gets recognition and respect. (as a verb) To participate in a battle.

BATTLE RECORD: A vinyl record compiled with a variety of music samples and sounds designed to provide material for a DJ to scratch with.

BEND: A prostitute.

(!) BITCH: 1) A prostitute. 2) A girlfriend. Not necessarily derogatory. 3) An insulting term for a man, implying he's weak or cowardly.

BITE: *(synonym: xerox)* To steal another rapper's lyrics, beats, etc.

"You're dumb anyway if you did **bite** off of him, cuz he ain't that good."

BLING BLING: Jewelry. More generally, wealth or expensive things.

BOMB: 1) (adjective) Very good; desirable 2) (noun) Something very fine. 3) (noun) Marijuana laced with heroin.

BONE: 1) (verb) To have sex with. 2) (noun) The penis. 3) (noun) One dollar.

see also: *to the bone, bone out*

BONE OUT: *(synonyms: bounce, jet, roll out)* To leave.

BOO: Darling, honey, sweetheart, baby. Term of affection for a significant other.

BOOSTER: 1) A shoplifter. 2) A car thief. 3) A thief of any kind.

BOOTY OR BOOTIE: 1) (as a noun) Backside. 2) (as an adjective) No good; worthless.

see also: *butt*

BOUNCE: *(synonyms: bone out, jet, roll out)* To leave.

BREAK: 1) (noun) A rhythmic section of a hip hop song with no rap over it. 2) (verb) To break dance. 3) (verb) To leave or go somewhere quickly.

BUDDY: (as a noun) A sexual partner. (as a verb) Seeming good at first, but later revealed as worthless; e.g., a pair of shoes, a friend.

BUG: To act crazy or act out.

see also: ill, wack

"I was about to order that sh*t last night with the Sweetwater Bill Me Later sh*t, but moms was **bugging** because I'm not 18 and don't have a 'credit history.'"

BUST SLUGS: Shoot bullets.

BUSTA: An unreliable person; a fake.

see also: bitch

BUTT: (adjective) No good; worthless.

CAP: A bullet.

see also: bust slugs, capped

CAPPED: Injured with a bullet; shot.

see also: bust slugs, cap

"But it goes deeper than "he was black and rapped, and got **capped**" like all the other authors."

CHEESE: *(synonyms: bank, chips, cream, duckets, ends, mail, paper, scrilla or scrillah)* Money.

CHILL: (as a verb) To calm down or relax. (as an adjective) Relaxed or in control.

CHIPS: *(synonyms: bank, cheese, cream, duckets, ends, mail, paper, scrilla or scrillah)* Money.

CHROME: *(synonyms: glock, steel, strap)* A gun.

see also: piece

CLIQUE: (pronounced "cleek") The friends a person spends time with. This is a West Coast word; in other parts of the country, crew is more common.

see also: crew

COLD: 1) Dangerous. 2) Intense. 3) Very cool.

COME CORRECT: To do right; to do something in the proper way.

"You all are funny to the point where clowns got notepads in their hands. **Come correct**, b**ches."

CRAZY: Many, very, a lot.

"My grandpa got **crazy** rich from trading stocks."

CREAM: *(synonyms: bank, cheese, chips, duckets, ends, mail, paper, scrilla or scrillah)* Money.

CREW: *(synonym: posse)* The associates a person spends time with and depends on.

see also: *clique*

CRIB: A person's living space.

CRUNK: 1) Relating to having a very good time, often in the context of "get crunk." 2) Drunk, or high and drunk. This is a more recent usage and is not necessarily implied when the word is used in the first sense. 3) A particular type of energetic, dance-oriented, southern rap music.

CUH: *(synonyms: cuz or cuzz or cuzzo)* Friend; "cousin."

CUZ OR CUZZ OR CUZZO: *(synonym: cuh)* Friend; "cousin." Used especially among Crips.

DAWG: *(synonym: dog or dogg)* A friend or member of a person's crew.

DEF: Very good; excellent. This word is dated and not as widely used as it once was.

DIME: A very attractive woman; i.e., a "ten."

DIS OR DISS: *(synonym: disrespect)* To disrespect; i.e., treat a person badly.

DIS RECORD: A recording of rap music that taunts or belittles another rapper. Not to be confused with a battle record.

DISRESPECT: *(synonym: dis or diss)* To treat a person badly.

DJ: *(synonym: turntablist) (as a noun)* Short for "disc jockey," a person who is expert at using vinyl records on turntables (and more recently, CDs on specialized equipment) to create a range of sounds and pull together music samples. Rap music originated with DJs manipulating records to make dance music. A Master of Ceremonies (MC) would often speak over parts of the mix (i.e., rap). Over time, rappers rather than DJs have become more prominent. "DJ" is both a noun and a title. (as a verb) To manipulate vinyl records so as to make music out of samples of existing songs.

see also: *mix, scratch*

DOG OR DOGG: *(synonym: dawg)* 1) (as a noun) A friend or member of a person's crew. 2) (as a form of address) A friend, or sometimes a neutral acquaintance. A particularly close friend can be called a

"road dog." 3) (as a verb) To act insultingly toward someone.

see also: crew, homeboy, dis

DOME: A head.

DOPE: *(synonyms: fat, phat, live, slammin')* Excellent; very good.

see also: cold

DOWN WITH: 1) Willing; having no objection. 2) Part of; accepted by.

"Don't front, a lot of you who remember them were **down with** Terrible T. and Sweet L.D., even though we may not have been **down with** MC Hammer."

DROP A DIME: To inform on someone to the police.

DROP KNOWLEDGE: *(synonym: drop science)* To show knowledge or skill.

DROP SCIENCE: *(synonym: drop knowledge)* To show knowledge or skill.

"I haven't worked this hard to be pigeon-holed by any dumb f*ck racists that act like they can **drop science**, when they really as ignorant as any Adolf Hitler wannabee."

DUCKETS: *(synonyms: bank, cheese, chips, cream, ends, mail, paper, scrilla or scrillah)* Money.

EMCEE: *(synonyms: rapper, Master of Ceremonies or MC)* An artist who speaks rhythmic rap lyrics over hip hop or rap music.

ENDS: *(synonyms: bank, cheese, chips, cream, duckets, mail, paper, scrilla or scrillah)* Money.

FADE: To suppress or disregard.

FAT: *(synonyms: dope, phat, live, slammin')* Excellent; very good.

FLOW: 1) (verb) To rap with continuous rhyme. 2) (noun) A section of a rap that rhymes continuously. 3) (noun) Money.

FLY: Attractive; sexy; very fine.

FREAK: 1) (verb) To have sex. 2) (verb) In reference to a woman, to dance provocatively. 3) (noun) A woman who is very sexual.

FREESTYLE: (as a verb) To improvise a rap. (as a noun) An improvised rap.

FRESH: 1) New; innovative. 2) Fine; high quality.

FRONT: To pretend to be other than you are, especially to pretend to be tough.

"Did they agree? If yeah then it's cool, but if they never then no, 'cause I don't want 'em think we **frontin'**."

GAME: Real life, as opposed to things that aren't true or don't matter.

see also: playa

GANGSTA OR GANGSTER: 1) A gang member. 2) A criminal. 3) A formidable rapper.

GANK: To steal from or otherwise cause harm to.

GAT OR GATT: A gun, especially an automatic.

GET BUSY: To have sex.

GHETTO BIRD: A police helicopter.

GHOST: (as an adjective) Suddenly gone. (as a verb) To disappear.

GLOCK: *(synonyms: chrome, steel, strap)* A gun.

GO FEDERAL: To make it big; to become famous or very successful (figuratively, across the entire country).

GRIP: 1) Rapping ability; refers to the rapper's grip on the microphone. 2) Money. 3) A gun.

HARD: Tough; dangerous.

HARDCORE: Truly represented; real; straight.

HAWK: *(synonym: scope)* To stare or watch.

HEAT: A gun.

HELLA: Much; very; a lot of.

"They started coming to my events and showing me **hella** love."

- Candyman 187, in an interview with Real Hip Hop

HIP HOP OR HIP-HOP: Rap music or rapper culture. Hip hop encompasses DJing, rapping, dancing, the hip hop music club scene, and the street culture of people who listen to hip hop music.

The term "hip hop" is more closely associated with the dance/club scene than the term "rap." "Rap" also has other meanings.

see also: rap

HOMEBOY OR HOMEGIRL: *(synonyms:homes or homey or homie)* A friend or relative.

HOMES OR HOMEY OR HOMIE: *(synonyms: homeboy or homegirl)* A friend or relative.

HOOD: Short for "neighborhood." 1) A person's neighborhood,

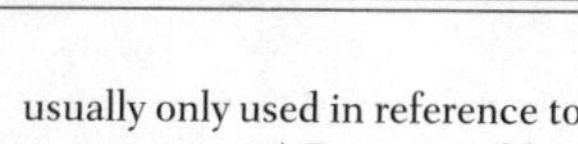

usually only used in reference to poorer areas. 2) Poorer neighborhoods in general.

HYPE: (as a noun) Media spin, advertising, or promotion. (as an adjective) Very good; excellent.

ILL OR ILLIN': 1) Strange; weird; crazy. 2) Really good; fine. 3) Bad; nasty.

see also: bug, wack

JACK: (as a verb) To steal or steal from. (as a noun) Nothing, or nothing worthwhile.

JAKES: *(synonym: one-times)* The police.

JAM: A rap song.

see also: mix

JANKY: No good, or fake.

> "You know I'm not some **janky** ass newbie."

JET: *(synonyms: bone out, bounce, roll out)* To leave.

LIVE: *(synonyms: dope, fat, phat, slammin')* Excellent; very good.

LOC: (pronounced "loke") 1) (noun) A term of address for a friend or acquaintance. 2) (adjective) Crazy. 3) (adjective) Cool; admirable.

MAD: Very many; a lot.

MAIL: *(synonyms: bank, cheese, chips, cream, duckets, ends, paper, scrilla or scrillah)* Money.

MARINATE: To hang out and relax.

> "While I was just **marinating** a few days ago, this thought popped into my head."

MARK: A sucker; someone who's an easy target. This word is borrowed from con artist and carnival slang (see pages 95 and 61).

MASTER OF CEREMONIES OR MC: *(synonyms: rapper, emcee)* An artist who speaks rhythmic rap lyrics over hip hop or rap music.

MIX: (as a verb) To time, combine, and manipulate music played on turntables as a means of making hip hop music. (as a noun) The music (rather than the rap) of a hip hop song.

see also: DJ, jam

MONEY: A name used for a friend or acquaintance. The word is also used in its traditional sense of "currency," but there are many other hip hop slang words for "currency" (for instance, bank).

see also: homeboy, bank

MOTHERFUCKIN': A word used for emphasis before a noun or verb. The meaning of the noun or verb isn't changed, but more attention is drawn to it, and the rhythm of the sentence is changed, which can be useful to rappers.

see also: ass

MOVE ON: *(synonyms: step to, step up)* To provoke someone.

(!) NIGGA OR NIGGER: 1) General use, non-derogatory term to use when addressing a friend or acquaintance. 2) An appellation for any person who understands the street and acts authentically.

Despite the widespread use of the word "nigga" in hip hop culture, the term still carries its history of persecution of blacks by whites, so non-blacks and even blacks who are considered to be more a part of mainstream culture than of street culture can't necessarily count on using the word without giving offense.

OG OR ORIGINAL GANGSTER: A title for a person who has knowledge and experience of gang life and is looked up to by gang members.

OFF THE HOOK: Wild; really exciting; impressive.

> "Your flow was **off the hook**."

OLD SCHOOL: Outdated or retro.

ONE-TIMES: *(synonym: jakes)* The police

PAPER: *(synonyms: bank, cheese, chips, cream, duckets, ends, mail, scrilla or scrillah)* Money.

PEACE: (as an interjection) Goodbye (or less often, "hello"). (as an adjective) Relaxed; calm; in control.

PEEPS: People, specifically in reference to those from the same area or same culture as the speaker.

PHAT: *(synonyms: dope, fat, live, slammin')* Excellent; very good.

PIECE: 1) A gun. 2) Sex.

see also: chrome, heat

PLAY: 1) To be part of, especially in the phrase "play that." 2) To try to deceive.

PLAYA OR PLAYER: Someone who's successful in life; e.g., a person who can get money, respect, and sex.

> "Keep on going Jeremy. You taken da game to a new height, **playa**."

PLAYA-HATA OR PLAYER-HATER: A person who speaks insultingly of people more successful than himself.

POINT BLANK: Right now; here in this situation.

POSSE: *(synonym: crew)* The associates a person spends time with and depends on.

PROPS: Gratitude or recognition; short for "proper respect."

PUNK: A person who isn't worthy of respect; a coward.

RAP: (as a verb) To speak lyrics rhythmically, as a rapper does. (as a noun) A rap song, or the lyrics to a rap song.

RAPPER: *(synonyms: emcee, Master of Ceremonies or MC)* An artist who speaks rhythmic rap lyrics over hip hop or rap music. The lyrics may be memorized or improvised. As a rule, rap artists don't perform other rappers' work.

RAW: True; real; straight.

REPRESENT: Stand up, or stand up for.

> "This is for people who are serious, people that are loyal, people who will **represent** to the fullest."

RIDE: A car.

see also: whip

ROLL OUT: *(synonyms: bone out, bounce, jet)* To leave.

ROLL WITH: To be part of a group; to hang out with.

see also: down with, crew

SCOPE: *(synonym: hawk)* To stare or watch.

SCRATCH: (as a verb, in reference to a DJ) To spin vinyl records back and forth to produce a scratching sound sometimes used in rap music. (as a noun) Money.

SCRILLA OR SCRILLAH: *(synonyms: bank, cheese, chips, cream, duckets, ends, mail, paper)* Money.

SCRUB: A lazy or worthless person.

SERVE: To defeat or outface.

SHIFE: In regard to a person: new, inexperienced, contemptible, or inconsequential.

SHORTY: 1) A younger person or child. 2) A woman, particularly one who looks like girlfriend material.

SLAMMIN': *(synonyms: dope, fat, phat, live)* Excellent; very good.

SMOKE: To kill, especially with a gun.

STEEL: *(synonyms: chrome, glock, strap)* A gun.

STEP OFF: To back off or stop provoking.

STEP TO: *(synonyms: move on, step up)* To provoke someone.

see also: step off

STEP UP: *(synonyms: step to, move on)* To provoke someone.

STRAIGHT: True; real; all right.

STRAP: *(synonyms: chrome, glock, steel)* A gun.

STUPID: 1) Funny or creative. 2) Very or extremely.

TAX: To steal.

TIGHT: Very good; fine. The word suggests that things are in order, that everything is in its proper place.

TO THE BONE: Completely; all the way.

(!) TRICK: A insulting term for a woman.

TURNTABLIST: *(synonym: DJ)* A person who is expert at using records or CDs to create a range of sounds.

WACK: Crazy; freaked out. A negative term, as contrasted with ill, which can be either positive or negative.

see also: bug, ill

> "You **wack**, yo. You gotta be kiddin' me, kid."

WHIP: A fine car.

see also: ride

(!) WIGGA OR WIGGER: A derogatory term for a white person who tries to be a part of black street culture but is not accepted by it.

WORD OR WORD UP: 1) That's the truth; I agree. 2) A general-use greeting.

"Word up" used to be used widely, but now "word" alone is more common.

WORD IS BOND: An expression of trust or a guarantee of honesty.

> "Yeah, it's very decent, **word is bond**. Supreme mad props on that sh*t."

XEROX: *(synonym: bite)* To steal lyrics.

Bibliography

I've arranged this bibliography by section to make it easier to research a particular subculture, and have mixed Web resources in with printed ones for the same reason. Some sections have few or no references here because the research was primarily with people within the subculture, and in fact, that kind of research was important throughout the book.

Since Web resources regularly change, expand, and disappear, you'll find a more up-to-date Internet bibliography as well as discussion groups and other resources on the *Talk the Talk* Web site at www.subculturetalk.com.

Introduction

Wikipedia, the online, collaborative encyclopedia: www.wikipedia.org

Robert L. Chapman with Barbara Ann Kipfer, *American Slang* (Harper Collins, 1998).

Steven A. Jacobson, *Yup'Ik Eskimo Dictionary* (Alaska Native Language Center, 1984).

John Simpson, Chief Editor, *The Oxford English Dictionary* (Oxford University Press, 1989).

Richard A. Spears, *Slang and Euphemism* (Signet, 2001).

Simon Winchester, *The Meaning of Everything: The Story of the Oxford English Dictionary* (Oxford University Press, 2003).

Anthony C. Woodbury, "Counting Eskimo Words for Snow: A Citizen's Guide" (1991): www.sfs.uni-tuebingen.de/linguist/issues/5/5-1239.html

Americans in Antarctica

The Seventh Continent, Ethan Dicks' Antarctic Home Page: penguincentral.com/penguincentral.html

Matthew Lazzara's Antarctic Journal: tellus.ssec.wisc.edu/outreach/antarctic

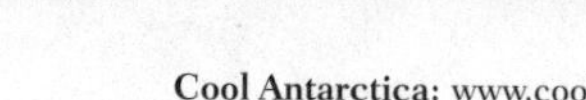

Cool Antarctica: www.coolantarctica.com

Guillaume Dargaud's Antarctic page: www.gdargaud.net/Antarctica

Anime and Manga Fans

Ryouko's Cave anime page: www.ryouko.demon.co.uk/animetop.htm

A shoujo anime page: www.naughtykitty.org/shoujo.html

Shunsuke's Anime Page: victorian.fortunecity.com/university/5

Yale Anime Society: www.yale.edu/anime

AnimeMetro.com: www.animemetro.com

The Anime Critic: www.animecritic.com

Absolute Anime: www.absoluteanime.com

Akemi's AnimeWorld: animeworld.com

Astrologers and Astrologists

Astrology.com: www.astrology.com

Astrology, Tarot & Jung: Home Page of Anthony Louis: members.aol.com/tonylouis/home

Lore of Astrology: www.elore.com/Astrology/contents.htm

Basic Astrology Lessons: astrologystudent.50megs.com

Astrology-Numerology.com: www.astrology-numerology.com

AstroCenter.com: www.astrocenter.com

Beekeepers

Beekeeping: The Beekeeper's Home Page: ourworld.compuserve.com/homepages/Beekeeping

Bee Happy: pages.prodigy.net/dscribner/bees

Bees and Beekeeping Home Page: www.main.org/cahbs

Betterbee (beekeeping supplies): www.betterbee.com

Virtual Beekeeping Gallery: www.beekeeping.com/_menus_us/index.htm?menu.htm&0

Beekeeping Tips for Beginners: extension.missouri.edu/explore/agguides/pests/g07600.htm

Bicyclists and Mountain Bikers

Bicycle Source: www.bicyclesource.com

EXPN BMX site: expn.go.com/bmx

Dictionary of Roadie Slang: embers.tripod.com/geert_pc/slang.htm

Bike Colorado: www.bikecolorado.com

Birders

About.com Birding/Wild Birds by Christine Tarski: birding.about.com

Birdforum.net: www.birdforum.net

Glossary of Birder Slang: home.pacifier.com/~mpatters/bird/slang.html

Randall T. Cox, Birders Dictionary (Falcon, 1996).

Bodybuilders

Getbig: www.getbig.com

BodybuildingPro.com: www.bodybuildingpro.com

Learn Bodybuilding: www.learnbodybuilding.com

Gordo's Fitness Emporium: www.goheavyorgohome.com

The Pumping Station: www.thepumpingstation.com

About.com Bodybuilding, from Hugo Rivera: bodybuilding.about.com

RosellaPurnetti.com: www.rossellapruneti.com

Carnival Workers

To the Hilt Sword Swallowing: www.swordswallow.com

Carny Lingo: goodmagic.com/carny

Cavers and Spelunkers

Glenn Baddeley—Caving: home.mira.net/~gnb/caving

Cat Fanciers

Cat Fanciers: www.fanciers.com

CatsPlay.com: www.catsplay.com

The Cat Fanciers' Association: www.cfa.org

Circus People

International Circus Hall of Fame: www.circushalloffame.com

The Ringling Bros. and Barnum & Bailey Circus: www.ringling.com

CircusNews.com: www.circusnews.com

Coin and Money Collectors (Numismatists)

Coin Market Slang: malakoff.com/cms.htm

site about paper money collecting: www.atsnotes.com

Professional Coin Grading Service: www.pcgs.com

Heritage Auction Galleries—Rare Coins: coins.heritageauctions.com

Centerville Coin & Jewelry: www.centercoin.com

Con Artists and Scammers

FraudAid.com: First Aid for Fraud Victims: www.fraudaid.com

Frank Abagnale, *The Art of the Steal* (Broadway, 2002).

Frank Abagnale, *Catch Me If You Can* (Grosset & Dunlap, 1980).

Harry Anderson, *Games You Can't Lose: A Guide for Suckers* (Burford Books, 2001).

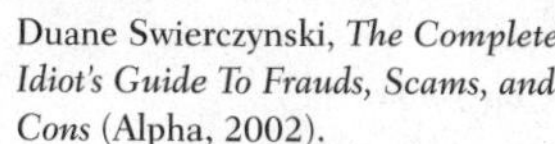

Duane Swierczynski, *The Complete Idiot's Guide To Frauds, Scams, and Cons* (Alpha, 2002).

Cowboys and Rodeo Riders

Cowboy Frank: cowboyfrank.net

TexianCowboy Enterprises: www.texiancowboy.com

CyberRodeo: cyberrodeo.com

Nevada Department of Cultural Affairs: dmla.clan.lib.nv.us/

Cowboy Showcase: www.cowboyshowcase.com

Carved Eggs partial vocabulary of cowboy terms: www.carved-eggs.com/cowboy_vocabulary.htm

Library of Congress: Buckaroos in Paradise: memory.loc.gov/ammem/ncrhtml/crhome.html

About.com Rodeo, from Ralph Clark: rodeo.about.com

Atlantic States Gay Rodeo Association: www.asgra.org/

Diana Rowe Martinez, "Rodeo Culture": www.suite101.com/article.cfm/rodeo_and_cowboys/47908

Drug Pushers and Users

Indiana Prevention Resource Center: www.drugs.indiana.edu

Addictions.org Guide to Recovery: www.addictions.org/

U.S. Office of National Drug Control Policy: www.whitehousedrugpolicy.gov

Flyfishers and Sport Fishermen

Arkansas Striper Fishing: www.arkansasstripers.com

Fishing in California: www.fishingnetwork.net

ActiveAngler.com: www.activeangler.com

Learn How to Flyfish: www.school-offlyfishing.com

Furries

Nadan's Watching Stone: www.watchingstone.com

Wabbit's Lair: www.chameleon.net/~deserthare/

Furry Internet Services and Hosting: www.furcen.org

Gamblers and Poker Players

Cardshark Online: cardshark.us

Gambling Il Dado: www.ildado.com

Casino Info: www.casino-info.com/

Allgam: All About Gambling: www.allgam.com

Gardeners

LewisGardens.com: Beginner's Guide to Perennial Gardening: www.lewisgardens.com

The Garden Helper (includes an active gardening forum): www.thegardenhelper.com

Gay, Lesbian, Transgendered, and Bisexual People

A Brief Dictionary of Queer Slang and Culture: www.geocities.com/WestHollywood/Stonewall/4219

Bisexual Resource Center: www.biresource.org

FastCat's Place, including the Gay Dictionary: www.fortunecity.com/village/birdcage/279

Robert Scott's Gay Dictionary: www.hurricane.net/~Ewizard/19a.html

Glossary of Gay Slang Terms: andrejkoymasky.com/lou/dic/0.html

Goths

Darkness.com forums: forum.darkness.com/index.php

Encyclopedia Gothica: www.waningmoon.com/gothica/

Graffiti Writers

Art Crimes: The Writing on the Wall: graffiti.org

New York City Cyber Bench: www.at149st.com

Gun Enthusiasts

Boomershot!: www.boomershoot.org

SavvySurvivor.com (gun-related survivalism): www.savvysurvivor.com

Hackers and Programmers

The Jargon File: www.catb.org/jargon/html

The Learning Channel: Hackers: tlc.discovery.com/convergence/hackers/hackers.html

Temple of the Screaming Electron: www.totse.com/en/hack/index.html

GameProgrammer.com: www.gameprogrammer.com

Ham Radio Operators

Ham Radio forum: www.hamforum.com

Amateur radio community site: www.qsl.net

Amateur Radio and DX Reference Guide: www.ac6v.com

Hikers and Backpackers

Trailplace: An Appalachian Trail Resource Guide: www.trailplace.com/

Whiteblaze.Net: A Community of Appalachian Trail Enthusiasts: www.whiteblaze.net

American Trails: www.americantrails.org

Appalachian Long Distance Hikers Association: www.aldha.org

Historical Reenactors

Teen Reenactors and Historians Site: rehisteens.tripod.com/indexdefault.html

Fanny & Vera's Helpful Hints & Timely Tips for Civil War Reenactors: www.shasta.com/suesgoodco/newcivilians/index.htm

Hot Rodders

Auto Hobby Page: www.carnut.com

Team Chevelle: www.chevelles.com

HotrodShows.com: www.hotrodshows.com

#1 Motormart Classic Car Glossary: www.1motormart.com/glossary.htm

Hotrods & Classics: www.hotrodsandclassics.net

Hunters

HuntingNet.com (with online forum): www.huntingnet.com

ButlerWebs.com hunting page: www.butlerwebs.com/hunting/

2001 National Survey of Fishing, Hunting, and Wildlife-Associated Recreation: www.census.gov/prod/2002pubs/FHW01.pdf

Bill Cochran, "How to Talk Like a Deer Hunter" (Roanoke Times, 11/11/2004). Available online at www.roanoke.com/outdoors/bill cochran/wb/wb/xp-13631

Kayakers, Canoers, and Rafters

Paddling.net: Canoeing and Kayaking Info: www.paddling.net

A Paddler's Glossary: www.kenduskeagstreamcanoerace.com/glossary.html

OutdoorPlaces.com Paddling Put In: www.outdoorplaces.com/Features/Paddle/

WetDawg: www.wetdawg.com

Paddling glossary and degrees of difficulty: suoc.syr.edu/suoc/paddling/glossary.html

Magicians

MagicTricks.com: www.magictricks.com

Simple Magik: www.angelfire.com/pe/SimpleMagik

Blifaloo.com magic: www.blifaloo.com/magic

Magic and Illusion from Wayne Kawamoto: magic.about.com

Mediums, Channelers, and Spiritualists

Phenomenal Evidence: nsacphenomena.com

SpiritWritings.com: www.spiritwritings.com

Model Builders and Radio-Controlled Model Enthusiasts

Essence's Model Rocket Reviews and Resources: www.rocketreviews.com

National Association of Rocketry: www.nar.org

International Electric Models, a model supplier site with model hobby resources: www.greatmodeldeals.com

Rocketry Online Reference Library: www.info-central.org

Great Planes model manufacturing company site, with model plane resources: www.greatplanes.com

Model Cars Online: www.modelcarsonline.com

Glossary of Common Model and High Power Rocketry Terms: my.execpc.com/~culp/space/glossary.html

Skip Perrine, "A Primer of Glossary Terms for the NASCAR Modeler." Available online at www.teamracin.com/Articles/2003/SP825.htm

Model Railroaders and Railfans

Bill's Galesburg Journal: www.billselleck.net

Lionel Trains getting started page: www.lionel.com/GettingStarted/

Railroad.net: The Railroad Network: www.railroad.net

Site for H&R trains, including model train resources: www.hrtrains.com

World's Greatest Hobby: Your Guide to the World of Model Trains: www.greatesthobby.com

National Model Railroad Association: www.nmra.org

Motorcyclists (Bikers)

Motorcycle Club & Riding Club Education: home.earthlink.net/~rcvsmc-edu/index.html

Rocky Mountain Harley Davidson Biker Glossary: www.rmh-d.com/info/glossary.php

Total Motorcycle: www.totalmotorcycle.com

Star Touring & Riding Southwest Territory #275: star275.org

Lone Star Ironworks Biker Dictionary: www.lonestarcc.com/dic.html

BMW Motorcycle dictionary: w6rec.com/duane/bmw/vocab.htm

Naturists and Nudists

Nudism and Naturism: Introduction, history, glossary of terms: www.religioustolerance.org/nudism4.htm

Rec.nude FAQs (nudism discussion group frequently asked questions): www.cs.uu.nl/wais/html/na-dir/nude-faq/part1.html

Online Gamers

Rei's Random Guide to M.M.P. Gaming Terms: stuff.mit.edu/people/rei/game-terms.html

The Video Game Critic: www.videogamecritic.net

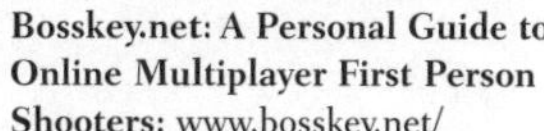

Bosskey.net: A Personal Guide to Online Multiplayer First Person Shooters: www.bosskey.net/

Flying Omelette: www.flyingomelette.com

New Museum of Contemporary Art Killer Instinct gaming site: www.newmuseum.org/killerinstinct/#

Parapsychologists

Paranormal Investigators & Research Association: mywebpages.comcast.net/parainvestigator/Index/Main.html

Parapsychological Association: www.parapsych.org

Politicians and Politicos

U.S. Political Glossary: www.killian.com/earl/glossary.html

Harvard University Institute of Politics: www.iop.harvard.edu

United States Political Glossary: www.uta.fi/FAST/GC/poliglos.html

Grant Barrett, *Hatchet Jobs and Hardball : The Oxford Dictionary of American Political Slang* (Oxford University Press, 2004).

Bill Doskoch, "Getting the Words Out: U.S. Political Glossary": www.ctv.ca/servlet/ArticleNews/story/CTVNews/1095635647727_25

Prisoners

Texas Department of Criminal Justice Institutional Division: The Correctional Officer's Guide to Prison Slang: members.tripod.com/catchout/dictionary/DictFrameSet3.html

The Best of "The Other Side of the Wall": www.prisonwall.org/

Prison Slang 101: www.geocities.com/waytoofunny_2000/prisonslang.html

Pro Wrestling fans

Pro Wrestling Torch newsletter site: www.pwtorch.com

Online Onslaught: www.onlineonslaught.com

The Rasslin' Ring Glossary of Pro Wrestling: www.shotgun-reviews.com/russ/glossary.html

Prostitutes and Other Sex Workers

The Escort Boards: escortboards.com

World Travel and Sex Guide: www.worldsexguide.com

Punk Rockers and Straight Edgers

GaragePunk.com: www.garagepunk.com

Ishkur's Guide to Rave Culture: www.ishkur.com/culture

The Punk and Ska Archive: voodooglowskulls.tripod.com

Renaissance Fairegoers

Renaissance Faire Home Page: www.renfaire.com

Scribe: The Renaissance Faire Information Clearinghouse: www.faire.net/SCRIBE

Ren-Fest Glossary: mrffriends.tripod.com/language/glossary.html

Rock Climbers

Bay Area Climbers: www.bayareaclimbers.com

RockClimbing.com: www.rockclimbing.com

Outdoor Adventures Network: www.myoan.net/climbing

Camp4 Rock Climbing: www.camp4.com/rock

Role-Playing Gamers

John Kim's RPG site: www.darkshire.net/~jhkim/rpg/site/about.html

Introduction to Roleplaying: www.geocities.com/daveshwz

The Handbook: Your Guide to Role-playing: www.angelfire.com/tx/afira

Roleplay.org: Roleplaying Games and Information: www.roleplay.org

Wizards of the Coast (the company that makes Dungeons & Dragons and other RPGs): www.wizards.com

RV Owners

RVNetLinx: www.rvnetlinx.com

RV Forum: www.rvforum.net

RVAdvice.com: www.rvadvice.com

RV-Coach Online: www.rv-coach.com

A Beginner's Guide to RVing: beginningrvers.com

RV.Net: www.rv.net

Sci-Fi and Fantasy Fans

C.M. Shaw's Fan Glossary: www.geocities.com/Area51/Shire/6930/

Jane's Story Page (with Ms. Nitpicker's Fanfic Glossary): littlecalamity.tripod.com

Stilyagi Air Corps (Ann Arbor Science Fiction Association): stilyagi.org

SiliCon's Fannish Vocabulary: www.siliconventions.com/faqs/vocab.html

Scuba Divers and Wreck Divers

Wrolf's Wreck: wrolf.net

NJSCUBA.Com: The Online Resource for New Jersey Divers: www.njscuba.com

Skateboarders

Exploratorium Skateboard Science: www.exploratorium.edu/skateboarding/

EXPN Skateboarding Glossary: expn.go.com/glossary/skt/index.html

Skateboard Dictionary: www.geocities.com/Pipeline/Slope/4774/sk8dictionary.html

Skiers

Hikok Sports: www.hickoksports.com

Ski Smarts: www.skismarts.com

ABC-of-Skiing.com: www.abc-of-skiing.com

Arizona Ski Guide: www.azcentral.com/travel/seasonal/skiing/ski-slang.html

Skydivers and B.A.S.E. Jumpers

Flag Day Festival Glossary of Skydiving Terms: www.flagday.com/about/skydiver/terms_glossary/index.shtml

DropZone.com: www.dropzone.com

Adventure Skydiving, with glossary of skydiving terms within FAQ: adventureskydiving.mtsyellowpages.com

United States Parachute Association: www.uspa.org

Snowboarders

Adventure Sports Online Snowboarding Glossary: www.adventuresportsonline.com/snowboardglossary.htm

Outboard: Gay & Lesbian Snowboarders: www.outboard.org

ABC-of-Snowboarding.com: www.abc-of-snowboarding.com

Transworld Snowboarding: www.transworldsnowboarding.com

Society for Creative Anachronism Members (SCAdians)

Golden Stag Productions: www.goldenstag.net

The Dictionary of SCA Slang, by Ioseph of Locksley: www-cs.canisius.edu/~salley/Articles/slang.html

Society for Creative Anachronism College of Svatý Sebesta: www.usd.edu/orgs/socrean/

Stamp Collectors (Philatelists)

AskPhil stamp collecting resource: www.askphil.org/

Surfers

Riptionary Surfer Lingo Lexicon: www.riptionary.com/

SurfHumor.com: www.surfhumor.com

Sustainable Living Advocates

EcoIntegrity Center of Bellingham: www.attractionretreat.org/ecobell/

Fifth World Network Glossary: www.5thworld.net/HTML/MS_Glossary.htm

Permaculture.net: www.permaculture.net

Intentional Communities Web site: www.ic.org

Tattoo Artists and Tattoo Enthusiasts

About.com Tattoos/Body Piercings, from Karen Hudson: tattoo.about.com

2003 Harris Interactive poll on tattoos:

www.harrisinteractive.com/harris_poll/index.asp?PID=407

Thespians and Stage Crew

CATCo Theatre Terms: www.geocities.com/jegoldston/CATCo_TheatreTerms.html

Sapsis Rigging: Resources: www.sapsis-rigging.com/Resources.html

Theatrecrafts.com: theatrecrafts.com

Truckers

Layover.com Info Center: www.layover.com/infocenter

Glossary: Terms Used in Intermodal Transportation: www.ecargotport.com/indexpages/glossary.htm

Bear's Trucking Page: www.bearspage.info/h/tru.html

The Trucker's Place: www.geocities.com/TheTropics/1608

U.S. Department of Labor Bureau of Labor Statistics: Truck Transportation and Warehousing: www.bls.gov/oco/cg/cgs021.htm

U.F.O. Believers

TruthNet International: www.geocities.com/CapitolHill/8167

UFOpsi: www.ufopsi.com

Mark's U.F.O. page: members.aol.com/mddunbar1

Steelmark: www.steelmarkonline.com

Appendix: The Language of Hip Hop

Rap/Hip-Hop from Henry Adaso: rap.about.com

Bay Area Hip Hop Dictionary: www.riceplate.com/rap/rap.php

Hip-Hop Dictionary: hhdictionary.blogspot.com

The Ultimate Rap Dictionary: the_yz.tripod.com/dictionary

The Rap Dictionary (wiki): www.rapdict.org/Main_Page

General References for Subculture Slang

The University of Oregon Slang Dictionary (material compiled by students in introductory linguistics): babel.uoregon.edu/slang/

Glossarist: A searchable directory of glossaries and topical dictionaries: www.glossarist.com

YourDictionary.com specialty glossaries: www.yourdictionary.com/specialty.html#table

Open Directory dictionaries by subject: dmoz.org/Reference/Dictionaries/By_Subject

Index

#

187, 373; 2000-miler, 172; 40-miler, 56; 411, 373; 419, 88; 5-0, 373; 50-miler, 56; 73, 167; 86'ed, 56; 88 (skinheads), 317; 88 (ham radio), 167

A

abductee, 357; abduction, 357; abortion, 249; abs, 46; abscond, 31; abseil, 276; academy, 271; accidental, 42; accumulation, 82; acid head, 108; acronym agency, 236; action, 128; active, 128; active cave, 70; actor (thespians), 349; actor (fairegoers), 271; actorvist, 236; ACW, 177; add 'em up, 56; addict, 88; advance, 236; Advance Fee Scheme, 88; advance man, 56; aerophilately, 333; afflicted, 25; after-market, 211; agency, 258; agent (carnival), 56; agent (mediums), 201; aggro, 337; aid climbing, 276; air, 310; air hog, 306; air rappel, 70; air sign, 25; airdog, 325; alarm odor, 31; albino, 333; ALF, 357; alibi store, 56; all breed, 66; all in, 128; all lit up, 115; all that, 373; allbreed, 66; all-city, 153; alligator (truckers), 354; alligator (ham radio), 167; all-terrain biking, 35; ally, 138; alpha, 224; alphabet agency, 236; alpine skiing, 314; alpine snowboarding, 325; alpine start, 276; alter, 66; amateur radio, 167; amateur rocketry, 208; amen corner, 236; amendment, 135; anchor (rock climbers), 276; anchor (bicyclists), 35; angle, 249; angles, 25; anime, 16; aniparo, 17; annex, 57; Annie Oakley, 73; Anno Societatis, 328; announcer, 73; anon, 271; Antarctic 10, 12; ante, 128; anthro (SF/fantasy), 294; anthro (furries), 123; antique, 181; Any Other Variety, 66; anyfur, 123; AOV, 66; APA, 294; ape hangers, 216; apes, 216; apex, 35; apparition, 201; apple, 128; apport,

201; approach, 276; appropriate technology, 342; approvals, 333; après-ski, 314; Area 51, 357; armchair caver, 70; aroint, 271; artificial climbing, 276; artificial spit, 306; artillery, 108; artist, 73; artiste, 73; AS, 328; Asatru, 363; ascendant, 25; A-show, 249; Asian Flew, 42; Asian Flu, 42; aspect, 25; asport, 201; ass, 373; astral body, 231; astral projection, 231; astral travel, 231; astrologer, 26; astrologist, 26; AstroTurf, 236; at your back door, 354; ATB, 35; athame, 363; attack politics, 236; auger, 35; Auguste clown, 73; aura, 231; author, 108; authorized, 328; autocrat, 328; Autograph Scam, 88; automagically, 160; automatic drawing, 201; automatic painting, 201; automatic speaking, 201; automatic writing, 201; automatism, 201; avatar, 224; average, 103; Award of Arms, 328; axed, 337; aye, 271

B

baby bat, 148; baby butch, 138; baby dyke, 138; baby habit, 108; baby harp seal, 328; babyface, 249; babygoth, 148; babyheads, 35; back channel, 236; back door, 73; back end, 57; back piece, 346; back up, 108; back yard, 73; backscatter, 306; backslide, 320; backstage, 271; back-to-back, 153; backyard, 73; bacon, 35; bad trip, 108; badge name, 294; Badger Game, 88; bafflegab, 237; bag bride, 108; bag drag, 12; bag lock, 320; bag man, 57; baggies, 337; baked, 108; baldie, 186; balefire, 363; ball, 31; baller, 374; balloon, 108; bally, 57; ballyhoo (circus), 73; ballyhoo (carnival), 57; bammer, 109; ban, 224; banana, 237; bane, 363; bang, 109; banger, 374; bank (hip hop), 374; bank (skateboarders), 310; Bank Examiner Scheme, 89; bank scout, 190; bankroll, 128; bar (hackers), 161; BAR (models), 208; bar fine, 258; bar hopper, 216; bareback, 258; barker, 57; barking head, 237; barn door, 276; barn queen, 216; Barney (surfers), 337; Barney (fishing), 120; barnstorm, 237; barrel, 337; base (skiers), 314; base (drugs), 109; base (skydivers), 320; BASE jumping, 320; basement, 289; basher, 138; bashing, 337; Basic Faire Accent, 271; basic strategy, 128; basket case, 216; bat sweat, 271; batt, 109; battle (graffiti), 153; battle (hip hop), 374; battle record, 374; be stole, 244; beaker, 12; beamer, 109; bean chute, 244; bean slot, 244; bear (truckers), 354; bear (GLTB), 138; bear bag,

172; bear off, 190; beard, 139; beat, 349; beat artist, 109; beatdown, 317; beauty contest, 237; beaver, 306; bedbug, 109; bedroll, 103; bee blower, 31; bee space, 31; bee suit, 31; bee yard, 31; beef (carnival), 57; beef (prisoners), 244; beef (con artists), 89; bee-haver, 31; beer-and-pretzel gaming, 284; beeyard, 31; beginners, 349; belay, 276; belay monkey, 276; belay slave, 276; belike, 271; bells and whistles, 160; below, 190; belt voice, 349; Beltane, 363; belted fighter, 328; bench, 46; benchwork, 213; bend, 374; bends, the, 306; Benny, 337; bent (surfers), 337; bent (SCUBA), 306; beret, 258; besom, 363; beta (SF/fantasy), 294; beta (rock climbers), 277; beta (gamers), 224; beta reader, 294; Betty (bicyclists), 35; Betty (snowboarders), 325; BFA, 271; bi, 139; bid party, 294; biff, 35; big con, 89; big eye, 12; Big Government, 237; big tent, 237; big top, 73; big ups, 172; bigfoot, 237; big-name caver, 70; biker, 216; Bilbo thumper, 284; bill, 73; billet reading, 201; bilocation, 231; binders, 181; 'biner, 277; bing, 109; biodiesel, 342; bio-PK, 231; bio-psychokinesis, 231; bioregion, 342; bird, 167; birder, 42; birdie, 167; birdy, 186; bis, 46; bisexual, 139; bishojo, 17; bishonen, 17; bishoujo, 17; bishounen, 17; bit (fairegoers), 271; bit (prisoners), 244; bitch, 374; bitch tits, 46; bitch up, 244; bite (hip hop), 374; bite (graffiti), 153; black book, 153; Black Dollar Scam, 89; black project, 357; black tank, 289; black water, 289; blacks, 266; blade, 249; blade glommer, 57; blank, 109; blast (drugs), 109; blast (bodybuilders), 46; blast a joint, 109; blast a roach, 109; blast a stick, 109; blasted, 109; blaze (hikers), 172; blaze (drugs), 109; blazer, 82; bleeding heart, 237; bleep, 148; blessed be, 364; blind bet, 128; bling bling, 374; block, 213; Block Hustle, 89; blockbuster, 153; blow, 109; blow a fix, 109; blow a shot, 109; blow a stick, 109; blow off, 249; blow up, 249; blowdown, 73; blowfish, 148; blown out, 337; blowoff, 57; Blue Book, 358; blue pill, 258; blue steel, 258; blue-blazer, 172; blues, 73; blunt, 110; BNC, 70; board, 310; boat scout, 190; bobber, 216; bobpoint, 277; bobtail, 354; body bag, 82; body composition, 46; bodysuit, 346; boffer, 328; boil, 190; boiler room, 89; boing-boing, 35; boline, 364; bolline, 364; bomb (snowboarders), 325; bomb (graffiti), 153; bomb (bicyclists),

35; bomb (hip hop), 374; bomber (hunters), 186; bomber (rock climbers), 277; bombproof, 277; bone, 374; bone out, 374; bone smuggler, 139; bone yard, 244; bonehead, 317; boneyard, 216; bonk (bicyclists), 35; bonk (snowboarders), 325; Bonneteau, 89; bonus delay, 208; bony, 190; boo, 374; boobtube, 70; boof, 190; boogie, 320; book of shadows, 364; book test, 201; booker, 250; bookie, 128; bookmaker, 128; boomer, 157; boomerang, 12; boondocking, 289; booshway, 177; boost, 110; booster (hip hop), 374; booster (con artists), 89; boot, 110; boot party, 317; booted, 224; booth, the, 349; boothie, 271; bootie, 374; bootlegger, 167; booty (hip hop), 374; booty (rock climbers), 277; booty (cavers), 70; BOP, 42; bore holes in the sky, 210; boss (hunters), 186; boss (prisoners), 244; boss (gamers), 224; boss canvasman, 74; boss clown, 74; boss monster, 224; bot, 224; bottle, 306; bottom, 139; bottom time, 306; bottoms, 46; boulder garden, 35; bouldering, 277; bounce (skydivers), 320; bounce (hip hop), 374; bounce (politicos), 237; bounce (SCUBA), 306; bounce box, 172; bounce dive, 306; bouncer, 57; bourse (stamps), 333; bourse (coin), 82; box, 181; boxed, 110; box-pusher, 349; boy, 139; boy scout, 354; boys, 250; Bozo, 57; braces, 317; brah, 337; Braille dive, 306; brain bucket (bicyclists), 36; brain bucket (motorcyclers), 216; brain bucket (rock climbers), 277; brake check, 354; brass, 157; break (magicians), 196; break (hip hop), 374; break a leg, 349; break off, 320; breakable crust, 314; breakaway, 320; breed true, 66; breeder, 139; breezers, 120; brewery, 110; bridge up, 110; bring home a Christmas tree, 36; bring up, 110; bro, 337; broach, 190; broad tosser, 90; broadcast, 167; Broads, the, 90; broadsheet, 271; broke, 103; broken wand ceremony, 196; broker, 110; bronc buster, 103; bronc peeler, 105; bronco, 103; bronco buster, 103; brood, 31; Brookings Report, 358; bruiser, 186; brushing, 172; brute force (and ignorance), 160; BSG, 35; Bubba factor, 238; bubble, 289; buck fever, 186; buckaroo, 103; bucket, 277; bucking chute, 104; buckle bunny, 103; buckskinner, 157; buddy, 374; buddy box, 210; buff (gamers), 224; buff (graffiti), 153; buff (bodybuilders), 46; buffed, 46; buffer, 110; bug (hip hop), 375; bug (fishing), 120; bug (SCUBA), 306; bug (hackers), 160; buildering, 277; build-up, 58; bulk up, 46; bull (GLTB), 139; bull (prisoners), 244; bull (circus), 74; bull dyke, 139; bulldyke, 139; bullet hose, 157; bully pulpit, 238; bum beef, 244; bump (wrestling), 250; bump (drugs), 110; bump (gamblers), 128; bump a nose, 74; bumper belay, 277; bumper sticker, 354; bunco, 90; bunco artist, 90; bunco squad, 90; bunk, 110; bunny boots, 12; bunny hop, 36; bunny hunt, 167; bunny slope, 314; burble, 320; burn (graffiti), 153; burn (drugs), 110; burn (bodybuilders), 46; burner, 153; Burning Times, 364; burnout, 216; bury, 250; bushytail, 186; business (thespians), 349; business (drugs), 110; bust (hunters), 186; bust (gamblers), 128; bust slugs, 375; bust up, 186; busta, 375; busted call, 167; butch, 139; butcher, 74; butt, 375; butter butt, 42; button, 128; button pisser, 177

C

C joint, 110; C-1, 190; C-2, 190; Cabala, 367; cabinet, 202; cackle bladder, 90; Cadillac, 244; café racer, 216; cage, 216; cager, 217; call (gamblers), 128; call (cat fanciers), 66; call (carnival), 58; call a dive, 306; call boy, 258; call girl, 258; call sign, 167; calliope, 74; call-shy, 186; callsign, 167; cam, 277; cameling, 172; cameling up, 172; camp (GLTB), 140; camp (gamers), 225; campaign, 284; can, 157; Can I roll to disbelieve?, 285; cancelled to order, 333; Candlemas, 364; candy, 120; candy goth, 148; candy man, 110; candyman, 110; canned heat, 250; cannon, 271; canon, 294; canopy, 320; canopy relative work, 320; cans, 349; canuding, 222; canvas, 346; canyon, 36; cap (bodybuilders), 46; cap (hip hop), 375; cap (graffiti), 153; capped, 375; capper, 90; carabiner, 277; caravan, 289; carb up, 47; carbon condition, 271; card, 250; card counting, 129; card tosser, 90; cardician, 196; carding, 90; carnage, 190; carney, 58; carnie, 58; carny, 58; carpet clown, 74; carpet joint, 129; carpet patrol, 110; carry, 250; cartomancy, 202; carve (skiers), 314; carve (skateboarders), 310; carving, 217; case money, 129; cash and dash, 258; cash register, 354; cashed, 110; cast, 272; casual, 42; cat fancier, 66; cat fancy, 66; catch, 129; catch air (bicyclists), 36; catch air (skiers), 314; catch and release, 120; catch out,

244; catcher (GLTB), 140; catcher (circus), 74; CATO, 208; cattery, 66; cattle boat (SCUBA), 306; cattle boat (fishing), 120; cattle drive, 103; cattle show, 238; catwalk, 217; CAVE, 238; cave diving, 70; caver, 70; C-card, 307; CD, 140; CE, 358; cellie, 244; center joint, 58; center pole, 74; CHAD, 208; chain, 244; chain suck, 36; chalk, 278; chamber ride, 307; channel, 110; channel swimmer, 110; channeled, 181; channeler, 202; channeling, 202; chaparral, 103; chaps, 103; chapstick lesbian, 140; chara, 17; character clown, 74; charge, 364; charged up, 110; charismatic leader, 342; chart, 26; chase, 111; chase the tiger, 111; chaser, 111; chatelaine, 328; ChCh, 12; cheap heat, 250; cheat (gamers), 225; cheat (bodybuilders), 47; cheat reps, 47; check (gamblers), 129; check (drugs), 111; check in, 244; cheese, 375; Chelsea, 317; chemical persuasion, 70; cherry pie, 74; chew the scenery, 349; chibi, 17; chibi eyes, 17; chicken (GLTB), 140; chicken (fishing), 120; chicken coop, 354; chicken lights, 354; chicken scratch, 111; Chicken Stick, 210; chicken strips, 217; chicken tractor, 342; chickenhead, 278; chill (hip hop), 375; chill (con artists), 90; chillax, 337; chimney, 278; chinks, 104; chip (drugs), 111; chip (gamblers), 129; chips, 375; chirurgeon, 328; chopped, 181; chopper, 217; choss, 278; choss pile, 278; chrome, 375; chuck, 104; chum, 307; chummer, 120; chump, 58; chunder, 36; chute (paddlers), 190; chute (cowboys), 104; chute (rock climbers), 278; chute assis, 320; Ciazarn, 58; cinch, 104; Cinderella, 334; Cinderella fella, 258; circle, 364; circus jump, 58; claim skinhead, 317; clairaudience, 231; clairvoyance, 231; clairvoyant, 231; clan, 225; class A, 289; class B, 289; class C, 289; clean (rock climbers), 278; clean (bicyclists), 36; clean and jerk, 47; cleanup wave, 337; clear!, 328; clem, 58; cliché, 334; clip in, 278; clip out, 36; clip-ons, 217; clique, 375; clocker, 111; clockwatcher, 258; clone, 217; close encounter, 358; close spot, 47; closed boat, 190; closet, 140; closet champion, 250; close-up magic, 196; closing gate, 272; clothespin vote, 238; clothing optional, 222; cloud swing, 74; clown alley, 74; clown stop, 75; cluck, 111; clucked, 337; cluster, 31; coach, 289; coattails, 238;

cob, 342; cockpit, 191; COD Scam, 90; code, 160; code monkey, 160; cohousing, 342; co-housing, 342; cold (gamblers), 129; cold (hip hop), 375; cold bust, 111; cold frame, 135; collector, 346; colony, 31; color, 251; color up, 129; colors, 217; combust, 26; come correct, 375; come down (thespians), 349; come down (drugs), 111; come home, 111; come in, 75; come out, 140; come through, 90; comeback call, 186; come-in, 75; come-on, 91; comic book, 354; commemorative, 334; commercial company, 258; commitment ceremony, 140; commitment holder, 91; commune, 342; communicator, 202; comp (circus), 75; comp (gamblers), 129; companion planting, 135; company, 350; composite chart, 26; compost tea, 135; compulsory pose, 47; con (SF/fantasy), 294; con (furries), 123; con (con artists), 91; con (anime), 17; con artist, 91; con man, 91; con suite, 295; ConCom, 295; Condon Report, 358; cone of power, 364; confidence decoy, 186; confidence game, 91; confidence man, 91; confidence scheme, 91; confidence trick, 91; confidence trickster, 91; ConOps, 295; conrep, 295; consensus, 343; console, 225; consuite, 295; contactee, 358; contemporary counterfeit, 83; control (mediums), 202; control (puppeteers), 266; controller, 266; conversion, 211; convict, 244; convincer, 91; cook shack (carnival), 58; cook shack (circus), 75; cookhouse, 75; cooperative, 343; cop, 111; copy, 167; core, 337; core sample (models), 208; core sample (bicyclists), 36; cork, 321; corndogged, 36; corpgoth, 148; Corpora, 328; corporate goth, 148; correspondences, 364; cosplay, 18; count store, 58; coupon, 217; courtesy gobble, 186; coven, 364; covenstead, 365; cover (sex workers), 258; cover (stamps), 334; cover (cowboys), 104; covered, 337; cow horse, 104; cow puncher, 104; cowboy (gamblers), 129; cowboy (cowboys), 104; cowgirl, 104; cowpoke, 104; crack (carnival), 59; crack (hackers), 161; crack gallery, 111; crack head, 111; crack house, 111; crack spot, 111; cracker, 161; crackerjack, 111; Craft, the, 365; cram, 92; cranial disharmony, 36; crank (rock climbers), 278; crank (bicyclists), 36; crank up, 112; crash, 112; crashocrat, 328; crater (snowboarders), 325; crater (rock climbers), 278; crayon, 37; crazy, 375; cream, 375; credit card generator, 92; credit glide, 217; creeper, 321; cretin con, 295; crew (surfers), 338; crew (graffiti), 153; crew (hip hop), 376; crew (skinheads), 318; crib, 376; crimp, 278; crimper, 278; crippler, 42; crippleware, 161; cross dresser, 140; cross out, 153; cross quarters, 365; cross-country skiing, 314; crossdresser, 140; cross-dresser, 140; crossover, 295; cross-quarter days, 365; crotch rocket, 217; crow hop, 104; crow makeup, 148; crowd surf, 263; crownie, 328; crud, 314; Crud, the, 12; crufty, 161; cruise missile, 208; cruiser, 217; crunk, 376; crust, 314; Crust Punk, 263; crux, 278; cryptomnesia, 202; cryptorchid, 67; crystal gazing, 232; cuh, 376; cull (coin), 83; cull (birders), 42; cup of coffee, 258; curbstomping, 318; curbstoner, 92; curler, 191; curtain of light, 266; cusp, 26; custom, 181; customize, 181; cut (gamblers), 129; cut (bodybuilders), 47; cut (cowboys), 105; cut card, 129; cut up, 47; cut up jackpots, 59; cutaway, 321; cutting house, 92; cuz, 376; cuzz, 376; cuzzo, 376; cybergoth, 148; cycle (astrologers), 26; cycle (bodybuilders), 47; cylinder, 307; Czech black, 266; Czech zone, 266

D

da kine, 338; dab, 37; dabbler, 42; daemon, 202; daimon, 202; dally, 105; dam, 67; damp, 328; dance, 37; Dane, 272; 'dane, 272; dark horse, 238; dark lark, 42; Dark Path, 365; darktime, 354; date, 259; dawg, 376; day money, 105; daylight disc, 359; daylight disk, 359; dead dog party, 295; dead zone, 167; deadhead (railroad), 213; deadhead (truckers), 354; dead-head, 135; deadpoint, 278; deal, 112; Deal, the, 251; dealer, 92; death cookies, 37; death dive, 208; death march, 37; death match, 225; deathbed experience, 202; deathbed visions, 202; deathmatch, 225; debuff, 225; deck (skateboarders), 310; deck (rock climbers), 278; deck (thespians), 350; deck (prisoners), 244; decked, 181; deco, 307; dedication, 365; de-dyke, 141; def, 376; defarb, 177; defined, 47; definition, 48; degree, 365; delts, 48; Demican, 238; Demopublicrat, 238; demoscene, 161; deosil, 365; dequeen, 31;

dermography, 202; design type, 83; detailing, 211; detriment, 26; device, 83; DFL, 37; dial it in, 48; dialed in, 37; Dianic, 365; die, 161; diesel dyke, 141; diesel puller, 289; diesel pusher, 289; digisub, 18; dignity, 26; dime (bodybuilders), 48; dime (hip hop), 376; dime bag, 112; dime's worth, 112; ding, 244; ding-dong, 153; dinghy, 289; dink, 120; dip (coin), 83; dip (birders), 42; dip out, 42; direct, 26; direct drawing, 202; direct painting, 202; direct voice, 203; direct writing, 203; dirt dive, 321; dirt me, 279; dis, 376; dis record, 376; disappearance, 196; disaster mail, 334; disaster march, 75; discarnate, 203; disqualified, 59; disrespect, 376; diss, 376; dissociation, 203; ditch, 197; ditch parrot, 186; ditch weed, 112; divemaster, 307; diver, 42; DIY, 263; DJ, 376; DM, 285; do a line, 112; do business, 251; do it yourself, 263; do your own time, 245; doctored, 83; documentary interpretation, 177; dodge, 92; dog, 376; dog soldier, 177; dogg, 376; dogie, 105; doll, 267; doll wiggling, 267; dome, 377; dome slug, 13; donation, 259; doniker (circus), 75; doniker (carnival), 59; doniker joint, 59; doom cookie, 148; doors!, 75; dope, 377; double, 232; double blaze, 172; doujinshi, 18; down, 245; down range, 157; down to the felt, 130; down with, 377; downclimb, 279; downhill, 310; downhill skiing, 314; downstage, 350; downtown brown, 112; dowsing, 232; drabble, 295; drag, 141; drag king, 141; drag queen, 141; drag race, 208; dragon piss, 272; Drake Equation, the, 359; drama CD, 18; draw, 59; draw up, 112; Dreamland, 359; dress the house, 75; dresser, 217; drift, 32; drift dive, 307; drillium, 37; drop (gamblers), 130; drop (paddlers), 191; drop (drugs), 112; drop a dime, 377; drop in (skateboarders), 310; drop in (surfers), 338; drop knowledge, 377; drop science, 377; drop zone, 321; drown some worms, 120; Druidism, 365; dry (SCA), 328; dry (thespians), 350; dry bag, 191; dry camping, 290; dry snitch, 245; dry suit, 307; dry weight, 290; D-seg, 244; dual boinger, 37; dub, 18; ducat, 75; duck, 172; ducket, 75; duckets, 377; duckunder, 213; dude, 42; dukey run, 75; dukie run, 75; dumb cancellation, 334; dumb patron story, 177; dummy wagging, 267; dump station, 290; dungeon crawl, 285; dungeon master, 285; dust on crust, 314; DV, 12; DX, 168; DXer, 168; dyke, 141; dykon, 142; dynamiter, 213; dyno, 279; DZ, 321

E

ears, 157; earth religion, 365; earth sign, 27; Easter egg (gamers), 225; Easter egg (hackers), 161; eat it, 338; EBE, 359; ecchi, 18; eclectic, 365; ecovillage, 343; ectoplasm, 203; ECW gear, 13; eddy fence, 191; eddy hop, 191; eddy line, 191; eddy wall, 191; educated, 59; e'en, 272; effect, 197; egg lofter, 208; egoscan, 295; elbow, 112; electron hose, 350; electronic voice phenomena, 203; electrotype, 83; elegant, 161; elephant, 168; elmer, 168; Elvis, 279; emanations, 232; emblem, 83; emcee, 377; emergency gun, 112; Emo, 263; end user, 164; ender, 191; endo (bicyclists), 37; endo (motorcyclers), 217; ends, 377; end-to-ender, 172; enforcer, 251; engine, 208; enow, 272; entrance fever, 70; epic, 37; equestrian director, 75; Equity, 350; Eric, 329; esbat, 366; escape, 197; escort, 259; escort service, 259; Eskimo roll, 191; ESP, 232; ET, 359; etchi, 19; etheric body, 232; etiquette, 334; even money, 130; evergreen, 92; everyfur, 124; EVP, 203; exchange club, 334; exhibitor, 67; exogamy, 359; exotic, 135; experimental rocketry, 208; exploit, 225; exposure, 279; extra-sensory perception, 232; extraterrestrial, 359; eye appeal, 83; eyeball, 168; eyecatch, 19; eyes, 157

F

F/F, 296; faaan, 296; faan, 296; face, 251; face fault, 19; face plant (snowboarders), 325; face plant (skateboarders), 310; factory, 112; fade, 377; Faerie, 366; Faery, 366; fafiate, 296; fag, 142; fag hag, 142; faggot, 142; failure, 48; faire boogers, 272; fairing, 217; fairy, 142; fairy ring, 272; faith healing, 203; fakie (skateboarders), 310; fakie (snowboarders), 325; fall line, 314; fallen flag, 213; false cut, 197; false floor, 70; family, 142; fan, 296; fan fiction (SF/fantasy), 296; fan fiction (anime), 19; fan service, 19; fanac, 296; fanboy, 297; fancy cancel, 334; fancy pants, 75; fandom, 297; fandub, 19; faned, 297; fanfic (SF/fantasy), 297; fanfic (anime), 19; fanfiction (anime), 19; fanfiction (SF/fantasy), 296; fangirl, 297; fannish, 297;

fanon, 297; fansub, 20; fantasy, 297; fantasy note, 83; fantasy piece, 83; fantasy stamp, 334; fanzine, 298; farb, 177; farmer, 120; fat, 377; fat load, 354; FDGB, 37; feastocrat, 329; feed, 251; feed the fish, 307; feghoot, 298; female/female, 296; female-to-male, 142; femme, 142; femmefan, 298; femslash, 298; fen, 298; fence mending, 238; fence-walker, 318; Feri, 366; Fermi's Paradox, 359; ferry, 191; festival, 272; feud, 251; FIAWOL, 296; Fiddle Game, 92; fie, 272; field, 83; fifth wheel, 290; fifth wheel trailer, 290; figure 9, 210; FIJAGH, 296; filk, 298; filksong, 298; fill (hot rodders), 181; fill (graffiti), 154; fill-in, 154; filth, 338; Find the Lady, 92; finger, 83; fink, 42; fire, 112; fire bottle, 168; fire sign, 27; fire up, 112; fireball, 59; fireball show, 59; first count, 59; first generation, 148; first of May, 75; first person interpretation, 177; first personal, 168; first-person shooter, 226; fish (GLTB), 142; fish (prisoners), 245; fish (con artists), 93; fish (gamblers), 130; fish cop, 186; fish line, 245; fishing expedition, 238; fishing line, 245; five-oh, 245; fiver, 290; fix, 112; fix up, 245; fixed line, 279; fixed rope, 279; fixed star, 27; flail, 325; flame thrower, 181; flamed, 279; flamethrower, 181; flaming, 142; flapper, 279; flapping, 267; flare (hunters), 186; flare (SF/fantasy), 298; flare (skydivers), 321; flash (models), 211; flash (rock climbers), 279; flash (tattoo), 346; flash (carnival), 59; flat (bodybuilders), 48; flat (thespians), 350; flat (graffiti), 154; flat joint, 59; flat store, 59; flat water, 192; flatlander, 178; flattener, 70; flattie, 60; fleece, 112; flex, 112; flight, 318; flight box, 211; flimflam artist, 93; flimflam man, 93; flip, 83; flip flop, 354; flip topping, 267; flip-flop, 172; float, 93; float hunt, 187; floater, 321; flock shooter, 187; floof, 124; floofy, 124; flourish, 197; flow (snowboarders), 325; flow (hip hop), 377; fluff, 350; fluffbunny, 366; fluffy bunny, 366; flush, 48; fly, 377; fly catching, 267; flyer, 76; flying, 112; flyman, 350; FNG, 13; foamer, 213; focus (puppeteers), 267; focus (skateboarders), 310; fog lifter, 354; fold, 130; Follow the Lady, 92; foo, 161; foo fighter, 359; fool hen, 187; force (magicians), 197; force (gardeners), 135; forced rep, 48; forecaster scam, 93; formation skydiving, 321; forsoothly, 329; foul air, 71; fourth wall, 350; four-wheeler, 354; fox hunt, 168; foxhunt, 168; FPS, 226; frag, 226; frame, 32; frank, 334; freak (bodybuilders), 48; freak (hip hop), 377; Fred, 38; free beach, 222; free climb, 279; free diver, 307; free posing round, 48; free solo, 279; free weights, 48; Free World, the, 245; freebase, 113; freeflying, 321; free-form, 285; freelance, 213; freelancer, 259; freeride, 325; freestyle (hip hop), 377; freestyle (skateboarders), 310; freestyle (skydivers), 321; freestyle (snowboarders), 325; freestyle skiing, 314; french press, 49; frenched, 181; fresh (coin), 84; fresh (hip hop), 377; fresh (stamps), 335; freshcut, 318; fresh-cut security, 93; freshies, 13; friend of Dorothy, 142; frig, 338; FROG, 290; front (hip hop), 377; front (carnival), 60; fruit booter, 310; fruitbooter, 310; fry, 49; full, 49; full gallon, 168; full hookup, 290; full meal deal, 259; full service, 259; full-timer, 290; funambulist, 76; funder, 93; funnel, 321; fur, 124; fur trade rendezvous, 178; furcon, 124; furridom, 124; furry (furries), 124; furry (SF/fantasy), 298; furrydom, 124; furson, 124; fursuit, 124; fursuiter, 124; furvert, 124

G

gaff, 60; gaffed, 93; gaffel, 113; gaffer, 76; gaffus, 113; gafiate, 299; gag, 76; gallon, 168; game, 378; game master, 285; gameplay, 226; gamer, 285; gamer crack, 285; gaming, 285; gangsta, 378; gangster, 378; gank (hip hop), 378; gank (drugs), 113; gap, 325; gaper, 314; garage kit, 20; garb (fairegoers), 272; garb (SCA), 329; garbage wrestling, 251; Gardnerian Wicca, 366; gas, 251; gashawk, 42; gat, 378; gate, 245; gate money, 245; gate time, 245; gatt, 378; gauge, 213; gay, 142; gay basher, 138; gaydar, 143; gear, 49; gee-fink, 43; geek (wrestling), 251; geek (carnival), 60; gen, 299; gender f*ck, 143; gender identity, 143; genderqueer, 143; genset, 290; George, 130; gerry line, 307; gerrymander, 238; get air, 38; get busy, 378; get hung, 120; get off, 218; get through, 113; get wet, 307; ghetto bird, 378; ghost, 378; ghost flames, 182; ghost light, 350; ghostbust, 113; giblets, 38; gifting circle, 93; gifting club, 93; gig, 272; gilly, 76; gilly wagon, 76; gimmick (drugs), 113; gimmick (wrestling), 251; gimmicked, 197; girl, 143; girlfriend experience, 259; give wings to, 113; giving club,

94; glamgoth, 149; glass (hunters), 187; glass (hot rodders), 182; 'glass, 182; glass axe, 338; glass gun, 113; glissade, 279; glock, 378; glossolalia, 203; glove, 259; glutes, 49; GM, 285; go Federal, 378; go off, 338; go over (wrestling), 252; go over (graffiti), 154; go south, 60; go up, 350; gobbler, 187; gobi, 280; God, the, 366; Goddess, the, 366; goff, 149; golden hour, 49; gonzo, 38; good hand, 252; goofy, 310; goofy foot (skateboarders), 310; goofy foot (snowboarders), 325; Goofy Gauge, 213; go-round, 105; gospel magic, 197; goth, 149; goth as f**k, 149; goth card, 149; goth code, 149; goth points, 149; goth test, 149; gothic, 149; gothic rock, 149; gothic Slide, 150; grab joint, 60; grade, 84; graft, 32; grain, 157; gramercy, 272; grandstands, 76; granny gear, 38; granny line, 307; grass roots, 238; grassroots, 238; graver, 150; gravity check, 38; gray tank, 290; gray water, 291; Grays, 360; grease gun, 157; grease joint, 76; Great Rite, 366; Green Man, the, 366; green room (surfers), 338; green room (thespians), 351; green tunnel, 172; green water, 192; greenhead, 187; greymuzzle, 125; Greys, 360; grid, 272; griefer, 226; grifter, 94; grimoire, 366; grind, 310; grind it out, 49; grind show, 60; grinder, 130; grinner, 187; grip, 378; grip off, 43; gripped, 280; grocery getter, 182; grognard, 285; grok, 299; grom (snowboarders), 325; grom (surfers), 338; grom (skateboarders), 311; grommet (surfers), 338; grommet (snowboarders), 325; Groom Lake, 360; grot hole, 71; ground control, 113; ground man, 113; ground shrinkage, 187; ground trog, 71; group, 157; growl, 43; G-top, 60; guardian spirit, 203; Guardians, 366; Guardians of the Watchtowers, 366; guide, 203; guiding spirit, 204; guild, 226; gum, 32; gum hive, 32; Gumby, 280; gun (surfers), 338; gun (drugs), 113; gun (tattoo), 346; gunch, 329; guns, 49; gutter, 113; gutter bunny, 38; guy, 76; gym rat, 49

H

H (anime), 20; H (SF/fantasy), 299; h/c, 299; hack (hackers), 161; hack (prisoners), 245; hack and slash, 285; hackamore, 105; hacker, 162; Hacker Ethic, the, 162; half pipe (snowboarders), 325; half pipe (skateboarders), 311; halfpipe, 325; hall costume, 299; ham, 168;

ham radio, 168; hamfest, 169; hammer (bicyclists), 38; hammer (snowboarders), 325; hammer down, 354; hammerhead, 38; hams, 49; hand and rod, 267; handfasting, 367; handle, 60; handler, 182; handrail, 173; hand-to-hand, 113; hand-to-hand man, 113; hang, 162; hanky code, 143; hanky-pank, 60; hard, 378; hard core, 178; hard money, 239; hardbody, 49; hardcore (punk rockers), 263; hardcore (hip hop), 378; hardcore wrestling, 252; harden off, 135; hard-way, 252; harmonic, 169; hasbian, 143; hat, 329; hat production, 197; hatchet job, 239; haul bag, 280; hawk, 378; hawker, 272; hazard tree, 173; head, 105; head bobbing, 267; head shop, 113; header, 299; header info, 299; headwall, 192; heat (wrestling), 252; heat (carnival), 60; heat (hip hop), 378; heat wave, 245; heavy, 252; heavy racket, 94; heavy weapons, 329; heel, 252; heirloom, 135; heli-skiing, 314; hella, 378; hello world, 162; helo, 13; hemoed, 338; henshin, 20; hentai, 20; hep, 94; herald, 76; Herbie, 13; hereditary witch, 367; het (GLTB), 143; het (SF/fantasy), 299; heterosexism, 143; hey, Rube!, 76; hi hi, 169; hides, 182; high, 113; high magic, 367; high magick, 367; high roller, 130; high side, 218; high wire walker, 76; hiker box, 173; hip, 311; hip hop, 378; hip-hop, 378; hippodrome, 76; hir, 143; hit (fishing), 120; hit (circus), 76; hit (graffiti), 154; hit (models), 211; hit (gamblers), 130; hit house, 113; hit the hay, 113; hit the needle, 113; HO scale, 213; hoard, 84; hoarder, 84; hobble, 105; Hobby, the, 259; hobby rocketry, 209; hobbyist, 259; hobo clown, 77; hodad, 338; hog, 218; HOG, 218; hog tie, 272; hold, 280; hold!, 329; hole, the, 245; hole (carnival), 60; hole (paddlers), 192; hole card, 130; Hollywood shower, 13; home, 245; homeboy, 378; homebrew, 307; homegirl, 378; homes, 378; homesteaders, 343; homey, 378; homie, 378; honey flow, 32; honeyflow, 32; honker (birders), 43; honker (hunters), 187; hood, 378; hoofstock, 77; hook (a person) up, 114; hooker, 259; Hoover, 307; hop, 169; hope spot, 252; hopped up, 114; horary astrology, 27; horn, 114; Horned God, the, 367; horoscope, 27; horseshoe, 321; hose, 162; hospitality suite, 299; hot check, 94; hot rod,

182; hot snake, 60; house (prisoners), 245; house (thespians), 351; house (astrologers), 27; house (gamblers), 130; house (circus), 77; house edge, 130; house fee, 114; house mouse, 13; house piece, 114; house rule, 285; household pet, 67; huck, 38; hucker, 325; huckster, 314; hump, 77; hung up, 192; hurt/comfort, 299; hustler, 94; hybrid, 67; hydraulic, 192; Hynek Classification System, 360; hype (drugs), 114; hype (hip hop), 379

I

Ice, the, 13; ice cream habit, 114; identify as, 144; ill, 379; illin', 379; illo, 299; illusion, 197; image album, 20; Imbolc, 367; impersonation, 204; impersonator scam, 94; import scene, 182; in sooth, 272; in the car, 245; in the life, 144; in the scene, 150; in very sooth, 273; in-call, 259; independent (motorcyclers), 218; independent (sex workers), 259; indie, 259; inferior planet, 27; ink (motorcyclers), 218; ink (tattoo), 346; ink slinger (motorcyclers), 218; ink slinger (tattoo), 346; inmate, 245; inside man, 94; inside talker, 61; inside the Beltway, 239; insides, 154; instagoth, 150; intentional community, 343; interpreter, 259; intersex, 144; invasive exotic, 135; invisible primary, 239; invitation, 355; involuntary dismount, 38; iron butt, 218; iron jaw act, 77; iron jaw trick, 77; isolation, 49

J

jab, 114; jack, 379; jack shack, 259; jack up, 114; jacket, 246; jackknife, 355; jackpot, 77; jafa, 13; jag (drugs), 114; jag (surfers), 339; jailhouse tattoo, 346; jake, 187; jakes, 379; jam (hip hop), 379; jam (rock climbers), 280; jam (skateboarders), 311; Jamaican Switch, 94; janky, 379; Japanimation, 20; Jesus clip, 218; jet, 379; jib, 326; jinx bird, 43; jizz, 43; job, 252; jobber, 252; Joey, 77; jog, 197; John, 259; Johnnie, 246; Johnny, 246; joint (carnival), 61; joint (drugs), 114; jointee, 61; jolly pop, 114; jolt, 246; jones, 114; J-punk, 263; jug (rock climbers), 280; jug (motorcyclers), 218; juice (bodybuilders), 49; juice (gamblers), 130; juice (wrestling), 252; jump (carnival), 61; jump (circus), 77; jump out, 246; jump run, 322; jumper, 187; jungle fowl, 43; jungle primary, 239; junk, 114; junk gun, 157

K

K-1, 192; K-2, 192; Kaballah, 367; kayfabe, 252; keeper, 192; keister, 246; key (coin), 84; key (drugs), 114; key to the midway, 61; key up, 169; keyframe, 20; kick (carnival), 61; kick (gamers), 226; kick (drugs), 114; kicker (skateboarders), 311; kicker (snowboarders), 326; kid show, 77; kidnapping, 239; kiester, 77; kill (graffiti), 154; kill (thespians), 351; killer, 335; killer app, 162; kiloware, 335; kindergoth, 150; king, 154; king pole, 77; kingdom, 329; kink, 311; kinker, 77; kip, 77; Kirlian photography, 232; kissing John Barleycorn, 273; kit, 114; kitbash, 209; kitbashing, 213; kite (gamers), 226; kite (prisoners), 246; kludge, 162; kluge, 162; kook, 339

L

lady, 130; lag (prisoners), 246; lag (gamers), 226; lame duck, 239; Lammas, 367; lampie, 351; lampy, 351; land shark (surfers), 339; land shark (models), 209; landed nudist club, 222; lane splitting, 218; lapping, 95; lariat, 105; LARP, 285; Larry, 77; lasagna bed, 135; lasso, 105; lats, 49; laugh and scratch, 114; laughing group, 38; launch, 38; laundry, the, 209; Law of Threefold Return, 367; lawn carp, 43; lawn dart, 209; lay down, 218; lay up, 154; lay-in, 246; layout, 214; layup, 154; LBJ, 43; LCO, 209; lead, 280; leak, 95; leathers, 218; lecturer, 61; Left-Hand Path, 367; left-handed monkey wrench, 61; leg, 329; leggings, 105; leggy, 136; legit voice, 351; lemon, 21; lesbian, 144; LesBiGay, 144; Less-Cash Deposit Scheme, 95; let it ride, 131; LETS, 343; letter of comment, 300; letterhack, 300; leveling, 291; liberty, 77; liberty horse, 77; lid (ham radio), 169; lid (motorcyclers), 218; lid (bicyclists), 38; life list, 43; lifer (prisoners), 246; lifer (birders), 43; lifestyler, 125; lift, 335; lifted, 115; light, 253; light bulb grease, 61; light line, 267; light weapons, 329; lightly, 253; lines, 351; lip, 311; lipstick lesbian, 144; list field, 330; lit up, 115; Litha, 367; live (hackers), 162; live (hip hop), 379; live hands, 268; live steel, 330; llama, 226; loaded, 115; loc (carnival), 61; LoC (SF/fantasy), 300; loc (hip hop), 379; local currency, 344; local yokel, 355; lockdown, 246; log, 339; long con, 95; long odds, 131; longbeard, 187; loose, 131; lop, 246; lord, 28; lot (carnival), 61; lot (circus), 77; lot lice, 61; lot lizard, 259; loud pedal, 182; loud powder, 315; low magic, 367; low magick, 367; low side, 218; lowboy, 182; lowrider, 182; Lughnassadh, 368; lumasuck, 351; lumosuck, 351; lunar mansion, 28; lunch, 38; lunch bucket, 239; lunge rope, 77; lunker, 120

M

M/F, 300; M/M, 300; Mabon, 368; macrofurry, 125; Mactown, 14; mad, 379; magic, 368; magic triangle, 268; magical girl, 21; magick, 368; magnumitis, 187; maho shojo, 21; mahou shoujo, 21; mail, 379; mail drop, 173; main, 322; main line, 214; mainbody, 14; mainline, 115; mainstream (reenactors), 178; mainstream (punk rockers), 263; maintainer, 173; majoko, 21; make, 144; make a station, 28; make game, 187; male/female, 300; male/male, 300; male-to-female, 144; Managed Earnings Scam, 95; manager, 253; mandatory pose, 50; manga, 21; manga CD, 22; mangaka, 22; manky, 280; Mansonite, 150; marinate, 379; mark (gamblers), 131; mark (con artists), 95; mark (carnival), 61; mark (hip hop), 379; mark (wrestling), 253; mark out, 253; marker, 131; marriage, 253; Mary, 144; Mary Sue, 300; mashed potatoes, 315; mashie pow, 330; massage, 163; master model railroader, 214; Master of Ceremonies, 379; materialization, 204; maverick, 105; max out, 50; mayhap, 273; Maytagged, 192; MC, 379; meat, 347; meat actor, 268; meat shield, 286; meat theater, 268; mech, 268; mecha, 22; mechanic (circus), 77; mechanic (gamblers), 131; medevac, 14; media con, 300; mediafan, 300; medium, 204; mediumship, 204; megadose, 50; megatick, 43; melt, 84; melt value, 84; Men in Black, 360; Men in Gray, 360; menage, 78; mental telepathy, 232; merchandise, 115; MIBs, 360; Michigan roll, 95; Midsummer, 368; midway (circus), 78; midway (carnival), 62; mileage, 259; mill, 182; minac, 300; mind reading, 232; minmaxer, 286; min-maxer, 286; miss, 115; Miss Thang, 144; Miss Thing, 144; missing time, 360; mitt camp, 62; mix, 379; MJ-12, 360; MLM, 95; MMR, 214; mo, 239; mob, 227; mogul, 315; molded, 182; money, 379; money match, 253; money store, 62; monoculture, 344; monorchid, 67; monosexism, 145; monosexual, 145; monster (coin), 84;

monster (gamers), 227; monster heel, 253; Monte, 95; Monty Hauler, 286; mooch, 62; mooch list, 95; mook, 22; moose, 84; moo-tweet, 43; mopeygoth, 150; morph, 125; morrow, 273; mosh pit, 263; moshing, 263; mossback, 239; motel militia, 178; motherfuckin', 380; motion tagging, 154; motioning, 154; motor, 209; motorboating, 169; motorcoach, 291; motorhome, 291; mountain biking, 38; mountain money, 173; mouse hanger, 173; mouse trapeze, 173; mouthpiece, 253; move on, 380; mow the grass, 115; Mr Sands, 351; MTB, 38; MUD, 227; mud duck, 355; mud show, 78; mudpecker, 43; mule (prisoners), 246; mule (drugs), 115; mule (gamers), 227; multi-level marketing, 95; multi-user dungeon, 227; munchkin, 286; mundane (furries), 125; mundane (SF/fantasy), 301; mundane (SCA), 330; mundane astrology, 28; muppet, 326; muscle car, 183; muscle confusion, 50; muscle reading, 233; mustang, 105; Mustard Squirter, 96; my time, 178; mystery move, 192

N

narc, 115; nard guard, 38; natal astrology, 28; native, 78; natural contest, 50; naturist, 222; nay, 273; NDE, 204; near-death experience, 204; necromancy, 204; nectar, 339; nectarflow, 32; negative, 50; negative rep, 50; Nelly, 145; neo, 301; neofan, 301; neo-pagan, 368; Neptune cocktail, 339; nerd gate, 71; nerf, 227; nervous water, 120; net, 169; netgoth, 150; new old stock, 183; new school, 263; newspaper test, 204; nickel, 50; Nigerian letter fraud, 96; Nigerian money transfer fraud, 96; nigga, 380; nigger, 380; NIMBY, 239; NINny, 150; NOBO, 173; nocturnal light, 361; no-grade, 84; non-morphic, 125; non-player character, 227; noodled, 339; nooner, 260; nose, 311; no-sell, 253; note, 85; NPC, 227; nuc, 32; nucleus, 32; nudist, 222; nudist colony, 222; nut (carnival), 62; nut (con artists), 96

O

OAV, 22; OBE, 233; obliterator, 335; odd-eyed, 67; oddroc, 209; Odinism, 368; off belay, 280; off book, 351; off side, 193; off the clock, 260; off the hook, 380; offgassing, 307; off-trails, 315; oft, 273; OG, 380; oi!, 263; oil, 50; old Antarctic explorer, 14; Old Path, 368; Old Religion, 368; old school (graffiti), 154; old school (punk rockers), 263; old school (hip hop), 380; Old Ways, 368; Olympic plate, 50; on a mission, 115; on a trip, 115; on belay, 280; on book, 351; on ice, 115; on side, 193; on the leg, 246; on the money, 50; on the send, 96; on the show, 78; on tilt, 131; on time, 51; one and one, 115; one percenter, 218; one rep max, 51; one-times, 380; onsight, 280; OOBE, 233; open source, 163; opening gate, 273; operation, 214; operator (ham radio), 169; operator (con artists), 96; Orange Book, 209; orb, 28; organ donor, 38; Original Gangster, 380; Ostara, 368; otaku, 22; out, 145; out of the closet, 145; out-call, 260; outgassing, 307; outlaw, 105; out-of-body experience, 233; outside man, 96; outside talker, 62; OVA, 22; over (wrestling), 253; over (ham radio), 169; over the falls, 339; overcall, 62; over-dipped, 85; overgunned, 339; overhead, 339; overshadowing, 204

P

pack, 322; package bees, 32; pad boy, 330; paddle, 169; pagan, 368; paint, 131; painted pony, 78; palm, 197; panic, 115; paper (magicians), 198; paper (wrestling), 254; paper (circus), 78; paper (hip hop), 380; paper player (con artists), 96; paper player (gamblers), 131; paperboy, 115; paperhanger, 96; papers, 67; parapsychology, 233; park model, 291; parlor magic, 198; participant, 273; party hat, 260; party hunting, 187; pass (GLTB), 145; pass (gamblers), 131; pass-along plant, 136; patch (carnival), 62; patch (birders), 43; pax, 14; PC, 227; peace, 380; peace bond, 301; peak bagging, 173; peaking (drugs), 115; peaking (bodybuilders), 51; pecs, 51; pedigree, 85; pedigreed, 67; peeler, 105; peep, 44; peeps, 380; pell, 330; pentacle, 368; pentagram, 368; perchance, 273; performer, 273; period, 330; period-correct, 178; perkygoth, 151; permaculture, 344; perp, 116; persona, 330; personal, 169; personal flotation device, 193; personal zine, 301; persuadables, 240; perzine, 301; PFD, 193; phase of the moon, 163; phat, 380; philately, 335; phishing, 96; phreak, 163; pickled punk, 62; pickup man, 106; picture taker, 355; pie, 44; pie car, 78; pie-car, 78; piece (tattoo), 347; piece (hip hop), 380; piece (graffiti), 154; piece book, 154; pig (birders), 44; pig (cavers), 71; pig (prisoners), 246; pigeon, 96; Pigeon Drop, 97; Pig-in-a-Poke, 97;

pike, 214; pileup, 169; pillion, 218; pillow, 193; pin, 116; pinch back, 136; pinch off, 136; ping, 227; pinner, 116; pipe, 116; pipe dragon, 326; pipero, 116; pipes (bodybuilders), 51; pipes (motorcyclers), 219; pirate, 169; pish out, 44; pit, 131; pit boss, 131; pitch (cavers), 71; pitch (carnival), 62; pitcher, 145; pitchman, 78; pitted, 339; PK (gamers), 227; PK (parapsychologists), 233; plain wrapper, 355; planet, 28; plate, 51; play, 380; play a mark, 63; play flight, 32; playa, 380; playa-hata, 381; playboard, 268; player (hip hop), 380; player (RPGs), 286; player character, 227; player killing, 227; player-hater, 381; playtron, 273; plugged, 85; plushophile, 125; poach, 326; pogo, 264; point blank, 381; point break, 339; poke, 97; poker run, 219; politainer, 240; politico, 240; poltergeist, 204; pony, 307; pony car, 183; pony cylinder, 307; Ponzi Scheme, 97; pop (drugs), 116; pop (coin), 85; pop (wrestling), 254; pop punk, 264; popcorn match, 254; pop-out, 291; population, 85; pork barrel, 240; porn star experience, 260; porpoise, 291; portage, 193; posedown, 51; posing routine, 51; posse, 381; possum belly, 78; posthole, 173; post-op, 145; post-revel, 330; pot, 131; potato chip, 39; poundage, 51; pow, 326; pow pow, 326; powder, 315; power lifting, 51; power prang, 209; powerlifting, 51; practical hands, 268; prang (bicyclists), 39; prang (models), 209; pray, 273; precognition, 233; prefix, 67; pre-op, 145; press, 131; prime bank, 97; primitive camping, 291; prithee, 273; privy, 273; privy monster, 273; pro (sex workers), 260; pro (rock climbers), 281; production, 198; profonde, 198; program (bodybuilders), 51; program (wrestling), 254; progression, 28; Project Aquarius, 361; Project Redlight, 361; projective energy, 369; promo, 254; proof, 85; prop, 63; proper person, 369; proposition, 63; proposition bet, 131; props, 381; protection, 281; protest vote, 240; prototype, 214; provenance, 85; provider, 260; pruno, 246; psi, 233; psychic, 233; Psychobilly, 264; psychokinesis, 233; psychometry, 233; pucker factor (surfers), 339; pucker factor (motorcyclers), 219; puddle duck, 187; PUDs, 173; puffer, 116; puller, 291; pull-through, 291; pump (drugs), 116; pump (bodybuilders), 51; pump iron, 51; pumped, 281; punch, 193; punch a cloud, 322; puncher, 106; punk (hip hop), 381; punk (prisoners), 246; punk (punk rockers), 264; punk (carnival), 63; puppet actor, 268; purist, 173; push (wrestling), 254; push (gamblers), 132; push (drugs), 116; push poll, 240; pusher, 291; put down, 121; put over, 254; put the mark up, 97; put-in, 193; pyramid scheme, 97; pyramiding, 51; pythons, 52

Q

Q signal, 170; Qabala, 367; QSL, 170; quads (gamblers), 132; quads (bodybuilders), 52; quarter, 52; Quarters, 369; queen (GLTB), 145; queen (cat fanciers), 67; queen cage, 32; queenright, 33; queer, 145; querent, 369; quiver, 339

R

rabbit, 246; rack (hunters), 187; rack (graffiti), 154; rack (rock climbers), 281; rack (prisoners), 246; ragchewing, 170; raincoat, 260; raise, 132; rake (motorcyclers), 219; rake (gamblers), 132; Ramada rangers, 178; random bred, 68; rangy, 63; rap, 381; rappel, 281; rapper, 381; raps, 205; raptivist, 240; rat bike, 219; rat rod, 183; ratchet jaw, 355; rattan, 330; rattle can, 211; raudive voices, 205; rave, 116; raw (hip hop), 381; raw (coin), 85; read, 146; read the water, 193; readers, 198; reading, 205; real life fiction, 302; real people fiction, 301; Real person slash, 301; real-time, 228; receipt, 254; receptive energy, 369; Red Baron, 209; red wagon, 78; red-headed Eskimo, 240; redpoint, 281; re-dyke, 146; registered, 68; regular, 311; regular foot (skateboarders), 311; regular foot (snowboarders), 326; rehash, 63; re-kitted, 209; relative work, 322; relaxacon, 301; relaxicon, 301; reloader, 97; remainder (stamps), 335; remainder (coin), 85; remote viewing, 233; remuda, 106; ren faire, 273; ren fest, 273; Renaissance faire, 273; rennie, 274; renny, 274; rep, 52; represent, 381; representative interpretation, 178; Republicrat, 241; Republocrat, 241; requeen, 33; reserve, 322; resistance, 52; retrocognition, 233; retrograde, 28; retro-grouch, 39; rettysnitch, 170; reversal, 193; 'rhoid buffing, 39; rice boy, 183; rice burner (hot rodders), 183; rice burner (motorcyclers), 219; rice rocket, 183; ricer, 183; rickt, 339; ride (prisoners), 246; ride (hip hop), 381; ride jock, 63; ride the hook,

308; rider (motorcyclers), 219; rider (bicyclists), 39; ridgerunner, 173; ridgie, 154; ridgy, 154; riding bitch, 219; riding leg, 246; riffles, 193; rig (ham radio), 170; rig (skydivers), 322; rig (SCA), 330; rig (truckers), 355; rig (drugs), 116; rigger (skydivers), 322; rigger (circus), 78; rigging, 78; ring, 79; ring curb, 79; ring rat, 254; ringer, 79; ringmaster, 79; rinse cycle, 339; riot grrrl, 264; rip (surfers), 339; rip (fishing), 121; rip (coin), 85; ripped, 52; rising sign, 29; RL fiction, 302; roach, 116; road rash (motorcyclers), 219; road rash (bicyclists), 39; roadie, 39; robber bee, 33; rock garden, 193; rock house, 116; rock scramble, 174; rock solvent, 71; rock!, 281; rocker, 219; rocket fuel, 39; rocketeer, 210; Rock-in-a-Box, 97; rockpecker, 44; rod, 184; 'roid rage, 52; 'roids, 52; roll, 132; roll down the windows, 326; roll out, 381; roll with, 381; roller coaster, 174; roller skate, 355; roof sniffing, 71; roost, 39; root-bound, 136; rope wrench, 351; roper, 98; rosinback, 79; Roswell, 361; roughy, 63; rounder, 132; roundup, 106; roustabout, 79; rout, 71; routine, 52; RPS, 302; RTFM, 163; RUB, 219; rubber, 219; rubber side down, 219; rube, 98; rube act, 98; ruck, 174; ruler, 29; rules lawyer, 286; ruling planet, 29; rump, 44; rump session, 241; run, 219; run a book, 132; run-in, 254; runout, 281

S

sabbat, 369; salad, 121; salami attack, 98; sallyport, 247; salting, 98; Samhain, 369; sand facial, 339; sandbag (wrestling), 254; sandbag (rock climbers), 281; sauce, 52; save versus, 286; scab, 339; Scadian, 330; SCAdian, 330; scale (models), 211; scale (railroad), 214; scam, 99; scam artist, 99; scam baiting, 99; scammer, 99; scenicked, 214; schmecker, 116; schuss, 315; schuss-boomer, 315; science fiction, 302; scientifiction, 303; scifi, 303; sci-fi, 303; scoop, 71; scoot, 219; scooter, 219; scope (hip hop), 381; scope (birders), 44; score (drugs), 116; score (con artists), 99; Scottish Play, the, 351; scratch, 381; scratch-build, 214; scratcher, 347; screamer, 281; screw job, 254; scrilla, 381; scrillah, 381; scripophily, 85; scrub, 381; scrying, 233; SCUBA, 308; scum, 281; scuz, 281; SD, 23; sea chicken, 120; seance, 205; séance, 205; seat cover, 355; second generation, 151; second sight, 234;

secondary market, 99; Secret Master of Fandom, 303; section hiker, 174; sectioned, 184; security through obscurity, 163; seeing daylight, 106; seeker, 344; seg, 247; segregation, 247; seiyuu, 22; self-deploying cargo, 14; self-liquidating loan, 99; sell, 255; sensitive, 234; separation, 52; sercon, 303; series, 85; servante, 198; serve, 381; server, 116; session (skateboarders), 311; session (snowboarders), 326; session (sex workers), 260; set (bodybuilders), 52; set (drugs), 116; set (skateboarders), 311; sewer, 116; sewing machine leg, 281; sex worker, 260; SF, 302; shacked, 339; shaggy dog story, 303; shake and bake, 268; shaking the dollies, 269; shank, 247; shark, 132; shark biscuit, 339; sharp, 132; sharpie, 44; shaved, 184; sheeple, 241; Sheldon Scale, 85; shibby, 340; shife, 381; shill (gamblers), 132; shill (carnival), 63; shill (con artists), 99; shiny side up, 219; shire, 274; shoe-polisher, 187; shojo, 22; shonen, 23; shonen ai, 23; shoot, 255; shoot a bag, 308; shoot up, 116; shooter, 188; shooting gallery, 116; shore power, 291; short, 247; short con, 99; short odds, 132; short set, 335; shorty, 381; shot down, 211; shot on goal, 260; shotgun (drugs), 117; shotgun (bodybuilders), 52; shoujo, 23; shoulder surfing, 100; shounen, 23; shounen ai, 23; shoving rubber, 269; show light, 255; show quality, 68; showman, 63; shralp, 340; shred (surfers), 340; shred (snowboarders), 326; shred (models), 210; shredded, 52; shuttle bunny, 193; side story, 23; sidewall, 79; sie, 146; sign, 29; signature fraud, 100; silent key, 170; silt-out, 308; sim, 228; simp heister, 63; single-O, 63; sire, 68; sissy bar, 220; sit flying, 322; sit in, 39; sit on, 39; sitter, 205; sitting, 205; sitzmark, 315; six pack, 53; six-pack, 308; sixth sense, 234; ska punk, 264; skacore, 264; skanking, 264; skeezer, 117; sketch, 326; sketchy, 311; ski porn, 315; skid lid (motorcyclers), 220; skid lid (bicyclists), 39; skiffy, 303; skimmer, 100; skin, 308; skin money, 352; skinhead, 188; skull crusher, 53; sky busting, 188; skyboard, 322; skybusting, 188; skyclad, 370; skygod, 322; skyhook, 170; skysurfing, 322; slab (hikers), 174; slab (motorcyclers), 220; slab (coin), 86; slab (rock climbers), 281; slabland, 86; slackpack, 174;

slam (drugs), 117; slam (prisoners), 247; slammed (hot rodders), 184; slammed (fishing), 121; slammer, 211; slammin', 381; slamming, 100; slan, 303; slan shack, 303; slang, 117; SLAPP, 241; slash, 303; sled, 220; sleeper, 184; sleepwalker, 117; sleeve (magicians), 198; sleeve (tattoo), 347; sliced, 53; sliced and diced, 53; slick, 63; slickhead, 188; slicks, 39; slide, 198; slide-in, 291; slide-out, 292; slider, 86; sling a stick, 188; sling lead, 188; slinging ink, 347; sloper, 281; slum, 63; slumgum, 33; smalls, 331; smark, 255; smart, 255; smear, 281; SMOF, 302; smoke, 381; smoker, 33; smoothed, 184; snake (skateboarders), 311; snake (surfers), 340; snake (snowboarders), 326; snatch, 53; SNI, 210; sniff, 117; snort, 117; snotty, 308; SNP, 210; soap eater, 178; SOBO, 174; soft money, 241; solitary, 370; sour soil, 136; source, 163; source code, 163; space opera, 303; space-filler, 335; spaghetti code, 163; spam, 228; spare change, 53; spatula, 44; spawn, 228; spawn point, 228; spec, 79; specklebelly, 188; speculative fiction, 303; speed goat, 188; speed rig, 157; speleologist, 71; spellcaster, 286; spelunker, 71; spike (drugs), 117; spike (thespians), 352; spirit communication, 205; spiritual healing, 205; spiritualism, 206; spiritualist, 206; spit out, 39; Split Deposit, 100; sponge, 340; spoof (hackers), 163; spoof (carnival), 63; spoofing, 100; spook, 132; spooky kid, 151; spool truck, 79; spool wagon, 79; sport bike, 220; sport climbing, 281; spot (bodybuilders), 53; spot (wrestling), 255; spot (skydivers), 323; spotter (bodybuilders), 53; spotter (guns), 158; sprawk, 44; spray skirt, 193; springer, 100; sprint, 39; spur, 170; squad, 315; square, 247; squash, 255; squawk, 100; squib, 352; squick, 304; squid (motorcyclers), 220; squid (surfers), 340; squirt boat, 193; stack (gamblers), 132; stack (bicyclists), 39; stack (bodybuilders), 53; stack (magicians), 198; stage dive, 264; stage left, 352; stage right, 352; stalls, 79; stance (skateboarders), 312; stance (snowboarders), 326; stand, 79; standard plate, 54; standing wave, 193; stand-up magic, 198; stargazing, 269; stash, 117; steal, 198; stealth camping, 174; steed, 39; steel, 382; step off, 382; step on, 117; step to, 382; step up, 382; steward, 331; stick (carnival), 64; stick (SCA),

331; stick (surfers), 340; stick (snowboarders), 326; stick jock, 331; stiff, 255; stigmata, 206; stinger, 247; stink-eye, 340; stomp, 326; stone butch, 146; stoned, 117; stoppie, 220; store (carnival), 64; store (con artists), 100; straight (hip hop), 382; straight (GLTB), 146; straight edge, 264; strainer, 194; strap (wrestling), 255; strap (hip hop), 382; straw house, 79; straw poll, 241; strawbale, 344; street (fairegoers), 274; street (skateboarders), 312; street action, 260; street rod, 184; street skating, 312; stretch, 255; strike (thespians), 352; strike (fishing), 121; stringer, 44; stringers, 79; stringy, 44; stripe, 80; stroke, 308; stroll, 260; strong, 64; strung out, 117; stud cat, 68; stuff, 117; stuffed, 340; stump, 241; stupid, 382; sub, 23; succession planting, 136; sucker (carnival), 64; sucker (gamblers), 132; sucker (con artists), 100; sucker effect, 198; sucker list, 100; suffix, 68; sugar snow, 315; suicide door, 184; Sun sign, 29; sunny, 260; super, 33; super user, 164; superdeformed, 23; superior planet, 29; superset, 54; superuser, 164; surface interval, 308; surfology, 340; survival, 206; survivalist, 158; suss, 318; sustainable, 344; Svengali Deck, 199; swamp donkey, 188; swazi, 318; sweet soil, 136; swerve, 255; swing, 352; swish, 146; switch stance, 312; sword sponge, 286; sXe, 264; symmetry round, 54; synastry, 29

T

table tilting, 206; table turning, 206; tabletop, 269; tabletop gaming, 287; tack, 247; taco, 40; tactical voting, 241; tag, 155; tagger, 155; tail (birders), 44; tail (skateboarders), 312; tailgunner, 292; tailor-made, 247; take, 100; take care of business, 260; take!, 282; takeoff, 340; take-out, 194; take-out fee, 260; talker, 64; talking, 199; tap out, 256; target panic, 188; Tarot, the, 206; tat, 347; taunt, 228; taur, 126; 'taur, 126; tax, 382; tea bagging, 269; tea kettle, 214; tea party, 40; team kill, 228; techie, 352; technical (skateboarders), 312; technical (paddlers), 194; telefrag, 229; telekinesis, 234; Telemark skiing, 315; telepathy, 234; tell, 133; tenderfoot, 106; ten-in-one, 64; tension!, 282; tent master, 80; terrain park, 326; textile, 222; thematic collecting, 335; therianthropy, 126; thermos bottle, 355; thigh biceps, 54; thirst monster,

117; thoroughbred, 117; thrash (bicyclists), 40; thrash (bodybuilders), 54; thread counter, 179; thread Nazi, 179; Three Card Molly, 101; Three Card Monte, 100; Three-Card Monte, 133; Three-Card Trick, the, 101; three-finger salute, 164; Threefold Law, 370; three-hour tour, 40; through-hiker, 174; throwie, 155; throwup, 155; throw-up, 155; thumb, 86; T-hunt, 170; ti, 40; ticket, 170; tight (hip hop), 382; tight (gamblers), 133; tight (wrestling), 256; tightrope walker, 80; timberdoodle, 188; tin can, 355; tin teepee, 179; tip (carnival), 64; tip (graffiti), 155; tip-out, 292; title, 68; to the bone, 382; toad, 292; TOAD, 292; toast, 14; toke (drugs), 118; toke (gamblers), 133; toke up, 118; tom (cat fanciers), 68; Tom (gamblers), 133; tongue (paddlers), 194; tongue (coin), 86; toning, 86; tools, 118; top (GLTB), 146; top (circus), 80; top to bottom, 155; top world bank, 101; topfree, 222; topit, 199; top-to-bottom, 155; torch, 54; tosser, 101; touch, 101; tourer, 220; touring bike, 220; touron (reenactors), 179; touron (hikers), 174; towed, 292; town clothes, 174; towner (carnival), 64; towner (circus), 80; townie (carnival), 64; townie (circus), 80; tox, 308; toy, 155; toy box, 292; toy hauler, 292; track (drugs), 118; track (skydivers), 323; tracks, 118; trad climbing, 282; trader, 101; tradition, 370; traditional climbing, 282; traffic, 170; trail, 106; trail angel, 174; trail magic, 174; trail name, 174; trailer queen, 220; train, 229; tramp clown, 80; trans, 146; transfiguration, 206; transgendered, 146; transit, 29; transition, 312; transplant shock, 136; transsexual, 146; transvestite, 146; trash bird, 44; travel agent, 118; travel trailer, 292; traveler, 274; traverse, 14; tree rat, 188; Trek, 304; Trekker, 304; Trekkie, 304; trick (hip hop), 383; trick (sex workers), 261; trike, 220; trip, 118; tripping, 118; trips, 133; tris, 54; tri's, 54; tri-set, 54; trog up, 71; Trojan, 164; Trojan horse, 164; troll (sex workers), 261; troll (surfers), 340; troll (SCA), 331; troll gate, 331; troupe, 80; trouper, 80; trudge mode, 175; true odds, 133; trufan, 304; trustee, 101; tube, 340; tubed, 340; Tuckerize, 304; tunnel of fun, 287; turf surf, 323; turkey, 274; turkey farm, 242; turkey with dressing, 274; turn, 256; turn out, 247; turnaway, 80; turn-based, 229; turned on, 118; turntablist, 383; turtle, 175; turtled, 194; TV, 44; tweak (punk rockers), 264;

tweak (skateboarders), 312; tweak out, 264; tweener, 256; twenty-four hour man, 80; twilight zone, 71; twink (gamers), 229; twink (GLTB), 146; twink (RPGs), 287; twisties, 220; twisty, 220; twitch, 44; twitcher, 44; two-planker, 326; two-sided die, 287; two-wheeler, 355; type, 86

U

U-barrel, 14; UFO, 361; Ufology, 361; UFOnaut, 361; ugly season, 242; ultragoth, 151; umbrella, 261; uncast, 370; uncle, 118; unconcede, 242; uncovered, 261; undeserved hit, 308; unobtainium, 40; up, 155; upstage, 352; user, 164; user error, 164

V

vanish, 199; vanishing, 199; vaporware, 164; vaquero, 106; vegetable tunnel, 40; veggie tunnel, 40; verily, 274; vert skating, 312; vest pocket dealer, 86; vig, 133; vigorish, 133; village, 274; vintage, 184; virtual caver, 71; vis, 308; viz, 308; volunteer, 136; volunteer plant, 136; Vulcan nerve pinch, 164

W

wack, 383; wad, 133; waddie, 106; waddy, 106; wagging the dummies, 269; wagon, 80; wahine, 340; wah-wahs, 308; walk on, 355; walkaround, 80; walk-around, 80; walk-on, 352; wall (skateboarders), 312; wall (bicyclists), 40; wall-hanger, 188; war canoe, 194; warez, 164; warez d00dz, 164; warlock, 370; wash, 101; wash out, 40; washboard, 54; Washington read, 242; wasted, 118; Watchers, 370; water sign, 29; wavy, 188; weather guesser, 14; web, 80; webify, 165; wedge issue, 242; weed tree, 136; weekend goth, 151; weekender, 151; weenie, 86; well-behaved, 165; wench, 274; wet, 331; wet exit, 194; wet weight, 292; wetware, 165; whale, 133; whelped, 126; wherefore, 274; whip (hip hop), 383; whip (politicos), 242; whipper, 282; white meat, 133; whiteface clown, 80; white-handled knife, 370; whiz, 86; whoosh generator, 210; whore, 261; whuffo, 323; Wica, 370; Wicca, 370; Wiccan Rede, 370; widdershins, 371; wide open, 64; widowmaker, 175; wigga, 383; wigger, 383; wiggling the dollies, 269; wild pigs, 40; wild style, 155; wildstyle, 155; Willy Weaver, 355; wind doping, 158; windage, 158; windjammer (circus), 80; windjammer (truckers),

355; winky, 40; winter quarters, 80; winter-over, 14; wire weenie, 331; wired (drugs), 118; wired (rock climbers), 282; wise, 101; witch, 371; witchcraft, 371; wolf ticket, 247; wonder coin, 86; wonk, 242; wood-pusher, 312; word, 383; word is bond, 383; word up, 383; work (wrestling), 256; work (ham radio), 170; workamping, 292; workaround, 165; worked, 340; working girl, 261; works, 118; World, the, 247; World Guide, the, 222; wouff hong, 170; wrangler, 106; wrap, 194; wreck mail, 335; wrench (motorcyclers), 220; wrench (bicyclists), 40; writer, 155; WYSIWYG, 164

X

x/o, 304; XC skiing, 314; xenoglossy, 206; xerox, 383; xover, 304; x-over, 304

Y

yak, 101; yaoi, 23; yard sale (skiers), 315; yard sale (bicyclists), 40; yard shark, 220; yardstick, 355; yea, 274; yiff, 126; yiffy, 126; yogi, 175; your time, 178; yo-yo, 175; yoyo mode, 165; Yule, 371; yuppie larva, 179; yuri, 23

Z

zanie, 80; zany, 80; zero day, 175; zipper, 282; zippering, 210; Zodiac, 29; zombie gimmick, 199; zone bending, 136; zoomer, 118